Out of the Nest,

into the Frying Pan

. . . a cookbook for kids who have left home and other fledgling gourmets.

Written and Illustrated by Eileen Lafferty

BIRD IN HAND
PUBLISHING

© Copyright 1984
Bird in Hand Publishing

Library of Congress Catalog Card Number 84-72116
ISBN 0-9613994-0-6

Typesetting by I'm Your Type

**Published February 1985
Second printing June 1985
Third printing October 1987**

For ordering information, see back page.

To RUSSELL, RANDY and SYDNEY

. . . and to all those other kids who have left home knowing every way to make chocolate chip cookies known to man but no idea what to do when the gravy lumps . . .

To the bachelor who's trying to make it on Big Macs and six packs . . .

And to the career girl who is bringing home the bacon and wondering how to cook it.

acknowledgements

More people were involved in this project than I can ever acknowledge. But I owe particular thanks to Kathryn Roos who did all the typing and added some really hysterical notes in the margins. And Anne Graves, Godmother and great grammarian, who volunteered to slog through the proofing.

I am also beholden to Walker Propst, calligrapher extraordinaire, who did the pretty lettering — and Mark Robinson, an artist of great perception and patience, who did what he could to keep the graphics from getting too crazy.

Most of all, I want to thank my long-suffering husband, Jim, who kept encouraging me in the backhanded way of the Irish. All along, he would growl, "Look, if you're going to do it, for God's sake, do it right."

I hope I did.

CONTENTS

Introduction

... in case you're wondering how
this whole thing came about

This book started off to be a sort of survival kit for my three kids — a gathering of quick-fix foods and old family favorites. Everyone was on his own, no one could cook, yet there was no way anybody could possibly get through Christmas without Grandma's persimmon pudding and turkey stuffing.

Then, as the project gathered steam, friends and acquaintances began volunteering recipes for the casseroles **their** kids took off to college, plus other fail-safe shortcuts their families have come to love best.

And so the whole thing grew into a freewheeling collection of recipes for the amateur epicure. This includes the student who just left home, the bachelor who will probably never own a Cuisinart and the bride who flunked Home Ec and now needs to have the boss and his wife over for dinner.

To these new and late-blooming gourmets, I say, "Bon appetit and be of good cheer. Help lies directly ahead."

Happily, cooking is a game anyone can play. If you are hungry enough, you can cook. Keep it up, and you may even be a great cook.

In the process you will learn that a really good meal can be prepared in an hour, whereas one that was three days in the making isn't necessarily better. Worse, probably. You have that much more time to mess things up.

In the beginning stages, it is okay to read fancy gourmet magazines and sigh over the pretty pictures. But, after that, they are best left on the coffee table. Certainly I would steer clear of menus that have lists of ingredients as long as your leg and would have you running all over town hunting for dried morels and Black Forest truffles. You don't need to spend $80 for something that took days to track down and wasn't that good in the long run.

Which is not to say that all gourmet cooking is all that involved. It isn't. A lot of so-called epicurean cookery is an absolute snap. Vichyssoise is only slightly harder to prepare than Jello, and if you can poke a snail in a hole, you can make escargots bourdelaise.

Obviously, the beginner cook should lose no time nailing down a couple of these grandstand plays that will throw everyone off the track.

For example, you wouldn't believe the mileage you can get out of making your own mayonnaise. Or a great steak tartare. Come sailing out of the kitchen with one of these zingers, and no one will believe the rest of dinner came out of a box.

Speaking of boxes, this is where the crafty use of shortcuts comes into play. The experts will sniff, but many of the so-called convenience foods can be real life savers. Muffin mixes, top-of-the-stove dressings, pop-out biscuits, packaged salad dressings, sauces and gravies can be dependable stopgaps where you are hanging on the ropes and there's no time for finer efforts. Even canned stew and bottled spaghetti sauce will pass muster, given a splash of wine and a dash of herbs.

However, if anyone asks, deny that you have ever heard of them before. Your reputation as a cook — and you can't start playing that part too soon — hinges on the illusion that everything short of churning the butter is something you do all by yourself. So lie a little.

If you feel guilty over stashing Sara Lee and Chef Boyardee in the closet, tell yourself it is only temporary.

The big trick is not to get permanently fixed in the shortcut category. To learn, one must advance. After you have made a half-dozen pies with readymade crusts and aerosol cans of whipped cream, it is time to push on.

Accordingly, you will find that the recipes in this book range from super simple to slightly more complex. None is really difficult, and they are all very good.

Recipes with a single star (*) are for the headstart group. A two-star (**) recipe is only marginally harder and is still well within the grasp of the beginner. Get your stripes here, then proceed to the three-star (***) sensations.

Just remember, nothing can teach you how to cook like getting in and doing it. If you experience a few flops along the way, that's okay. You will learn from your mistakes. And short of burning the house down, you won't kill anyone in the process.

As you work along, your confidence should grow apace. This will come as the troops you are feeding start approaching the table with cries of joy and anticipation. But be realistic. Occasionally your efforts may be met with grunts or outright groans. **Do not be put off.** Press on.

And trust me.

Kitchen Stuff

. . . what you need, and don't need, to get started

Gourmet cooking does not depend on a lot of fancy or expensive equipment. Some of the simplest things — a chef's whisk, a nutmeg grater — have great authority and don't cost more than a few dollars.

A few of these minor props, plus some well-calculated hype (chill the salad forks, light a lot of candles) will create the ambiance you are after.

Unlike a lot of basic cookbooks, there is no attempt here to catalog all the equipment you will need for your kitchen. Everyone needs a rolling pin and a set of measuring cups, but not every cook needs a muffin tin. These are the things you have to decide as you go along.

The following observations are mere guidelines to help you get going.

Supermarket cookware is no bargain. Good pots and pans cost more, but you need the kind with heavy bottoms — and the heavier the better for the beginner who is apt to be doing something else when the pot boils dry.

If you already have a set of pans with pretty copper bottoms, make a simple polishing mix of 1 cup vinegar, 1/4 cup cleanser and 1/4 cup salt. This will help you keep them bright until you get sick of all that scouring. Then hang them up for show and get some plain pans for serious duty.

Don't get conned into buying a set of knives. You only need three or four, but they ought to be good ones, and good ones are pretty expensive. Stainless steel knives may look good, but they are hard to sharpen and don't hold an edge. Carbon steel isn't as pretty but it stays lots sharper. Keep your knives sharp and hang them in a rack on the wall. Dumping sharp cutlery in a drawer is crazy.

In my opinion, a good heavy-duty pepper mill is well worth the price. Good cooks also grind their own salt and nutmeg. These are the kinds of things you can do with a flourish that is bound to impress. Besides, fresh grinds are better.

The same goes for coffee. Nothing in this world smells more heavenly than the fragrance of freshly ground beans. If you use instant coffee when you are alone, don't for heaven's sake trot it out when company is coming. And hide the jar.

Well-constructed pepper grinder and coffee mills are available in the housewares sections of all department stores. You will also find them in the kind of gourmet shops that are proliferating in shopping malls all over.

Incidentally, as your interest in cooking develops, the lure of these specialty cookware stores will grow apace. Well, let me warn you: they are full of things you can do nicely without.

Special crepe pans, for instance. A teflon-lined skillet works just as well. Quiche pans are pretty, but a plain pie pan will do the job. And I can't think of **anyone** who really needs a shrimp de-veiner, cherry pitter or hot dog cooker.

On the other hand, I couldn't get through one day without a rubber spatula for scraping pots and bowls. Or one of those swivel-handled peelers for paring spuds. And everyone needs a good can opener.

For my money, a heavy-based electric opener is ideal. Just make sure its cutting wheel is designed for easy cleaning. Sometimes the best housekeepers overlook this minor chore, then wonder why the applesauce tastes like catfood.

We don't fry enough food at our house to justify a deep-fat fryer. But if your family is big on French fries and low on cholesterol, you might love one.

I don't own an electric ice cream freezer, nor do I want one. Nor am I into crockpot cookery. But that is another personal prejudice. Some people —mostly absentee cooks — swear by these slow-motion stew pots.

You will also notice that there are no recipes in this book for micro-cookery. While I wouldn't take anything for my ancient microwave oven for re-heating the breakfast coffee and thawing out the roast I forgot to take out of the freezer yesterday, that pretty well covers the territory. I have yet to microwave a muffin without turning it into a cueball. Besides, I am not really psychologically conditioned to cope with anything in this life that hinges on split-second timing.

This has nothing to do with short cuts. I adore my food processor that makes short work of shredding cabbage and mincing parsley. I love its powerful chop-chop. But I know some good cooks who don't share my enthusiasm.

Whether or not you should invest in one depends on your budget (good ones aren't cheap), how much chopping and slicing you do and how much work surface you can spare. If the processor isn't where you can get at it, you will not use it.

A hand-mixer is a handy gadget to have. It is also cheaper by an order of magnitude than the conventional stand mixer with all the bowls and attachments. These are great but, again, they take up space. And I repeat: if these appliances aren't up front and on top, you will not use them. The effort involved in dragging a mixer or toaster out of the cupboard and getting it plugged in will be enough to discourage its regular use.

The one item every kitchen should have is a timer. When you put something on to boil or bake, set it. Put it in the pocket of your chef's apron. That way, if you get distracted and end up out in the garage dipping candles or sorting through the kids' Halloween costumes, the bell will remind you to take the pudding out of the oven before it burns its buns off.

Entertaining

. . . look fancy, but keep it easy

Now let us talk about entertaining — how you can have people over for dinner and impress them with your razzle-dazzle. How a little advance planning and calculated chutzpah come into play.

If you work for a living or are otherwise occupied, do not plan on launching even a minor bash in the middle of the week. Even if you are convinced you can race home, throw the roast in the oven, the body in the tub, the wine on ice and still come out with five minutes to spare, this is bound to be a cliffhanger. What if the lid sticks or you drop the gin?

Wait for a weekend. Work up a menu that is dependably familiar. Make a list of what you need and where things go. Give yourself plenty of time.

And keep it simple. A five-course feast with a harried host or hostess is no treat. A simple menu and a serene cook is a delight.

Wine and cheese may have been run to death, but that's still a viable way for the beginner to break into the party traffic. Four wines, that many good cheeses — plus a few really great breads — will do the trick nicely.

For an informal drop-in dinner, soup and salad can have a nice Bohemian flair. Make a rib-sticking peasant soup, toss a salad, heat a long loaf of crusty bread, and that's it.

This approach makes particular sense if your dining space is limited or nonexistent. Simply serve from the living room coffee table (which could be a couple of crates cleverly disguised with an Indian shawl), and ask people to sit on the floor. Offer pillows and keep the wine flowing.

Some of the most successful dinner parties I have ever attended spotlighted a particular dish for which the host or hostess was famous among their friends. There's a bachelor in town whose single claim to culinary fame is a Brazilian stew he concocts out of beef, yams and hot peppers. That is the one and only thing he ever cooks. Or serves. And people kill for invitations to his dinner parties.

So if a dynamite Texas chili is your specialty, serve it. Again. And again. Or your mother's special recipe for scallopini. Or an unbeatable beef bourguignonne (an unpronounceable name for beef stew). Once you have established your specialty, and can make it blindfolded, the rest of the spread is a snap — a make-ahead appetizer, a fail-safe accompaniment, a fret-free dessert.

Beyond this basic blueprint, there are a few ploys you can pull off and look like the real pro.

Having allowed yourself sufficient tailwind, there are a few easily maneuvered ploys that will make you look like a real pro.

Hot foods are much better served on heated plates. Ten minutes in a low oven does the trick.

Chilling the salad plates and forks in the freezer a half hour before serving is a nice touch. Just don't forget where you put them.

Use cloth napkins. Paper is out.

Get good at garnishing. Food that looks good always tastes better. Obvious garnishes include, but aren't limited to, parsley. Grape leaves work well. I have even decorated with nasturtium leaves and ferns — for garnishing, not eating.

Fresh flowers are lovely. They also cost an arm and a leg. As an alternative, start collecting some really good-looking silk flowers (in general, white ones seem to work best). Then, when a party is in the offing, plump out your fake bouquet with real ferns. Fifty cents worth of baby's breath from the corner florist will also give your arrangement credibility. But if all this fakery really offends you, just clump fresh ferns and leaves in a bowl, and let it go at that.

Use candles. Apart from the fact that candlelight is the most flattering illumination in the world, it makes everything look like a party. It also obscures the fact that the umbrella rack in the corner didn't get dusted.

You don't need Waterford candelabra to set the scene. Clusters of votive candles that cost mere pennies will do the trick.

And serve wine — with confidence. Admittedly this can take a bit of doing for the novice who is apt to be turned off by all the hype that makes wine tasting about as much fun as flunking your driver's test.

The way around this is to pick two wines — one red and one white — and go for it. Better yet, make that **three** wines — one red and two white, a dry white wine and a fruitier variety. Then, no matter what you are serving, you're covered.

Pour with panache. And if some crashing bore who has just finished a two-day wine tasting class wants to debate your choices, stand your ground. Wine is a subjective thing. It's your word against his.

So keep pouring. And don't invite him again.

The
Laudable Larder
. . . beating the Mother Hubbard rap

I knew a lady once who, being a free and unfettered spirit, was forever skidding into her kitchen, huffing and puffing, and a half-hour late to be starting dinner. She would jam her golf clubs in the broom closet, peel off her sweater, than chop an onion.

Up to this point, there was no variation in her plan of attack. What followed was chancier, however. Dinner pretty much depended on what fell out of the pantry next.

That kind of seat-of-the-pants cookery takes confidence. You also need to have a working stash of canned and packaged edibles on hand.

People who buy canned guavas or hearts of palm in 100-lot cases might be considered eccentric. But those who keep a working inventory of emergency rations stashed on their kitchen shelves are **smart.**

Laying in a few cans of beans and bouillon against the time you crave chili at midnight or limp home, slack-jawed, from the dentist's, is only showing foresight. Furthermore, you will never be caught empty-handed if someone drops in and shows signs of sticking it out through dinner. (See Desperation Dishes, **page 39.**)

If you are stocking your pantry from scratch, the following check lists could help you beef up your inventory.

Bedrock Basics . . . stocking the bare essentials

The following list contains the fundamentals — items you should always have on hand on a catch-as-catch-can basis. You will note the omission of such essentials as salt, catsup and tea bags. These were purposely omitted on the assumption that you weren't born yesterday and are already armed with the bare-bottom basics.

Evaporated milk	**Packaged whipped cream**
Powdered milk	**Rice (regular and instant)**
Dehydrated potatoes (not bad	**Pasta (noodles, spaghetti,**
if you doctor them up enough)	**macaroni)**

Canned vegetables (keep a
few cans chilled for salads)
Canned fruits (keep a few cans
chilled for salads)
Canned soups (the creamed ones
are great sauce shortcuts)
Tomato sauce
Tomato paste
Dried onion flakes
Dehydrated onion soup
Canned tuna (only white,
preferably in spring water)
Canned meats (beef stew,
corned beef hash, dried beef)
Canned beans (chili, kidney,
refried, pork and beans)

Parmesan cheese
Packaged bread crumbs
Pudding mixes
Cake mixes
Pie crust mix (until you have the
homemade kind down pat)
Pie shells (frozen)
Bouillon granules (beef
and chicken)
Mayonnaise
Reconstituted lemon juice (not
as good as fresh, but okay in
a squeeze)

Gourmet goodies . . . putting a little class in the cupboard

This second-string shopping list contains some of the fancier foodstuffs you will
want to acquire as you go along. Fling a couple in your market basket this week,
and one or two more next week. By stringing it out, you won't miss the money.
Well, not as **much**, anyhow.

Canned nuts (cashews, almonds,
pecans — smoked and salted)
Smoked oysters and clams
Canned crabmeat
Frozen uncooked shrimp
Artichoke hearts (frozen
and marinated)
Canned Camembert cheese
(and other cheesey imports)
Escargots (buy one set of shells,
then save them)
Cocktail franks
Bamboo shoots
Mushrooms (canned — button
and slices)

Olives (green and black —
jumbos for cocktails)
Caviar (red and, if you can
afford it, black)
Wild rice (canned
and packaged)
Canned puddings (babas,
plum, date)
Instant espresso coffee (almost
as good as the real thing)
Liqueurs (any and all kinds;
start a collection)

Actually the list of lily-gilders could go on and on. The next time you are
wheeling through the gourmet section of your supermarket, stop and browse a
bit. You may be surprised to find chocolate-covered grasshoppers a skip and a
jump away from the dog biscuits and laundry bleach. Along with the oddities,
there are loads of gourmet items worth stashing away for future cocktail bashes
and company drop-ins.

Seasonings

. . . keeping a handle on the spice shelf

Beyond such standbys as salt, pepper and cinnamon, it is to be supposed that you already have the working rudiments of a spice shelf at your disposal. However, if you are hesitant as to how to use — or supplement — your stash, read on.

In an over-zeal to "create," the novice is apt to get carried away when it comes to seasoning. A curry that raises beads of sweat on the brow may have authority but be deadly on the digestion. And too much turmeric won't have anyone coming back for seconds, either.

The same note of caution goes for extracts. I knew a young woman once who, in a burst of inspiration, poured vanilla in the tomato soup. No family can survive that kind of creativity very long.

But back to the spice shelf. Remember that the life of most herbs and spices is limited. Buy in small quantities and keep the boxes and bottles in a dark, cool place. And sniff before you sprinkle. If your basil has the blahs, dump it.

It takes fresh and frisky seasonings to do the job — to impart the gentle herbal hint that enhances without knocking your hat off.

Experiment until you know which seasonings you like in one dish, what herb you prefer in another. It's **your** taste, after all. There are no hard and fast rules about what goes where.

The following guidelines are offered merely as a place for you unseasoned cooks to start. From there feel free to blaze your own trails.

Allspice . . . shows up in everything from pickles to cakes and cookies. A dash goes nicely in baked beans and spaghetti sauce. Adds that certain something.

Anise seeds . . . a must for those rock-hard Christmas springerle cookies. And for those who love licorice, sprinkle some seeds on the baking sheet before you bake sugar cookies.

Anise extract . . . more licorice flavor for those who like it. A drop or two in white cake icing makes a surprising taste change. Kids, especially, go for it. A drop or two in cooky dough is okay, too.

Basil . . . goes anyplace tomatoes go. Fresh basil leaves can be processed in a blender with pine nuts and olive oil to make a divine pesto sauce for pasta. This is an easy-to-grow backyard herb. Fresh or dried, it can be sprinkled on lamb and also does nice things for cheese and fish dishes.

Bay leaf . . . a dominant herb (a couple of leaves will do the trick). Makes a flavorful addition to soups and stews. Pea soup, in particular, likes a little bay leaf to give it a boost.

Caraway seeds . . . good for gussying up homemade breads and rolls. Also a neat additive for sauerkraut. Can be added to buttered noodles for a little unexpected crunch. Dieters can sprinkle it on cottage cheese to break the monotony.

Cardamom . . . goes in Christmas cookies and all kinds of baked goods in the Scandinavian tradition. It's a natural for fritter batter and all sorts of sweet doughs. Can be used to tasty advantage in pickle brines, wine punches, and meat marinades. Can be hard to find, however. Your best sources are stores in neighborhoods where Scandinavian families congregate.

Cayenne . . . a little dash will do you. It imparts more pure "hot" than any discernible flavor. If you are looking for a hair-raiser, this is it.

Chervil . . . a delight in fish dishes. Ditto for scrambled eggs and omelets. Also good in Sauce Verte, Remoulade and Bearnaise sauces.

Chili powder . . . for chili, naturally. Just be sure it is fresh. (Old chili powder definitely lacks pizazz.) Apart from its necessary presence in Mexican dishes, a little dash of chili does wonders for the whole gamut of cheese dishes, like Welsh rabbit and cheese stratas.

Cinnamon . . . you can't make cinnamon toast without it, or apple pie or baked apples. Applesauce needs a drift of cinnamon, too. It goes like a hand-in-glove with ham and does surprisingly well in beef stew. **Honest.**

Cloves . . . make nice polka-dot trims for baked hams and spiced peaches. A dash of powdered cloves isn't all bad for livening up a beef stew (just don't use too much).

Coriander . . . toss in a couple of seeds in stews and soups and see if you don't like the results. Used extensively in commercial sausages and luncheon meats, coriander can do lovely things for your homemade meatballs and meat loaves, too.

Cumin . . . this gives Mexican dishes the right accent. And it's good on pork chops and roasts. Try a pinch in the flour the next time you dredge chicken pieces for frying. A modest sprinkling can also do mysterious things on sugar cookies and fruit pies. But don't get carried away — a smidge is what you're after.

Curry . . . this is generally a blend of turmeric, ginger, pepper, mace and cloves. Hot stuff. Domestic blends are generally milder than imported curries that can raise beads of sweat. Apart from curry dishes where it is imperative, try a sprinkle in potato salads, deviled eggs, and over broiled tomatoes.

Dill . . . beautiful in the green, leafy fresh state, but more often available dry (in seeds and weed). For a change, try dill seed in mashed potatoes. And dill weed is marvelous sprinkled over any kind of potatoes — scalloped, au gratin, etc. It's a natural go-along for any tomato dish and blends beautifully anyplace sour cream is present. And don't serve salmon, poached or baked, without it.

Fennel . . . crush a teaspoonful in a mortar, then toss into spaghetti sauce or sauce for lasagna. Good on pizza, too. It tastes vaguely like licorice and imparts a very authentic paisano accent to dishes of Italian or Sicilian conviction.

Ginger . . . powdered is potent, so use it with discretion. However, a dash gives pumpkin pie pizazz, and where would gingerbread be without it? For a change of pace, try it in butter sauces for fish and chicken.

Mace . . . a stronger version of nutmeg. Goes in pound cake and cherry pie. Good in chicken dressings and does surprisingly lovely things for mashed potatoes. Just a **drift,** mind you.

Marjoram . . . this is for lamb. A nice addition to oil and vinegar dressings, too. A fairly subtle spice, it goes on delicate things — like mushrooms, omelets, cream sauces. Teams nicely with spinach, too — in soups, souffles, etc.

Nutmeg . . . use in almost any creamed sauce. Goes beautifully sprinkled over baked squash (with plenty of butter and black pepper). Baked apples cry for it as do baked custards. Freshly grated nutmeg, from a whole seed-like nut, is vastly superior to the pre-ground, canned stuff.

Oregano . . . necessary for any and all kinds of Italian cuisine (spaghetti and pizza are zilch without it). Just be sure your oregano is frisky fresh. Oregano that is over the hill doesn't have it.

Rosemary . . . easy to grow in the garden. Needle-like leaves are a super additive to spaghetti sauces, all kinds of tomato dishes. Great in vinegar dressings, too. And try it in butter sauces for fresh vegetables.

Saffron . . . so costly it'll make your hair stand on end. But if you can afford it, it does wonderfully mystic things for sweet breads, casseroles with rice, chicken, fish, and soups — especially bouillabaisse. If you do spring for some, use it sparingly. It's not only expensive, it is also very strong. Imparts a deep yellow color, too. So be forewarned.

Sage . . . a positive must for the Thanksgiving bird's stuffing. Equally essential in all manner of sausage and pork dishes.

Sesame seeds . . . sprinkle them on homemade rolls and breads. And do try toasting them for a wonderfully nutty flavor. Add a handful to any cocktail dip and vegetable salad.

Thyme . . . the universal herb. Goes nicely with any vegetable and is great in chicken and turkey salads. Again, make sure it's fresh. This is no time to try old thyme!

Tarragon . . . if you're lucky, you can grow it outdoors. Pinch off the leaves and add them to your vinegar cruet. Tarragon is imperative for Sauce Bearnaise, and adds a nice touch to chicken and egg dishes. Very distinctive, and very, very good.

Turmeric . . . like saffron, it gives off a deep yellow color which is nice provided that's what you had in mind. Turmeric is a natural for pickled eggs and, combined with butter, makes a rich-looking basting sauce for chicken and ribs. Imparts a kind of nice indoor tan.

What's Ahead in Constant Nibblers

Constant Nibblers

. . . closet munchies for the cocktail crowd

Nibblers are made up of things you can keep, more or less indefinitely, in the fridge or the kitchen cupboard. Their actual shelf life will depend on how successful you are at keeping your roommate, spouse or whomever you live with from digging into the inventory.

The beauty of the first dozen or so recipes that follow is twofold: one, they are ready to go; and, two, they are a snap to prepare.

Further on down the line are ideas for appetizers that are just as easy but that call for ingredients you are less likely to have on hand — ground beef, chicken wings, etc. If you have time for a quick run to the market, these, too, are winners.

Onion-Mayo Puffs*

Here is, without question, the easiest, least expensive and most readily available canape in captivity. I first sampled these little gems at a posh wedding reception on Nob Hill in San Francisco, and have been boggled ever since over how good — and simple — these puffy, cheese-like goodies are. Men, especially, love them. And nobody ever guesses exactly what's in them!

Soft white sandwich bread,	**Mayonnaise**
cut in 2-inch rounds	**Parmesan cheese**
Sweet Bermuda onion,	
sliced paper-thin	

Cut the bread into rounds (an empty frozen orange juice concentrate can works just fine for a cutter-outer). Place rounds on a cookie sheet and lightly toast under the broiler. Turn rounds over and on the untoasted sides place a thin round of sliced onion. Then, on each one, spoon a fat tablespoon of real mayonnaise (salad dressing doesn't work here — you need *mayonnaise*). Sprinkle with parmesan and place canapes under a hot broiler until the mayonnaise puffs up and turns a delicate brown. Serve hot. Get raves!

Panic Buttons*

Got a package of refrigerated biscuits languishing in the fridge? If you do, you are in luck, for the biscuits can be pressed into a number of notable emergency roles, one of which follows. These onion-crunchy tidbits go great with cocktails and are sensational with salads.

1 8-ounce tube refrigerated biscuits 1 envelope onion soup mix	1/2 cup butter Parmesan cheese

With a sharp knife, cut each biscuit in quarters. Mix soup mix and butter in a small skillet, melting the butter. Toss in the biscuit bits, tossing and turning until each piece is well coated with the butter mixture and is lightly browned. Arrange the biscuit bits on a baking sheet and bake for 5 minutes in a 425° oven. Sprinkle with Parmesan cheese and serve hot.

Cheesy Bread Sticks**

The following chunky bread squares make great go-alongs with cocktails and are equally good as an accompaniment for a salad lunch. On either kind of occasion, make plenty. They disappear fast!

1 large loaf unsliced white bread 1/2 pound processed cheese brick, grated 1 pound margarine	1 egg white 1 teaspoon Worcestershire sauce 1 clove garlic, minced

Cut crusts from bread, then cut into cubes approximately 1-1/2 by 4 inches long. Place on a cooky sheet and lightly toast one side. Remove and set aside.

Mix remaining ingredients until well blended. Spread generously on bread cubes, covering all sides but the one toasted side.

When ready to serve, broil at 400° F. with pan 5 to 6 inches from the broiler element. Watch closely. When cubes are lightly browned and bubbling, remove and serve.

Chile Toasts*

Here's another "let 'em eat bread" appetizer that comes forth from the oven gorgeously crunchy — so good you may spend the evening cranking out more.

1/4 pound margarine
1 cup canned green chiles,
  chopped
2 cloves of garlic, crushed
1/2 pound Jack cheese, shredded
	1 cup mayonnaise
	1 loaf thin-sliced white bread,
	  lightly toasted

Combine margarine, chiles and garlic. Spread on toast slices. Mix mayonnaise with cheese and spread over the chile layer. Don't skimp. Spread the cheese to the edges. Cut the bread into quarters (triangles) and place on an ungreased cookie sheet. Broil until bubbling. Makes approximately 5 dozen appetizers.

English Muffin Snack Bites*

English Muffin Snack Bites prove that the best things are often the very easiest. The blend of flavors — cheese, olives and curry — makes these cocktail nibbles worth serving, time and time again.

1 package English muffins	**1/2 cup mayonnaise**
1/2 cup green onion, minced	**1 teaspoon mild curry powder**
1-1/2 cups shredded Cheddar cheese	**1 cup chopped black olives**

Cut muffins in fourths. Blend remaining ingredients and spread thickly on the muffin pieces. Broil until cheese melts and muffins get lightly browned around the edges. Makes enough spread for 1 package of muffins.

Sardine Roll-Ups*

Like many simple but satisfying things, Sardine Roll-Ups come out tasting a lot better than their humble ingredients would lead one to expect.

1 can sardines packed in oil	**Juice of 1/2 lemon**
1 teaspoon fresh horseradish	**Melted butter**
6 slices white bread, thinly sliced, crusts removed	

Drain oil from sardines and mash fish with horseradish and lemon juice. Spread on thin slices of bread and roll up, jelly-roll fashion, and fasten with toothpicks. Brush with melted butter and bake at 400° F. for 5 or 6 minutes, or until lightly browned and toasty.

Smoky Sardine Spread*

This next one is a real rock-bottom emergency measure, but don't underestimate it. It makes a super short-cut spread that tastes lots better than it sounds.

Drain and mash one can of sardines (don't worry about the skin, just mash). Blend in cream cheese — a half package or whatever happens to be on hand. When smooth, sprinkle in 2 to 3 drops liquid smoke. Mound mix in a small serving bowl and sprinkle with chopped parsley or nuts or whatever surfaces in the way of garnish. Serve with crackers.

Chutney Butter Canapes*

A good cook always has a jar or two of chutney hanging around. Assuming you have some in your inventory, try teaming it with peanut butter and cream cheese for a cocktail spread that will stop everyone in his tracks. Very good — very different.

1 3-ounce package cream cheese	Dash Worcestershire sauce
1/2 pound chunky peanut butter	1/4 teaspoon garlic salt
4 ounces chutney	Orange juice

Blend all ingredients together in a small bowl, using only enough orange juice to moisten the mixture to spreading consistency. Spread can be kept in the refrigerator for weeks and actually improves with a day or so of aging. Serve with firm crackers, such as Triscuits.

Hot Chipped Dip**

A funny thing . . . nobody ever guesses what's in this one (answer: chipped beef). **Do** try this one. It is one of the best hot dips in captivity.

1 8-ounce package cream cheese	1 5-ounce jar chipped beef,
2 tablespoons milk	snipped in shreds
2 tablespoons minced green onion	1/2 cup sour cream
2 tablespoons dried onion flakes	1/2 cup diced walnuts

Mix everything but the nuts, and spoon into a shallow ovenproof ramekin. Sprinkle with walnuts and bake at 350° F. for 15 minutes. Serve hot with whole wheat crackers.

Baby Tomato Cocktail Buds*

Edith, my interior designer friend, is a wizard with colors but a dead loss in the kitchen. She is always on the lookout for things that require little or no cooking, and quite often she comes up with a real winner. Witness her quick solution of what to serve with martinis when time (and talent) has run out.

Wash a basket of cherry tomatoes and pat dry. (Leave the little green tops on, if possible.) Pile tomatoes in a basket and pour two inches of gin, or vodka, in a small bowl. In a second small bowl put some seasoned salt. Furnish toothpicks.

Instruct your guests to spear a tomato, dunk it in booze, then dip in the salt. They will love it and will think you're a genius for dreaming up such a smart trick.

Snappy Snow Peas*

Another super quickie involves nothing more than a clutch of crisp, chilled snow peas and a dunk made of sour cream and mayonnaise.

Wash and pat dry about a half-pound of snow peas. Mix 1/2 cup sour cream with 1/2 cup mayonnaise. Season to taste with prepared mustard — about 1-1/2 teaspoons — and a hefty sprinkle of dillweed. Serve dunk-mix in a bowl surrounded by the snow peas arranged spoke-fashion all the way around. Well-chilled young peas are as crisp as chips, and lots better for you!

Pickled Mushrooms*

Is there a soul alive who doesn't like pickled mushrooms? I haven't met one yet! Everyone in our family seems to think these are the very best of the bunch.

2 baskets of mushrooms, about 1/2 pound	Salad oil
1 cup cider vinegar	1 clove garlic, minced
1/3 cup wine vinegar	2 tablespoons finely chopped parsley
1 teaspoon salt	Salt to taste

Bring vinegars to a boil, add cleaned mushrooms and simmer 1 minute. Drain, saving vinegar. Place mushrooms in a mason jar and add just enough oil to make the mushrooms glossy (about 1 tablespoon). Add garlic and parsley, then pour in enough reserved vinegar to come part way up the jar. Refrigerate, shaking the jar occasionally, and serve after 3 to 4 days.

Shrimp-Stuffed Tomatoes*

If you are a slam-and-cram kind of cook, the prospect of standing around filling cherry tomatoes might not be your idea of something to do for a cocktail party. On the other hand, once you get underway, the job goes pretty fast and the result pays handsome dividends.

1 basket cherry tomatoes	1 green pepper, minced
1 6-ounce can cocktail shrimp, drained	Juice of 1 lemon
1 onion, chopped fine	Salt and pepper

With a sharp teaspoon (a grapefruit spoon works well), scoop out the tomatoes, being careful not to pierce the shells. Invert on paper towels to drain. Lightly sprinkle cavities of the tomatoes with salt. Mash well-drained shrimp with minced onion, pepper and lemon juice in a small bowl. Season with a drift of salt and pepper. With a small spoon, gently fill the scooped-out tomatoes. Cover with plastic wrap and chill until serving time.

Note: A little finely minced parsley makes an attractive garnish.

Nancy's Super Shrimp Mold**

Much as I tend to be anti-gelatin in general, this next jelled shrimp mold is quite exceptional. My friend Nancy never has a cocktail party without it.

1 can tomato soup	Dash Worcestershire sauce
1 8-ounce package cream cheese	Dash hot pepper sauce
1 package unflavored gelatin	1 cup cooked and cleaned shrimp (or crab)
1/2 cup celery, finely chopped	
1/2 cup green onions, minced	

Heat soup, cream cheese and blend well. Sprinkle gelatin on top and mix well. Take off heat. Add the remaining ingredients and pour into a greased mold. Chill until set. Serve with crackers.

Ceviche***

*When you sally forth bearing a bowlful of ice-cold ceviche, nothing says you **have** to tell everyone that the fish in it hasn't been cooked. For one thing, that is not an entirely accurate statement. While ceviche isn't cooked calorically, it really **is** poached — or pickled — in lime juice. That ought to take care of the queasies if, indeed, you encounter any.*

1 pound scrupulously fresh white fish (sea bass, red snapper, scallops, etc.)	1/2 teaspoon oregano
	1 teaspoon salt
	Freshly cracked pepper
Juice of 4 to 5 limes (about 1/2 cup juice)	2 teaspoons finely minced cilantro (optional)
3 peeled and chopped tomatoes	1 avocado, peeled and diced
2 chopped canned green chiles	4 green onions, minced
3 tablespoons olive oil	

Cut fish into dice (slice scallops) and place in a glass bowl to marinate in lime juice for at least 4 hours. Stir occasionally and keep refrigerated.

Drain fish and combine with everything but the avocado and chopped green onion. Cover and refrigerate 1 hour before serving. Spoon mixture into individual scallop shells (or small serving dishes) and garnish with avocado and green onions. Serves 4.

Nacho Platter***

Served bubbling hot from the oven, nachos make a marvelous grab 'n snack appetizer for an informal gathering. This meltaway combination of cheese, chiles and chips is so good, in fact, that you can figure on six couples taking less than 10 minutes to demolish two platters.

1 dozen corn tortillas	1-1/2 cups refried beans
Shortening	1 cup finely diced tomatoes
Salt	1 cup finely diced green onions
1 cup shredded Jack cheese	1/2 cup finely diced cilantro (optional)
1 cup shredded Cheddar cheese	
3 jalapeno chiles, finely chopped	

Cut tortillas in quarters and fry in hot shortening until crisp. As quarters brown, remove with a slotted spoon and drain on paper towels. Salt lightly. Arrange tortillas in a single layer on a large ovenproof platter. (If you can't fit all the pieces on one platter, use two.) Sprinkle half the grated Jack and cheddar cheeses over the chips, then sprinkle with diced chiles. Dollop spoonfuls of refried beans over the chips, then top off with the remaining cheese. Sprinkle with chopped tomatoes, onions and cilantro and bake at 375° F. for 10 to 15 minutes or until bubbly. Makes 12 to 14 appetizer servings.

Note: If you lack the time or inclination to make your own tortilla chips, you can substitute the ready-made kind. Just make sure to get large size dippers. (Dinky tortilla strips don't really work for nachos. Everything keeps falling through the cracks.)

Mock Crab Spread*

*If the price of fresh crab has you blanching, try this sleight-of-hand recipe for Mock Crab Spread the next time you serve cocktails. If you can keep a secret — and a straight face — chances are no one will ever guess they're not really eating ten dollar a pound crab. I've tried it, and I **know**.*

1/2 pound grated Swiss cheese	1/2 cup finely chopped tomato
3 tablespoons green	1/2 cup mayonnaise
olives, chopped	2 green onions, minced
2 tablespoons green	(use part of green tops)
pepper, chopped	

Lightly combine ingredients, tossing with a fork. Season to taste with salt and pepper and serve — silently. Makes enough spread for approximately 12 munchers.

Pool Hall Pickled Eggs**

One of our town's best-known saloons has been doing a landslide business for more than 50 years. Beer flows in tall frosted mugs, and huge glass jars back of the bar are afloat with the best pickled eggs this side of the Rockies. Here's how they are done.

8 eggs	1 cup water
1 12-ounce jar pickled	1 tablespoon sugar
yellow chile peppers	1 teaspoon tumeric
2 tablespoons pickling spice	2 teaspoons salt
1 cup wine vinegar	2 peeled cloves garlic

Hard cook eggs. Mix remaining ingredients and add the peeled eggs while they are still warm. Do not refrigerate as this will toughen the eggs. Keep in a sealed jar for 2 days. When the eggs are gone, the marinade can be reused 3 or 4 times.

Saloon-Type Pickled Knockwurst*

Pickled Knockwurst are reminiscent of the treats saloons in the old West used to serve on the counters with their nickel lunches. Goes great with beer. Make up a batch the next time the poker club convenes.

1-1/2 pounds knockwurst	1 teaspoon salt
1 onion, sliced	1 teaspoon whole allspice
2-1/2 cups water	1-1/4 teaspoons crushed
1-1/2 cups vinegar	dried red chiles
2 tablespoons sugar	1 teaspoon whole black peppercorns
1 tablespoon pickling spices	

Cut knockwurst in diagonal 1/4-inch chunks. Separate onions into rings and layer, with knockwurst pieces, in a 2-quart glass jar.

Bring remaining ingredients to a boil, reduce heat and simmer 5 minutes. Pour over knockwurst, cover and set aside to cool. Refrigerate 4 to 5 days before serving. Makes about 5 cups.

Red-Hot Cocktail Cookies**

When we first encountered these "cocktail cookies" they were being passed around to a group of imbibers by a young thing with the face of an angel. We all thought those goodies on her tray were sugar cookies. One bite — wow! — proved how wrong we were.

1/4 pound butter or margarine	3 tablespoons dried onion soup mix
1/2 pound grated Cheddar cheese	(1/2 package) crumbled
1 cup flour	1 teaspoon cayenne pepper
1/4 teaspoon salt	

Mix all ingredients by hand until thoroughly blended. Roll dough into a cylinder about the diameter of a quarter. Wrap in foil and place in the freezer.

To serve, take roll from freezer and slice, with a very sharp knife, into 1/8-inch slices. Bake on an ungreased cookie sheet at 375° F. until golden.

Note: Feel free to add a bit more cayenne if you really want to wake up the crowd. But proceed with caution. That stuff is **hot.**

Crunchy Cocktail Wafers*

A lady friend of mine who is famous throughout the territory for her sumptuous cocktail parties served these crisp cheese crackers at a recent do, and everyone begged for the recipe. Getting the combination took a bit of doing (some people don't like to share their secrets), but we finally found the crunch came from Rice Crispies.

2 cups sharp cheese, shredded	Pinch garlic powder
2 cups flour, sifted	Pinch cayenne (more if you like
1 cup butter	inner fire)
2 cups Rice Crispies,	Dash salt
slightly crushed	

Mix ingredients and form into small walnut-size balls. Flatten slightly with a fork. Bake on an ungreased baking sheet for 20 minutes at 350° F.

Chile con Queso**

Chile con Queso always goes well at informal cocktail gatherings. The trick is to keep it warm throughout the festivities without burning its bottom. Keep an eye on the flame and stir it now and then. And make sure the chips don't run out. You don't want people sticking their fingers in the pot.

1 pound processed cheese, diced	1 7-ounce can green chile salsa
1 4-ounce can whole green	1 brown or white onion,
chiles, diced and seeded	finely chopped

Heat cheese over a low fire until melted, stirring to prevent sticking. Add the salsa, the chopped chiles and the onions and continue to heat slowly. The mixture will be thin but will thicken as it cools. Allow to cool for one-half hour before serving. Just before trundling into the party, spoon the mix into a chafing dish or one of those serving dishes that sets over a candle flame to keep things warm. Serve with plenty of crisp tortilla chips.

Chicken Liver Paté**

Chicken livers, blended to a paste, are the mainstay of this next easy-to-make paté. Another time try chopping the livers instead of processing them in your blender. The chopped version is a divine sandwich spread for Jewish rye or pumpernickel.

1/2 cup sweet butter	1-1/2 tablespoons brandy
1 large onion, sliced	1/2 teaspoon salt
1-1/4 pound chicken livers	Pepper
1 hard-cooked egg	3 green onions, finely chopped

Saute sliced onion in 2 tablespoons butter until onion is tender but not browned — about 7 minutes over low heat. Remove from skillet and set aside. In same pan, heat remaining butter and add livers. Saute over low heat for 5 minutes — until golden brown. (Don't overcook. Livers should still be pink inside.)

Place half the livers, onion and the remaining ingredients in a blender and process on low speed until smooth. Repeat with remaining ingredients. Stir together in a bowl, test for seasonings and pack into a crock or small serving bowl. Refrigerate until thoroughly chilled. Serve garnished with finely chopped green onions. Makes about 3 cups.

Frosted Party Paté**

If you decide to mold your paté, why not go a step further and "ice" it with a creamy cheese frosting?

Molded pate (any kind)	1 tablespoon cream
1-1/2 packages (3-ounce size)	or evaporated milk
cream cheese	1 small can sliced black olives

Pack pate into a round bowl or fancy mold and chill until firm. Unmold on a serving dish and frost with a mixture of cream cheese and cream that has been whipped smooth. Decorate pate with slices of olive.

Note: capers make a pretty garnish, too.

"Smoked Salmon" Paté**

My friend Nancy, who caters elegant parties, dreamed up this elegant paté that everyone thinks is made from smoked salmon. It isn't, but she isn't telling!

1 8-ounce package cream cheese	1/3 teaspoon liquid smoke
1 7-3/4-ounce can red salmon	Dash Worcestershire sauce
2-1/2 teaspoons horseradish	1 teaspoon lemon juice
2 teaspoons finely minced onion	Salt and pepper

Soften cheese, then beat until fluffy. Fold in remaining ingredients and pack into a lightly greased mold (a fish mold is ideal). Chill overnight. Unmold and garnish with capers or minced parsley or chopped walnuts or all three!

Date Rumaki**

Date rumaki is one of those things that sounds pretty awful but comes out tasting dreamy. The sweet and smoky combination of dates and bacon is a surprise palate-pleaser. Just keep your wits about you when they cook. They burn easily, so don't stray far from the oven door.

Dates	Bacon slices, cut in half
Sharp Cheddar cheese, cubed	

Pit as many dates as you intend to use, or buy the pitted kind. Cut cheese in small cubes, and fit one cube in each date, pressing slightly to close. Wrap a half slice of bacon around each date and secure with a toothpick. Toast under broiler until bacon is crisp (you will need to turn the dates over as they broil). Drain on paper towels before serving. Serve hot — but not **red** hot.

Rumaki Cocktail Spread**

If you adore rumaki but find it a bit of a bother to assemble, here is a quick spread that goes together in minutes and has the same delectable blend of texture and flavor.

1/2 pound chicken livers	Pinch dry ginger
1/4 cup butter	1 clove garlic, minced
2 tablespoons lemon juice	1 5-ounce can water chestnuts,
1 tablespoon soy sauce	drained and chopped
4 to 5 green onions, chopped	4 slices crisp bacon, crumbled
1/2 teaspoon dry mustard	

Cook livers in butter until browned but still pink in the centers. Cool. Blend livers with lemon juice in a blender, pushing down with a rubber spatula as necessary. Add soy sauce, sugar, mustard, ginger and garlic and process until smooth. Scoop into a bowl and add chopped chestnuts and bacon. Garnish with green onions. Serve with crackers.

Jalapeno Quiche**

Here is another quick-mix, no-crust party quiche that speaks for itself with a decided Mexican accent. If you serve these peppery little squares along with frosted margaritas, so much the better. Ole!

1 pound Jack cheese, shredded	1/4 cup margarine, melted
1 cup milk	1 small can minced olives (optional)
1 cup flour	1 4-ounce can Jalapeno peppers,
1 pint cottage cheese	seeds removed
6 eggs, beaten slightly	

Combine all ingredients, mixing until thoroughly blended. Pour into a greased 9 x 13-inch baking pan and bake at 375° F. for 30 to 40 minutes, or until eggs are set. Cut into small squares and serve warm for a spirited party appetizer. This can be prepared early in the day and briefly reheated at 400° F. for 5 or 6 minutes.

Potato Skin Crisps**

Potato skins, melty with cheese and sour cream, make a rib-sticking cocktail snack. Save the insides of the baked potatoes for use later.

2 large Idaho baking potatoes	1/4 cup bacon bits
1/2 cup butter	Garlic salt
1/2 cup shredded	1 cup sour cream
Cheddar cheese	3 green onions, minced
1/2 cup shredded Jack cheese	

Early in the day, bake potatoes until fork-tender. With a sharp knife, cut in half lengthwise and carefully scoop out the centers, leaving a 1/4-inch shell. Cut each half lengthwise into thirds if the potatoes are large. Otherwise, cut each piece in half. This much may be done ahead.

Before serving, brush the inside of each potato skin with butter and place, skin side down, on a cookie sheet. Bake at 450° F. until hot and crisp —about 10 minutes. Divide cheese among the potato skins and top with bacon bits and a sprinkling of garlic salt. Place under a hot broiler until cheese melts. Top each piece with a dollop of sour cream and a pinch of minced onion. Serve piping hot. Serves 6.

Note: Another excellent option is to fill the shells with refried beans and cheese. Broil until bubbly, then serve with chopped onion and salsa.

Pinata Party Platter***

Here is a colorful chip-and-dip appetizer that is bountiful enough to keep eight guests happily munching all through the cocktail hour.

It looks — and tastes — a lot like a Mexican tostada that you dig into with corn chips. For the best visual effect, make each layer a little smaller in diameter than the one below, which mounds up the platter and shows off all the layers to colorful advantage.

2 cans (10-1/2 ounces each)	1/4 teaspoon cumin
jalapeno bean dip	1 medium tomato, chopped
1/2 cup sour cream	8 ounces Cheddar cheese, grated
1/2 onion, finely chopped	3 to 4 green onions, chopped
2 ripe avocados,	1 small can chopped black olives
peeled and mashed	8 ounces Jack cheese, grated
Salt and pepper, to taste	2 tomatoes, chopped
1 tablespoon lemon juice	

Mix bean dip with sour cream and spread over a 10-inch serving platter. Top with guacamole layer (avocados mashed and mixed with the next 4 ingredients). Sprinkle with grated Cheddar cheese. Over the cheese, distribute the chopped green onion. Top with a smaller circle of chopped olives, topped with grated Jack cheese; lastly, the chopped tomatoes. Alongside the Pinata Party Platter provide a big bowlful of corn chip dippers. Be sure the chips are large enough to make good "scoopers".

Sausage Mushroom Caps**

Sausage-stuffed mushroom caps always go fast with the nip-and-nibble cocktail crowd. This recipe makes a lot, but don't worry . . . there won't be any left.

2 pounds large mushrooms
3 to 4 tablespoons butter
1 12-ounce package sausage

1 8-ounce package cream cheese
Parmesan cheese

Gently twist stems from mushrooms and chop. Saute in melted butter until soft. In another pan, saute the sausage, breaking up with a fork as it cooks. When crumbly and lightly browned, drain well. Mix cheese into the sausage and blend. Stir in the sauteed mushroom stems. Fill mushroom caps with the mixture and sprinkle lightly with Parmesan cheese. Place under a broiler until cheese is lightly browned and mushrooms are piping hot — about 5 minutes.

Artichoke Cocktail Squares**

This quiche-like artichoke hors d'oeuvre is one of the very best. If you want to make it ahead of the party, that's fine. It warms up nicely in a slow oven.

2 (6-ounce) jars marinated
   artichoke hearts
1 small onion, finely chopped
1 clove garlic, minced
4 eggs
1/2 cup fine dry bread crumbs

1/4 teaspoon salt
Dash pepper
Dash oregano
Sprinkle hot pepper sauce
1/2 pound sharp cheese, grated
2 tablespoons minced parsley

Drain marinade from artichokes into a skillet. Chop the artichokes and set aside. Heat marinade and add the onion and garlic to the skillet. Saute slowly, until onion is golden. Beat the eggs with a fork, add the crumbs and seasonings, and then fold in the grated cheese, parsley, chopped artichokes and the sauteed onions. Turn into a greased 7 x 11-inch baking pan and bake at 325° F. for 30 minutes or until set. Serve warm or cold in small squares.

Note: This can be made ahead and reheated in the pan at 325° F. for 10 minutes before serving.

Antipasto, Anyone?*

There is something wonderfully bountiful-looking about an antipasto tray, lovingly and artistically prepared by you ahead of time — a factor that has the added bonus of getting you out of the kitchen before your guests arrive.

On a small tray or platter, arrange as many mini nibblers as you can gather up . . . fresh cauliflowerets, carrot sticks, celery, radishes (leave the stems on if they are presentable), green onions, sliced unpeeled zucchini, plump mushrooms.

Punctuate the garden stuff with Italian peppers, black olives, paper-thin slices of hard salami, a mound of marinated garbanzo beans.

Provide small dishes and plenty of finger napkins. A small bowl of sour cream dunk would go nicely with the raw veggies even though dips are not part of the typical Italiano-type spread.

Deviled Lobster Canape*

*Face it: sometimes the emergency tidbits one whips up from provisions on hand come out looking a bit desperate even though they **do** fill the chink. But not this one. If you had the foresight to lay in a can of lobster meat against the time you need a hurry-up nosh, you will come out very much on top. This canape is **terrific.***

1 can (small) lobster meat	2 tablespoons fresh bread crumbs
1 tablespoon butter	Sprinkle dry mustard
1 tablespoon rum	Sprinkle cayenne pepper
Juice of 1 small lemon	Toast rounds or crackers

Mash the lobster meat with the butter, pounding to a smooth paste. Add the lemon juice and rum and continue mashing until thoroughly mixed. Add bread crumbs, blending well. Season mix to taste with dry mustard and cayenne. (Don't over-season . . . a sprinkle should do.) Spread mix on small toast rounds or crisp crackers. Slip under the broiler a minute or two. When piping hot, serve.

Poor Man's Paté**

Like many other vestiges of the good life, pate has soared beyond the reach of most mortals. Happily, a creditable sustitute is here at hand — an easily concocted mix that goes together in a flash, for pennies. Liverwurst is the magic ingredient.

1/2 pound liverwurst	1 tablespoon sherry
1 small package cream cheese	Pinch garlic salt
1/2 cup cream	White pepper, about 1/4 teaspoon
1 tablespoon melted butter	Curry powder (add by pinches)
1 teaspoon Worcestershire sauce	

Mash liverwurst with cream cheese, moisten with cream and blend in remaining ingredients. Taste and adjust seasonings accordingly. You may want a speck more curry powder or pepper, but proceed with caution. The flavors intensify as the pate sets. Refrigerate overnight, but allow to come back to room temperature before serving.

Dorothy's Divine Spinach Dip*

Here, I promise, is the very best spinach dip you will ever dig into.

2 cups sour cream	1/2 cup onion, chopped
1 cup mayonnaise	1/2 cup parsley, chopped
1 envelope dried leek soup	1 teaspoon dry salad seasoning mix
1 package frozen chopped spinach, thawed and drained	1 teaspoon dillweed
	1/2 teaspoon garlic powder

Mix and chill several hours for flavors to ripen. Serve with vegetables or chips.
Note: After spinach has been drained thoroughly, chop into finer bits if you want a smoother dip.

A Word About Filo

In the last couple of years, the popularity of filo dough pastries has really soared. So let's talk about it for a minute or two.

First of all, no matter **what** the cookbooks tell you, this paper-thin dough can be **murder** to handle. This is especially true if the packaged dough has been languishing over long in the freezer case. Alas, this is something you cannot judge until you get it home, start unfolding it, and it falls apart in shreds.

This is a disappointment, but it needn't mean disaster. Simply slather the pieces of filo with melted butter and stack them into a layered rectangle that can be rolled around your filling.

This will seen pretty willy-nilly, but take my word for it — it works.

Place your filling along one edge and start rolling, tucking in the tag ends as you go. Once it is baked, you will have a crisp and flaky pastry roll that can be cut in sections and served.

If you luck out and get a package of pliable filo, you can proceed with the tuck-and-fold technique for making packets.

The only caution here is to be careful to keep the dough from drying out as you work. As you use one sheet, be sure to keep the rest of the filo under wraps — topped with a sheet of plastic and a damp tea towel.

Filo Party Poufs***

Properly executed, the following recipe yields beautifully crisp and compact filo packets, called poufs. Just remember: thaw the dough according to the package instructions. Then, if the dough won't fold, roll it. The end product will be just as good.

1/2 pound filo dough, thawed	1 tablespoon dill weed
1/2 cup butter, melted	Salt and pepper
1/2 pound ricotta cheese	Grated Parmesan cheese

Unroll filo dough and cut the stack in half. Next, cut each section lengthwise into 2-inch wide strips. Place one stack of strips on a board and cover first with plastic, then with a damp cloth. Wrap the remaining dough with another damp towel and place in the refrigerator.

Combine ricotta cheese with dill weed, salt and pepper.

Taking one strip of filo dough at a time, brush with melted butter, and spoon about 1 teaspoon of the ricotta cheese mixture on the corner of one end of the filo strip. Fold up diagonally, flag style, to form a triangle. Brush the triangular packet with more melted butter and sprinkle with Parmesan cheese. Repeat with remaining strips, being careful to keep the dough covered until ready to be folded. When all the strips have been filled and folded, brush with melted butter, place them on a baking sheet and bake at 350° F. for about 8 minutes, or until puffed and golden. Makes about 5 dozen poufs.

Garlic Stuffed Eggs*

*There are stuffed eggs and there are stuffed eggs. Regrettably, nine out of ten suffer terminal blahs. If nothing more inventive has gone into the works than a glop of mayonnaise and mustard, I am for forgetting the whole thing. This next one represents a significant improvement over those bland picnic eggs that just sit there blinking their pale yellow eyes. The difference is garlic — **lots** of garlic — cooked to a creamy paste and stirred into the mix.*

6 eggs	Dash tabasco sauce
6 to 8 fat cloves of garlic, unpeeled	1 teaspoon prepared mustard
1-1/2 tablespoons mayonnaise	Salt and pepper to taste
1-1/2 tablespoons softened butter	1-1/2 tablespoons minced parsley

Cook eggs and unpeeled garlic cloves in hot water for 12 to 15 minutes. Plunge eggs into cold water, then peel. Cut eggs across and scoop yolks into a bowl. Squeeze cooked garlic cloves gently — the pulp will ooze out like toothpaste — and add to yolks. Mix with butter, mayonnaise, tabasco sauce and mustard. Season with salt and pepper. Fill reserved whites with the mixture and refrigerate until serving time. Just before serving, sprinkle with parsley.

Note: If you have time and feel fancy, pipe the yolk mixture into the whites with a pastry bag and star tip.

Steak Tartare*

*Some of the fanciest gourmet fare is the easiest food in the world to prepare. Steak Tartare is a case in point. Guaranteed to impress the daylights out of your epicurean friends, this classic appetizer isn't even **cooked**.*

1 pound top round steak	1 teaspoon Worcestershire sauce
1 tablespoon minced onion	Salt and ground pepper, to taste
1 tablespoon minced parsley	3 tablespoons drained capers
1 tablespoon anchovy paste (optional)	

Have butcher put meat through a medium grinder (don't get the grind too fine). With two forks, lightly mix the rest of the ingredients, except the capers, into the meat. Toss until lightly but thoroughly blended. Shape into a smooth mound on a serving dish. Stud the surface with capers. Serve with toast rounds or crackers.

Tartare-Stuffed Tomatoes**

Next time you are planning a cocktail buffet, set out a tray of tiny tartare-stuffed tomatoes. Real show-stoppers, these! Easy to make, too.

1-1/2 to 2 pints cherry tomatoes (about 60)	1 recipe Steak Tartare
	2 bunches fresh parsley

Cut tops off tomatoes and scoop out seeds and pulp with a grapefruit spoon or small melon baller. Turn tomatoes upside down on a rack to thoroughly drain. Fill with Steak Tartare, garnishing each one with a tiny sprig of parsley.

Raw Beef Appetizer*

If you like steak tartare, you will love this one. Even people who think they don't keep coming back for more.

1 pound beef filet, sliced paper-thin	1/3 cup brandy (optional)
1/2 cup olive oil	1-1/2 teaspoon salt
1/4 cup wine vinegar	1 teaspoon cracked pepper
1/4 cup soy sauce	1 large onion, chopped
	2 cloves garlic, minced

Place filet in the freezer long enough to firm up. Slice as thinly as possible. Discard any visible fat. Combine remaining ingredients and pour over the beef. Allow to marinate 4 to 6 hours. Drain and granish with parsley. Serve with thin slices of buttered pumpernickel or rye bread.

Caviar Pie**

Caviar, the world's all-time top lily-gilder, is easy as 1-2-3 to serve. Just open and offer. Unless you make a caviar pie, of course. It is a little more effort, but considering the raves you'll get, well worth it.

8 hard-cooked eggs	3/4 cup sour cream
3 tablespoons soft butter	1/2 onion, minced very fine
Dash tabasco sauce	Sour cream
Sprinkle of dry mustard	1 small jar red or black caviar
Salt and white pepper	

Peel and mash hard-cooked eggs. Blend in butter and stir to a smooth, pale yellow paste. Flavor to taste with salt, pepper, a dash of tabasco sauce and a sprinkle of dry mustard. Mixture should be zestful but not overpowering.

Pat egg mixture in a smooth layer in a glass pie plate. Sprinkle with finely minced onion and top with an icing of sour cream. Now sprinkle on the caviar. Cover plate with plastic wrap and refrigerate until serving time. Serve accompanied with crisp whole wheat crackers.

Eggplant Caviar**

No matter how you slice it, Aubergines Caviar doesn't taste the least bit like real caviar. But no matter. It is really very good, easily prepared and offers a nice relief from those ubiquitous cream-cheese-and-whatever dips.

1 large eggplant	1/2 cup olive oil
1 large onion, chopped	Seasoned salt
1 green pepper, chopped	Pepper
1 clove garlic, minced	2 to 3 tablespoons dry red wine
2 tomatoes, chopped	

Bake whole eggplant in 400° F. oven for about an hour, or until soft. Meantime, simmer onion and green pepper in olive oil until soft. Add garlic, chopped tomatoes and eggplant that has been peeled and chopped fine. Season to taste with salt and pepper and add wine a little at a time until mixture is fairly smooth. Continue cooking until fairly thick, then cool and refrigerate overnight. Serve with pumpernickel or rye bread.

Escargots a la Bourguignonne***

*Snails with garlic butter are one of the world's greatest delicacies. Never mind any mind-set about snails. Just close your eyes and dig in. They are **divine**. And be sure to provide plenty of crusty French bread for mopping up. The garlic butter is too heavenly to waste one drop.*

1 shallot (or white parts
  of 2 green onions),
  finely chopped
2 cloves garlic, minced

2 tablespoons chopped parsley
1 cup butter (not margarine)
36 snail shells
36 canned snails, drained

Blend shallot (or green onion), garlic and parsley into butter, making a smooth, pale green paste. Season with salt and white pepper. Spoon about 1/2 teaspoon of the butter into each shell, poking it down into the cavity. Place 1 drained snail in each shell and cover with remaining butter.

If you have those special little snail plates, put filled shells in the depressions.* Otherwise, fill a shallow baking pan with rock salt and fit the shells, top side up, in the pan. Bake at 350° F. for 10 to 12 minutes, or until red-hot and bubbling. Serves 6.

*Small forks are usually sold in sets along with escargot plates. If you don't have any, simply provide small cocktail forks for dainty digging. And remember to save the snail shells (which initially can be purchased along with the canned snails in a kind of two-for-one rumble-seat type package).

Garlic-Cheese Popcorn*

If you think the flavor of hot buttered popcorn can't be topped, try seasoning the puffy kernels with garlic and cheese. A big bowlful goes great at a backyard barbecue or cocktail party.

2 quarts popped corn
1/3 cup butter
1/2 cup grated Parmesan cheese

1-1/2 tablespoons minced garlic
Salt

Spread popped corn out in a shallow baking pan and keep warm in a 250° F. oven. Melt butter, stir in cheese and garlic and mix well. Drizzle over popped corn, tossing until coated. Salt to taste. Makes about 2 quarts.

Note: For added zap, add 1 tablespoon chili powder to the mix.

What's Ahead in
Desperation Dishes

Desperation Dishes

. . . first you chop an onion

A desperation dish is something that can bail you out when the ship is sinking. Ideally it consists of ingredients you already have on hand — onions, canned soups, tunafish, etc. If you have a pound of ground beef hanging around, that can't hurt either.

So armed, you can cope with those crises when your company show no signs of budging, there's not time to thaw out the turkey and even the corner deli can't throw you a line.

The following recipes are faithful standbys. Your gourmet friends may sniff, but don't fret. **People who drop in unannounced deserve what they get. They should expect pressed duck or something. Pressed *you*, maybe . . .**

Easiest Enchiladas*

Provided your tortillas are fresh enough to roll, this version of enchiladas is easy enough for the greenest one-star (*) cook to master. (To soften tortillas, either flip, over and over on a hot, dry skillet, or wrap in foil and heat in a moderate oven until pliable.)

1 dozen corn tortillas	1 cup sour cream
2 8-ounce cans enchilada sauce	1/2 teaspoon cumin
2-1/2 cups grated Cheddar	1/2 cup canned chopped green chiles
(or Jack) cheese	Grated cheese

Heat enchilada sauce in a skillet. Quickly dip each tortilla in the hot sauce and lay in a baking pan. Mix the grated cheese with the sour cream, seasonings and finely chopped chiles. Spoon the cheese mixture — about 1 rounded tablespoon — onto each of the tortillas, then roll and place, seam side down, in the baking pan. Do not crowd.

Top with the remaining enchilada sauce and bake at 375° F. for 20 minutes. Serves 6.

Note: Additional cheese may be sprinkled on the enchiladas just before taking from the oven.

Last Resort Casserole*

Last Resort Casserole is just that — an emergency measure you can fall back on before walking off the end of the pier.

1 6-1/4-ounce package corn chips	1 cup shredded Jack cheese
1 onion, chopped	2 15-1/2-ounce cans chili con carne with beans

Crush enough of the corn chips to make 3 cups. Pour half the crushed chips into a greased 2-quart casserole. Distribute chopped onion and shredded cheese over the chips, then top with chili and beans. Smooth out, then sprinkle the remaining corn chips over all and bake at 350°F for 30 minutes. Serves 6.

Next-to-the-Last-Resort Casserole*

The reason casseroles like this don't just fade away is because they are so easy you could toss them together blindfolded. (Just make sure you know where the can opener is before you tie the knot.)

1 pound ground beef	Pinch sugar
1 large onion, chopped fine	8-ounce package noodles, cooked
1 can tomato soup	and drained
1 can chili beef soup	3/4 to 1 cup grated cheese
3/4 can water	

Brown ground beef with chopped onion. Then add soups, water and a few grains of sugar. Blend thoroughly. Fold this mixture into the drained noodles and spoon into a greased casserole. Sprinkle with grated cheese and bake at 350°F. about 20 minutes — until cheese is melted and casserole is lightly browned and bubbly. Serves 4.

Burger-Stuffed Spuds*

If you can lay your hands on a pound of ground beef and a half dozen potatoes, you can have the crammers next door over for Burger-Stuffed Spuds. Be it ever so humble, it sure fills those mid-term gaps.

1 pound ground beef	5 to 6 tablespoons milk
1 large onion, chopped	2 tablespoons butter
Salt and pepper	1 egg, beaten
6 large baking potatoes	Grated cheese

Brown beef, discarding fat if any. Add onion and sprinkle with salt and pepper. Cook until onion is tender. Set aside.

Meantime, pierce potatoes with a fork and bake at 375°F. until done. Cut a thin slice off the top of each potato. Carefully scoop out the centers and mash with a fork, adding milk, butter, egg and ground beef. Pile back into the potato shells and sprinkle with cheese. Bake at 350°F. until piping hot. Serves 6.

Ravioli Divan*

Ravioli Divan doesn't taste one bit like chicken divan, but that's okay. It is quicker than greased lightning and needs nothing more than French bread and red wine to make a meal.

1 15-ounce can beef raviolis	1 10-ounce package frozen broccoli
1 8-ounce container sour cream	1 cup shredded mozzarella cheese

Gently mix raviolis and their sauce with sour cream. Steam broccoli until tender-crisp (do not overcook!) Place a layer of broccoli in an oiled 8 x 13-inch baking dish. Spoon ravioli over and garnish the top with the rest of the broccoli spears. Sprinkle with cheese and bake at 350° F. for 25 minutes, or until heated through and melty. Serves 4.

Starving Student's Chili**

When you hanker for chili and have no time to stand around soaking beans and stirring the pot, here's a shortcut that starts out, logically enough, with canned chili and beans and comes out tasting like the real McCoy.

1 pound ground beef	Salt and pepper
1 large onion, chopped	1 cup grated Cheddar cheese
1 15-1/2-ounce can chili and beans	1 cup chopped onions
1 8-ounce can enchilada sauce	

Saute ground beef with onion until onions are slightly soft and meat has lost its pink color. Drain off any excess fat and add chili beans, sauce and seasonings. (A dash of cumin is good, too.) Bring to a simmer and serve up in bowls topped with coarsely chopped onions and grated cheese. Serves 4.

Busy Student's Chili Stuffers**

This simple dish has vague south-of-the border overtones . . . somewhat like chiles rellanos, similar to Spanish rice, but easier than either to assemble.

1 package beef flavored Rice-a-Roni	1 pound Jack cheese, cut in 1/2 x 2-inch strips
1-1/2 pounds ground beef	1 large carton sour cream
2 7-ounce cans whole green chiles	Salt and pepper, to taste

Cook Rice-a-Roni according to package directions. Cook ground beef, drain off excess fat, and add the cooked rice.

Stuff chiles with cheese strips and set aside.

Place rice and beef mixture in a flat, well-greased baking dish. Place chiles stuffed with cheese on top. "Frost" the whole thing with sour cream. If prepared ahead, refrigerate until ready to bake. (The flavor improves with standing.) Bake in 350° F. oven for 30 minutes or until thoroughly heated through and bubbling. Serves 8.

More Desperate Measures

For the student or working type whose middle-of-the-week approach to cooking is strictly slam-and-cram, here are four easy options. Any one will keep body and soul together until payday.

Student's Stew*

3 pounds stew meat or round steak cut in 1-inch pieces	1 package onion soup mix
2 cans cream of mushroom soup	1 can water
	1/2 soup can sherry

Dump everything in a 2-quart casserole. Cover and bake at 325°F. for 2-1/2 to 3 hours. Stir occasionally. Add a little liquid — water or wine — if it gets too thick. Serve over rice or noodles. Serves 6.

Quick Burgundy Beef*

This is the same thing as Student's Stew, only you substitute 1 cup Burgundy wine for the sherry.

B&M Fix-Up*

To one tall can of B&M baked beans stir in some chopped onion (one small or half a large one), a glob of chili sauce and some brown sugar — 1 tablespoon, say. If you like your beans really sweet, you can add a tablespoon of molasses, too. That will also make the beans darker. A teaspoon of prepared mustard adds zip.

From here, you can fold in the contents of a can of apple slices and some bits of leftover ham or a can of luncheon meat cut into cubes. Bake the whole thing in a greased casserole at 325° F. for about a half hour and there you have it — a best-bean dinner for 4.

Stir-Fry Tuna*

Bored with tuna and noodles? Fair enough. Here is another way to turn a can of tuna into tonight's dinner.

1 teaspoon oil	2 teaspoons instant chicken bouillon
3/4 cup thinly sliced carrots	
1/2 cup thinly sliced green pepper	1 teaspoon soy sauce
3 green onions chopped, with tops	1 cup water
1 6-1/2-ounce can water-packed tuna	1 rounded tablespoon cornstarch
1 6-ounce can sliced bamboo shoots	Hot cooked rice or canned chow mein noodles

Stir-fry carrots, pepper and onions in oil over medium heat until vegetables are tender-crisp. Do not allow to brown. Drain tuna and add to vegetables. Stir for 2 minutes.

In a small bowl, mix cornstarch with water, bouillon and soy sauce. When smooth, add to vegetables and heat to boiling. Cook 1 minute, or until sauce is clear and thickened. Serve over rice or noodles. Serves 2.

Poached Eggs Florentine*

One staple everyone should always have on hand in the freezer is a package or two of spinach. All it takes is a quick thaw and presto! — you can turn almost anything into a Florentine fix-up. Like this one.

1 can white sauce	1 10-ounce package frozen chopped
Dash nutmeg	spinach, thawed
1/4 cup grated Swiss cheese	4 eggs
or Parmesan	Salt and pepper

Season white sauce with a sprinkling of nutmeg. Stir in cheese. Drain spinach in a seive, pressing out as much liquid as possible. Add white sauce to spinach and mix well. Spoon into a shallow baking dish. Bake at 350° F. until heated through — about 15 minutes.

Meantime, poach eggs. When eggs are done, gently transfer with a slotted spatula to the casserole, arranging them on top. Sprinkle with salt and pepper and, if desired, a drift of Parmesan. Serves 2.

Quick Spinach Pie*

*Here's another speedy combo that turns a package of frozen spinach into fit-for-company fare (if the company isn't **too** fancy.)*

1 cup biscuit baking mix	1 cup grated Jack cheese
1/4 cup milk	1 12-ounce carton creamed
2 eggs, slightly beaten	cottage cheese
1/2 onion, minced	Salt and pepper
1 10-ounce package frozen	2 cloves garlic, minced
chopped spinach, thawed	2 eggs, slightly beaten
1/2 cup Parmesan cheese	

Combine biscuit mix with milk, 2 eggs and minced onion. Spread in a greased 7 x 12-inch baking pan. Set aside.

Mix well-drained spinach with remaining ingredients. Spoon over biscuit mix. Bake at 375° F. for about 30 minutes, or until set. Let stand 5 minutes, then cut into servings. Serves 6.

Clam Bake*

A clutch of crackers and a can of clams are about all that's needed for this one.

12 soda crackers, crumbled	1/2 small onion, minced
1 cup milk	1/2 green pepper, minced
1 8-ounce can minced	Salt and pepper
clams, undrained	2 eggs, beaten
1/4 cup melted butter	

Combine crumbled crackers, undrained clams and milk in a bowl. Let stand 10 minutes. Add butter, onion, green pepper, salt, pepper and beaten eggs. Pour into a buttered 9-inch baking pan. Bake at 325° F. for 30 to 40 minutes, or until puffed and delicately browned. Serves 4.

*Taquitos***

Taquitos resemble tacos except that the corn tortillas are tightly wrapped around shredded beef, then pan-fried until crisp.

Note: The falling-off-the-bone beef needed for taquitos requires you either start early and slow-cook a pot roast or save enough of Sunday's leftover roast for this purpose.

2 cups slow-cooked beef, shredded	2-1/2 teaspoons chili powder
	Salt and pepper
3 tablespoons minced onion	1/2 teaspoon cumin
2 tablespoons oil	12 corn tortillas

Heat beef with onion in hot oil until onion is soft. Add chili powder, cumin, salt and pepper. Lightly grease a griddle and heat the tortillas one at a time, until soft enough to roll. Spoon about 2 tablespoons beef in a narrow strip down the center of each tortilla, roll tightly, and secure with toothpicks. Heat 1/2-inch oil in a skillet until it ripples when the pan is tilted, then fry each taquito over medium-high heat until crisp and golden. Drain on paper towels, sprinkle lightly with salt and serve with sour cream and guacamole. Makes 12.

*Fall-Out Frittata**

Fall-Out Frittata is so named because almost anything that falls out of the fridge can go into it — chopped leftover meat, cheese, veggies — what have you. Here we use a potato and a couple of zucchini. Try it or ad lib at will.

1 potato	Salt and pepper
2 zucchini	3 eggs
3 tablespoons oil or margarine	Parmesan cheese

Peel potato. Scrub zucchini but don't peel. Grate potato and zucchini with a medium to coarse grater.

Heat oil (or margarine) in a large skillet. When sizzling, add grated vegetables and stir-fry until tender crisp. Season with salt and pepper and pat flat. Beat eggs. Pour over grated potato and zucchini and turn heat low. Sprinkle with Parmesan cheese. Cover pan and cook until eggs are set. Cut in wedges. Serves one. Can be doubled. Or tripled. Just get a larger pan.

*Apple-Kraut Bavarian**

1 pound sausage links	1 1-pound can sauerkraut, rinsed
1 1-pound can applesauce	and drained

Brown sausage links and drain off most of the fat. Pour applesauce and sauerkraut over the links, cover and cook gently until thoroughly heated through — about 20 minutes over low heat. Brown bread makes a good accompaniment. Serves 4.

Hash Quiche*

Got a can of corned beef hash in the pantry? Good. Within minutes, you can have a beefy quiche if you follow the following.

1 15-ounce can corned beef hash	3 to 4 tablespoons minced
2 tablespoons flour	green onions
3 eggs	1/4 teaspoon salt
1 cup half and half	1/4 teaspoon hot sauce
1/2 cup shredded Swiss cheese	Parmesan cheese

Mix hash with flour and one egg. Press against bottom and sides of an ungreased 9-inch pie pan. Bake at 375° F. for 10 minutes. Lower heat to 350° F. Beat remaining two eggs. Add everything else but the Parmesan cheese. Pour into hash shell and sprinkle with Parmesan.

Bake at 350° F. for 40 minutes or until a knife inserted in the center comes out clean. Let stand 15 minutes before serving.

Saucy Chicken Lickin'*

Face it: that frigid fried chicken that comes boxed up in the freezer case of the supermarket is never going to measure up to a crusty, freshly fried bird. But when you're caught in a revolving door and time has run out, here is how to gussy up a freezer fryer that's good enough for company.

Note: You can work the same trick on take-out chicken from the Colonel's corner franchise.

1 32-ounce package pre-fried frozen chicken (or take-out chicken for 4)	1/2 cup chopped onion
	Pinch fresh grated (or powdered) ginger
1 cup apricot-pineapple preserves	2 tablespoons soy sauce
1/2 cup bottled barbecue sauce	

Place chicken in an ungreased 9 x 13-inch baking dish and cook according to package instructions. (If you are using over-the-counter fried chicken, you skip this part).

Combine apricot-pineapple preserves with the onion, soy sauce, barbecue sauce and ginger. Spoon over chicken and bake for 20 minutes. Chicken should be hot through and richly glazed. Serves 4.

Sour Cream Enchilada Stack*

The laziest way of all to make enchiladas is to simply layer the tortillas with plenty of filling and serve the stack in fat wedges.

1 pound ground beef	5 to 6 corn tortillas
1 onion, chopped	1 cup sour cream
1 tablespoon oil	1 cup shredded Jack or
1 teaspoon salt	Cheddar cheese
1 7-ounce can green chile salsa	1 2-1/4-ounce can sliced olives

Cook beef and onion in oil until meat loses its red color. Break up meat with a fork as it cooks. Stir in salt and salsa, cover and simmer 5 minutes. In a shallow baking dish layer meat-salsa sauce, sour cream, cheese and olives between tortillas. End with a liberal sprinkling of cheese. Bake at 350° F. for 20 minutes or until cheese is melted and stacks are piping hot. Cut in wedges. Serves 4.

Strip-Tease Tacos**

Ready-made taco shells need nothing but a handful of filling and they're ready to go. If you prefer softer tacos, skip the store-bought shells and pile the following filling onto steamed flour or corn tortillas.

8 packaged taco shells	1/4 teaspoon cumin
1 pound top round steak, cut in	1/2 teaspoon salt
strips 3/4-inch thick	4 tablespoons taco sauce or salsa
2 tablespoons oil	1-1/2 cups shredded lettuce
1 onion, chopped	2 cups shredded Jack cheese
2 cloves garlic, minced	Guacamole

Wrap taco shells in foil and heat in 350° F. oven for 10 minutes. Heat oil in a heavy skillet and gently saute onion until golden. With slotted spoon, remove onion and set aside. Saute meat slices in same pan, stirring only until pink disappears. Add garlic, cumin, salt, sauce and the sauteed onion. Simmer for 2 minutes. Spoon meat into hot taco shells and serve with bowls of shredded lettuce, cheese and guacamole to spoon over. Serves 8.

Humongous Bean Pot*

When a hungry mob descends, minutes count and the budget is busted, this hefty big bean combo could really save the day.

1 16-ounce can baked beans	1 cup chopped green pepper
1 15-ounce can kidney beans,	1 16-ounce can tomatoes
drained	1 1-1/2-ounce package Sloppy Joe
1 15-ounce can navy or pinto	seasoning mix
beans, drained	3/4 cup shredded Cheddar cheese

Combine everything but the cheese and pour into a buttered 2-quart casserole. Top with cheese. Bake at 375° F. for 30 minutes. Serves 8.

Joe's Special**

Legend has it that a well-known San Francisco eatery in North Beach was once jammed with an unexpected mob of after-hours customers, and there was nothing left in the kitchen but ground beef, onions, spinach and eggs.

Undaunted, the chef deftly tossed it all together and came up with a concoction that has been a favorite of San Franciscans ever since.

Note: this stuff tastes a lot better than it looks.

1 pound ground beef (lean)	1 teaspoon salt
2 tablespoons oil	Cracked pepper
1/2 cup chopped onion	6 eggs, lightly beaten
1 package frozen, chopped spinach, drained	

Cook beef in oil, breaking it up with a fork as it cooks. When it has lost its red color, add the onion and continue to cook until the onion is tender but not brown. Squeeze as much liquid from the thawed spinach as possible, then add to the meat. Cook until the pan juices have evaporated. Add the beaten eggs. Cook and stir occasionally, just until the eggs are set. Don't overcook. Serves 4.

Note: If the fixings in the skillet look a little skimpy for the bunch you are trying to feed, don't panic. Open a can of kidney beans, drain and toss into the pot. This adds a nice touch of color along with the needed heft.

Pork and Green Chili Stew**

The next time you make burritos, try this hefty pork and chili filling. Just remember to start early. Slow simmering makes all the difference.

2-1/2 to 3 pounds boneless pork butt	1-1/2 teaspoons ground cumin
2 14-ounce cans chicken broth	1/2 teaspoon crushed red chili peppers
1 16-ounce can tomatoes, undrained	1/2 teaspoon pepper
2 7-ounce cans diced green chiles	1/2 cup water
	1/4 cup flour
	Fresh cilantro

Cut fat off pork, then cut into 1-inch cubes. Brown meat in batches in a heavy kettle. When all is browned, add broth, tomatoes, chiles, cumin and peppers. Bring to boil, then cover and lower heat. Cook at a simmer for about 1-1/2 hours, or until meat is fork-tender. If made ahead, this is the time to cover and refrigerate.

Before serving, blend flour with 1/2-cup water, making a smooth paste. Stir into heated stew and cook until smooth and slightly thickened. Serve with a garnish of cilantro. Serves 6.

What's Ahead in Potluck Portables

Potluck Portables

. . . coping with the PTA and other mob scenes

Even if you don't belong to the PTA, ERA or other assorted orders, sooner or later you are going to be roped into a potluck. And when the time comes, you probably won't be able to weasel out by volunteering to bring the plastic forks and cups.

People who organize potlucks are like drill sergeants. Before you know it, they will have you pressed to the wall and promising to bring "a hot dish for 12." Feeble attempts to get off the hook with a three-bean salad from the deli won't· work, either.

Before you go stomping off to doctor up six cans of baked beans, check out the following recipes. Any one of them could do noble duty at the office get-together. They are all very good — everyone will want the recipe — and you will make points as a willing and innovative contributor.

You may even find that you like potlucks. On the other hand, if dipping potato salad out of a communal trough is **not** your idea of a good time, try to be out of town the next time plans start brewing for one of these shindigs.

Chalupas**

Here's a big, fat make-ahead casserole that feeds a mob. Take the recipe along. Everyone will want it.

2 pints sour cream	12 corn tortillas
2 4-ounce cans diced green chiles	1/2 cup oil
1 onion, grated	3-1/2 pounds cooked chicken
1 green pepper, chopped	or turkey
3 large cloves garlic, minced	2 pounds American cheese, grated

Combine sour cream, chiles, pepper, onion and garlic. Soften tortillas in hot oil (and be quick! Don't let them get crisp). Cover bottom of a flat 3-quart casserole with 6 tortillas, top with part of the chicken (or turkey) cut in small pieces, and half of the sour cream mixture. Sprinkle with cheese. Repeat the layers, topping casserole off with the grated cheese. Let stand a minimum of 8 hours before baking in a 350° F. oven for 1 hour. Serves 16.

Encinitas Casserole**

This hefty casserole combines all the good things that go into Mexican cookery —
cheese, chiles, green onions and corn tortillas.

2 large chicken breasts (4 halves) 1 cup milk
12 corn tortillas   1 large onion, chopped
1 pound Cheddar cheese, grated   1 7-ounce can chopped green chiles
1 can cream of chicken soup   1 7-ounce can green chile salsa
1 can cream of mushroom soup

Simmer chicken breasts in a small amount of lightly salted water until tender.
Set aside to cool. Cut tortillas in 1-inch strips and use half to line the bottom and
sides of a buttered 2-quart casserole.

Skin and bone chicken and cut in large pieces. Place half over the tortilla layer,
then cover with a mixture of soups, milk, onion, chiles and salsa. Add another
layer of tortilla strips, a layer of chicken and more sauce. Top with shredded
cheese and bake 1-1/2 hours at 300° F. Serves 8 bountifully.

Chula Vista Casserole**

Three cheeses and ground beef give this mob-sized dish real heft. Don't let the long
list of ingredients throw you. Just assemble the elements, toss it all together, then
stand back and accept raves. Everyone **loves** *this one!*

4 pounds ground beef   24 corn tortillas
2 large onions, chopped   Oil
3 cloves garlic, minced   4 cups cottage cheese
1/4 cup chili powder   2 eggs
6 cups tomato sauce   1 pound Jack cheese, coarsely
1 teaspoon sugar   grated
1 tablespoon salt   2 cups Cheddar cheese, grated
1 cup sliced black olives   1-1/2 cups chopped green onions
2 4-ounce cans diced   1 cup sour cream
   green chiles   Cilantro

Brown meat in a large, heavy skillet. (Do not add all the meat at once — it is
better to cook it in batches.) When meat is nicely browned, add onions and garlic.
Mix in chili powder, then add tomato sauce, sugar, salt, olives and chiles. Simmer
slowly for 15 minutes.

Fry tortillas in hot oil, one at a time, removing before they are brown or crisp
(they should be soft and pliable). Drain on paper towels, then cut in quarters.

Beat cottage cheese with eggs until smooth.

Spread 1/3 of the meat mixture in a large 6-quart casserole. Cover with half the
Jack cheese, half of the cottage cheese mixture and half of the tortilla wedges.
Repeat, ending with a top layer of meat. Sprinkle with grated cheese.

Bake at 350° F. for 30 minutes. Serve with chopped green onions, sour cream
and cilantro as "toppers." Serves 12.

Broccoli Rice Casserole**

A friend of mine who considers herself quite a gourmet cook sniffed at this recipe, intimating that she wouldn't be caught dead with Cheese Whiz in her house. Well, that's too bad, for she's the loser. This dish is really delicious and could be served, without apology, to company. (But play it safe. Hide the empty Cheese Whiz jar and don't give anyone the recipe.)

3 cups cooked rice	1/4 pound fresh mushrooms, sliced
1 large bunch broccoli	1 can cream of celery soup
(about 20 ounces)	Grated onion, to taste
1 6-ounce jar Cheese Whiz	Salt and pepper

Trim and cut broccoli into bite-size pieces. Steam until tender-crisp (don't overcook!). Fold all ingredients together and bake at 350° F. about 15 to 20 minutes — just long enough to heat through and bubble. Serves 6.

Teeny Tamale Casserole**

This quick-fix casserole calls for canned tamales. Crank open the can, peel off the papers, and you're off and running.

1 large onion, chopped fine	Salt and pepper to taste
1 tablespoon margarine	1/2 teaspoon cumin
1 pound ground beef	1 teaspoon chili powder
1 large 1 pound-12-ounce can	2 cans tamales (about 12 total),
stewed tomatoes	sliced
1 3-ounce can tomato paste	2 cups sour cream
1 package taco seasoning	2 cups grated Cheddar cheese
1 package onion soup mix	

Saute onion in margarine until tender-crisp. Add beef and saute until cooked through. Drain off fat and liquid. Add undrained tomatoes, tomato paste, taco seasoning and onion soup mix. Season and cook for 20 minutes.

Place the sliced tamales in a flat 9 x 13-inch baking dish. Cover with meat sauce and top with a mixture of sour cream and grated cheese. Bake at 350° F. for 35 to 40 minutes. Serves 8.

Cheesy Stove Top Casserole*

The mainstay of Cheesy Stove Top Casserole is, not surprisingly, a package of Stove Top dressing. This makes a quiche-like treat that's as good cold as it is hot. And that's a nice feature if you have leftovers, which you probably won't. Everybody always goes back for seconds.

2 packages Stove Top dressing	1 pound Jack cheese, grated
8 medium size zucchini, chopped	1 pound Cheddar cheese, grated
2 large onions, chopped	8 eggs, beaten

Prepare the dressing according to the package instructions. Then stir in the remaining ingredients, mix well, and place in a well-greased flat baking dish. Bake at 350° F. for 45 minutes. Serves 12.

Beef Noodle Stroganoff**

Beef Noodle Stroganoff is one of those quick-mix casseroles that can be doubled, tripled and then some without losing its integrity. When you need food for a mob, this could be the answer.

1/4 cup butter or margarine	2 cans beef bouillon
4 onions, chopped	2/3 cup red wine
2 pounds ground beef	1 pound wide noodles
4 4-ounce cans canned	2 cups sour cream
mushrooms, sliced	Salt and pepper to taste
1/4 cup lemon juice	Finely minced parsley

Saute chopped onion in butter or margarine. When lightly browned, add beef, browning a bit at a time and breaking up with a fork as it cooks. Drain off excess grease. When beef has lost its pink color, add mushrooms and lemon juice, bouillon and wine. Simmer gently for 5 minutes. Meanwhile, cook noodles in rapidly boiling salted water until tender. Drain and fold into meat and mushrooms. Just before serving, add sour cream and season to taste with salt and pepper. Take care not to boil, but serve piping hot. Serves 8.

Chiles Rellenos Casserole**

Chiles Rellenos are good, but are also something of a pain to prepare. This casserole, by contrast, is a snap to assemble and comes out with all the fluffy, cheesy qualities of rellanos with minimum fuss.

1-1/2 pounds Jack cheese, grated	4 eggs, beaten
2 4-ounce can whole	1 small can evaporated milk
green chiles, seeded	2 tablespoons flour
1-1/2 pounds sharp Cheddar	
cheese, grated	

Layer chiles and grated cheese in a greased casserole. Combine eggs and milk and blend in flour until smooth. Pour over chiles and cheese and bake at 350° F. for 35 minutes. Top casserole with the following sauce:

Chiles Rellenos Sauce

1 8-ounce can tomato sauce	1 teaspoon sugar
1 7-ounce can green chili salsa	

Combine ingredients and pour over casserole. Bake an additional 15 minutes. Let casserole stand for 8 to 10 minutes before serving. Serves 8 to 10.

Florentine Fill-Up**

A friend of mine who has six kids, and who is a genius at stretching a pound of ground beef into infinity, gave me this recipe. Try it when your budget's hurting.

1 pound ground beef	2 packages frozen spinach, chopped
1 4-ounce can mushrooms, sliced	1 can cream of celery soup
1 onion, chopped	1 cup sour cream
2 cloves garlic, minced	4 rounded tablespoons pre-cooked
3 tablespoons butter	minute rice
1 teaspoon oregano	1 6-ounce package Mozzarella
Salt and pepper	cheese, sliced

Brown beef with next six ingredients. Drain off excess grease and place in a flat baking dish. Press as much liquid as possible out of the thawed spinach, then add, with the soup, sour cream and rice, to the meat layer, forking gently to mix it all together. (Don't overmix — just sort of "clump" everything together.) Bake at 350° F. for 20 minutes, then place Mozzarella cheese slices, cut in strips, over the top of the casserole. Return to the oven and cook another 15 minutes. Serves 6.

Note: If you double the recipe to serve 12, use two baking pans.

Spinach-Cheese Rice-a-Role**

Here's another casserole that does noble duty for potlucks and clan gatherings where heft counts for more than haute cuisine.

4 eggs, beaten	1/4 teaspoon dill weed
1 cup half and half	1 package frozen chopped spinach,
3 tablespoons minced onion	drained
1 tablespoon Worcestershire	1 pound sharp Cheddar cheese,
sauce	grated
2 teaspoons salt	4 cups cooked rice
1/4 teaspoon marjoram	5 tablespoons melted butter

To beaten eggs, add the half and half, onion and the seasonings. Then fold in the cheese and spinach that has been pressed in a sieve to remove excess moisture. Stir in the rice, blending lightly but thoroughly before pouring into a greased casserole. Melt butter and drizzle over the whole thing before popping it into a 375° F. oven for 35 minutes. Serves 6.

What's Ahead in
Brunch & Breakfast

Breakfast & Brunch

. . . and how to tell one from the other

Serious bacon-and-eggers regard breakfast as the best meal of the day and they don't cotton much to people messing with their menus. For these early birds, it is eggs over easy or sunny side up and spare them the Benedict bit.

And then you have the brunch bunch — people who are in no hurry to rise **or** shine, and are not at all adverse to finding blueberries in their waffles or gin in their juice.

Because they are informal and generally undemanding on the cook, brunches are a popular way to entertain on weekends. Menus can vary almost endlessly, although light repasts — quiches, stratas and crepes — are particularly appropriate.

As for washing it down, what could be better than Bloody Marys? Or chilled champagne? Or, better yet, **both?**

But you'd better make it coffee — black — for the bacon and egg gang. And because they are the first ones up, we will deal with the subject of breakfast in the pages that follow. Then, once we've fried a few eggs, we can work our way into the more exotic midday options.

The Shell Game

Eggs come from hen to housewife in nature's most perfect package . . . plump, pristine and ready to go. Why, then, one wonders, do so many people goof up when it comes to cooking them?

The problem is temperature. Brides, in blissful innocence, fry eggs to a frazzle over too hot a fire, sear omelettes to a crisp and boil eggs to the toughness of hockey pucks. The culprit, to repeat, is **heat.**

*Never Say "Boiled"**

"Soft boiled" eggs may be one of the biggest items on America's breakfast menus, but please note: eggs should never, ever, be boiled. Soft **simmered** eggs are what you are after.

Start with room-temperature eggs. Those straight from the fridge tend to crack when they hit the hot water, so either let them stand around on the sink for a half-hour or run warm water over them long enough to take off the chill. Poking a tiny hole in the blunt end of the shell with a pin also helps keep the egg from cracking.

Bring water in a saucepan to boil. Then gently lower the eggs into the water with a tablespoon. Immediately lower the heat so the water just simmers. Cook the eggs for 3 minutes for soft-cooked, 5 to 7 minutes for medium and 20 minutes for hard-cooked.

Or you can start the eggs in cold water and bring the pot to the boiling point. The minute the water boils, the eggs will be cooked if you like them very, very soft. For slightly firmer eggs, cover the pan and the let the eggs simmer another 2 minutes. For medium-soft, cook 3 to 4 minutes. Hard-cooked eggs should simmer 15 minutes.

Then stop. Long cooking causes the eggs to develop unattractive black "eye-liners" around the yolks, so don't over-do. Plunge the eggs in cold water and let stand until cool.

Another thing: keep hard-cooked eggs cool, but don't chill. Hard-cooked eggs toughen up in the fridge.

Fried Eggs*

For best results, use a heavy non-stick skillet. Heat 1 tablespoon butter until it sizzles, then break the egg(s) directly into the pan or into a saucer first if you opt for the crack-and-slide approach.

Lower the heat and add a bit more butter, if needed, to baste the eggs as they cook. Without turning, the eggs are "sunny side up." Flip them, and you have "once over lightly" eggs.

Either way — up or over — the yolks should be on the soft side. And never should the bottoms be brown or "sizzled." Keep the heat low. High heat and eggs don't mix.

Scrambled Eggs*

If you have the patience, you can scramble eggs in the top of a double boiler. This is a good option if you aren't sure they can be served up right away. Otherwise, use a heavy, non-stick skillet.

For 4 people, lightly beat 6 to 8 eggs and add 1/2 cup milk or half-and-half. Season with salt and pepper. Melt 2 to 3 tablespoons butter in the skillet over high heat. The minute the butter sizzles, lower the heat and pour in the beaten eggs.

Cook slowly, using a broad spatula to lift the eggs from the bottom as they cook. Serve while the eggs are still moist and creamy.

Cheesy Scrambled Eggs*

Beat eggs with milk or light cream, as for regular scrambled eggs, and fold in 1 cup of cottage cheese just before eggs set up. Or you can use 1 small package of cream cheese, crumbled. Eggs scrambled with cottage cheese or cream cheese are a wonderful brunch idea. Garnish with finely minced parsley.

Holdover Scrambled Eggs**

If you are planning a mid-morning breakfast and you are not sure just when the tennis players or joggers will trot in, these stay-at-home eggs will wait for the party to get started. The addition of white sauce keeps the scrambled-ahead eggs moist and creamy.

1/3 cup (rounded) butter or margarine	12 eggs
2 tablespoons flour	1 teaspoon salt
1-1/3 cups milk	Dash black pepper
	Dash hot pepper sauce

Melt 2 tablespoons butter in a saucepan and stir in flour, mixing to a smooth roux. Remove pan from heat and gradually stir in 1/2 cup of the milk, mixing until smooth. Return to heat and cook until sauce thickens, then add another 1/2 cup of the milk. Simmer for 5 minutes. Combine the remaining 1/3 cup of milk with the eggs, and beat with salt and pepper.

Melt remaining butter in an electric skillet set at 320° F. Add eggs and cook slowly, lifting with a broad spatula as the eggs begin to set up. While they are still soft, add the cream sauce, folding gently to mix. Do **not** overcook. Turn skillet heat down, cover and set at warm — 200°. These eggs will wait for late comers. Serves 6 to 8.

Early Scrambled Eggs**

Another way to hold scrambled eggs for a party is to add cream soup and cheese. These wait and wait — and they're wonderful!

1 can undiluted cream of mushroom soup	2 tablespoons milk
1/4 cup sherry	1 teaspoon dillweed
1-1/2 cups shredded Jack cheese	Dash white pepper
1-1/2 cups shredded Cheddar cheese	1/4 cup margarine
18 eggs, beaten slightly	1/4 pound mushrooms, sliced
	1/2 cup chopped green onion
	Parmesan cheese

Heat soup over low heat until smooth. Take from heat and add sherry. Toss grated Jack and Cheddar cheeses together to mix, then set aside.

Beat eggs with milk, dillweed and pepper, and set aside.

Melt margarine in a large skillet, then add the mushrooms and green onion. When onions are limp, add the beaten eggs and stir still eggs are set but still moist.

Spoon half the eggs into a buttered, 11 x 14-inch baking dish and top with half of the soup and sherry mixture. Sprinkle with half of the cheese. Repeat, layering on the rest of the eggs, soup and cheese. Sprinkle top with Parmesan, then cover and refrigerate. This much can be done the night before.

The next day, take pan from refrigerator and let mixture reach room temperature. Bake at 300° F. for 35 minutes, or until hot and bubbling. If the mixture goes into the oven straight from refrigerator, allow an hour heating time. Serves 10 to 12.

Omelets-To-Order**

Over-sized omelets are awkward to handle. Don't attempt making one with more than four eggs. Small omelets, made to order, work better.

For a standard omelet, beat 4 eggs, then add 4 tablespoons water. Season with salt and pepper. Melt 2 tablespoons butter in a heavy skillet and bring to a quick sizzle. Add the beaten eggs, reduce the heat at once, and as the mixture begins to set, gently lift the eggs with a spatula, allowing the uncooked part to run under until the whole thing is moderately set and creamy. *The omelet is ready when the bottom is set and the surface is still moist and shiny.*

Using a spatula, tilt the pan, fold the omelet and slide onto a hot platter. Serves 2 to 3.

Cheese Omelet**

Sprinkle 1/2 cup grated Cheddar cheese over the eggs a few minutes before the omelet is ready to fold. Gruyere and Jack cheeses may be used in place of Cheddar with excellent results. (Another time try teaming 2 or 3 tablespoons of chopped canned chiles with Jack cheese. Zesty!)

Brie Omelet**

One of the most heavenly omelets I ever had was in the coffee shop of the St. Francis Hotel in San Francisco. It was, quite simply, a regular omelet folded over a generous blob of ripe Brie cheese and topped with toasted almond slices.

This is something you **have** to try when you are feeling indulgent. To really gild the lily, serve the omelet with a warm croissant and strawberry preserves.

Huffy Omelet**

Because of its puffed-up qualities, Huffy Omelet seems to taste like **more** *. . . a point to consider if the larder is a little skimpy or if you're on a diet.*

3 eggs, separated	**Salt and white pepper**
3 tablespoons milk	**2 to 3 tablespoons butter**

Separate eggs and beat the whites until they hold stiff peaks. In another bowl, beat the yolks thoroughly, and then add milk and seasonings. Next, gently — very gently — fold the whites into the yolks, using a light up-and-over motion.

Heat the butter in a small skillet or omelet pan. When it sizzles, gently pour in the eggs. Lower heat. When the bottom begins to brown, pop the pan into a preheated oven — set at 360° F. — and watch it! When the top is set, sprinkle some cracked pepper or finely minced parsley over the top and serve. Serves 2.

Apple Pie Omelet**

Here is a sweet breakfast treat with a filling that calls to mind that all-American favorite, apple pie and Cheddar cheese.

1 cup canned apple pie filling	4 tablespoons water
1/4 teaspoon cinnamon	1/4 teaspoon salt
1/4 teaspoon nutmeg	2 tablespoons butter
4 eggs	1/2 cup shredded Cheddar cheese

Mix pie filling with cinnamon and nutmeg. Set aside. Mix eggs with water and salt, whipping with a fork. Heat butter in a medium-size skillet or omelet pan and heat until butter sizzles (don't let it brown).

Pour in eggs and swirl around pan, then allow to cook until edges set. With spatula, gently lift one edge of the omelet and tip pan so that uncooked portion of egg can run under to the bottom of the pan.

While the top of the omelet is still moist and shiny, spoon the apple filling over one half of the omelet and sprinkle on half the grated cheese. Tip pan and fold omelet in half and slide onto a warm serving plate. Top omelet with rest of cheese. (If your broiler is hot, you can slip the works in for a minute to melt the cheese, but this isn't really necessary.)

Omelet serves 2.

Poached Eggs**

Poached eggs are delicate but they aren't difficult provided you don't attempt cooking too many at one time. Four is a manageable number. Five at one time is maximum.

Lightly grease a wide, shallow skillet and fill with 1½-inches water. Add 1 teaspoon vinegar. Bring to a boil, then lower heat so water just simmers.

Slip eggs into the simmering water and cook 3 to 4 minutes — even 5 if you want the yolks a bit firmer (you can judge this by pressing gently with your finger). Remove eggs with a slotted spatula and drain well.

Pre-Poached Eggs**

Prepare eggs, as directed, except when they have been cooked 3 or 4 minutes, take from the hot water and slip into a shallow bowl filled with ice water. Refrigerate overnight.

Next day, bring fresh water to a boil, then turn off the heat. Transfer the chilled eggs to the hot water and let them stand until heated through — 5 to 7 minutes. Drain well before serving.

Eggs Benedict**

Easter morning, or any special Sunday morning, nothing is more festive than Eggs Benedict under a golden cloak of buttery Hollandaise. Frankly, I can't think of anything more gorgeously contrived to blow one's diet.

Hollandaise sauce (page 170)	**8 poached eggs**
4 English muffins	**Paprika and parsley**
8 slices ham or Canadian bacon	

Prepare Hollandaise and keep warm over hot (not boiling) water. Poach eggs. Split and toast muffins.

To assemble, place a slice of ham on each muffin half, top with a poached egg and dress liberally with Hollandaise. Sprinkle with paprika and garnish with parsley. Serves 4.

Buttoned-Down Benedict*

For this one-star (*) version, you skip making hollandaise from scratch. Whip up an envelope of hollandaise mix (which is good if you add a bit more butter), or crank open a can. You could also substitute a can of undiluted cheese soup, although that's stretching things a bit.

Eggs Florentine**

This is the same as Eggs Benedict except that you add spinach. Cook a 10-ounce package of chopped, frozen spinach, then squeeze as much liquid out of it as possible through a sieve. Place a mound of spinach over the ham and under the poached egg. Top with Hollandaise. This makes a great luncheon dish.

Union Street Eggs**

Here's another take-off on the standard Benedict bit. It originated in San Francisco in a superb patio cafe that specializes in great food and spectacular Bloody Marys. Every Sunday morning, the customers are lined up for blocks.

4 English muffins	**6 slices bacon, fried crisp**
8 poached eggs	**and crumbled**
2 tablespoons butter	**Hollandaise (page 170)**
8 thick slices tomatoes	**Cracked pepper**

Split and toast muffins. Poach eggs. Melt butter in a skillet and quickly saute tomato slices on both sides.

Place a tomato slice on each muffin half and sprinkle with crumbled bacon. Top with a poached egg and dress lavishly with Hollandaise. Sprinkle with cracked pepper. Serves 4.

Eggs in Nests*

Grease two small ramekins or small baking dishes and line them with canned corned beef hash, pressing the hash up the sides to form nests. Brush with melted butter or margarine and gently crack an egg into each dish.

Bake in a 350° F. oven just until the whites of the eggs are completely set (test gently with the tines of a fork or a sharp knife). Sprinkle with salt and freshly cracked pepper and top with a tablespoon of grated cheese. Let the cheese melt, then serve piping hot.

Brunch Egg Casserole**

This hearty casserole is a dandy choice for the busy cook looking for a quick brunch entree that can be tossed together the night before. It is also a good dinner dish for students, bachelors and career types on the run.

4 cups cheese croutons	1 tablespoon minced green
(Pepperidge Farms is good)	onions or chives
2 cups grated sharp cheese	Dash pepper
8 eggs, beaten slightly	8 to 10 slices bacon,
4 cups milk	fried until crisp
1 teaspoon mustard	

Butter a 9 x 12-inch baking dish. Sprinkle croutons over bottom, then top with cheese. Mix eggs with milk, mustard, onion and pepper. Add crumbled bacon. Pour mixture over cheese and croutons and bake at 325° F. for 1 hour. Serves 8.

NOTE: This dish can be prepared the night before, refrigerated, and baked the next day. If casserole goes into the oven chilled, it will take 10 minutes longer in the oven.

Dolan's Huevos Rancheros***

Dolan's approach to the standard huevos rancheros takes a radical curve — plumping poached eggs into avocado halves and topping the whole thing with cheese and chiles. Buttered tortillas and Bloody Marys are the perfect accompaniment.

1 onion, chopped	1 bay leaf
2 tablespoons oil	Salt and pepper
1 8-ounce can tomato sauce	6 poached eggs
1 clove garlic, minced	3 avocados, peeled and halved
2 tablespoons canned green	2 tablespoons lemon juice
chiles, chopped	1/2 cup shredded Jack cheese
1 teaspoon oregano	Lettuce
1 teaspoon cumin	

Cook onion in oil until limp. Add tomato sauce, garlic, chiles, oregano, cumin and bay leaf, and simmer for 10 minutes. Add salt and pepper, to taste. (This much may be done ahead — like the day before.) Remove bay leaf and bring sauce to a slow simmer just before serving.

Gently poach eggs. When firm enough to lift, transfer eggs to avocado halves that have been brushed with lemon juice and arranged in a 9-inch pie plate. Top avocado halves with sauce and sprinkle with cheese. Broil just until cheese melts. Serve on lettuce and pass extra sauce. Serves 6.

Eggs Rancheros**

Eggs gently poached in chile-tomato sauce, served on warm tortillas and topped off with cheese make a wonderful late-day breakfast for hearty appetites.

1 clove garlic, crushed	3 to 4 canned green chiles, seeded
1 onion, finely chopped	and chopped
2 tablespoons oil	Salt and pepper
2 1-pound cans tomatoes	6 eggs
1/2 teaspoon oregano	6 corn tortillas
1/4 teaspoon cumin	1 cup shredded Jack cheese
	Cilantro (optional)

In a large flat skillet cook garlic and onion in oil until tender but not browned. Add tomatoes, oregano, cumin, chiles, salt and pepper, and simmer about 15 minutes.

Break eggs in a saucer and slip into the simmering sauce. When all eggs are in the pan, cover and gently poach for about 6 minutes. Serve eggs on warm corn tortillas which have been sprinkled lightly with water, wrapped in foil and heated in the oven. Top each egg with a mound of cheese and serve. If desired, garnish with a few sprigs of cilantro. Serves 6.

Tortilla Breakfast Flap*

If your crew likes tortillas, why not try serving them some morning for breakfast wrapped around mounds of creamy scrambled eggs? Just moisten your hands with water, pat the tortillas one at a time and flip into a hot, dry skillet. Turn the tortillas over and over for several seconds until warm and pliable. Wrap the warmed tortillas in foil and stash in a warm oven until you are ready to serve.

Spoon scrambled eggs — along with crumbled crisp bacon and avocado chunks, if you have them — onto the tortillas, fold and serve. Aficionados will appreciate a bowlful of salsa to spoon over. Ole!

Make-Ahead Brunch Livers**

To go along with the make-ahead scrambled eggs, why not include Make-Ahead Brunch Livers? Richly glazed with mayonnaise (no one will ever guess what it is), these livers stay pink, plump and moist — up to an hour.

1 pound chicken livers	1-1/2 cups mayonnaise
1/2 cup flour	4 tablespoons Worcestershire
Salt and pepper	4 tablespoons minced parsley
6 tablespoons butter	

Dredge livers in flour. Sprinkle with salt and pepper. Melt butter. When it sizzles, add the livers and cook 2 to 3 minutes on each side. Transfer livers to a serving platter and set aside. Heat oven to 200° F.

Spoon mayonnaise into the skillet along with the Worcestershire and parsley. With a spatula, scrape up all the browned bits. Spoon sauce over the livers, turning until they are well glazed. Slip into the oven that has been preheated to 200° F. Turn off heat and let livers rest in the warm oven — from 15 minutes to an hour. Serves 6.

Fabulous Fruit Balloons*

Sears, San Francisco's famous breakfast house, built its reputation on its superb dollar-size pancakes. Almost as famous are their wonderful fruit bowls — jewel-like assortments of fresh fruits served in long-stemmed balloon glasses.

This is an elegant touch that would add great panache to any brunch. Chill some fat, stemmed wine glasses and fill them with chunks of whatever fresh fruit is available — melons, grapes, papaya, berries, apples, orange and pineapple. Garnish, if you wish, with a mint sprig.

And stand back for raves. This is a **very** impressive touch.

Pantry Shelf Pancake Mix*

Feeling thrifty? Make up a big batch of pancake mix that you can stash in the pantry — ready to make gorgeous flapjacks in minutes, for pennies!

8 cups flour	4 teaspoons soda
3/4 cup sugar	2 teaspoons salt
1/4 cup baking poweder	2 cups non-fat dry milk

Mix dry ingredients and keep in a tightly covered container in the refrigerator.

Pantry Shelf Pancakes*

2 eggs, beaten	1/4 cup vegetable oil
1 cup buttermilk	2 cups Pantry Shelf
1 cup milk	Pancake Mix

Beat eggs with milk and buttermilk. Add oil. Stir in pancake mix with a fork. Mixture will be slightly lumpy. Bake pancakes on a hot griddle, turning once. Makes enough to serve 4 to 6.

Speedy Blender Pancakes*

In a hurry? Out of pancake mix? Here's how to whip out a stack of flapjacks in jig time.

1 cup milk	2 teaspoons baking powder
1 egg	2 tablespoons sugar
2 tablespoons oil	1/2 teaspoon salt
1 cup flour	1/2 teaspoon vanilla (optional)

Dump everything in a blender and process until smooth. Spoon onto a hot griddle. Makes about a half dozen, 6-inch pancakes.

Blueberry Pancakes*

Prepare Speedy Blender Pancakes. Fold in 2 cups fresh blueberries or 2 cups well-drained frozen and thawed berries. Serve with warm blueberry syrup.

Banana Pancakes*

Prepare Speedy Blender Pancakes, adding 2 small ripe (or 1 large) bananas. Process until smooth. These are great with Coconut Syrup (page 67).

Andy's Hotcake House Flapjacks**

Andy's Cafeteria in downtown Long Beach used to have customers lined up in throngs for the house specialty — old-fashioned buttermilk pancakes. Someone finally got Andy to divulge the recipe for those flapjacks that had become a local legend.

2 eggs, separated	1/4 cup sugar
2 cups fresh buttermilk	3/4 teaspoon baking powder
2-1/3 cups all-purpose flour	1/2 teaspoon baking soda (rounded)
1/2 teaspoon salt (rounded)	1/4 cup melted butter

To the egg yolks, add the buttermilk and beat until well blended. Then combine the flour, salt, sugar, baking powder and soda, and sift into the buttermilk and egg mixture. Beat lightly with a fork just until the ingredients are blended. Do **not** over-mix. Add the melted butter and stir briefly.

Beat the egg whites until stiff. Gently fold into the flapjack batter, taking care not to over-mix. Bake cakes on a lightly greased griddle over moderate heat, turning the flapjacks once and baking until golden. Serves 6.

Cottage Cheese Pancakes**

Pancakes made with cottage cheese are incredibly light and fluffy. They would be great for waistline watchers, too, if it weren't for the sour cream. Well, you can't have everything.

4 eggs, separated	1 tablespoon sugar
1 cup sour cream	3/4 teaspoon soda
1 cup small-curd	1/4 teaspoon baking powder
cottage cheese	1/2 teaspoon salt
3/4 cup sifted flour	

Beat egg whites until stiff peaks form, then set aside. Beat egg yolks until light, then stir in sour cream and cottage cheese. Sift flour, sugar, soda, baking powder and salt together. Stir into cheese mixture. Gently fold in egg whites. Spoon batter by tablespoons onto hot lightly greased griddle. Turn pancakes as edges dry and cook until golden. Serves 6. Delicious served with hot maple syrup.

German Apple Pancake**

Here is a hefty breakfast pancake you whip up in a blender, bake in the oven and serve in fat, buttery wedges. A wonderful idea for a bleak winter Sunday morning when all hands need something substantial to warm their cockles.

3 eggs	2 tablespoons lemon juice
1/2 cup milk	4 tablespoons butter
1/3 cup flour	1/4 cup granulated sugar
1/4 teaspoon salt	1/4 teaspoon cinnamon
2 green apples	1/4 teaspoon nutmeg

In a blender combine the eggs, milk, flour and salt. Process until smooth. Let batter chill for 1 hour. Meantime, core and peel apples and cut into paper-thin slices. Sprinkle apple slices with lemon juice.

In a heavy skillet (about 11 inches) heat 2 tablespoons butter until it bubbles, then pour in the batter. As batter spreads out and begins to set, carefully place apple slices over the batter in rows. Slip the skillet into a preheated 375° F. oven and bake for 10 to 15 minutes, or until the pancake is puffed and set. Have a hot plate ready, and when the pancake is taken from the oven, quickly slip it onto the plate and spread with the remaining 2 tablespoons butter. Sprinkle with sugar, cinnamon and nutmeg and serve. Serves 4.

French Toast**

Does anyone ever have time during the week to monkey around with delicacies like French toast? Not at our house. But, that's okay . . . things like that are what help make Sunday mornings so special.

2 eggs	8 slices day-old,
1 cup sifted flour	firm, white bread
1 cup milk	7 tablespoons butter
1-1/2 teaspoons baking powder	or margarine
1/2 teaspoon salt	3 tablespoons salad oil
1 teaspoon cinnamon	Powdered sugar
1 teaspoon vanilla	Raspberry or pineapple jam

Process eggs in a blender until frothy. Add the flour, milk, baking powder, salt, cinnamon and vanilla, and whip until smooth. Pour batter into a shallow baking dish or pie pan.

Cut bread slices in half, forming triangles. Set aside while 2 tablespoons of butter or margarine and 1 tablespoon oil heat up in skillet. While this heats, soak bread in the batter, turning to absorb egg-milk mix on both sides. Drain and fry in the hot oil and butter, two pieces at a time. Add more oil and butter, as needed. Keep turning slices until they are golden brown on both sides. Remove to a heated platter while remaining bread is cooked. Dust toast with powdered sugar and serve hot with jam. Serves 4 to 6.

Coconut Crunch French Toast**

Along with the standard milk-and-egg dip, this version of French toast gets extra crunch with a coating of corn flake crumbs and coconut.

2 eggs	1 cup flaked coconut
2/3 cup milk	2/3 cup crushed cornflake crumbs
4 teaspoons sugar	6 tablespoons butter
1/2 teaspoon coconut flavoring	8 slices white bread

Whip eggs, milk and sugar together. Add coconut flavoring. In another bowl, combine coconut and crumbs. Dip bread slices first in egg mixture, then into coconut and crumbs.

Heat butter in a small heavy skillet. When butter begins to sizzle, brown bread on both sides until golden. Serve with powdered sugar. Serves 4.

*French Toast Grand Marnier***

Weekends are the time to trot out something special for a leisurely breakfast. If you can anticipate this the night before, you can put together the fancy fixings for French Toast Grand Marnier. It takes an overnight soak, so think ahead. And the next morning, sit back and enjoy.

8 slices French bread,	1/2 teaspoon vanilla
sliced 3/4-inch thick	1/4 teaspoon salt
4 eggs	2 tablespoons butter
1 cup milk	Confectioners sugar
2 tablespoons Grand Marnier	Apricot preserves
1 tablespoon sugar	

Place bread slices in a 12 x 8-inch shallow baking dish. In a small bowl, beat eggs with milk, Grand Marnier, sugar, vanilla, salt and butter until well blended. Pour over bread slices, turning to coat evenly with the liquid. Refrigerate, covered, overnight.

In the morning, heat butter in a heavy skillet and saute bread until golden — about 4 minutes per side. Keep warm in oven until all slices are cooked.

Serve with drifts of confectioners sugar on top and dollops of apricot preserves on the side. Serves 4 to 6.

*French Raisin Toastwiches***

A sweet takeoff on the standard Monte Carlo sandwich is this treat that puts raisin bread into the act. Raisin-nut bread works equally well.

8 slices day-old raisin bread	1/2 cup milk
4 thin slices ham	1/2 teaspoon salt
4 slices Cheddar or Swiss cheese	Butter or margarine
2 eggs, beaten	

Assemble four sandwiches with the bread, ham and cheese. In a bowl, combine eggs, milk and salt. Dip each sandwich in the egg mixture, coating well on both sides. Melt butter or margarine in a heavy skillet and cook sandwiches over medium heat until golden on both sides. Serve with powdered sugar and jelly.

Hawaiian Coconut Waffles**

This recipe for coconut waffles is a specialty of a popular gathering spot in Waikiki. Accompanied by a platter of fresh fruit and plump breakfast sausages, this would make a sumptuous mainland brunch.

2 cups flour	2 cups buttermilk
1 teaspoon salt	2/3 cup margarine, melted
1 teaspoon baking soda	1/2 cup flaked coconut
1 teaspoon baking powder	1/4 cup finely chopped macadamia
4 eggs	nuts (or pecans)

Sift dry ingredients together. Beat eggs until light. Add buttermilk and the dry ingredients alternately into the beaten eggs, ending with dry ingredients. Stir briefly, then add the margarine, coconut and nuts. Bake in a non-stick waffle iron that has been sprayed with a non-stick aerosol product. Bake waffles until golden brown and serve with Coconut Syrup (recipe below). Makes about 8 medium waffles.

Cherry Waffle Sauce*

A choice of toppings for one's hotcakes or waffles makes nice but modest luxury for a Sunday morning. Aside from that old standby, maple syrup, it's fun to slather flapjacks in blueberry syrup. Or how about cherry?

3/4 cup sugar	1 tablespoon lemon juice
1/4 teaspoon cinnamon	1 cup liquid (cherry juice) plus
3 tablespoons cornstarch	water to make 1 cup)
Dash salt	Red food coloring
1 cup canned cherries, drained and chopped	

Mix sugar, cinnamon, cornstarch and salt in a small saucepan. Add the rest of the ingredients, excluding food coloring, and bring to a boil. Stir constantly, allowing the mixture to simmer 1 minute. Add about 1 teaspoon of red food coloring. Serve over plain or Cinnamon Waffles.

Coconut Syrup*

In a small saucepan gently heat 1 cup canned cream of coconut syrup with 2 tablespoons margarine and 1 tablespoon lemon juice. Add a sprinkle of salt and serve warm.

Pineapple-Apricot Butter*

Here's a divine spread for Sunday morning's croissants. Pile the mix in a small crock and spread it lavishly on the hot, flaky rolls. And when the topping is gone, make up a new batch using strawberry or raspberry jam. It's equally delicious.

1 pound sweet (unsalted) butter	1 cup pineapple-apricot jam

Whip butter and jam together until blended.

Shall We Quiche?

These creamy custards-in-crusts are one of the best brunch ideas ever invented. Furthermore, they are an absolute snap to prepare.

If you've a mind to quiche from scratch, there are all kinds of fancy scalloped pans on the market. Otherwise, just use a plain pie pan. Fancier isn't necessarily better.

For you one-star (*) cooks, pick up a ready-to-bake crust at the corner grocery store and you're already half-way home. From there, whipping up the filling is a breeze.

Baking time averages 40 minutes in a moderate oven. When done, a knife inserted in the center will come out clean. Don't worry if the middle jiggles slightly when shaken. The filling will firm up as it cools.

Another thing: a quiche should never be served red-hot. Let it cool its heels 15 to 20 minutes before cutting. Then slice, serve and sit back. You will get more compliments than you rightly deserve. Quiches always look a lot more complicated than they really are.

Kirkwood Quiche*

Kirkwood Quiche, named for the lady who gave me the recipe, calls for ham, although I have found that mushrooms, chopped chicken and shellfish work equally well. The cottage cheese custard is foolproof and seems to team beautifully with anything you toss in.

1 9-inch unbaked pie shell	1/4 teaspoon sage
3 eggs, beaten	1/4 teaspoon salt
1 cup half-and-half	2 tablespoons Parmesan cheese
1 cup cottage cheese with chives	1 cup diced cooked ham
1 tablespoon flour	

Bake pie shell for 5 minutes at 375° F. Set aside to cool.

Beat eggs. Add half-and-half, cottage cheese, flour, sage and salt. Place ham in pie shell, pour over custard and sprinkle with Parmesan cheese. Bake at 350° F. for 35 to 40 minutes. Serves 6.

Chorizo-Chile Quiche**

If you have a mania for Mexican food, you will **love** *this chile-flavored quiche. Never mind that the traditional Mexican cook never head of — much less made — a quiche. We're not in this to nit-pick.*

1 9-inch unbaked pie shell	4 eggs, beaten
12 ounces Chorizo sausage	1 cup sour cream
1/4 cup sliced green onions	1/4 teaspoon cumin
1/4 cup bottled green taco sauce	1/4 teaspoon oregano
1 4-ounce can diced green chiles, drained	1/2 teaspoon chile powder
	Dash bottled hot sauce
1 2-1/4-ounce can sliced black olives, drained	1-1/2 cups grated Jack cheese

Bake pie shell in 375° F. oven for 5 minutes. Remove and set aside.

Saute crumbled sausage in a skillet until browned. Remove and drain on paper towels. Pour off all but 1 tablespoon fat in pan. Add green onions and cook 1 minute. Combine sausage and onions with taco sauce, chiles and olives.

To the beaten eggs add sour cream, cumin, oregano, chili powder and dash of hot sauce. Combine with meat mixture.

Sprinkle grated cheese into the pie shell. Pour in egg-meat mixture. Bake at 350° F. for 35 to 40 minutes. Let stand 15 minutes before serving. Serves 6.

Spinach and Feta Quiche**

Feta cheese and spinach make a delectable filling for this quiche that smacks, deliciously, of Greek cookery.

1 9-inch unbaked pie shell	1 small clove garlic, minced
2 packages frozen chopped	1 tablespoon olive oil
spinach, thawed	Dash basil
6 ounces Feta cheese, crumbled	Salt and pepper, to taste
1/2 cup cottage cheese	4 eggs, beaten
6 green onions, thinly sliced	3/4 cup half-and-half

Bake pie shell in a 375° F. oven for 5 minutes. Remove and cool. Drain spinach, pressing out excess moisture through a sieve. Set aside.

In a blender, combine the Feta cheese, cottage cheese, onions, garlic, oil, basil, salt and pepper. Process until smooth.

Beat eggs in a bowl, adding half-and-half. Add drained spinach. Add the blended cheese mixture and mix. Pour into the pie shell and bake at 375° F. for about 30 minutes. Serves 6.

Beefsteak Tomato Quiche**

You can also squash the rumor that real men don't eat quiche by serving hefty wedges of this next one alongside a small, well-seared steak. Trust me, this is really a great combination.

1 9-inch unbaked pie shell	1/2 cup sliced ripe olives
2 large, firm beefsteak tomatoes	1 cup minced green onions
1/4 cup flour	3 slices Provolone cheese
1/2 teaspoon salt	2 eggs, slightly beaten
Dash black pepper	1 cup grated Cheddar cheese
2 tablespoons oil	1 cup heavy cream

Bake pie shell at 375° F. for 5 minutes. Cool.

Cut tomatoes in 6 thick slices (total), and dip in flour. Sprinkle with salt and pepper. Saute quickly in hot oil. Arrange olives and 3 tablespoons chopped onions in pie shell. Add Provolone cheese and tomato slices.

Blend eggs with cream and cheese. Pour into shell. Bake at 375° F. for 40 minutes. Sprinkle with remaining onions, let stand for 10 to 15 minutes, then serve.

He-Man Quiche**

Men tend to find the average quiche a bit on the light side as a main dish. Not this one! Beef and plenty of cheese give it a very hefty quality.

1 9-inch unbaked pie shell	1 tablespoon cornstarch
1/2 pound ground beef	1/3 cup green onions, sliced
1/2 cup mayonnaise	3/4 pound Cheddar cheese, grated
1/2 cup milk	3/4 pound Swiss cheese, grated
2 eggs, slightly beaten	Salt and pepper, to taste

Bake pie shell in a 375° F. oven for 5 minutes. Remove and cool.
Saute ground beef until crumbly. Drain off fat.
Combine mayonnaise, milk, eggs, and cornstarch; mix well. Fold in meat, onion, cheeses and seasonings and put into pie shell. Bake at 350° F. for 35 to 40 minutes. Serves 6.

Zucchini Un-Quiche**

This next company casserole is not quite a quiche although it has many of the same puffed-up cheesy qualities.

1 can Betty Crocker crescent rolls	1/2 teaspoon salt
2 teaspoons Dijon mustard	1/2 teaspoon pepper
4 cups unpeeled zucchini, thinly sliced	1/4 teaspoon garlic powder
1 cup onion, chopped	1/4 teaspoon sweet basil
1/2 cup celery, chopped	1/4 teaspoon oregano
1/2 cup margarine	2 eggs, beaten
2 tablespoons parsley	8 ounces grated Mozzarella cheese

Unwrap crescent rolls and place in a greased 9 x 11-inch baking dish, pressing squares closely together. Spread with mustard. Saute zucchini, onions and celery in margarine until tender-crisp. Add parsley and seasonings. Beat eggs and mix in cheese. Combine with vegetables. Blend and smooth over dough. Bake at 375° F. for 20 minutes. Serves 5 to 6.

Stratas

Souffles — which can be sky-high one minute and flat on their backs the minute somebody slams the back door — are not something for the nervous cook to tackle. Stratas, on the other hand, don't pout, fall down or have a snit if brunch runs a little late.

The thing that props them up is bread — preferably the soft white store-bought kind that has been buttered, de-crusted and cut into cubes.

Another nice thing about these pseudo souffles is that they can be put together well ahead of time. In fact, an overnight headstart is ideal. And this makes stratas great party choices for the beginner cook who doesn't need anything more to do at the last minute than get out of her (or his) apron and answer the doorbell.

Cheese Strata*

*Here's a foolproof recipe that can be weasled around and changed at will. Try it in this basic cheesey form, then start tossing in a few touches of your own — green chiles, olives, minced meat, shellfish, **whatever.** You can innovate, ad infinitum, without upsetting the basic balance.*

4 slices white bread, buttered	2 cups milk
8 ounces Old English (or	1 teaspoon dry mustard
Cheddar) cheese, grated	1/2 teaspoon salt
3 eggs, beaten	1/2 teaspoon pepper

Butter bread, then trim off the crusts. Cut bread into 1-inch cubes and place in a greased casserole. Combine grated cheese with eggs, milk, mustard, salt and pepper; pour over bread cubes. Cover casserole and place in refrigerator overnight. Before serving, place casserole in a larger pan filled with hot water to a depth of 1 inch, and bake at 350° F. for 1 hour. Serves 4 to 5.

Pizza Strata**

Pizza for breakfast may not be everyone's idea of an ideal way to start the day, but for those who love 'em, here is a pizza-flavored strata that offers a lusty way to get late-mornings brunchers bright-eyed. Sangria and fresh fruit would go along nicely.

1/2 pound mild Italian sausage	1/2 teaspoon salt
2/3 cup chopped green onion	Dash garlic powder
1/2 cup chopped green pepper	4 tablespoons Parmesan cheese
8 slices white bread,	1/2 pound Mozzarella cheese, sliced
crusts removed	3 eggs, lightly beaten
2/3 cup tomato paste	2 cups milk
1-1/2 teaspoons Italian seasonings	

Strip casings off sausage and crumble into a large skillet. Add onion and pepper and saute until meat is lightly browned and crumbly. Pour off excess grease.

Place 4 slices bread in buttered 8-inch square baking pan. Combine tomato paste, Italian seasonings, salt and garlic; spread 1/2 of it over bread. Sprinkle with 2 tablespoons Parmesan cheese, half Mozzarella cheese slices, and half the sausage mixture. Top with remaining 4 slices of bread, remaining tomato paste, cheeses, and sausage.

Beat eggs with milk and pour over bread layers. Cover with plastic and refrigerate overnight. Before baking, sprinkle with additional Parmesan cheese. Place baking dish in a pan of hot water and bake at 350° F. for 45 minutes or until a knife inserted in the middle comes out clean. Serves 6.

Goober Sandwiches in Custard**

These strata-like sandwiches feature that old standby combo, peanut butter and jelly. Makes a great treat for the kids. Make them ahead. They can even stand overnight before baking. (The sandwiches, not the kids.)

8 slices white bread,	1-1/2 cups milk
crusts removed	2 tablespoons sugar
3/4 cup peanut butter	1/2 teaspoon vanilla
1/4 cup apricot preserves	Dash nutmeg
3 eggs	Powdered sugar

Spread 4 slices of bread with peanut butter, then preserves. Make sandwiches by topping with other 4 slices and place in a greased 9 x 9-inch pan. Combine eggs, milk, sugar, vanilla and nutmeg, beat until frothy, then pour over the sandwiches. Cover and let stand a minimum of 1 hour.

Place baking dish in a larger pan of hot water and bake at 350° F. for 40 to 45 minutes, or until puffed and golden. Let stand 10 minutes before serving. Cut and serve with powdered sugar. Serves 4.

Crepes

Crepes — and if you're saying it right, it comes out "kreps" — are tender little pancakes used to wrap everything from scallops to strawberries. There are a lot of special crepe pans on the market, but you really don't need one.

All it takes is a smallish eight- or nine-inch Teflon-lined skillet and a twist of the wrist to keep things moving.

Once swirled, lightly browned and flipped, the crepes can be used at once or stacked between sheets of waxed paper and frozen for later use.

Basic Crepes*
(Makes about 24 8-inch crepes)

No matter how you mix it, your basic crepe is no big deal. Just make sure the batter is about the consistency of heavy cream and is thoroughly chilled before using.

3 eggs	1-1/2 cups milk
1/4 teaspoon salt	1/4 cup butter
1 cup flour	

Mixer Method: Beat eggs with salt until thick. Gradually add the flour alternately with the milk. Beat in the melted butter. Refrigerate a minimum of 1 hour.

Blender Method: Place everything in the container and process until smooth, about 15 seconds. Scrape down the sides with a rubber spatula, if necessary. Refrigerate a minimum of 1 hour.

Heat a heavy 8-inch Teflon-lined skillet until drops of water dance on the surface. Butter lightly. Pour 1/4 cup of chilled batter into the pan, tilting and turning so the batter spreads evenly over bottom and part way up the sides of the pan in a thin, smooth film. Pour off any excess batter.

Cook until the underside is golden — 2 to 3 minutes. Then flip (you can use your fingers) to the other side and cook another couple of minutes. Slide crepes out onto a towel to cool. (If you plan to use them later, stack between sheets of wax paper.)

NOTE: As you cook the crepes, you will need to re-butter the pan lightly as you go along.

*Spinach Crepes**

12 crepes
2 10-ounce packages
  frozen chopped spinach
1/4 cup butter
1/4 cup flour
2 cups half-and-half

1 cup shredded Swiss cheese
1 teaspoon salt
Dash pepper
1/2 teaspoon nutmeg
Parmesan cheese

Cook spinach; press as much liquid as possible through a sieve and set aside. In a heavy saucepan, melt butter over medium heat and stir in flour, making a smooth roux. Gradually add the half-and-half, stirring constantly until smooth and thickened. Add the well-drained spinach and cheese. Season with salt, pepper and nutmeg.

As soon as the cheese has melted, take from heat. Spoon 3 to 4 tablespoons of the filling onto each crepe. Roll and place, seam sides down in a buttered baking dish. Brush lightly with butter and a drift of Parmesan cheese. Bake at 325° F. for about 20 minutes, or until bubbling and lightly browned. Serves 6.

*Broccoli Crepes**

Prepare as for Spinach Crepes, substituting chopped frozen broccoli for the spinach. If desired, top the rolled crepes with Hollandaise sauce prepared from scratch or from a packaged mix. Bake crepes until Hollandaise is lightly browned and bubbling.

*Sweet Crepes**

This slightly sweetened batter makes delicate crepes for filling with whipped cream, creamed cheese, creme fraiche, fruits and all manner of puddings and the like. Fresh strawberry crepes are one of the delights of summer.

4 eggs
3/4 cup water
3/4 cup milk
2 tablespoons sugar

1-1/2 cups flour
3-1/2 tablespoons brandy
1 teaspoon salt
3 tablespoons melted butter.

Combine all ingredients in a blender. Process until smooth. Refrigerate 30 minutes before using. Prepare the same as Basic Crepes.

What's Ahead in Salads

Salad Savvy

... how to turn over a new leaf

There is little reason why the greenest of cooks can't turn out the greatest of salads, if a couple of rules are followed.

Shop smart. Buy only the freshest greens possible. End-of-the-day bargains are no bargains, so skip the tag ends. You can't give an old lettuce new crisp.

Store smart. The minute you get them home, wash your salad goodies quickly, blot them as dry as possible and wrap in a clean, dry towel. From there, tuck the whole thing in a snug plastic bag and stash it in the refrigerator's crisper compartment.

Break it up. At serving time, break or tear the greens into bite-size pieces. Don't use a knife. (The one exception is iceberg, or head lettuce; that can be cut with a steel knife without discoloring.)

Keep it dry. Salad dressing slides off wet lettuce like rain off a duck's back and ends up in a sorry puddle in the bottom of the bowl. Besides making sure the works are dry, some experts claim it helps to "fatigue" the salad before adding the dressing. This involves dribbling a tiny amount of oil onto the greens and giving them a brief toss — just long enough to glaze each leaf — before adding the dressing. For some reason, this helps keep the dressing in place.

Under-dress. Too much dressing drowns the greens. If you are serving six, try four tablespoons of dressing to eight cups of greens. Toss, then stop and taste. Need more dressing? Add a spoonful, but go easy. You can add but you can't subtract. If you are serving a heavy dressing, like a thick bleu cheese, serve it separately and let everyone spoon on his own.

Freeze play. Serve your salads on ice-cold plates that have been slipped into the freezer a half hour before serving. Ditto for the salad forks. Fancy restaurants make a big thing about distributing salad forks cold enough to freeze your fillings, and this is a trick you can easily pull off at home.

Greens, Greens and More Greens

Almost anything leafy and green can be tossed into a salad, so feel free to fling. Some of the more obvious choices include escarole, chicory and watercress (which are slightly bitter and add bite to the mix), plus all the leafy members — Boston, bibb, romaine, spinach, and the ubiquitous iceberg head lettuce.

Some people like to pitch in a handful or two of alfalfa sprouts, although caution should be exercised lest the final mix takes on a hairy, bearded look. Sprouts are scraggly things to eat and tend to behave much better tucked into pita bread pockets and in sandwiches. But suit yourself on the sprout score.

As for specific combinations, this, too, is a personal matter although there is something to be said for moderation. Too many ingredients give your salad bowl a catch-all look that proves — once again, — that more isn't always better.

A good tossed green salad should probably combine two, certainly no more than three, of the following options: croutons, fresh mushrooms, crumbled bleu cheese, bacon bits, green beans, artichoke hearts, hearts of palm, tomatoes, cucumbers, chick peas and avocado.

The Story on Slaws

A really **good** cabbage slaw is hard to beat in the right setting. Crunchy, cold and dressed with appropriate tang, it is a winner at potlucks and picnics where good eating counts for more than sophistication. (Slaw is a lot of things, but sophisticated it isn't.)

This version features a thick creamy dressing that can be varied with the addition of such accoutrements as dill weed, celery seed — whatever strikes your fancy.

Unbeatable Slaw*

1 head cabbage, finely shredded	1/3 cup sugar
1 cup coffee cream, whipping cream or sour cream	1/4 cup cider vinegar
	1/2 teaspoon salt

Shred cabbage (and try to pick out a firm, bright green head) and place in a large bowl. Mix remaining ingredients, blending well. Pour dressing over cabbage and toss well. This version is best served right away.

NOTE: After shredding cabbage, try covering it with salted ice water for a half hour, then drain. This will keep it extra crisp through all the tossing and standing around that follows.

Super Slaw*

If you like slaw and aren't averse to gussying it up a bit, here's a way to do it with — of all things — peanuts and green peas.

2 small heads of cabbage, finely shredded	1 package frozen peas, thawed
1/2 cup chopped green onions	1 cup peanuts
1 cup raisins	2 tablespoons chopped parsley

Mix ingredients, tossing lightly to blend. Add dressing and chill before serving.

Super Slaw Dressing*

1 cup mayonnaise
1 teaspoon curry powder

Salt and pepper, to taste

NOTE: My friend Debby, who gave me this recipe, says it's even more sensational topped off with coconut chips.

Caesar Salad**

Waiters in fancy restaurants make a big show out of whipping up Caesar salads at tableside. But until your are sure of your footing, you'd best do the tossing in the kitchen.

1 large head romaine lettuce,
   broken in pieces
2 cloves garlic, minced
Juice of 1 lemon
1 tablespoon wine vinegar
1/2 cup olive oil
Dash Worcestershire sauce

3 drops tabasco sauce
1 teaspoon Dijon mustard
1 egg, soft cooked for 1 minute
1 2-ounce can anchovies
1/4 pound Parmesan cheese, grated
1 cup garlic-flavored croutons

Mince garlic and place in a bowl. Add the lemon juice, vinegar, oil, Worcestershire sauce, tabasco and mustard. Whip together. Add soft-cooked eggs and beat.

Break romaine into a large salad bowl, then toss with the dressing. Add in the croutons and the chopped anchovies, blend briskly and top with a thick drift of freshly grated Parmesan. Serves 6.

NOTE: If you are one of those people who cannot tolerate anchovies, leave them out. But be forewarned: you no longer have a genuine Caesar salad.

Chutney Chicken Salad**

A mid-summer treat is being invited to Susan's house for a luncheon featuring her special Chutney Chicken Salad. She serves it in crisp lettuce cups and dresses it up , with whatever perky fresh fruits are on hand.

1 cup mayonnaise
1/4 cup chopped chutney
1 teaspoon curry powder
2 teaspoons grated lime peel
1/4 cup fresh lime juice
1/2 teaspoon salt
4 cups cooked, diced chicken
   (white)

1 13-1/2 ounce can pineapple
   chunks, drained
1-1/2 cups diced celery
1 cup sliced green onions
   (with tops)
1/2 cup toasted whole
   blanched almonds

Combine mayonnaise, chutney, curry powder, lime peel, juice and salt. Mix well. Fold in remaining ingredients and refrigerate until serving time. Serves 6 to 8.

Serve salad on lettuce leaves with any or all of the following garnishes: sliced melon, sliced avocado, grape clusters, fresh pineapple spears, parsley sprigs.

*Palace Court Salad***

After landing our first jobs in San Francisco, my college roommate and I used to squander part of Friday's paychecks on lunch at the Palace Hotel. Memories of those Palace Court Salads still make me swoon!

Here's how to build one. You will probably want to make at least two. (Who would ever go to such bother when dining alone?)

1 cup finely shredded iceberg lettuce	3 tablespoons Thousand Island dressing
2 hard-cooked eggs, chopped	1 teaspoon capers
1 large slice of tomato	4 cooked asparagus spears
1 large artichoke bottom	2 large shrimp, cooked and split lengthwise
1/4 cup lobster chunks	6 pimento strips
1/4 cup crabmeat	
1 green pepper ring	

Arrange lettuce on a chilled salad plate. Top with chopped egg, pressing gently into a mound. Place tomato slice on top, then the artichoke bottom, cavity side up.

Firmly press lobster and crab into a cup. Unmold over the artichoke. Top with a ring of green pepper and fill with Thousand Island dressing. Sprinkle with capers.

Arrange shrimp, asparagus spears and pimento strips around base of salad. Pass additional dressing.

*Tostadas****

Tostadas provide one of the best ways in the world to eat one's salad. Even people who normally don't go much for greens can be counted on to plow through one of these layered lovelies with gusto.

4 corn tortillas	6 radishes, thinly sliced (optional)
1 cup heated refried beans	2 tomatoes, diced
1 cup shredded Jack cheese	1 1-1/4-ounce can sliced black olives
1 cup finely shredded lettuce	1 avocado, peeled and diced
1 onion, chopped (or 6 green onions, chopped)	1 7-ounce can green chili salsa

Heat about 1/2 inch of oil in a small skillet — slightly larger than the diameter of the tortillas. When the oil starts to smoke, quickly cook the tortillas, one at a time, in the hot fat. Turn each one until lightly browned on both sides and very crisp. Drain on paper towels.

Spread each tostada (as soon as a tortilla is fried, it becomes a tostada) with 2 or 3 tablespoons of the hot beans. Sprinkle grated cheese over the beans, then layer on the shredded lettuce and the rest of the garnishes. Top off each one with a generous portion of salsa and serve. Serves 4.

NOTE: For those that like it, you might add a sprinkling of freshly chopped cilantro. (I love it. My kids don't.)

Hot Seafood Salad Toss**

One of the city's shorefront restaurants serves a marvelous seafood salad in oversized shells that features scallops, bacon, shrimp and zucchini in white wine. Here is a close replica.

If you don't have big shells, use large dinner-size salad bowls. And top with plenty of cheese.

1 large bunch crisp romaine lettuce	1/3 cup white wine
1/4 pound bacon	2 tomatoes, cut in wedges
1/4 pound scallops	Lemon wedges
1/4 pound small frozen or fresh shrimp	1/2 cup coarsely chopped parsley
3 small zucchinis, unpeeled and sliced on the diagonal	Salt and pepper
	1/4 pound Jack cheese, coarsely shredded

Wash and chill romaine. Before serving, tear into bite-size pieces and divide between two dinner-size salad bowls.

Cut bacon in 1-inch pieces and saute until crisp. Drain on paper towels, reserving 2 to 3 tablespoons of the bacon fat. In the fat, quickly saute the scallops, shrimp and zucchini. Shake pan over high heat — just until fish is cooked and zucchini is tender-crisp.

Slosh wine into the pan, bring to a quick boil, then pour over the salad greens, equally dividing the fish and zucchini between the two servings. Garnish each one with tomato and lemon wedges. Sprinkle with parsley, bacon, salt and pepper and top liberally with grated Jack cheese. Serves 4.

Susan's Layered Salad*

The trouble with most layered salads is that the dressing on top never seems to quite make it to the bottom. This version solves that dilemma by tucking an extra layer of dressing in the middle. Use a clear glass bowl and don't let the layers get too deep.

2 cups Romaine lettuce, torn in bite-size pieces	1 16-ounce package petite frozen peas, thawed
2 cups iceberg lettuce, torn in pieces	1 cup mayonnaise
1 medium red onion, halved and sliced	2 to 3 teaspoons lemon juice
1-1/2 to 2 cups chopped celery	4 teaspoons sugar
1 cup sliced water chestnuts	Salt and pepper
6 slices Swiss cheese cut in bite-size pieces	Parmesan cheese (optional)
	6 slices bacon, cooked crisp and crumbled

In the following order, layer half of the lettuce, onion, celery, water chestnuts, cheese and well-drained peas in a glass serving bowl. Top with half of the mayonnaise (mixed with lemon). Sprinkle liberally with salt, pepper and sugar. Repeat layering remaining vegetables and spread with mayonnaise-lemon topping. Sprinkle with Parmesan. Cover tightly, and refrigerate overnight. Just before serving, sprinkle with crumbled bacon. Serves 8.

Chinese Chicken Salad***

Preparing Chinese Chicken Salad involves a certain amount of windup, but it's well worth it. You will need 3 whole chicken breasts — 6 halves — for this version. Go to an Oriental market for the rice sticks.

2 cups oil
1 package (6-3/4 ounces)
   rice sticks
1 head lettuce, finely shredded
1 basket mushrooms, sliced
1 fryer, cooked and diced
(or 3 chicken breasts)

1 cup chopped green onions
3 tablespoons chopped cilantro
1/4 cup toasted sesame seeds
1/2 cup chopped peanuts
Dressing

Heat oil in a deep saucepan and when hot (400° F) drop in the rice sticks, a few at a time. (They puff up almost immediately and need to be quickly removed from the hot fat before they brown. Cook sticks in small batches, draining on paper towels as you go.)

In a large bowl, combine the shredded lettuce, mushrooms, diced chicken, onions, cilantro, sesame seeds and peanuts. Toss with part of the dressing. Just before serving, add the rice sticks and the remaining dressing. Serves 6 amply.

Chinese Dressing*

1/4 cup sesame oil (available
   in Oriental markets)
1/4 cup salad oil

1/3 cup fresh lemon juice
Salt and pepper

Combine in a screw-top jar and shake well.

Take-Out Chinese Chicken Salad*

If you are put off by all the chop-chop and carrying on that goes into the traditional Chinese Salad, make a shortcut version using fried chicken breasts from a take-out franchise. (Bone the breasts, then chop the meat and skin into strips.)

Substitute a 3-ounce can of chow mein noodles for the fried rice sticks. Toss with Chinese Dressing and enjoy!

Rice and Artichoke Salad*

This hearty main dish chicken and rice salad makes a great summertime supper when everyone is hot and trying to cool it.

1 6-ounce package chicken-
   flavored rice (Rice-a-Roni, etc.)
3 green onions, chopped
1 6-ounce can water chestnuts,
   drained and chopped
2 6-ounce cans marinated
   artichoke hearts, undrained

5 to 6 stuffed green olives, diced
1/2 cup chopped peanuts
2 cups diced cooked chicken
1/2 teaspoon dry mustard
1 teaspoon curry powder
1/2 cup mayonnaise
1 teaspoon lemon juice

Cook rice according to package instructions. Cool. Add remaining ingredients, tossing lightly but thoroughly. Chill. Serve in lettuce cups. Serves 6 to 8.

Rice Picnic Salad**

It may never take the place of good old potato salad, but all the same this carry-along rice picnic salad is good enough to rate its own place in the sun. (Just keep it out of the sun when you get there.)

2 cups cooked white rice
1/2 cup diced red onion
1 large firm tomato, diced
6 green onions, thinly sliced
2 medium cucumbers, peeled
  and diced
1/2 cup sour cream

2 teaspoons mustard
1 tablespoon chopped parsley
2 teaspoons lemon juice
1/2 cup sliced ripe olives
1/2 cup slivered almonds
2 tablespoons butter

Combine rice with onion, tomato, green onions and cucumbers in a bowl. Toss lightly.

In another bowl mix the sour cream, mustard, parsley and lemon juice. Stir in drained olives.

Combine the sour cream dressing with rice mixture, tossing with a fork. Refrigerate for an hour or more, tightly covered. Before serving, saute almonds in melted butter until golden. Cool and sprinkle over salad. Serves 6.

Canny Combination Picnic Salad**

Here is another take-along picnic salad that involves a bit of putting together at the party site, but it is well worth the last-minute assembly. Just don't forget your can opener. Without it, all is lost.

1 1-pound can whole green beans
4 green onions, diced (including
  green tops)
3/4 cup Italian dressing
1 head romaine lettuce
2 cans water-packed tuna,
  drained
1 1-pound can whole boiled new
  potatoes, drained

1 tall can pitted black olives,
  drained
2 firm tomatoes
1/4 cup cubed Swiss or sharp
Cheddar cheese
1/2 cup slivered bologna or
  boiled ham
2 hard-cooked eggs, sliced

At home, open the beans and drain. Place them in a plastic container which has a tight-fitting lid. Add chopped onions to beans and toss with Italian dressing. Refrigerate.

Wash the romaine leaves and pat dry. Wrap in paper toweling, then tuck into a plastic bag and refrigerate. (If you are ready to go, just slip plastic bag into a larger bag into which you toss a few ice cubes. Secure with plastic tie.)

At serving time, break romaine into a large bowl and drizzle with Italian dressing drained from bean-onion mix. Sprinkle with crumbled tuna and garnish with bean-onion mix. Circle bowl with sliced potatoes and olives. Crown with tomato wedges, cheese cubes, meat slivers and eggs, making an attractive arrangement. Grate coarse pepper over all. Serves 6 to 8.

Steak Salad**

We love barbecued steaks well-seared but nearly raw in the middle. On those rare occasions when there are leftovers, this is something we do with the cold, super-rare meat: slice it and put it in a salad. (Heating the meat up only overcooks it, so this is one way to use it as-is.)

1/2 cup chopped green onions	2 cups leftover steak or roast, cut
1 cup sliced celery	in strips
1/2 cup chopped walnuts (not	1/2 cup mayonnaise
too fine)	1/2 cup sour cream
1/2 package frozen peas, thawed	Garlic salt and cracked pepper
	2 teaspoons prepared mustard

Place everything in a bowl and toss lightly, then refrigerate until thoroughly chilled . . . a minimum of 2 hours. Serve in a lettuce-lined bowl. Serves 4.

Peppy Garbanzo Salad Mix*

Garbanzo beans, also called chick peas, are those crunchy round white beans Italian restaurants serve on antipasto trays. They come in cans and need only a quick rinse before being spiked with garlic and a good oil and vinegar dressing.

1 20-ounce can garbanzo beans,	1 large clove garlic, minced
drained	1/4 cup olive oil
1/2 green pepper, slivered	3 green onions, chopped fine
1 small red onion, sliced	3 tablespoons wine vinegar
paper-thin	Salt and pepper, to taste
1 canned green chile, chopped	

Rinse beans and put in a large bowl with the rest of the ingredients. Toss, then cover and chill overnight. Serves 6.

Cantaloupe and Avocado Salad*

This next one might strike you as a strange combination of ingredients, and so it is. But don't knock it — try it. The mix of flavors is really quite sensational.

1 ripe, sweet cantaloupe, peeled,	6 firm radishes
seeded and cubed	1 sweet red onion, thinly sliced
2 small avocados, peeled and	Green grape clusters
cubed	Watercress
Lemon juice	

Make beds of watercress on 4 chilled salad plates. Over the greens arrange cubes of cantaloupe and avocado that have been sprinkled with lemon juice. Garnish each serving with thin slices of radishes and paper-thin onion slices (ringed). Stud with small clusters of grapes and pass Orange-Kissed Dressing. Serves 4.

Orange-Kissed Dressing*

6 tablespoons frozen orange
  juice concentrate
Juice of 2 lemons

1/2 cup salad oil
1 tablespoon sugar
Salt and white pepper

Combine all ingredients in a mason jar and shake vigorously to blend.

Japanese Summer Salad**

There is an elegant little restaurant in a refurbished San Pedro mansion where exquisitely presented salads are a midday specialty. Their Japanese noodle salad is particularly good, and this one is a close duplicate. You can buy udon — Japanese noodles — in Oriental food markets.

1 pound Japanese noodles (udon)
1 cup cooked chicken, shredded
1/2 cup chopped peanuts
3 tablespoons toasted sesame
  seeds

1/4 cup minced green onions
Cilantro
Marinated mushrooms (optional)
Peanut Dressing

Cook noodles according to package instructions. Drain and plunge into cold water. Chill, in water, for 2 hours. When ready to serve, drain thoroughly and place in a large salad bowl. Top with shredded chicken, sesame seeds and onions. Dress with Peanut Dressing, toss lightly and garnish with cilantro sprigs and mushrooms. Serves 6.

Peanut Dressing

1/4 cup water
3 tablespoons peanut butter
3 tablespoons oil
3 tablespoons rice or
  white vinegar

1 teaspoon sugar
Pinch powdered ginger
3 tablespoons soy sauce
1 tablespoon sesame oil (available
  in Oriental markets)

Combine ingredients in a jar and stir to dissolve peanut butter. Cover, shake well and chill.

Tak's Bean Sprout Salad**

In lieu of lettuce, this salad gets its crunch from bean sprouts that are blanched, then dunked briefly in ice water for extra snap.

1 pound fresh bean sprouts
1-1/2 tablespoons sugar
3 tablespoons vinegar
2 tablespoons soy sauce

3 tablespoons sesame seed oil
1/2 teaspoon MSG
1 tablespoon sesame seeds, toasted

Blanch bean sprouts in boiling water 1 minute, then chill in ice water. Drain well and toss with remaining ingredients. Refrigerate until serving. Serves 4.

Aztec Calendar Salad*

Presentation is the name of the game when you serve one of these masterpiece Mexican salads. Put together with all the symmetry of a mosaic, the colorful rings of beets and fruit make a stunning appearance on any buffet table. Drizzle on salad dressing at the last moment. No tossing, please.

4 small cooked beets	2 limes
2 peeled oranges	1/2 head iceberg lettuce
2 unpeeled red apples	2 tablespoons sugar
1/2 small jicama (optional)	1/2 cup chopped peanuts
1 small can pineapple chunks	Pomegranate seeds (optional)
1 banana	Mexican salad dressing

Thinly slice beets, oranges, jicama, bananas and apples (dip apples and bananas in lemon or lime juice to prevent discoloration). Slice limes and finely shred lettuce.

Place lettuce in the bottom of a large, shallow salad bowl. Arrange rows of apples, orange, beets and jicama in rings. Place pineapple in center. Garnish, around the edges, with sliced lime. Sprinkle with peanuts and pomegranate seeds.

Mexican Salad Dressing*

1/2 cup orange juice	Salt to taste
1/3 cup oil	1/2 cup mayonnaise
2 tablespoons red wine vinegar	

Blend ingredients well, chill, then dribble over assembled salad just before serving. Limes may be squeezed over individual servings for those that like it.

Fresh Fruit Ambrosia**

Ambrosia — that traditional mix of fresh fruits and coconut — has been around for years, performing lead roles at ladies' luncheons and afternoon teas. This recipe gets an added lift with a jolt of Cointreau. Use rum if you prefer.

2 oranges, peeled and sliced	Pinch salt
2 bananas, diagonally sliced	Fresh berries, in season
Juice of 1/2 lemon	Sugar to taste
4 large lettuce leaves	1/2 cup flaked coconut
1 papaya (or small cantaloupe), sliced	1 jigger Cointreau (or rum)

Place lettuce leaves on 4 salad plates. Arrange orange slices on greens and top with banana slices that have been dipped in lemon juice. Arrange slices of papaya alongside and sprinkle with a few grains of salt. Garnish with fresh berries, if available, and a light drift of sugar. Top with flaked coconut and enough Cointreau to make its presence known. Serves 4.

Melitzanoslata**

Translated, Melitzanoslata means eggplant salad. Of rather exotic dimension, it bears absolutely no resemblance to the standard tossed-green variety. It's good on a buffet and goes great with char-broiled beef.

1 small eggplant
1 clove garlic, crushed
2 tablespoons olive oil
Salt and cracked pepper
1 tomato, diced
1 tablespoon minced parsley

1 teaspoon grated onion
1/2 teaspoon oregano
1 tablespoon wine vinegar
1/2 teaspoon finely minced fresh
    mint leaves

Bake the whole eggplant in a 350° F. oven for 1 hour. Set aside to cool. When cool enough to handle, peel and dice pulp.

Combine garlic with olive oil. Mix with remaining ingredients and toss with the cubed eggplant. Chill thoroughly before serving. Serve in lettuce cups as a salad or as an accompaniment to meat. Serves 4.

Spaghetti Salad*

This pasta salad turned up recently at a big church social, and the lady who made it was besieged with requests for the recipe. The salad seasoning called for is available in the spices section of your supermarket.

1 pound spaghetti or linguini,
    cooked and drained
1 16-ounce bottle Wishbone
    Italian dressing
1 jar Shillings "Salad Supreme"
    seasonings

2 cucumbers, peeled and chopped
3 tomatoes, peeled and chopped
1-1/2 large red onions, chopped
1 large green pepper, chopped

The night before, cook the pasta, *al dente*. Drain and toss while warm with the Italian dressing and the entire jar of Salad Supreme seasoning. (Don't panic. It blends in very nicely.) Refrigerate. Early the next day, add the chopped vegetables. Cover and chill until serving time. Serves 8 to 10.

Horseradish Salad**

*Unlike most gelatin salads, this one has crunch **and** bite. Served in small squares, it makes a nice addition to a summer salad plate. It is also a nice — and unexpected — accompaniment to baked ham.*

1 small package lemon gelatin
1 cup boiling water
1 cup crushed pineapple,
    drained
1 cup small curd cottage cheese

1/2 cup chopped walnuts
1 teaspoon horseradish
1/2 cup mayonnaise
1/2 cup light cream

Dissolve gelatin in 1 cup boiling water. When gelatin is dissolved, pour into a larger bowl and add all the remaining ingredients, stirring until well-blended. Pour mixture into small individual molds or into a 9 x 9-inch cake pan, cutting the salad into squares at serving time. Makes 6 servings.

Avocado Cream Supreme**

This elegant pale-green molded salad is a creamy blend of avocado and — would you believe — ice cream. If you're looking for something different for the next office party, look no farther.

2 large ripe avocados
2 tablespoons lemon juice
1/2 teaspoon salt
2 packages lime gelatin
1 cup boiling water

1 pint vanilla ice cream
1 cup mayonnaise
1 cup canned crushed pineapple, drained

Peel and dice avocados. Sprinkle with lemon juice and salt, and set aside. Dissolve gelatin in boiling water. When completely dissolved, add the ice cream and mayonnaise. Chill until syrupy, then add the drained pineapple. Mix well; then fold in avocados. Pour into a lightly oiled mold and chill until firm. Serves 6.

Frosted Cranberry Salad

Ordinarily, this is not my very favorite kind of salad, but during the holidays when everything is over-extended (including our waistlines), this crunchy, icy-cold concoction is a relief.

1 14-ounce can evaporated milk
1/4 cup lemon juice
1 16-ounce can whole cranberries

1 20-ounce can crushed pineapple, drained
1/2 cup chopped nuts
1 9-ounce container whipped topping

Combine milk with lemon juice. Add pineapple, cranberries and nuts. Fold in whipped topping and spoon into a 9 x 13-inch baking dish. Freeze until firm. Take from freezer 10 minutes before serving. Cut into squares and serve on lettuce leaves. Serves 14 to 15.

Tabbouli**

Tabbouli, which seems to be spelled differently every time you see it, is an exotic stuff you scoop up with leaves. (Look Ma, no forks!) Its principal ingredient is bulgar wheat, one of those terribly earnest things people buy in health food stores. Good, though. Sort of nutty.

1/4 cup bulgar wheat
3/4 cup boiling water
1 cup finely chopped tomato
1/2 cup finely minced parsley
1/4 cup finely chopped fresh mint

1/4 cup minced green onion
2 tablespoons olive oil
2 tablespoons lemon juice
Salt and pepper, to taste
Romaine lettuce

Pour boiling water over bulgar and set aside for 1 hour. Then set in a strainer until fairly dry. Mix with remaining ingredients (except Romaine) and chill. Serve in a mound surrounded with small, crisp Romaine leaves. Use the leaves as scoopers for the Tabbouli. Serves 4.

Red Hot Gelatin Squares***

Snappy with cinnamon, this red-and-white striped jelled salad goes particularly well with ham, making it a natural for Easter festivities.

1/2 cup cinnamon "red hot" candies	2 tablespoons lemon juice
2-1/2 cups boiling water	Few grains salt
1 6-ounce package lemon flavored gelatin	4 to 5 drops red food coloring
2 cups sweetened applesauce	1 small package cream cheese
	3 tablespoons light cream or milk

Dissolve red hots in boiling water. Into this hot liquid, stir in the gelatin, stirring until completely dissolved. Stir in the applesauce, lemon juice, salt and red food coloring. Pour half of the mixture into a 9 x 9-inch baking dish and chill in refrigerator until set. (Keep second half of mixture at room temperature until ready to use.)

Whip cream cheese until fluffy with the milk or cream. Spread in a smooth layer over the firm gelatin. Then carefully spoon over the remaining gelatin. Chill in refrigerator until set. Cut in squares to serve.

A WORD ABOUT DRESSINGS

With very few exceptions, salad dressings should always be added at the very last moment before serving. Confident cooks can make a fine show of it by tossing at the table — a production that always gets dinner off to an impressive start.

The most popular dressing of all — French — is generally a mixture of three parts oil to one part vinegar. While the proportions are standard, the **kinds** of oils and vinegars you use can be anything that suits your whim.

By the way, that bottled bright orange abomination sold in grocery stores as French dressing really isn't French at all. What it **is** is plain awful. If you are lucky, you will never have to eat any, and there is no excuse whatever for buying it.

Some of the other bottled dressings are all right, but they are expensive and are rarely as good as the dressings you whip up at home.

In a hurry? Try a packet of dried salad mix. Properly blended with oil and vinegar — or, if it calls for it, mayonnaise, buttermilk or whatever — these quick mixes are really quite acceptable. Just steer clear of the bottled stuff. You can do better.

Short-Cut Packet Dressings

Quick-mix Italian is one of the best. Mix it with a good olive oil and wine vinegar and you have a fresh-tasting mix that's vastly superior to the bottled varieties. After you've made the basic blend a few times, try tossing in a little fresh tarragon or basil or garlic or whatever else strikes your fancy.

Continued

Packaged Ranch Dressing*

For a snowy-white, thick and creamy dressing, you just can't beat ready-to-mix Ranch. It is superb spooned over greens, goes great on baked potatoes and, in a pinch, makes a tasty dip for crudites.

Want an instant roquefort or bleu dressing? Just crumble in 1/4 to 1/2 cup of cheese and stir into basic Ranch. Beautiful!

Creamy Bleu Cheese Dressing*

This one doesn't use a ready mix, but it's almost as quick.

1/2 pint mayonnaise	1/2 pint sour cream
1/2 teaspoon garlic salt	1/4 pound bleu cheese, crumbled
1 tablespoon lemon juice	

Whip together until blended, then refrigerate. Makes 2 cups.

Basic French Dressing*

This one is a great standby for all kinds of green salads and also doubles handily as a marinade for vegetables (beets, green beans, etc.) and for priming meats for barbequing. A friend of mine always uses it to marinate chicken before tossing it on the coals. Says it works great.

1 cup vinegar (wine or tarragon)	1 teaspoon pepper
3 cups prime olive oil	1 clove garlic, finely minced
2-1/2 teaspoons seasoned salt	

Place ingredients in a jar with a tightly fitting lid. Shake well to blend. Bring to room temperature before using.

To this standard French dressing mix, you may add any or all of the following: minced parsley, fresh or dried basil, capers, curry powder, chopped olives, Italian seasonings, a handful of grated hard cheese — even finely chopped walnuts. This is a great place for the non-cook to innovate.

Basic Roquefort Dressing*

To Basic French Dressing add 1/2 pound crumbled Roquefort cheese blended with 1/4 cup Port wine and 2 cloves of minced garlic. This is especially good if the Basic French has been made with tarragon vinegar.

Mock Sour Cream Dressing*

Mock Sour Cream Dressing has a number of things going for it, not the least of which is its diminished calorie count. Make it sweet for fruit, zingy for vegetables.

1 pint imitation sour cream	Salt to taste
1/2 cup evaporated milk	White pepper
1 teaspoon lemon juice	Pinch sugar

Blend ingredients until smooth. Fresh chopped dill, parsley or chives may be added for a vegetable or green salad. To serve with fruit, add 2 tablespoons frozen orange juice concentrate, honey or a spoonful of currant jelly to the mix.

Great Green Salad Dressing*

This gorgeous jade-green dressing always scores big points with people who like guacamole-like toppings.

2 medium (or 1 large) avocado, mashed	1 envelope Green Goddess salad dressing mix
1/2 cup sour cream	1/2 cup buttermilk
1 clove garlic minced (or 1/2 teaspoon garlic powder)	1/2 teaspoon white pepper

Mix ingredients together until smooth. Refrigerate. Makes about 1-1/2 cups dressing.

Home-On-The-Range Bacon Dressing**

Served warm, this sweet-and-sour dressing is perfect for tender young lettuce or garden spinach.

5 slices bacon	1/4 teaspoon salt
1 egg	2 tablespoons vinegar
2 tablespoons sugar	1-1/4 cups milk
1 tablespoon flour	

Fry bacon crisp. Remove from pan, pat dry between paper towels, and crumble. Beat egg slightly, then add sugar, flour and salt, beating until smooth and well-blended. Add the vinegar and milk.

Drain all but about 2 tablespoons of bacon drippings from the skillet. Into pan add the egg-milk mixture and set over medium heat. Cook, stirring constantly, until smooth and slightly thickened. Serve hot over spinach or broccoli, or cool to lukewarm and pour over greens. Sprinkle with bacon bits. Makes 1 cup of dressing.

Red Devil French Dressing**

For some people, French dressing has to have a rosy glow. They probably grew up in households where that yukky store-bought orange stuff was a staple, and the poor things are on a nostalgia trip.

No matter. Here is a pink-cheeked dressing that is really very good. You will find it is a nice change from the day-in, day-out standard oil and vinegar blends.

1 cup bottled chili sauce	1 cup sugar
1 cup tomato catsup	2 teaspoons salt
1 cup cider vinegar	3 teaspoons Worcestershire sauce
1 cup tarragon vinegar	2 onions, chopped fine
2 cups salad oil	4 cloves garlic, minced

Combine ingredients, then pour into mason jars. Store indefinitely in the refrigerator. Makes 6-1/2 cups of dressing.

Mayonnaise

Homemade mayonnaise is only slightly harder to make than screwing the lid off a jar of store-bought mayonnaise. The big trick — the only trick, really — is to go slow. **You must take your time.**

It can be whipped up by hand, in a blender or a food processor. However you go about it, you must dribble in the oil very, very slowly — especially in the beginning. Once the mix begins to thicken, you can step up the stream a bit.

A small electric hand mixer is a good implement to use the first time around. *Hold the beater with one hand, dribble in the oil with the other, and you will be in perfect control of the situation.*

Mixer Mayonnaise**

1 egg	2 teaspoons wine vinegar
1 teaspoon salt	1-1/2 cups oil
1 teaspoon white pepper	2 teaspoons lemon juice
1 teaspoon mustard (optional)	

Beat egg with salt, pepper, mustard and vinegar in a small, straight-sided bowl. When thoroughly blended, start adding the oil, by droplets, beating continuously. As mixture starts to thicken, you can add the oil a bit faster until the entire 1-1/2 cups have been encorporated. When mayonnaise is thick, add the lemon juice and taste for seasonings. Store, tightly covered, in the refrigerator.

Fruit Salad Dressing*

This delicate pale pink dressing is a delight on fresh fruit. But save it for the ladies. Somehow men don't cotton much to combinations like this.

1 large carton sour cream	1/2 cup powdered sugar
1 small package cream cheese	1/2 cup grenadine syrup
2 tablespoons mayonnaise	

Beat until smooth and creamy. Can be kept up to two weeks in the refrigerator and is great served with any and all kinds of fruit. Not bad on coleslaw, either, if you leave out the grenadine.

Orange-Poppy Seed Dressing*

Lennie, who has no time for recipes that take a lot of time, whips this one up in seconds. She serves it over avocado, citrus fruits, kiwi and spinach toss-ups. And when she feels fancy, she tosses sliced mushrooms and Mandarin orange sections into the dressing. **Very** *tasty.*

2/3 cup salad oil	1/4 cup white vinegar
1 6-ounce can frozen orange	2 teaspoons poppy seed
juice concentrate, thawed	1/2 teaspoon celery salt
1/4 cup honey	

Combine ingredients, shake well and refrigerate.

Almond-Raspberry Sweet n' Sour Dressing*

Almond oil and raspberry vinegar go into this one, and a very exotic blend it is, too. The results are spectacular — well worth a trip to a gourmet specialty shop to get the ingredients.

1/4 cup almond cooking oil	2 tablespoons raspberry vinegar
1/4 cup honey	2 tablespoons lime juice

Combine ingredients, shake well and refrigerate.

Papaya Seed Salad Dressing*

The first time I tasted papaya seeds in salad dressing was in a restaurant in Maui. The pungent peppery-flavored seeds add a lot of zap to this basic oil-vinegar mix that's great over greens and good over fruit. (Use sliced papaya for the salad and scoop out the seeds for the dressing.)

1-1/2 tablespoons papaya seeds	2 tablespoons lime juice
1 cup oil	1 teaspoon salt
1/2 cup tarragon vinegar	1 teaspoon dry mustard
1/4 cup sugar	1 teaspoon instant minced onion

Process ingredients in a blender until papaya seeds are flecked through the mix like coarse-grind pepper. Chill. Makes 1-3/4 cups.

Not-So-Dry Martini Salad Dressing*

Vermouth and gin team up in this frisky salad dressing that gives you a chance to have a martini lunch without really drinking one!

1 tablespoon wine vinegar	1/4 teaspoon dry mustard
1 tablespoon dry vermouth	Pinch sugar
1 tablespoon gin	Salt and white pepper, to taste
2 cloves garlic, minced	1/2 cup oil

Combine all ingredients in a jar and shake vigorously. Let stand in refrigerator overnight before using. Makes about 3/4-cup.

What's Ahead in
Soup

Soup

... The Thick and the Thin of It

When the chill factor hits zero and you've missed the 4:30 bus, few things can restore one's soul like coming home to the sight and smell of a soup kettle bubbling merrily to itself.

Trouble is, soup making can be a day-long project. And working types who are out there missing buses rarely have that kind of a head start. So what do you do? You do the next best thing — crank open a couple of cans.

Some surprisingly exotic concoctions can be arrived at by simply blending a couple of cans of soup with a shot of sherry, a drift of herbs or a blob of sour cream.

All it takes is a bit of judicious flavoring-up to arrive at a point where you will wonder if starting from scratch would be worth the effort even if you did have the time. Of course if you find yourself home some Saturday morning with nothing to do and a soup bone in your hands, what better way to bubble away the day than with a lovely **pot au feu?**

The following soups run the gamut from one-star quickies to more complex combinations you could dish out for company. But actually there is nothing the least bit difficult about any of them, so if you toddler cooks feel adventurous, by all means go to the head of the class. Short of scalding the cat or dumping too much salt in the pot, there is little you can do to go astray.

Onion Mushroom Soup

Some of the neatest gourmet soups the beginner can pull off come straight out of soup cans. The following clutch of catch-as-catch-can recipes proves it.

1 can cream of mushroom soup	**1 can onion soup**
1/2 soup can of milk	**1/2 soup can of water**

Combine, heat, serve and enjoy. A delectable combination! Serves 4.

Instant Borscht*

1 1-pound can beets
1 can beef bouillon

1 pint sour cream
Salt and white pepper to taste

Drain beets, discarding juice. Place in a blender along with the bouillon and process until smooth. Pour into a bowl and blend in half of the sour cream. Stir until smooth. Season to taste with salt and pepper. Refrigerate until icy cold. Serve in chilled bowls topped with dabs of the remaining sour cream. Serves 4.

Lazy Day Pea Soup*

4 cans split pea soup
2 cans tomato soup
2 soup cans milk
2 onions, chopped

4 carrots, cut in thick slices
1 cup leftover baked ham, cut in
chunks

Mix everything together and simmer over low heat for about 2 hours. Stir now and then. Serves 8.

NOTE: You don't absolutely **have** to have ham for this, but the soup won't be nearly as hefty without it. In a pinch, you could toss in a couple of knockwurst, cut in chunks.

Sherried Mushroom Soup**

1 pound fresh mushrooms,
thickly sliced
1/4 pound butter
3 cans cream of mushroom soup

1 can cream of celery soup
1 cup sherry
2 soup cans filled with water
Salt to taste

Saute mushrooms in butter until limp. Add soups and water to the same pan and bring slowly to a simmer. Add the sherry, correct the seasonings, to taste, and serve. Serves 8.

Cashew-Mushroom Soup**

A rich, fresh mushroom soup is hard to beat for pure elegance. This one goes a step further — gilding the lily by tossing cashews into the pot.

2 tablespoons margarine
2 tablespoons flour
1-1/2 cups canned chicken broth
1-1/2 cups light cream

Dash nutmeg and white pepper
MSG
1-1/2 cups fresh mushrooms, sliced
1 cup cashews, coarsely chopped

Melt margarine and stir in flour, making a smooth roux. Gradually add the chicken broth and cream, stirring over low heat until smooth and thickened. Add the nutmeg, a pinch of white pepper, and a sprinkle of MSG. Stir in the mushrooms and half of the cashews. Simmer for 3 minutes more. Pour soup, in batches, into a blender and process until smooth. Return to the saucepan and slowly heat. Stir in the remaining chopped nuts. Serve in heated bowls. Serves 6.

Chinese Egg Flower Soup**

*Egg Flower Soup is delicate, different and so simple that you will never be able to convince anyone what a snap it is, so don't even bother. Just serve it like the Chinese do: be **inscrutable**.*

2 10-1/2-ounce cans chicken
broth or consomme
1 can water
1 teaspoon soy sauce
1 6-ounce can sliced mushrooms,
with liquid

1/4 cup bamboo shoots, finely
slivered
1/2 cup water chestnuts, thinly
sliced
2 eggs, beaten
2 green onions, minced

Combine chicken broth, water, soy sauce and mushrooms in a small saucepan and slowly bring to a boil. Add the bamboo shoots and water chestnuts and bring back to a boil. Reduce heat to a slow simmer. As the soup slowly bubbles, add the eggs in a slow drizzle, stirring briskly to separate the egg into thin threads. Remove from the heat and add the minced green onion. Serves 4.

Minestrone***

*Minestrone is hearty fare that needs nothing more than crusty chunks of sourdough bread and dry red wine to round it out. (Eat enough and it will round **you** out, too, but what a way to go!)*

Please don't let the long list of ingredients throw you. Once you have assembled all the fixings, it's just a matter of tossing everything into the pot. And if you are very lucky, you will have leftovers. Next day it's better than ever.

1/4 pound bacon, chopped
1/4 pound ham, chopped
1/2 pound Italian sausage
3 cloves garlic, minced
1 large onion, chopped
3 stalks celery, diced
2 small zucchinis, sliced
1 leek (or 3 small green onions),
thinly sliced
Salt and pepper

2 quarts beef soup stock (canned or
made from bouillon)
2 cups cabbage, finely shredded
1 cup canned kidney beans, drained
1 cup dry red wine
1 large can whole tomatoes
1/3 cup elbow macaroni
1/4 cup dried basil
Parmesan cheese, freshly grated

Saute bacon, ham and sausage. Drain off excess fat and add garlic. As soon as the garlic starts to brown add the onions, celery, zucchini, leek (or green onions), and season with salt and pepper. Lower heat, cover and cook for 10 minutes.

In a deep kettle bring the beef stock to a simmer. Add the bacon-ham-sausage-vegetable mixture to the pot. Bring back to a simmer and add the cabbage, drained beans and wine. Cover and simmer slowly for an hour.

Add tomatoes and macaroni and cook an additional 15 minutes. Just before serving, add the basil. Stir and serve, piping hot, with drifts of freshly grated Parmesan cheese atop each bowl.

NOTE: If soup gets too thick, thin with a little tomato juice or additional beef bouillon. Serves 8 generously.

Minute Minestrone*

Caught in a bind for time? Here is how to have a rich minestrone soup in minutes.

1 1-pound can beef stew
1 1-pound can tomatoes
1 16-ounce can new potatoes, sliced
2 tablespoons dried onion soup mix

1 teaspoon chicken bouillon granules
1/2 teaspoon oregano
1/2 green pepper, minced
1 cup cooked and drained spaghetti
Red wine
1/2 cup Parmesan cheese

Combine everything but the Parmesan cheese in a heavy saucepan and simmer 25 minutes. Ladle into two heated bowls and top with Parmesan. Serves 2 bountifully.

Ravioli Soup**

Canned ravioli add plump little pasta packets to this quick vegetable soup.

1 10-ounce can beef consomme
1 cup tomato juice
1 cup red wine
2 cups water
3/4 cup diced carrot
3/4 cup diced green pepper
1/2 cup sliced celery
1/2 cup chopped green onion

1/4 cup chopped parsley
1 teaspoon salt
1 teaspoon sugar
Dash pepper
1 cup chopped fresh spinach
1 15-ounce can ravioli with sauce
1 cup grated Parmesan cheese

Combine consomme, tomato juice, wine and water in a soup kettle. Bring to a boil, add the vegetables, salt, pepper and sugar and lower heat. Simmer, covered, about 10 minutes, or until vegetables are tender.

Wash and chop spinach. Add to soup and cook 5 minutes. Add ravioli with sauce, cover, and simmer an additional 10 minutes. Ladle into shallow soup bowls and sprinkle heavily with Parmesan cheese. Serves 6 to 8.

Green Chile Meltaway Chowder**

Cheese lovers, gather round! As the Jack cheese melts into gorgeous gobs in this spicy chili-corn chowder, every bite is pure joy. Just watch out for the strings when you dip in. Or wear a bib.

1 7-ounce can diced green chiles
2 12-ounce cans whole kernel corn, undrained
1-1/2 pounds ham, chopped in bite-size chunks

2 14-ounce cans chicken broth
1 teaspoon oregano
8 ounces Jack cheese, shredded
1 large onion, chopped

Combine chiles, corn, ham, broth, oregano and onion. Bring to a boil, then turn heat down and simmer 10 minutes. Ladle hot soup into heated bowls and add a handful of cheese to each one. Serve piping hot. Serves 6.

Watercress Soup**

Watercress is one of those under-used and largely misunderstood greens that can be the mainstay of a perfectly marvelous soup. The Arches Restaurant in Newport Beach, California, was famous for its watercress soup. For years people used to drive miles for that special treat.

1 bunch fresh, tender watercress	1 tablespoon butter
1 pint chicken broth (canned is good)	1 small onion, minced
	Salt and white pepper
2 slices lean bacon, fried crisp and crumbled	Nutmeg
	1 cup cream

Chop watercress fine. Simmer in chicken broth for 15 minutes. Fry bacon until crisp, towel-dry and crumble. Chop onion and cook in butter until limp. Add the onion and bacon bits to the watercress.

Turn the heat low and continue cooking for another 10 minutes. Add the cream last, slowly bringing soup to a simmer. Season with salt and white pepper, dust with nutmeg. Serves 4.

NOTE: This may also be served ice-cold, in which case it should be processed, before chilling, in the blender.

Black Bean Soup Baja**

One of the big specialties in Puerta Vallarta restaurants is Black Bean Soup — a thick and dusky brew that is served with a lot of condiments on the side — much like the side boys that accompany curries. This is a meal in itself, so make plenty, and make a lot of people happy.

1/4 cup oil	1/4 teaspoon cayenne
1/4 pound bacon, diced	2 teaspoons ground cumin
1/4 pound smoked ham	2 dried red chiles, crushed
4 large onions, chopped	3 quarts chicken broth
5 cloves garlic, minced	4 tablespoons wine vinegar
4 stalks celery, chopped	1/2 cup dry Sherry
1 pound dried black beans, sorted and rinsed	Soup garnishes

Saute bacon, ham, onion, garlic and celery in hot oil, stirring over medium heat until vegetables are lightly browned. This will take 30 to 40 minutes. Add beans, cayenne, cumin and chiles. Stir in broth and bring to a boil. Cover, reduce heat and cook, at a simmer, for 2½ to 3 hours. Let cool to lukewarm.

Process, a portion at a time, in a blender, leaving a few beans whole. Before serving, bring soup back to a simmer, adding the vinegar and sherry. Serve in heated bowls and provide any or all of the following garnishes to spoon over. Serves 10.

Garnishes: hot cooked rice, polish sausages (cut in 1-inch pieces), chopped onion, chopped fresh or canned chiles, lime wedges.

Mexican Pozole**

Properly presented, Mexican soups are not for the timid. Every helping needs a hefty heap of chopped onion and a good squeeze of lime. Hot buttered tortillas are mandatory go-alongs.

2 pounds oxtails	1 29-ounce can white hominy,
1-1/2 cups dry pinto beans	rinsed
1 large onion, sliced	3 tablespoons coarsely chopped
6 cloves garlic	fresh cilantro
1 tablespoon salt	Shredded lettuce
Water	1 cup chopped onion
1 10-ounce can red chili sauce	2 limes, quartered
(Las Palmas is a good one)	

Place oxtails, beans, onion, garlic and salt in a large soup kettle. Cover with water, filling the pot about 3/4 full. Bring to a boil, then lower heat and simmer. Cook slowly until beans are tender, adding water as necessary to keep mixture "soupy."

When meat is falling off the bones and the beans are tender, add the chili sauce. Taste for seasonings. Remove oxtails to a smaller pan and, when cool enough to handle, take meat off the bones and return meat to the pot along with the hominy. Cook another half hour, then serve. Top each serving with chopped onion, shredded lettuce, cilantro and pass quartered limes. A couple of squeezes really puts zest in this south-of-the-border soup. Serves 6.

Lime Soup La Paz**

Here's another bountiful soup from Baja that puts chicken in the pot, zips it up with salsa and gets crunch from tortilla strips. And as far as I am concerned, the more cilantro, the better.

1/4 cup minced onion	Juice of 2 limes
1 small green pepper, minced	3 cups cooked, shredded chicken
3 stalks celery, minced	6 corn tortillas, cut in strips
2 tablespoons butter	Oil
1 16-ounce can stewed tomatoes,	Cilantro
undrained	Lime slices
1 8-ounce jar red salsa	1 large onion, chopped
1-3/4 cups chicken broth	

Saute 1/4 cup minced onion, green pepper and celery in butter until vegetables are tender. Add tomatoes, salsa, broth, lime juice and chicken. Heat slowly to boiling, then reduce to a simmer.

Heat oil (about 1/2 inch deep) in a small skillet. Fry tortilla strips, a few at a time, until crisp. Remove with a slotted spoon and drain on paper towels.

Distribute tortilla strips among 6 bowls, then pour in hot soup. Serve with sliced limes, cilantro and chopped onions. Serves 6.

NOTE: If you don't want to fry tortilla strips, substitute a bag of tortilla chips.

*Tavern Cheese Soup***

Cheese soups are rich. As a first course, make the portions small.

1/4 cup butter
1/2 cup shredded carrots
1/2 cup chopped onion
1/4 cup flour
Dash salt and cracked black
pepper

2 cups milk
1/2 cup half-and-half
1/2 teaspoon dry mustard
3/4 cup beer
1/2 pound shredded sharp cheese

Melt butter and add the carrot and onion, cooking until tender. Stir in the flour, salt and pepper, stirring to make a smooth roux.

Stir milk into half-and-half, then add to the flour mixture, whisking to keep smooth. Add the mustard. Cook and stir until smooth and thickened. When bubbling, add the beer. Whisking continuously, add the shredded cheese, taking care that the heat does not exceed a simmer. Serves 4.

*Onion Soup Gratinee****

Onion Soup Gratinee is one of the most heavenly concoctions ever invented. Alas, more often than not, it is served up with soggy toast and pallid cheese — a sorry substitution for the real thing. Properly compounded, the brew should be dark, rich, and capped with a solid, pungent crust of freshly grated Gruyere cheese. Admittedly it takes a bit of engineering to keep everything properly afloat, but when it's done right, it is pure ambrosia.

3 tablespoons butter
4 cups thinly sliced Bermuda
  onions (3 to 5 onions)
10 cups light stock (beef or
  chicken, not too salty)
1 teaspoon salt

1 teaspoon white pepper
2 cloves garlic, finely minced
12 slices French bread, sliced very
  thin
1 pound Gruyere cheese (or Swiss),
  grated

Melt butter in a heavy pan and add the onions. Cook for 6 minutes, stirring to brown the onions evenly and lightly. Add the stock, salt, pepper and garlic; simmer for 30 minutes. Meantime, place bread under the broiler to lightly brown.

Set 6 ovenproof bowls on a large cookie sheet. Place 2 slices of the toast in each one. Now carefully pour in the hot soup, filling the bowls **half** full. As the bread starts to absorb the hot soup, very slowly add more liquid to the bowls, filling each one to the top. When the soup is level with the tops of the bowls, carefully sprinkle on the cheese, taking care not to push it into the liquid. This will take a good 1/2-cup loosely grated cheese per bowl. With your fingers, very gently press the cheese all around the edges of the bowl, effecting a seal. Bake at 400° F. for 35 minutes. Serves 6.

Broccoli Cheese Soup**

Broccoli topped with cheese sauce is a lovely green and gold duo. The same combination shows up in this creamy soup. With salad and crusty bread, it makes a meal.

1 pound broccoli, trimmed and chopped	3-1/2 cups evaporated milk
1-3/4 cups boiling water	4 cups milk
1 teaspoon salt	3-1/4 cups shredded Cheddar or Tillamook cheese
2-1/2 tablespoons minced onion	Salt and pepper, to taste
1/4 cup melted butter	Sprinkle nutmeg
3 tablespoons flour	

Cook broccoli in salted, boiling water until tender (don't overcook). Drain and set aside. Cook onion in butter until tender, then blend in flour. Add evaporated and regular milk, stirring constantly, and cook until thickened and smooth. Add cheese and broccoli and season to taste with salt and pepper. Sprinkle in nutmeg. Heat until cheese is melted, but don't boil. Serves 8.

Garlic Soup Mexicana**

Garlic Soup Mexicana is very big with people who love garlic and don't care who knows it. (And everyone within shouting distance will know it, all right.)

1/4 cup butter	Salt and pepper
1 onion, chopped	1 tablespoon minced parsley
17 cloves garlic, minced	Lime wedges
1 large tomato, peeled and processed in a blender	Tortilla chips
4 cups chicken broth	Assorted garnishes

Melt butter and slowly saute onion and garlic, stirring constantly. Don't let garlic brown. Puree tomato in a blender, then stir into the garlic mix. Simmer 1 minute, then add the broth. Season to taste with salt and pepper. Simmer an additional 20 minutes, then ladle into bowls. Sprinkle with parsley. Serve with lime wedges and crisp tortilla chips.

Additional garnishes, to be sprinkled into the soup at the table, include chopped onions, cilantro, diced tomatoes, grated sharp cheese (or Jack cheese), diced avocado, crisp bacon bits and chopped green pepper. Include as many, or more, as you wish. (The more the better, of course.) Serves 4.

Peanut Soup Pronto*

For a flash-in-the-pan, one-star (*) peanut soup, try a blend of canned chicken soup and Skippy. It's good and it's rich. A little dab will do you.

1 can cream of chicken soup	1/4 cup super-chunky peanut butter
1 can whole milk	

Stir ingredients together and bring to a slow simmer. Serves 4.

Belgian Beer Soup*

Here is a more streamlined takeoff on the classic French onion soup. This one gets a nice little kick from beer, but don't worry. No one would ever guess what's in it.

4 onions, thinly sliced	1/2 teaspoon pepper
3 tablespoons butter	4 slices French bread, toasted
3 cups beef broth	1 cup grated Swiss cheese
1 12-ounce can of beer	

Cook onions in butter until soft. Add broth, beer and pepper. Bring to a boil, then lower heat to a simmer, cover and cook for 30 minutes. Ladle into 4 heat-proof bowls. Float a slice of toast in each one, sprinkle with cheese and broil until cheese is melted. Serves 4.

Goober Soup**

I first tasted peanut butter soup in the grand old Roanoake Hotel where it was served by waiters in tuxedos and white gloves. They were too tony to call it Goober Soup, but that's how it translates here.

1/4 cup butter	1 cup peanut butter, creamy
1 onion, chopped fine	style
1 cup celery, sliced thin	1 cup light cream or
2 tablespoons flour	half-and-half
2 quarts chicken broth	

Melt butter and cook onion and celery over low heat. When tender, stir in flour and then gradually add the chicken broth. Bring to a gradual boil, stirring constantly. When smooth and simmering, add the peanut butter and cook an additional 15 minutes. Stir in cream just before serving. Adjust seasonings — adding a sprinkle of salt and pepper, if desired. Serves 8.

Mulligatawny Soup**

What better way to spend a wintry Saturday afternoon than to curl up with a good book, a steaming bowl of Mulligatawny Soup and watch the rain stream down the windows?

1/2 cup butter	3 cups milk
1 teaspoon curry powder	2 cups cooked chicken,
1/2 cup chopped onion	chopped
1/2 cup chopped celery	1 10-ounce can condensed
1/2 cup thinly sliced carrot	chicken broth
1/2 green pepper, chopped	1 cup chopped unpeeled green
1/3 cup flour	apple
1 teaspoon salt	

Melt butter, then stir in curry powder, onion, celery, carrot and pepper. Cook until vegetables are tender-crisp. Add flour, salt, milk, broth, chicken and apple. Cover and simmer 10 minutes. Serve in heated bowls. Serves 4.

Very Best Clam Chowder**

This sensational chowder was served every Friday for years in a small restaurant where the chef guarded the secret of this very special soup. Finally, when the restaurant closed, the cook gave out the recipe. Until then, no one knew that mushroom soup was one of this super chowder's main ingredients.

1 6-1/2-ounce can minced clams	1/4 teaspoon salt
Reserved clam liquid	1/4 pound butter
Pinch of soda	3 tablespoons flour
1/2 cup minced onion	1 quart whole milk
1/2 cup minced celery	1 can cream of mushroom soup

Drain clams, reserving liquid. Cook the reserved clam liquid, with a pinch of soda added, with the minced onion and celery until vegetables are tender-crisp. Add salt and set aside.

Melt butter in a heavy saucepan and stir in flour, mixing to a smooth roux. When flour and butter are well incorporated, gradually stir in the milk.

Combine clam broth mixture with the hot milk mixture and heat gradually. Add the clams and the undiluted soup. Stir to blend. Bring to a simmer and serve piping hot. Serves 4.

The Cool Soups

When hot weather hits, enthusiasm for cooking can hit an all-time low. Be prepared! Mix up a batch of Icy Soup Base, stash it in the fridge and you'll be ready to knock out a variety of cold soup pick-ups designed to refresh and refuel.

Icy Summer Soup Base*

2 2-3/4-ounce packages dried	4 cups cold milk
leek soup mix	1 cup light cream
4 cups cold water	MSG

Combine soup mix and water and bring to a slow boil. Lower heat, cover pan and simmer for 10 minutes. Set aside to cool. Process soup in batches in a blender until smooth. Add milk and light cream to the base, and sprinkle with MSG. Pour into two glass jars, cover and refrigerate until well chilled. Makes about 9 cups of base.

Cucumber Quickie*

In a blender, puree 1 small, peeled and seeded cucumber. Combine with 1 cup Icy Soup Base and 1 cup buttermilk. Sprinkle in 1 teaspoon dill weed. Add salt, to taste. Chill and serve. Makes 2-1/2 cups.

Hurry-Curry Asparagus*

Drain 1 8-ounce can asparagus and process in a blender until smooth. Combine with 1 cup Icy Soup Base, 1 teaspoon curry powder and a pinch of freshly grated nutmeg. Add a pinch of salt, then chill until ice cold. Serve in chilled bowls topped with finely chopped apple. Makes a scant 2 cups.

Vichyssoise on the Double*

Melt 1 tablespoon butter in 1/2 cup boiling water. Stir in 1-1/2 tablespoons instant mashed potato flakes, mixing well. Stir in 1 cup Icy Soup Base and 2 tablespoons sour cream. Add freshly snipped chives or 1 tablespoon frozen chopped chives. Chill well before serving. Makes enough for 1 serving.

Instant Cream of Carrot*

Drain 1 8-ounce can of carrots and put carrots in a blender. Process until smooth. Combine pureed carrots with 1 cup Icy Soup Base, a dash powdered thyme, a sprinkle of ground nutmeg and 1/4 teaspoon rosemary. Add a pinch of MSG, cover soup and chill. Serve topped with sour cream and a sprinkling of grated orange peel. Makes 1 serving.

Vichyssoise**

Mention a chilled soup, and everyone thinks of vichyssoise, which isn't all that bad. Still, I never cease to be amazed at what gourmet billing this plain old potato and leek soup gets. It really isn't that fancy!

1 large onion, cut fine	2 stalks celery
4 leeks (white part only), chopped	2 medium-sized potatoes, sliced
4 tablespoons butter	Salt and white pepper, to taste
4 cups chicken stock (may be canned)	Few grains nutmeg (optional)
	1 cup heavy cream
	Finely chopped chives

Cook onion and leeks in butter over a low fire until the vegetables are soft. Take care that they don't brown. When they are cooked, add the stock, celery and potatoes; simmer until the potatoes are soft. Then season to taste with salt, pepper and nutmeg. Process in a blender until the mixture is smooth. Pour into a container and add the cream. Refrigerate, preferably overnight. Serve in chilled bowls. Sprinkle with finely chopped chives. Serves 8.

Picnic Senegalese*

My friend Aida brought this soup to one of our Hollywood Bowl picnics — carried it in a thermos and dished up the chutney on the spot. Everyone loved it.

1/2 cup shredded apple	1 can cream of chicken soup
1/3 cup chopped onion	1 soup can half-and-half
1-1/2 teaspoons curry powder	Chutney
2 tablespoons butter	

Cook apple, onion and curry powder in butter until onion is tender. Stir in soup and half-and-half. Simmer 5 minutes. Cover and chill 8 hours. Serve in chilled bowls with a dollop of chutney in the middle of each one. Serves 4.

Chunky Gazpacho**

*There are as many versions of gazpacho as there are Spanish cooks, but I feel a good gazpacho should be **chopped**, not pulverized — something like salsa in a bowl. If you don't have a food processor to help with the chopping, roll up your sleeves, get a sharp knife and go to it. Shortcutting the process by running the works through a blender makes mush of it, so **don't**.*

3 tomatoes, peeled and cut in dice
3 stalks celery, finely chopped
2 green peppers, finely chopped
1 bunch cilantro (optional), chopped
2 cucumbers, peeled and diced
1 large onion, finely diced
2 cloves garlic, minced
1/4 cup canned green chiles, diced
1 46-ounce can tomato juice
1 teaspoon hot pepper sauce (or more)
1 teaspoon sugar
1 tablespoon red wine vinegar
1 tablespoon olive oil
Salt and pepper, to taste
1 cucumber, scored and coarsely chopped
Ice cubes

Chop vegetables, taking care not to "mush" tomatoes. Add remaining ingredients, except the coarsely chopped cucumber and ice cubes. Taste and correct seasonings. Refrigerate several hours or overnight, allowing flavors to blend. Serve in cold bowls topped with coarsely chopped cucumber. Place an ice cube in each bowl and pass additional hot sauce for those who hanker for extra heat. Serves 6 to 8.

Beer Soup*

*Next summer when the temperature hits sizzle, try cooling off with a cup of cold Beer Soup. (If you're out of sour cream and short on cucumbers, you might have to settle for beer, **period**.)*

1 can or bottle of beer
1/2 cup sour cream
2 cucumbers
Salt
1/2 teaspoon garlic salt
Accent

Add beer to sour cream. Chop cucumber (leaving skin on if the cucumber is a tender, young specimen). Put sour cream and beer — plus cucumber — in blender, adding pinch of salt, garlic salt, and Accent. Buzz until smooth. Pour in chilled soup bowls and garnish with a light sprinkling of very finely minced chives. Serves 2.

Vodka Soup**

Here is an icy soup that, to put it politely, will knock your hat off. Between the garlic (three big fat cloves) and the vodka (a whole cupful), this combo's a real whizbang. Just the thing to show off your culinary inventiveness. But I wouldn't serve it when Aunt Maude comes visiting from Des Moines. (And get someone else to drive home.)

3 large cloves garlic, crushed	2 tablespoons tarragon vinegar
1 large onion, chopped	1 cup beef bouillon or stock
6 ripe tomatoes, peeled and chopped	1-1/2 teaspoons salt
	Cracked pepper
Parsley — a half a small bunch, minced	1 cup vodka
	Assorted garnishes
3 tablespoons salad oil	

Crush garlic buds in blender and add the onion. Process until smooth, then toss in the tomatoes that have been peeled and chopped. Add the remaining ingredients (dividing the soup in two batches if your blender gets too full) and process until smooth. Taste and correct seasonings if necessary; then chill the soup in refrigerator until icy. Serve in cups that have been chilled 10 or 15 minutes in the freezer. Serves 4.

Pass separate bowls of chopped cucumber, onion, green peppers, diced green chiles, croutons and cilantro for your guests to sprinkle in and over, as they wish.

NOTE: You don't have to have **all** those things but, like side-boys for a curry, the more the merrier.

Icy Avocado Soup**

This summer smoothie is a great idea for a luncheon served with crusty rolls and platters of fresh fruit. This recipe makes a lot — you may have to process it in batches for your blender. Make it far enough ahead to get thoroughly chilled. White wine is a natural accompaniment.

3 ripe avocados, peeled and mashed	1 teaspoon minced onion
	3 tablespoons sherry
4 cups chicken broth	1 cup sour cream
1/4 cup lemon juice	Dash hot pepper sauce
1/2 teaspoon salt	1/2 cup finely chopped chives
1/4 teaspoon white pepper	

Mix avocado with chicken broth, lemon juice, salt, pepper, onion and sherry. Process in a blender until smooth. Add sour cream, a bit at a time, until well-blended. Chill 2 hours or more. Serve in chilled bowls garnished with chopped chives. Serves 8.

What's Ahead in
Vegetables

. . . .Eat your Carrots or you can't have Dessert

A generation or two ago the woods were full of meat-and-potatoes diehards who wouldn't touch vegetables with a hoe handle. And now there seems to be as many young things romping around who won't eat anything **but.**

Apart from showing how the pendulum swings, another reason vegetables are so in is because they are being prepared so much better. Southern cooks who used to cook greens all day and into the night are a dying breed, and even restaurants have done an about-face. (Restaurant veggies used to be cooked to pieces; nowadays they are coming out of the kitchen practically **raw.** Where, one wonders, is the happy medium?)

Happily, the proper cooking of vegetables just couldn't be easier. The way to go is simple but strict. Read, please, and **heed.**

Always buy the freshest produce available. Look for crispness, bright colors, tender leaves, beans with snap. Shun the wilties.

Wash with the speed of light. A steady stream of cold water is all it takes to rinse away the silt and sand. Don't soak. And don't peel, pare or cut until immediately before using.

Don't store too long. Except for the root family — potatoes, carrots, parsnips, etc. — two days are the most that vegetables should cool their heels in the fridge. Remember, you are after **fresh** vegetables.

Lower the waterline. Keep the cooking water to a minimum. Bring it to a boil, then lower the heat so the vegetables cook in their own steam. A collapsible steamer basket will keep the beans and brussels sprouts above the water level. If you buy one, be sure to check the water as things cook. More than once I have forgotten to peek and have burned the buns off my best pans.

Stop cooking while the vegetables are still crisp. When in doubt, opt for under-doneness.

And don't over-salt. A half teaspoon is about right for every pound of produce. A new cook would be well advised to salt after the food is cooked. That way there is less danger of overdoing it.

A word about pans. The heavier the better. To minimize cooking time, pick a wide, shallow pan in preference to a deeper pot. And if the water boils away before the vegetables have reached the **al dente** stage, add a bit more boiling water. And keep watching.

Once they're cooked, dress the vegetables with a lump of butter, a dribble of lemon juice, or whatever. Then whisk to the table. Too much standing around undoes all your lovely handiwork, so **hustle.**

Buttery Glazed Carrots*

Nine out of 10 kids grow up being told they can't have ice cream until they eat their carrots. And that explains why carrots get such rotten ratings with nine out of 10 adults. And that's too bad. They're bright and sunny and taste very good if you glaze them with honey and butter. (And eat them all or you can't have dessert.)

2 pounds small, young carrots
1/4 teaspoon salt
1/2 stick butter (margarine isn't as good here)

1 tablespoon honey or light brown sugar
Dash nutmeg

In a heavy pan, cook small whole carrots in a small amount of salted water, cooking only until tender. (The pan will be almost dry.) Melt butter in a heavy skillet and, when it sizzles, add the carrots, shaking the pan and rolling the carrots around until they are thoroughly coated. Add the honey and continue shaking the pan. Then lower the heat, cover tightly, and cook for 5 minutes, or until the carrots are beautifully glazed. Sprinkle with nutmeg and serve. Serves 6.

NOTE: Be sure to use the sweetest, youngest carrots you can lay your hands on. Old-timers simply won't do.

Baked Zucchini Boats**

Plant one zucchini, and by midsummer you will be hip-deep in the prolific little squash. And that isn't all. A zucchini can be two inches long one day and big as an inner tube the next. So pick fast. You need small to medium-size squash for this next one.

6 medium zucchini
6 tablespoons butter
2 rounded teaspoons dehydrated onions

1 tablespoon minced parsley
Garlic salt and pepper
Freshly grated Parmesan cheese

Scrub the zucchini briskly with a vegetable brush. Don't peel. Cut in half lengthwise and simmer 6 to 8 minutes in salted water, or until barely tender. Place squash in a shallow baking dish, cut side up. Sprinkle with Parmesan cheese. Melt butter in a small pan and stir in the dried onion flakes and the parsley. As the mixture bubbles, add 1 teaspoon water — just enough to keep things from sticking. Spoon over the zucchini and sprinkle with garlic salt and pepper. Place in a 350° F. oven for 15 minutes. Just before serving, slip under the broiler a minute or two to brown.

NOTE: If you want a crustier topping, sprinkle a bit more Parmesan over the zucchini just before going under the broiler. Serves 6.

Tomato Zuccini Pie**

This hearty, quiche-like vegetable pie offers one more way to use up some of your garden's excess zucchini.

1 8-ounce can of refrigerated crescent rolls	1/2 cup chopped onion
2 tablespoons bread crumbs	1/2 cup evaporated milk
3 zucchini cut into 1/8-inch slices	1 egg, beaten
1/4 cup olive oil	1/8 teaspoon oregano
1 tomato, cut in wedges	Pepper
1/2 cup chopped green pepper	2 tablespoons Parmesan cheese
	2 tablespoons bread crumbs

Heat oven to 325° F. Unroll crescent rolls and press into a greased pie pan. Completely seal dough. Sprinkle with bread crumbs. Saute zucchini until tender-crisp and arrange in pie shell. Top with tomato wedges. Saute green pepper and onion and sprinkle over tomatoes and zucchini. Blend milk with egg and pour over vegetables. Mix Parmesan cheese with oregano and remaining 2 tablespoons crumbs and sprinkle over pie. Bake at 325° F. for 35 minutes. Serves 6.

Garlicky Broccoli**

Looking for a lift for fresh broccoli? Try dressing it with lemon juice, olive oil and a drift of garlic.

1 pound broccoli	1/2 cup freshly grated Parmesan cheese
1/4 cup olive oil	
1 large clove garlic, minced	Salt and cracked pepper
1 teaspoon lemon juice	

Strip broccoli stems, cut into long uniform sticks and break off flowers. Steam the stems for 5 minutes before adding the flowers. Cook over high heat only until tender-crisp — 3 to 4 minutes. Then drain. Heat olive oil in a small skillet, add the minced garlic and then the broccoli, stir-frying for 2 minutes. Sprinkle with lemon juice, salt, pepper and Parmesan and serve piping hot. Serves 5 or 6.

Wok Tok Spinach*

Cooked this way, spinach keeps its brilliant green and comes out of the pan delightfully "al dente".

3 slices bacon	2 tablespoons French dressing
1-1/2 pounds fresh spinach	Salt and pepper

Wash spinach in several waters and trim off the coarse stems. Wrap in a towel and refrigerate until ready to serve.

Saute bacon until crisp, then remove and crumble. In a wok or heavy skillet heat 2 tablespoons of the bacon fat. Add the chilled spinach, stirring and tossing until the leaves are wilted and bright green. Don't overcook. Stir in the French dressing and season to taste with salt and pepper. Garnish with the chopped bacon. Serves 4.

Lawry's Creamed Spinach**

Lawry's famous prime rib house in Los Angeles is almost as well-known for its delicious creamed spinach as it is for its gorgeous beef. The recipe has appeared in the food pages of local newspapers countless times, and requests still keep coming.

1 10-ounce package frozen chopped spinach	1 teaspoon seasoned salt
3 slices bacon, chopped	Dash seasoned pepper
1/2 cup finely chopped onion	1 clove garlic, minced
2 tablespoons flour	1 cup whole milk

Cook and drain the spinach. While spinach is draining, cook the bacon and onions until tender, about 10 minutes. (Don't let the mixture get too brown — keep the heat low.) Remove the skillet from the heat and stir the flour into the pan drippings. Add seasonings. Return the pan to the stove and slowly add the milk, stirring and cooking until the sauce is smooth and thickened. Add the drained spinach, heat through and serve. Serves 4.

Easiest-Ever Creamed Spinach*

An even easier way to cream spinach is to fold in a package of cream cheese.

2 10-ounce packages chopped frozen spinach, thawed and drained	1 8-ounce package cream cheese
	Salt and pepper to taste

Cook spinach, then drain thoroughly. Add cream cheese in chunks and stir until melted. Reheat briefly, season to taste, and serve with a sprinkle of nutmeg. Serves 6 to 8.

Broccoli Cheese Casserole**

This broccoli casserole has been making the rounds at ladies' club meetings in our town lately. Anyone who doesn't already have the recipe makes sure to get a copy before the party is over.

2 10-ounce packages frozen chopped broccoli	2 eggs, beaten
3/4 cup mayonnaise	1-1/2 cups grated Longhorn or Cheddar cheese
1 onion, chopped	1 can cream of mushroom soup
3/4 stick margarine	1 cup cheese cracker crumbs

Cook broccoli tender-crisp, then drain thoroughly. Fold in remaining ingredients and spoon mixture into a greased 9 x 13-inch baking dish. Sprinkle with crushed cheese crackers before baking. Bake uncovered at 350° F. for 40 minutes. Serves 6 to 8.

Mushrooms Elegant***

Mushrooms Elegant is an elegant overnight casserole that puffs up into a creamy, cheesy delight. Apart from its sumptuous "company" quality, the beauty of this entree is that it can be assembled a day ahead — a marvelous plus for a busy cook.

1 pound mushrooms, sliced fairly thick	1/2 cup chopped celery
1/2 cube butter	1/2 cup finely chopped green pepper
8 slices soft white bread, crusts removed	2 eggs, slightly beaten
1/2 cup chopped onion	1-1/2 cups milk
1/2 cup mayonnaise	1 can cream of mushroom soup
Salt and white pepper	1 cup Cheddar cheese, grated

Saute sliced mushrooms in 3 tablespoons of butter just until they are soft. Do not overcook. Meanwhile, spread bread with remaining butter and cut into cubes. Put 1/3 of bread in greased 9 x 13-inch baking dish.

Combine mushrooms with mayonnaise, salt and pepper, onion, celery and green pepper. Spread over bread in casserole. Top with another 1/3 bread cubes. Blend beaten eggs with milk; pour over casserole. At this point it should be covered and refrigerated, preferably overnight.

An hour before serving, spoon 1 can undiluted soup over whole thing and top with remaining 1/3 buttered bread cubes. Bake 300° F. for 1 hour. Sprinkle with grated cheese; pop back into oven till cheese melts. Serves 6 to 8.

Eggplant Souffle***

Here is a nice cheesy souffle that puts eggplant in the mix. It would be a lovely accompaniment for lamb, but is hearty enough to stand on its own.

1 medium eggplant, peeled and diced	3/4 cup soft bread crumbs
2 tablespoons butter	2 tablespoons grated onion
2 tablespoons flour	1 tablespoon catsup
1 cup milk	Salt and pepper
1 cup grated Cheddar cheese	2 eggs, separated

Cook diced eggplant in a small amount of lightly salted water until tender. Drain and mash. Melt butter in a heavy saucepan, stir in flour until all the butter is absorbed; gradually add the milk, stirring briskly and continuously until the sauce is smooth and thickened.

Fold the mashed eggplant into the white sauce along with the grated cheese, bread crumbs, onions, seasonings and beaten egg yolks.

Beat egg whites until stiff peaks form, then gently fold into the eggplant mixture. Spoon into a straight-sided 1-quart casserole and bake at 325° F. for 1 hour. Serves 4.

Spaghetti Ratatouille***

Even if one adores eggplant, it's easy to run out of ideas on what to do with those purple blobs. Spaghetti Ratatouille offers an interesting way to have your eggplant and eat your pasta, too.

1 8-ounce package spaghetti (cooked al dente and drained)	1 cup canned stewed tomatoes
	2 cloves minced garlic
1 cup pared and diced eggplant	1/2 teaspoon thyme
1 cup unpeeled zucchini, sliced	1 teaspoon dried basil
1 yellow onion, peeled and sliced	Salt and pepper
1 green pepper, seeded and cut in strips	Parmesan cheese

While spaghetti is cooking, prepare sauce by combining all the remaining (except Parmesan cheese) ingredients, in a large skillet. Cover and cook sauce at a simmer for 10 minutes.

Uncover skillet, stir vegetables and continue cooking until sauce thickens. (Do not overcook. The vegetables should retain some crispness.)

Drain pasta and place in a large serving bowl. Spoon eggplant-tomato sauce over the pasta, top with grated Parmesan cheese and serve. Serves 4.

Broiled Tomatoes*

When tomatoes are at the peak of their season, don't overlook the simplest cooking method of all — broiling. Prepared this way, they make an excellent accompaniment for chops or roasts.

4 firm, ripe tomatoes	1/2 teaspoon basil
5 tablespoons butter	Dry bread crumbs
Salt and cracked black pepper	Parmesan cheese

Cut tomatoes in half and squeeze gently to remove some of the seeds and juice. Sprinkle with salt, pepper, basil, bread crumbs and Parmesan. Drizzle melted butter over all and slip under the broiler for 10 minutes, or until tomatoes are bubbly and the topping is lightly browned. Serves 4.

Mushrooms and Snow Peas*

Snow peas, in their bright-green prime, are so sweet and tender they can be eaten raw. It follows, then, that split-second timing is called for in their cooking. Just a quick steaming — say 2 minutes — is generally all the heat they need.

1/2 pound fresh mushrooms	Dash monosodium glutamate
2 tablespoons butter	Salt and pepper
1/4 pound fresh snow peas	

Gently clean mushrooms by wiping with a damp cloth. Don't soak! Slice and saute the mushrooms in butter until delicately colored a pale golden brown. Meantime, steam peas until barely tender. Drain and add to the mushrooms. Sprinkle lightly with monosodium glutamate (MSG) and taste for salt and pepper. Add a bit more butter and serve. Serves 4.

Baked Acorn Squash Cups*

In the fall of the year, acorn squash swimming with melted butter has a very special appeal. Just cut one in half and there you have — voila! — two individual scalloped cups, just right for filling with something else, like buttered peas or creamed spinach. Or spiced applesauce. For pennies a pound, who could ask for anything more?

2 small acorn squash, cut in half	1/2 teaspoon salt
2 tablespoons honey	2 tablespoons butter
	Nutmeg

Cut squash in half horizontally, remove seeds and rinse. If necessary to make the cups stand steady, pare a little of the stem ends off. Divide honey, butter and seasonings between the four "cups". Bake in an upright position in a pie plate in a 375° F. oven. This will take 45 minutes to an hour. When squash is fork-tender, it's ready. Serve as is, or fill with tiny peas or applesauce. Serves 4.

Glazed Party Onions**

These richly glazed onions make a great go-along with turkey, chicken or roast pork. Very festive.

4 large Bermuda onions, peeled and halved crosswise	1/2 teaspoon salt
1/4 cup oil	1/2 teaspoon nutmeg
2 tablespoons vinegar	1/2 teaspoon paprika
2 tablespoons honey	Dash rubbed sage

Fit onions, cut side up, in a large skillet. Add about 2 inches of boiling salted water, cover pan and simmer for 10 minutes. Drain. Mix remaining ingredients and pour over onions. Cover and cook over low heat for 30 minutes, basting occasionally. Serves 4.

Cheese-Crowned Cauliflower**

*I adore steamed and buttered cauliflower although I admit it **does** look a bit bland sitting there on a white china plate. For more pizazz, steam the cauliflower whole, then lather the whole thing with a crown of creamy cheese and walnuts. Superb!*

1 medium head cauliflower	1/2 cup shredded Cheddar cheese
1/2 cup mayonnaise	1/4 cup finely chopped walnuts
1 teaspoon prepared mustard	

Trim and wash cauliflower, leaving the head whole. Place stem side down in a large kettle and add 2 inches of salted water to the pan. Cover and bring to a boil. Lower heat and simmer until cauliflower is tender, about 20 minutes. Take care not to overcook, or the "flower" will fall apart!

Drain and place the whole cauliflower in an ovenproof serving dish. Mix mustard with mayonnaise and spread over cauliflower. Sprinkle with grated cheese and place in a 350° F. oven just until cheese melts. Sprinkle with chopped nuts. Serves 6.

Brussels Sprouts Sauterne**

Probably more than any other single vegetable, Brussels sprouts suffer from overcooking. To keep these little devils sprightly and green, cook fast. The trick is to cut a fairly deep X in the stem end of each sprout which allows the firm centers to cook as fast as the loose outer leaves.

In this version, they are spiked with sauterne and sprinkled with green grapes.

1 pound fresh Brussels sprouts	1 cup seedless green grapes
Boiling salted water	4 tablespoons sauterne
4 tablespoons butter	Salt and pepper, to taste
4 tablespoons blanched slivered almonds	

Trim ends off the sprouts and cut an "X" in the bottom. Cook in boiling salted water until tender-crisp — about 15 minutes. Drain and set aside. Melt butter in a heavy skillet and saute almonds until golden. Remove nuts with a slotted spoon. In the same skillet heat the grapes; add the sprouts, turning rapidly to glaze. Season with salt and pepper. Add sauterne and almonds, toss gently and serve. Serves 6 to 8.

Beer Batter for Fried Onion Rings*

Beer is the secret ingredient in this bubbly batter for crispy onion rings. This makes enough for about four onions, but should you have any batter left, it can be refrigerated and used again, up to one week.

4 Bermuda onions, thinly sliced	1 tablespoon paprika
1 12-ounce can beer, flat	1 tablespoon salt
1 cup flour	

If beer isn't already flat, pour it into a bowl and set aside long enough to lose its fizz. Mix flour, paprika and salt together, add the beer and beat until frothy. Separate onion slices into rings and dip first into a little dry flour, then into the batter. Without crowding, fry rings in 2 to 3 inches of fat heated to 375 - 380° F. When golden brown and crunchy, drain rings on paper towels.

Cabbage au Gratin*

*I **adore** cooked cabbage and resent the cliche that tenement hallways are always supposed to smell of it. Provided you don't cook it all day, the aroma of cabbage cooking can be perfume to those who know a good thing when they smell it. The trick is to quit cooking when it gets to the tender-crisp stage. (That way, it won't smell up your hallway, either.)*

1 head young green cabbage	1/2 cup seasoned crumbs
1 cup rich cheese sauce	

Cut cabbage in one-inch slices and steam until tender. Drain and place in a 2-quart casserole. Cover generously with cheese sauce and sprinkle with seasoned crumbs. Bake at 350° F. for 15 minutes. Serves 6.

Pat's Corn Pudding**

A friend of mine who is a great cook and a gracious hostess often includes this custardy corn pudding in her buffet menus. Everyone who tastes it raves.

1-1/2 16-ounce size cans creamed corn	1 tablespoon melted butter
4 eggs, well beaten	1-1/2 cups milk
1 tablespoon flour	1 teaspoon salt

Beat eggs well, then fold in remaining ingredients, mixing well. Pour into a 2-quart casserole and bake at 350° F. for 1-1/2 hours. Check for doneness. If casserole is still jiggly in the center, leave it in to bake another 15 minutes or so. Serves 6.

Fresh Corn and Chile Casserole**

Next summer, when fresh corn on the cob is bountiful, remember to try this marvelous sour cream and corn casserole. It would make a sensational accompaniment for burgers at a backyard barbecue.

5 ears of corn, kernels cut off cobs	1 cup grated Jack cheese
1 stick butter	1/2 cup cornmeal
2 eggs	1 4-ounce can diced green chiles
1 cup sour cream	1-1/2 teaspoons salt
	1/2 teaspoon cumin

Butter a 2-quart casserole. Puree corn kernels with butter and eggs in a food processor or blender. Mix with remaining ingredients and pour into casserole. Bake, uncovered, 50 to 60 minutes. Serves 6.

Cider-Baked Parsnips*

Interesting discovery: parsnips baked in cider seem to go down well with people who normally put parsnips on their hit list. (Face it, popularity polls on parsnips rarely score more than a 3).

Here's a recipe designed to convert the Doubting Thomases. Just be sure to get very tender, young parsnips. Elder members tend to get woody and just won't do.

6 small parsnips, pared and cut in half lengthwise	2 teaspoons brown sugar
1 tablespoon butter	Dash nutmeg
	1/3 cup cider

Cook parsnips in a small amount of salted water until tender. Drain and place on a greased baking dish. Dot with butter and sprinkle with brown sugar and nutmeg. Pour cider around the parsnips and bake at 375° F. for about 20 minutes, basting, until they are golden and glazed. Serves 6.

What's Ahead in
Rounder-Outers

Rounder-Outers

. . .usually, but not always, potatoes

Pity the poor spud. It is forever playing second fiddle to the meat and fish it accompanies.

Now that hardly seems fair considering how often a crusty baked Idaho, swimming in butter and chives, tastes better than the prime rib it goes with.

Looking farther afield, you can say the same thing for those other so-called side dishes.

Besides filling up the plate and making the meat go farther, well-dressed noodles can add a nice foreign accent to the goings-on. Pasta can come on as Italian or Asian while rice, depending on its makeup, can be Mexican, Chinese, Japanese or Indonesian in character.

With the possible exception of wild rice — which, by the way, isn't a rice at all — these starchy sidekicks are inexpensive, easily prepared and wonderfully filling. Their only possible drawback is that too many second helpings of rounder-outers can round **you** out, too.

Party Mashed Potatoes**

*No matter **what** the purists preach, one of the niftiest timesavers ever invented is instant dehydrated potato flakes. The trick is to avoid using them "as is." A little dressing up handily eliminates the straight-out-of-the cardboard box blight.*

1-1/2 cups water	1/2 teaspoon salt
3 tablespoons butter	1 egg
1-1/2 cups instant dehydrated potato flakes	1/2 cup shredded Cheddar cheese (optional)
1/2 cup whole milk	Paprika
1/2 cup sour cream	

Combine water and butter and heat to boiling. Remove from heat and stir in potato flakes and milk. Whisk until fluffy. In another bowl combine the sour cream, salt and egg. Whip, then stir into the hot potatoes. Beat until fluffy, then spoon into a buttered 1-quart casserole. Top with shredded cheese, if desired, and sprinkle with paprika. Bake at 350° F. for 15 minutes. Serves 4.

*Spuds From Heaven**

This next gorgeous fluff is not for weight watchers. But, then, weight watchers aren't supposed to nuzzle into mashed potatoes, anyhow. (All right, maybe a teeny spoonful . . .)

Whip 1 small package of cream cheese into 6 cups of hot, mashed potatoes. Beat until creamy. Good? It's **scandalous!**

*Family Favorite Potatoes***

As the name suggests, these are my family's favorite potatoes. They can be put together hours ahead of any clan gathering, they heat up slowly (or in a flash, depending on your time schedule), and everyone loves them. Make a lot. A little is never enough!

8 large potatoes, peeled and cubed	1 tablespoon dehydrated onion flakes
4 cups rich white sauce	1 teaspoon dillweed
1 teaspoon chicken-flavored bouillon granules	1 to 1-1/2 cups grated Cheddar cheese (optional)
	Parmesan cheese

Cook cubed potatoes in lightly salted water until tender but still fairly firm. Prepare white sauce and season, to taste, with chicken-flavored bouillon granules (this takes the place of salt). Add onion flakes and dillweed. If desired, add grated cheese — these potatoes are great either way. Spoon potatoes and sauce into a flat baking dish and sprinkle liberally with Parmesan cheese. Slowly heat at 300° F. for 40 minutes or until bubbly and piping hot throughout. Serves 10.

*Duchess Potatoes***

Duchess Potatoes are perfectly marvelous as-is, but they are also perfect for piping in fancy flourishes around the edge of scallop shells or individual meat platters. (After the potatoes are squeezed into fat ribbons, the whole thing should be slipped under a hot broiler until the potatoes are lightly browned.)

2 cups hot mashed potatoes (instant or otherwise)	1 teaspoon salt
2 eggs	Dash black pepper
2 egg yolks	1 tablespoon mayonnaise
2 tablespoons melted butter	Dash nutmeg
	Parika or parsley

Beat eggs and yolks until fluffy and set aside. Add butter, salt, pepper, mayonnaise and a sprinkling of nutmeg to the hot potatoes. (Be sure the potatoes are piping hot!) Beat eggs into potatoes until mixture is very fluffy. Sprinkle with a drift of paprika or finely minced parsley. Serve immediately or pipe in squiggles and brown lightly under the broiler.

Potatoes Chantilly**

Potatoes Chantilly can be a lovely addition to any company dinner. If you are running behind, instant mashed potatoes can be pressed into quick service here.

3 cups mashed potatoes
Salt and white pepper
3 tablespoons butter

1/2 cup whipping cream
2 tablespoons Parmesan cheese

Prepare potatoes (from scratch or from a packaged mix). Season with salt, pepper and butter. Pile into a greased baking dish. Whip cream until stiff peaks form (you need real whipping cream for this one — substitutes won't work), then 'frost' the potatoes and sprinkle with Parmesan cheese. Bake in a preheated 425° F. oven about 8 minutes or until the top is nicely browned. Serves 6.

Company Hashbrowns*

*This is a **wonderful** buffet dish. People keep coming back for seconds (and thirds), so make plenty.*

When I described it to a friend — who happens to be a very good cook — she asked why I didn't use plain potatoes instead of frozen hash browns. "Because it's lots faster this way," I replied. And I think that said it all.

2 pounds frozen hash brown
  potatoes, thawed
8 ounces sour cream
2 cans (10-1/2-ounce size) cream
  of potato soup

1 pound shredded Cheddar cheese
1 large onion, chopped
1/2 cup Parmesan cheese
Paprika

Combine everything but the Parmesan cheese and paprika, stirring well. Spoon into a greased baking dish and sprinkle with cheese and a drift of paprika. Bake at 300° F. for 1-1/2 hours. Serves 8.

Tater Toss-Up*

Here's another potato casserole quickie. You start with Tater Tots, those crusty potato nuggets sold in bags in the frozen foods section of the supermarket. Rounded out with sour cream and cheese, these ready-to-go taters make a great party filler-upper.

2 pounds frozen Tater Tots,
  thawed
1 pint sour cream
1 can (10-1/2-ounce size) cream
  of chicken soup
1/2 pound grated Cheddar cheese

1 cup melted margarine
1/2 cup chopped onion
Sprinkle of salt
3 cups crumbled potato chips (or
  corn flakes)

Reserve 1 cup of the crushed chips. Fold the rest of them into the remaining ingredients, tossing lightly until mixed. Spoon into a flat, buttered baking dish and top with the remaining crumbs. Bake at 300° F. for 1-1/2 hours. Serves 8.

Potatoes Anna***

Potatoes Anna is a classic dish with its potato slices molded into an interesting mosaic. (You get this by carefully arranging the first layer of potatoes in an even spiral. After the first layer is set, the rest of the slices can go in willy-nilly; they won't show when the pan is inverted.)

3 to 4 potatoes (about 1-1/2 pounds)	6 tablespoons butter
2 tablespoons oil	Salt and pepper, to taste
	Sprinkle of nutmeg

Before peeling the potatoes, prepare the pan — a 7- to 8-inch heavy skillet with rounded sides and an ovenproof handle. Heat oil and butter in the pan, swirling so that the sides of the pan, as well as the bottom, are completely covered. Keep the pan warm while you peel and cut the potatoes in 1/8-inch slices.

Work quickly — before the potatoes have a chance to turn dark. Arrange the slices, overlapping, pinwheel style. Over this first layer, distribute the remaining slices and pat down snugly.

Sprinkle with salt, pepper and a drift of nutmeg. Set the skillet back over medium heat and cook until the potatoes are nicely browned on the bottom — 10 to 15 minutes. (With the tip of a sharp knife, lift occasionally and peek. Is the bottom nice and crusty?)

Then put the skillet in a 400° F. oven for 25 minutes, leaving the pan uncovered for a very crisp crust. For a softer Anna, cover the skillet with foil before baking.

To serve, gently loosen the edges of the potatoes and invert onto a heated platter.

NOTE: This can be made ahead, turned out onto a platter and kept at room temperature. Just before serving, reheat at 350° F. until piping hot.

Sweet Potato-Almond Puff**

*If you like sweet potatoes sweet — that is, **sweeter** — there really is something to do besides shake out the marshmallows. In this light and puffy version, brown sugar, orange juice and almonds do the honors.*

2 cups cooked and mashed sweet potatoes or yams	4 tablespoons melted butter
2/3 cup orange juice	2 eggs, separated
Dash salt	1/2 cup almonds, chopped
8 tablespoons brown sugar	1 teaspoon finely grated orange peel
	Nutmeg

Blend orange juice, salt, sugar and butter into potatoes. Beat egg yolks until light and add to the potato mixture along with the chopped nuts and orange peel. Beat the egg whites until stiff peaks form, then fold gently into the potatoes. Spoon into a greased 1-1/2-quart baking dish, sprinkle with nutmeg and dot with a bit more butter. Bake at 350° F. for 25 minutes or until puffed and lightly browned. Serves 4.

NOTE: I vastly prefer yams to sweet potatoes. Try them both, then make up your own mind.

Two-Times Baked Potatoes*

*If you never thought that six baking potatoes could feed six people **twice**, look again. Here's how!*

6 plump baking potatoes	3/4 cup grated Cheddar cheese
1/3 cup hot milk	1/2 cup finely chopped green onions
1/3 cup margarine or butter	6 to 8 slices bacon, fried and
Salt and pepper	crumbled
1/2 cup margarine or butter	Sour cream

Pierce scrubbed and dried potatoes with a fork. Place on a baking sheet and bake at 375°F. for 1 hour or until soft to the squeeze. Cool, then cut in half lengthwise and scoop out the centers. Shells should be about 1/8-inch thick. (Be careful not to poke holes in the skins as you scoop.) Cover the shells and chill for use later.

Mash the centers until fairly smooth, then gradually add the hot milk, whipping until fluffy. Add 1/3-cup margarine or butter, season with salt and pepper and serve piping hot. Serves 6.

Next day, melt 1/2-cup margarine or butter and brush in chilled potato shells. Arrange, cut sides up, on a cooky sheet and bake at 475° F. for 15 minutes, or until crisp. Sprinkle grated cheese into each shell and top with minced onion and bacon. Heat until cheese melts. Serve with dollops of sour cream. Serves 6.

Latkes*

Crunchy, hot-off-the-griddle Latkes — Jewish potato pancakes — make a quick and delicious accompaniment for any kind of meat or oven roast. If the menu and your waistline warrant, serve with fat dollops of sour cream.

4 large raw potatoes, peeled	4 tablespoons flour
and grated	1/2 teaspoon baking powder
1 large onion, chopped	Oil
2 eggs, beaten	Sour cream

As potatoes are grated, drop immediately into cold water to cover (which keeps the potatoes from turning dark). When they are all grated, drain well and squeeze dry in a towel. Then combine with onion, eggs, flour and baking powder.

Heat oil — about 1/4-inch in a heavy skillet — until almost smoking. Spoon potato mixture by heaping tablespoons into the hot fat. Salt and pepper to taste. Fry cakes on both sides until golden, then drain on paper towels. Serves 6 to 8.

NOTE: Along with the sour cream, applesauce is a traditional go-along.

Baked Bouillon Rice*

This rice casserole bakes all by itself in the oven — no babysitting or last-minute fuss required.

1 stick butter or margarine	1 can onion soup
1 cup raw white rice	1 4-ounce can mushrooms
1 can beef bouillon	

Melt butter and add rice. Toss until grains are well-coated and starting to turn color. Combine remaining ingredients and pour into a casserole. Bake, uncovered, at 350° F. for 1 hour. Fluff with a fork occasionally as the rice cooks. Serves 6.

Chinese Fried Rice**

Chinese Fried Rice goes beautifully with any kind of Oriental entree. Make enough and it's a meal in itself.

8 cups cooked white rice, chilled	3/4 pound medium shrimp,
1 cup frozen peas	cleaned and chopped
2 eggs	1-1/2 cups diced cooked
Dash salt	roast pork
1/2 cup oil	3 tablespoons oyster sauce
	3 teaspoons soy sauce

Fluff cold rice with a fork to remove lumps. Pour boiling water over peas in a small bowl and set aside.

Beat eggs with a pinch of salt. Heat 2 tablespoons oil in a small skillet and quickly fry beaten eggs, letting them form a smooth, thin skin. Slip out of skillet and cut in slivers.

In same pan, add a bit more oil and saute shrimp, cooking just until they turn pink. Remove. Add pork to the pan and heat through.

In larger skillet, stir-fry rice with remaining oil, oyster sauce and soy sauce. When heated through, toss in the shrimp, pork and peas. Toss and heat until piping hot. Serves 8.

Creamed Chile-Rice**

This casserole is a breeze to put together and goes beautifully with any kind of beef. (If you're broke, serve it by itself with a pile of buttered tortillas.)

3 cups sour cream	Salt and pepper, to taste
2 4-ounce cans chopped	3/4 pound Jack cheese, cut in strips
green chiles	1/2 cup grated Cheddar cheese
3 cups cooked white rice	

Mix sour cream with chopped chiles. Sprinkle cooked rice with salt and pepper, to taste. Spoon half of rice into a greased 1-1/2-quart casserole. Spoon sour cream and chile mixture over the rice, then top with Jack cheese strips. Cover with remaining rice. Bake at 350° F. for 30 minutes. Ten minutes before taking from the oven, sprinkle with grated Cheddar cheese. Serve when cheese has melted and casserole is bubbling. Serves 6.

Greek Rice**

Next time you have a leg of lamb for dinner — or a brace of sweet and succulent lamb chops — serve Greek rice alongside.

2 tablespoons margarine	3/4 cup long grain white rice
1 small eggplant, peeled and diced	1 cup chicken bouillon
4 large mushrooms, chopped	2 teaspoons finely minced fresh mint (optional)
2 tomatoes, peeled and diced	1 teaspoon salt
1 onion, chopped	Cracked black pepper

Melt margarine, then saute eggplant, mushrooms, tamotoes and onions until tender — about 14 minutes. Stir in uncooked rice and cook over low heat for 10 minutes, stirring occasionally. Add bouillon, mint, salt and pepper and cover pan. Cook slowly for 20 minutes, or until rice is tender and liquid is absorbed. Fluff with a fork and serve. Serves 6.

Good Green Rice**

Here's another mouth-watering rice concoction that has spunky flavor and comes forth a gorgeous green. (Prettier, really, than most rice fixups.)

2 cups cooked rice	1 cup finely chopped green pepper
2 eggs, beaten	2 cloves garlic, minced
2 cups milk	1/2 cup oil
1 cup finely chopped parsley	Salt and pepper, to taste
2 cups grated Tillamook or Cheddar cheese	

Mix rice with eggs and other ingredients and pour into a greased 2-1/2-quart baking dish. Bake, uncovered, at 350° F. for 45 minutes. Serves 12 as a side dish.

Chili Grits*

Remember this one when you're looking for a way to fill up a crowd and keep everybody happy. Goes nicely with steak and burgers plus any kind of Mexican food.

6 cups water	1 7-ounce can diced green chiles
1 teaspoon salt	1/4 cup margarine
1-1/3 cups quick-cooking hominy grits	4 eggs, slightly beaten
1 pound grated Cheddar cheese	1/2 teaspoon chili powder

Bring water and salt to a boil in a large saucepan. Gradually stir in grits, stirring vigorously until smooth. Turn heat low, cover kettle and cook 5 minutes, stirring occasionally. Take off heat and add cheese, chiles, margarine, eggs and chili powder. Turn into a greased 9 x 13-inch baking dish. Bake, uncovered, at 350° F. for 1 hour. Let stand 10 minutes before serving. Serves 12 to 14.

Mexican Rice**

This blushing pink Mexican Rice is a dandy side dish for burgers. And, of course, it's a natural to go along with tacos, enchiladas and all like that.

2 tablespoons margarine	1 tablespoon chili powder (rounded,
2 cups uncooked long-grain	if you like it hot)
white rice	3-1/2 cups water
1 8-ounce can tomato sauce	1 large tomato, diced
2 cloves minced garlic	1 green pepper, diced
1/2 teaspoon salt	1 brown onion, diced
1 tablespoon chicken stock base	3 stalks celery, cut in 1/4-inch slices
	1/4 cup minced cilantro (optional)

Melt margarine in skillet. Add the rice and saute until golden. Add tomato sauce and cook slowly until liquid has evaporated. Add garlic, salt, stock base, chili powder and water. Cover and simmer for 20 minutes. Add remaining ingredients and steam an additional 20 to 25 minutes. Serves 8.

Rice Pilaf**

No matter how it's spelled — pilaf, pilaw or pilau — rice and broth or bouillon, cooked together, make an excellent accompaniment for all manner of meat dishes. The following approximates the near-Eastern version of pilaf and is extraordinarily good.

2 tablespoons oil	1/2 teaspoon salt
2 tablespoons butter	3 cups chicken broth (canned)
1/2 cup fine egg noodles	1/2 cup finely chopped green onion
1-1/2 cups long-grain white rice	tops

Heat oil and butter in a heavy pan. Break up noodles and drop into the hot oil and butter, stirring briskly so they don't burn. Turn heat down and continue cooking for 4 minutes. Then stir in rice and continue stirring, over moderate heat, until the rice appears opaque — 3 to 4 minutes. Add salt and broth and bring mixture back to a boil. Then lower heat, cover pan tightly, and simmer for 15 to 20 minutes. Stir in the chopped green onion tops, cover and cook an additional 5 minutes. Taste rice for seasoning and fluff up with a fork. Serves 8.

Easy Cheese Bake*

*This super-simple souffle-like side dish is a light and lovely accompaniment to baked ham. But don't limit it to just that. It's great with **anything**.*

3/4 pound shredded Jack cheese	6 tablespoons margarine
1 cup buttermilk biscuit mix	4 tablespoons cottage cheese
1/2 cup milk	1/2 teaspoon dill weed (optional)
4 eggs, lightly beaten	

Combine all ingredients and whip until blended. Butter a 2-quart baking dish and turn mixture into it. Bake at 350° F. for 45 minutes, until puffed and lightly browned. Serves 8.

Fast Fettucine**

This creamy pasta combination makes a magnificent side dish and can pinch-hit as a main course, too. The whole thing goes together in minutes and makes enough for six accompaniment servings or four main entrees.

1/2 stick butter, room
   temperature
2 tablespoons minced parsley
1 teaspoon dried basil
1 8-ounce package cream cheese
Cracked pepper

2/3 cup boiling water
1/2 stick butter
2 large cloves garlic, minced
1 8-ounce package fettucine,
   cooked and drained
1 cup freshly grated Parmesan
   cheese

Combine first 1/2 stick of butter with parsley and basil. Add softened cream cheese, mix well, and add cracked pepper. Mix in boiling water, stirring to blend thoroughly. Place bowl over a pan of hot water and set aside.

Melt second 1/2 stick of butter in a large skillet. Add garlic, taking care that it doesn't burn. Add the cooked and drained pasta and toss until heated through. Pour cream cheese mixture over the fettucine and toss with part of the grated Parmesan cheese. Heap onto a heated platter. Top with remaining cheese and serve. Serves 4 (or 6).

Noodles Romanoff*

Noodles Romanoff served alongside a steak or burgers hot off the grill is nifty and very easy.

1 cup cottage cheese
1 cup sour cream
1 8-ounce package noodles,
   cooked
Salt and pepper, to taste

1/2 large onion, finely minced
Sprinkle of garlic powder
Dash of tabasco sauce
1 cup grated Cheddar or Longhorn
   cheese

Place cottage cheese and sour cream in a blender and process until smooth. Combine with cooked noodles. Toss with salt, pepper, onion, garlic powder and tabasco. Spoon into a 2-quart baking dish. Top with grated cheese and bake at 350° F. for 35 to 40 minutes. Serves 6.

Pineapple Souffle*

This unusual souffle-like accompaniment goes particularly well with pork chops or ham.

1/2 stick butter or margarine
1 cup sugar
4 eggs
1 15-ounce can crushed
   pineapple, drained

5 slices soft white bread, crusts
   removed and bread cubed

Cream butter with sugar. Add eggs and beat well. Fold in pineapple and bread cubes. Bake at 350° F. in a greased casserole for 50 minutes. Serves 4.

What's Ahead in
Meat

Meat

. . . first you butter up the butcher

With the price of steak right up there with the national debt, it's no wonder housewives hang over meat display cases as if they were buying rare editions. Getting saddled with a tough rump is like finding out your new ninety-dollar pumps pinch. It **hurts**.

The problem is that a cut of meat, like a diamond, is something most people can't judge just by looking. Only your butcher knows for sure what's in the meat case. And in markets where everything is wrapped and packaged, it's hard to even **see** a butcher, let alone get one to tell you which chops are tops.

Look around and see if you can locate a market where meat can be bought by the piece instead of in a package. It may cost a little more, but it's usually worth it.

The next thing is to curry the favor of the butcher. He may look like a gorilla and have forearms to match, but remember — what Balenciaga can do for a ballgown, your butcher can do for meatballs.

Tell him you wouldn't know a saddle of lamb from first base, and that you need his help. Butchers, like anyone else, need to be needed; and if you can get one to feel tenderly for you, he won't give you a bum steer.

Wonder Roast*

At last! A good rare oven-cooked roast that needn't break your budget. Try slow-cooking an inexpensive boned chuck roast and see what a tender delight it is.

1 boned chuck roast, trimmed and tied — about 6 pounds	**2 teaspoons minced garlic** **Cracked black pepper**

Sprinkle meat with garlic and pepper and place in a shallow roasting pan. If you have a meat thermometer, insert it in the center of the roast. Cook roast 1 hour per pound in a slow — 200° F. — oven. The meat thermometer will register 120° F. for very rare, and 130° F. for medium rare. A 6-pound roast will serve 12 (or 8 with loads of leftovers). To reheat, heat meat in 200° F. oven.

Foolproof Rib Roast*

Foolproof Rib Roast is just what the name implies — a guaranteed way to turn out a gorgeous roast every time. Just be sure to follow the directions to the letter, and plan your day so you won't need the oven for anything else.

The trick is to precook the beef early in the day for one hour (no more, no less), and then leave it unattended in the closed oven until one hour before serving time. In between, **don't peek!** *Keep the oven door shut and your mitts off.* **No cheating.**

1 standing rib roast, *any* **size**	**2 cloves garlic, minced**
Pepper	

Early in the day bring the roast to room temperature. Rub the surface of the meat with garlic and pepper, and place on a rack in a shallow pan, rib side down. Preheat oven to 375° F. Place roast in the oven, close the door and roast for 1 hour. When hour is up, turn the oven off — **do not open the door** — and let the roast stay in the oven the remainder of the day. **At no time open the door!** The larger the roast, the longer it will continue to cook after the oven is turned off.

About 45 minutes before serving time, turn the oven back on, without opening the door, and again set the temperature for 375° F. After that temperature has been reached, start timing.

The meat will be rare and ready to serve after 20 minutes. Add another 15 minutes for medium rare (20 minutes for well done). Remove roast from oven and let stand 10 minutes before carving.

Chicken Fried Steak**

Face it: there is something hopelessly declasse about Chicken Fried Steak. But the truth is, it's **good.** *And if anyone gives you a hard time about this steak you serve swagged in milk-and-flour gravy, just say it's a nice bit of Early Americana and let it go at that. And watch them come back for seconds!*

2 pounds round steak, thinly sliced	**1/4 cup shortening**
1/2 cup flour	**1/4 cup water**
Dash garlic powder	**2 cups whole milk**
1-1/2 teaspoons salt	**2 teaspoons instant minced onion**

Trim fat from meat and pound with the edge of a saucer until tenderized. Combine 1/4 cup flour, salt and garlic powder and pound into steak. Cut meat into serving-size pieces and brown on both sides in hot shortening. When browned, add water and simmer slowly for 30 minutes in covered pan. When meat is fork-tender, remove to a warm platter.

Pour off all but 4 tablespoons of the pan drippings. Scrape up brown bits from the bottom of the pan with a spatula, then blend in remaining 1/4 cup flour. Cook until bubbly, then slowly add the milk, stirring vigorously. Add minced onion. When gravy is thickened and smooth, season with salt and pepper. Serve gravy with steak and mashed potatoes. Serves 4.

Beautiful Bifteck**

Here is a gorgeous way to cook steaks indoors when you — or your outdoor barbecue — are out of commission. Pan-searing steaks produces beautifully juicy steaks although the process is apt to smoke up the kitchen a mite. (Open the windows.) Serve the steaks with fat slices of tomatoes and mushrooms.

2 New York steaks, cut 1-1/2- inches thick	1 teaspoon Worcestershire sauce
1 teaspoon coarse black pepper	1 pinch MSG
2/3 cup dry red wine	2 teaspoons green peppercorns (sold
1 teaspoon Dijon mustard	in gourmet groceries)
	Salt

Heat oven to 400° F. Trim fat from steaks and rub fat over a hot black iron skillet until it sizzles. With the palm of your hand, press ground pepper into both sides of the steaks. Then, when the pan is smoking, quickly sear steaks on both sides. As soon as they are brown, slip them onto an ovenproof pan and pop into the preheated oven. Cook 7 to 9 minutes.

While steaks are in the oven, pour wine into the iron frying pan and scrape up brown bits from the bottom of the skillet. Set over heat, adding the mustard and Worcestershire. Toss in the peppercorns. When steaks are done, pour the wine sauce with peppercorns over them, whisk to the table on a heated platter and serve immediately. Serves 2.

Short-Cut Steak Diane***

Steak Diane is one of those razzle-dazzle things waiters prepare table-side in swank restaurants. You can enjoy the same results, minus the hassle, by putting the sauce together ahead of time and performing the pyrotechnics in the kitchen. (When you get surer of your footing, you can move the whole show into the dining room.)

1/2 stick butter	1/2 teaspoon Dijon mustard
1/2 cup finely minced green onions	2 pounds thinly sliced top sirloin
1/2 cup finely snipped parsley	1-1/2 ounces brandy
Salt and pepper	1 jigger white wine
2 tablespoons Worcestershire	

In a small saucepan, melt half the butter, then add the onion, parsley, Worcestershire, mustard, salt and pepper. Keep warm over a very low fire.

Melt remaining butter in a skillet. Cook the steaks over high heat, 1 or 2 minutes per side. Place on a warm platter and slip into 250° F. oven while the sauce is readied.

Heat brandy in small saucepan. When heated, pour into the same skillet used to cook the steaks. Swish around and light with a kitchen match. (Stand back!) As flames subside, add the wine and warm butter sauce. Pour hot sauce over the steaks, and serve immediately. Serves 4.

Broiled Filet Mignon*

Filet mignon, cut from the tenderloin, is considered one of the finest cuts of beef available. (You will see why when you price it.) Ideally, a filet should be no less than 3/4-inch thick.

After the broiler has been preheated to 500° F., broil each steak 1 inch from the flame (or element). Broil 5 minutes on the first side, then turn and broil no more than 2 to 3 minutes on the other side. This gives you a deliciously rare steak, which as any beef lover knows, is the only way to have it. Serve immediately — with or without a pat of butter melting scandalously over its surface.

NOTE: In the minds of many, you can't beat topping off a filet with a dollop of Bearnaise Sauce, but this, I think, merits second thoughts. Lots of people feel putting anything but a knife and fork to a fine filet is sacrilege.

Swimmin' Swiss Steak**

Swiss Steak is another item that will never make the Cordon Bleu hall of fame, but it always gets high marks with the men in the family (the kind with appetites out to **here***). Another plus: this recipe makes lots of good gravy.*

With the edge of a saucer, gently but firmly pound as much flour into a 2- or 3-pound top-quality piece of round steak as the meat will hold. Sprinkle with pepper and then brown quickly on both sides in hot fat in a heavy skillet. Once the steak is turned, sprinkle with salt.

When both sides are nicely browned, cover the steak with thinly sliced onion (don't skimp). Mix equal parts canned onion soup and sour cream — 1 cup each, or more — and spread over the steak. Cover pan and bake in a 350° F. oven for 2 hours. This makes its own gravy in the process — a great cover up for mashed potatoes. Serves 4 to 6.

Quick Pepper Steak**

Pepper Steak, not to be confused with **Peppered** *Steak, smacks slightly of Chinese fare, and very good it is, too. Being a real quickie, it is a good thing to keep in mind for those days when there isn't time for much of anything, much less dinner.*

1 round steak, about 1-1/2 pounds	1/2 cup sliced (not too thin) celery
2 tablespoons oil	3 tablespoons cornstarch
2 tablespoons minced onion	2 tablespoons white wine
2 cloves garlic, minced	1 cup consomme (or bouillon made from granules)
2 large green peppers, sliced	1 teaspoon soy sauce

Put the steak in the freezer until firm, then cut in thin diagonal slices. Sear quickly in hot oil over a hot fire. Add onion, garlic, seeded and sliced peppers and celery along with 1/2 cup of the consomme or bouillon.

Cover the pan, lower the heat and simmer for 5 minutes.

Blend cornstarch into the wine, making a smooth paste. Add this to the pan, stirring vigorously. Add the remaining consomme and soy sauce. Simmer for 5 minutes, and serve over white rice. Serves 4 to 5.

Stuffed Flank Steak Florentine***

Stuffed flank steak is not something to launch when time's running out and your apron is caught in the oven door. However, if you have 3 hours to spend and a good tail wind, this may be just what's needed to put an outstanding dish on the table tonight.

2 pieces (1 pound each) flank
  steaks
1 slightly beaten egg
1 10-ounce package frozen
  chopped spinach, cooked
  and drained
1/2 cup Cheddar cheese, grated
1/2 teaspoon sage
1/4 teaspoon salt
Pepper

1 slice white bread, torn into
  crumbs
2 tablespoons oil
1 8-ounce can tomato sauce
1/2 cup dry red wine
1/2 cup chopped onion
1 clove garlic, minced
2 tablespoons flour
1/4 cup cold water

Pound each steak with a mallet until meat is 1/4-inch thick. Set aside. Combine egg, spinach, cheese, salt, pepper and sage. Stir in bread crumbs. Spread dressing over steaks. Starting from narrow side, roll up and tie with string.

Brown steak rolls in hot fat in heavy skillet, turning to sear evenly. Remove to a baking dish. Combine tomato sauce, wine, onion and garlic and pour over the meat. Cover with foil and baked 1-1/2 hours at 350° F. Remove to hot platter.

Measure pan juices, adding enough water to make 1-1/4 cups. Turn into saucepan. Add flour that has been blended with cold water. Cook sauce till thick and bubbling. Pour over steak rolls. Slice. Serves 6.

Steak au Poivre**

Some people want their peppered steak (called Steak au Poivre on French menus) so heavily peppered it looks like it fell into a gravel pit. If you are tender-hearted, scrape off some of the pepper before the steaks or cooked, or don't put so much on in the first place.

2 pounds sirloin or tenderloin
  steak
2 tablespoons coarsely cracked
  pepper
4 tablespoons butter

2 tablespoons olive oil
3/4 teaspoon cornstarch
1-1/2 tablespoons white wine
2 tablespoons brandy
1/4 cup bouillon

Place steak on waxed paper. With the heel of your hand, firmly press the pepper into the meat.

Heat butter and olive oil until sizzling in a heavy skillet. Sear steak on both sides for 3 to 5 minutes per side (depending on how rare you want it). Salt lightly as you turn the meat. Remove to a heated platter.

Mix cornstarch with wine, then add to meat juices in the pan. Stir in the brandy, loosening any particles on the bottom of the pan. Add the bouillon and simmer 5 minutes. Pour sauce over the steak. Serves 4.

NOTE: If your pepper mill grinds too fine, put some whole peppercorns in a plastic bag and bash them with a rolling pin.

Hero's Pot Roast**

A Sunday down-home dinner of pot roast and potatoes might not send Escoffier into a fit of ecstasy, but it's always a first-place winner with the men in the family.

4 pounds chuck, rump or round of beef	6 stalks celery, cut in chunks
3 tablespoons bacon fat	4 small onions, cut in half
2 tablespoons flour (seasoned with salt and pepper)	6 carrots, scraped and cut in chunks
2 cups boiling water	6 small potatoes, halved
	Worcestershire sauce
	1/2 cup red table wine

Rub meat with flour, salt and pepper. In a heavy Dutch oven, brown meat on both sides in hot bacon fat. Add boiling water, cover, and lower fire. Cook very slowly for 2 to 3 hours. When meat is nearing tenderness, add the celery, potatoes, carrots and onions. Cook until vegetables are tender-done. At the last 15 minutes, stir in the red wine and a dash of Worcestershire sauce. Taste for seasonings. Serves 4 to 6.

The meat and juices are ready to serve as-is, or the gravy may be thickened slightly be adding flour and water. (Stir 3 tablespoons flour into 1/2 cup cold water, then add, a little at a time, to the boiling liquid. Keep stirring and boiling until gravy is smooth and satiny.)

NOTE: A dash of soy sauce or a rounded teaspoon of dried onion soup mix adds wonderful zest to meat gravies like this.

Stove-Top Stroganoff**

What comes next are four distinctly different approaches to that old classic, Beef Stroganoff. The first one is cooked on top of the stove. The second bubbles merrily away in the oven. And the last two are penny-pinching alternatives — one uses hamburger while the other cuts corners with quick-cooking minute steaks.

2-1/2 pounds round steak	1/2 envelope onion soup mix
Flour	1 small can button mushrooms, undrained
Salt and pepper	
Garlic powder	3/4 cup water
1 onion, chopped	1/2 cup sherry wine
1/4 cup oil	1 large carton sour cream

Pound flour (seasoned with salt and pepper) into steak. Tenderize with the rim of a saucer, pressing as much flour into the meat as it will take. Cut meat into 1-inch strips.

Saute chopped onion in a little hot oil until onion is tender-crisp. Remove with a slotted spoon and set aside.

Add a bit more oil to the pan, heat to sizzling, then add meat strips and brown well. Return onions to the pan along with the mushrooms and their juice. Add the onion soup mix, a sprinkle of garlic powder and blend. Stir in water, cover pan and simmer for 5 minutes. Add sherry. Quickly stir in sour cream, taking care that the sauce does not boil. Remove from heat and serve Stroganoff over hot rice, noodles or mashed potatoes. Serves 6.

Skid Row Stroganoff**

A poor student or a bride on a budget would do well to consider this one before throwing in the towel (or cranking open another can of beans).

1 pound ground beef	MSG
1/2 cup chopped onion	1/2 teaspoon paprika
1 clove garlic, minced	1 6-ounce can mushrooms, drained
1 teaspoon salt	1 can cream of chicken soup
1/2 teaspoon pepper	1 cup sour cream

Brown meat with onions. Pour off excess fat. Add next six ingredients and saute for five minutes. Add the undiluted soup and simmer an additional 10 minutes. Fold in sour cream and heat — don't allow to boil. Serve over rice. Serves 4 starving students.

Flash-In-The-Pan Stroganoff**

The trick with this next one is to avail yourself of those skinny fast-cooking minute steaks and then proceed with stopwatch timing. (As long as you stay ahead of the noodles, you're okay. But keep moving.)

1 package (5 to 6 ounces) noodles	3 minute steaks, cut in strips
1 tablespoon margarine or butter	1 can cream of mushroom soup
1 tablespoon poppy seeds	1 cup sour cream
(optional)	1 3-ounce can mushrooms, drained
1 large onion, sliced	2 tablespoons catsup
2 cloves garlic, minced	2 tablespoons Worcestershire sauce

Put noodles on to cook in boiling salted water, and as the noodles cook, cut the steaks in strips and lightly dust with flour. Brown in 2 tablespoons of hot fat. Add the onion and garlic and cook 5 minutes. As this cooks, combine the soup, sour cream and mushrooms. Stir in catsup and Worcestershire. Add to the meat and heat gently over lowered heat. Drain noodles and toss with butter and poppy seeds. Serve the Stroganoff over the hot noodles. Serves 4.

Oven Stroganoff*

1-1/2 pounds round steak	1/2 package dehydrated onion soup
Flour	1/2 cup Sherry
1 can cream of mushroom soup	1 cup sour cream

Cut off visible fat and cut meat into strips — about 1/2 by 2 inches. Dust meat lightly in flour and brown quickly in small amount of fat or cooking oil. As meat strips brown, remove them to an ovenproof casserole.

Combine soups and wine and pour over the meat. Cover and bake at 325° F. until mixture begins to bubble. Turn heat down to 300° F. and continue cooking for 2-1/2 to 3 hours. Just before serving, stir in the sour cream, taking care that the sauce does not boil. Check for seasoning, then serve over fluffy white rice or buttered noodles. Serves 4.

Sticky Bones**

*Sticky Bones are a snap to prepare but are a mess to eat. You **have** to pick them up, but gooey fingers are a small enough price to pay for the flavor which is heavenly. (One way to minimize the trauma is to serve the bones with dampened face cloths or finger towels to mop with as you go.)*

1 cup vinegar	1 teaspoon dry mustard
1/2 cup honey	1 teaspoon paprika
2 tablespoons Worcestershire sauce	Dash pepper
	2 cloves garlic, minced
1/2 cup catsup	Dash hot pepper sauce
1 teaspoon salt	4 pounds meaty beef ribs

Combine all ingredients but ribs and bring to a boil. Cover and simmer for 15 minutes. Place ribs in a single layer in a large baking pan and cover with hot marinade. Let stand 3 hours. Drain off but save marinade. Bake the ribs at 325° F. for 1 hour, or until done, turning and basting with the marinade. Serves 6.

Bul Kogi*

I always thought short ribs were pretty dull until I tried barbecuing them Korean style. Try them this way and see if you don't think it's a big improvement, too.

3 cloves garlic, crushed	2 cups soy sauce
1/4 cup sesame seeds, toasted and crushed	1 teaspoon liquid smoke
	1 teaspoon dried red pepper flakes
1 cup finely chopped green onions	1 cup sugar
	1/4 cup oil
1 teaspoon black pepper	4 pounds beef short ribs
2 teaspoons sesame oil	

Make a marinade of the first 10 ingredients. Pour over ribs in a large bowl. Turn to coat well, cover, and let stand at room temperature for 2 to 4 hours. Barbecue over coals or under a broiler, basting with the marinade. Serves 5 to 6.

Teriyaki Finger Steaks*

Here's a steak you can eat with your fingers. Serve it with corn on the cob and forget the forks.

1 pound top round steak, cut 3/4 inch thick	1 tablespoon sugar
	2 tablespoons sake (or sherry)
1/2 cup soy sauce	1 teaspoon fresh ginger, grated
2 cloves garlic, minced	

Cut steak into strips 3/4-inch wide. Marinade in sauce made of the remaining ingredients and let stand 1 to 3 hours.

Drain meat and barbecue over glowing coals, turning meat as soon as it sears. The idea is to have the steak fingers crunchy outside, pink on the inside, so work fast. Serves 4.

Pot Roast in Beer**

This make-ahead pot roast simmered in beer makes divine next-day sandwiches.

3 large onions, sliced
1 3-pound pot roast
1 package onion soup mix
1 teaspoon thyme
2 bay leaves

4 carrots, sliced
4 stalks celery, sliced
2 12-ounce cans beer
Salt and pepper to taste

Cover bottom of a Dutch oven with slices of onion. Place pot roast on top of the onions and pour over remaining ingredients. Cover and cook in the oven at 350° F. for 2-1/2 to 3 hours.

Make this the day ahead. Next day, slice meat and reheat in marinade until hot through. Serves 6 to 8.

Beef Bourguignon**

No matter how you cut it, a stew is a stew is a stew. But if you give it a fancy French name and a nice slosh of red wine, what you get is Beef Bourguignon.

2-1/2 pounds lean stewing beef
2 tablespoons butter
3 tablespoons flour seasoned
   with salt and pepper
1-1/2 cups red wine
2 onions, chopped
2 tablespoons butter

2 carrots, coarsely chopped
2 cloves garlic, minced
Pinch marjoram
Pinch fresh or dried parsley
2 tablespoons brandy
1/2 pound raw mushrooms, sliced

Brown beef cubes in butter, then sprinkle with the seasoned flour. Stir until the flour is absorbed. Add wine and bring to a simmer.

In a small skillet, cook onions in butter until limp. Add onions, carrots, garlic, marjoram and parsley to the meat along with just enough water to barely cover. Cover the pot and simmer slowly for 3 hours. At that point, the meat should be fork-tender and the gravy a rich, dark brown.

One-half hour before taking the stew off the stove, stir in the brandy and mushrooms. Serves 6.

Teriyaki Marinade*

Teriyaki Marinade is one of the biggest blessings that ever befell a tired cook or a tough cut of beef. The trick is to give the chuck steak or round bone roast enough time to arrive at tender surrender. Cover the meat and marinate it in the refrigerator for 8 hours or so, piercing it several times with a fork during the soak.

1 tablespoon crushed fresh
   ginger
1/4 cup sake or dry sherry
2 tablespoons sugar

3/4 cup soy sauce
1/2 cup salad oil
2 cloves garlic, crushed

Crush fresh ginger in a garlic crusher or pound with a mallet. Combine with other ingredients, and pour over meat. Place in a glass container, cover and refrigerate at least 8 hours.

Charlotte's Carbonnade**

My friend Charlotte says her carbonnade is always a big hit with her party guests. It can be prepared well ahead of the festivities and isn't all that fussy about when it gets served up — two big pluses for the laid-back party thrower.

4-pound rump roast	3 tablespoons dark brown sugar
1 tablespoon oil	1/4 cup water
1 onion, sliced	3/4 cup dried apricots
1 teaspoon cinnamon	3/4 cup dried prunes
1 teaspoon pepper	1 can beer
2 teaspoons salt	1/2 teaspoon fresh grated ginger
4 tablespoons honey	

Brown meat in hot oil. Add onion, salt, cinnamon, pepper, honey, sugar and water. Cover tightly and cook slowly on top of the stove. Meantime, combine prunes and apricots, adding beer and ginger. Let fruit soak for 2 hours.

When meat has cooked 1-1/2 hours, drain the beer from the fruit and add it to the meat. Cover and cook for 1/2 hour. Then add the fruit and cook an additional 1/2 hour. If desired, gravy may be thickened with flour before serving. Serves 8.

Roulatin**
(Danish Round Steak)

When round steak goes on sale it can be the best meat buy in town. Having located the bargain, the next thing is to decide how to serve it. Here is a slow-cook method with a rich sour cream sauce that teams deliciously with mashed potatoes.

2 pounds round steak	Salt and pepper
Flour	2 tablespoons bacon fat
4 slices bacon, cut in half	1 cup sour cream
2 small onions, thinly sliced	

Pound steak with flour until thin (use a meat mallet or the edge of a saucer). Cut meat into 8 pieces. Place one piece of bacon and one slice of onion on each portion of steak. Sprinkle with salt and pepper and roll up. Tie each bundle with string and cook in hot bacon fat, turning as the rolls brown. Add 1/2 cup water to the pan, cover and simmer slowly for 1-1/2 hours, or until meat is tender. Place rolls on a heated platter and remove the strings. Add sour cream to the reduced liquid in the pan. Don't let it boil! Adjust seasonings, and pour sauce over the meat. Garnish with chopped parsley. Serves 6.

Bourbon Soak*

Another good tough-meat marinade uses bourbon to help boost the tenderizing process. This one omits ginger, which takes it out of the teriyaki class, but use it the same way.

1/2 cup soy sauce	Dash hot pepper sauce
1-1/2 cups water	1 tablespoon lemon juice
1/2 cup bourbon	1 clove garlic, minced
1/2 cup brown sugar	1 chopped onion
1 teaspoon Worcestershire sauce	

Mix everything together and let flavors steep 1 hour. Pour marinade over meat in a bowl and let meat soak in the marinade for 8 to 12 hours.

Roast Pork Loin*

One of the best of all oven roasts is the loin of pork that looks like a bunch of pork chops, still attached. Easy, too.

For an oven roast, select a small loin — one having 5 to 6 "chops". Ask the butcher to saw through the bone so that you can neatly cut through the whole thing when you serve it.

Sprinkle roast lightly with salt and pepper. A fine drift of thyme or marjoram is nice but optional. Bake in an uncovered pan at 325° F. for 40 minutes per pound. Better yet, use a meat thermometer and remember: pork is the one meat you really want well done.

Pork Roast Gravy*

Drain excess fat from the baking pan, retaining about 3 tablespoons for the gravy. Place the pan on top of the stove over moderate heat and quickly stir in 2 tablespoons flour. Cook and stir to a smooth paste. Gradually add 1 cup hot water, continuing to stir. When gravy is thickened, season to taste with salt and pepper.

NOTE: A tablespoon of soy sauce gives a deeper color and a wonderful flavor. If you use soy, go easy on the salt.

Pork Chops and Sour Cream*

Sour cream with a drift of rosemary makes a delicious gravy to go along with pork chops.

6 medium-thick pork chops	1/2 teaspoon rosemary
Oil	1 cup sour cream
Salt and pepper	Chopped parsley

Lightly grease a heavy skillet and brown chops on both sides. Pour off any excess fat and season meat with salt and pepper. Sprinkle with rosemary. Add a tablespoon or two of water, cover tightly and simmer over low heat until chops are tender. This should take from 20 to 30 minutes. Just before serving, spoon sour cream over the chops, turning and stirring the sour cream into the pan juices. Serve with noodles or mashed potatoes. Serves 6.

Gourmet Orange Pork Chops**

*If you have ever had **Duck a l'Orange** you already know what a succulent delicacy that is. Well, what's good for the duck is good for pork chops, too, as the following recipe deliciously proves. Here the chops get nicely browned on top of the stove, then go into the oven where they develop a rich glaze. For a festive (and easy) touch, top the chops with a few thin slices of orange about 20 minutes before taking from the oven.*

6 pork loin chops, 1 inch thick	3 tablespoons Curacao (orange
Fat cut from chops	flavored liqueur), optional
2 onions, sliced	2 tablespoons brown sugar
1 6-ounce can frozen orange	1-1/2 teaspoons ground ginger
juice, thawed	1 teaspoon poultry seasoning
2/3 cup water	1 teaspoon marjoram
1 tablespoon lemon juice	Salt and pepper
Grated rind of 1 orange	

Cut fat from pork chops and render in a hot skillet until there is sufficient grease to saute chops. Brown meat on both sides. Add the sliced onion, cover skillet and cook until meat is tender, about 35 minutes.

When chops are cooked, add the undiluted orange juice, water, lemon juice, grated peel and Curacao. Transfer meat to a shallow baking dish. Add dry ingredients to skillet, stirring to loosen brown particles at bottom of pan. Pour over the chops, cover with foil and bake at 350° F. for 1 hour. Serves 6.

Ribs, Kraut and Stuffing Balls***

Here is another winner for hearty souls who love pork and sauerkraut combinations. Nestled into the mix are rib-sticking stuffing balls — plumped up with steam and light as clouds. Some winter afternoon, when the rain is beating on the windowpanes, try this one.

3 pounds lean pork spareribs	2 tablespoons brown sugar
2 teaspoons salt	2 teaspoons caraway seeds
1/4 teaspoon pepper	2/3 cup water
1 can (1 pound, 11 ounces)	1/4 cup butter
sauerkraut, undrained	1-1/2 cups packaged bread stuffing
1 tart apple, chopped	mix
1-1/2 cups tomato juice	1 egg, beaten slightly

Season ribs with salt and pepper. Add sauerkraut, apple, tomato juice, sugar and caraway seeds. Cover and simmer over low heat for 2 hours.

Heat water and stir in butter. Lightly fork stuffing mix into liquid and add the egg. With a light touch, gently shape the stuffing mixture into 6 balls. Pull ribs to top of kraut and place stuffing balls on top. Turn up the heat a bit and closely cover the kettle, taking care not to peek for 15 minutes. Let contents steam, undisturbed, for 15 minutes. Stuffing balls will be light and puffy, like dumplings. Serves 6.

Mainland Laulaus

Anyone who has ever been to a Hawaiian luau knows that, to make laulaus, one needs ti leaves. That being the case, it is easy to see that this next recipe really doesn't make laulaus at all.

What we have here is a reasonable substitute using leaves of romaine. If you live outside of Hawaii, that may be the closest you are going to get to the real thing.

2 pounds boneless pork shoulder,
   cut in 1/2-inch cubes
2 teaspoons salt
2 teaspoons grated fresh ginger
   (or 1 teaspoon powdered)
1 teaspoon paprika
2 tablespoons flour

1 cup water
1 1-pound, 4-ounce can pineapple
   tidbits, drained
1/2 cup flaked coconut
16 large leaves romaine (outside
   leaves from 2 heads)
Ginger Sauce

Brown pork cubes in their own fat in a heavy skillet. As meat browns, sprinkle with salt, ginger and paprika. Cover, lower heat, and cook for 40 minutes. Remove cooked pork with a slotted spoon and set aside.

Blend flour into pan drippings and stir. Add water, cooking and stirring until smooth and thickened. Pour over pork. Add coconut and pineapple.

Wash romaine and remove 16 large leaves. Trim off coarse bases and pare out heavy ribs of leaves. Blanch, a couple of leaves at a time, in boiling water — just long enough to soften, about 15 seconds. Drain on paper towels.

Spoon 1/3 cup of filling on the base of each leaf. Fold bottom end up and over filling, then fold both sides toward the middle and roll into a compact cylinder. Fasten with toothpicks.

Place rolls in a baking pan. Cover and thoroughly chill. When ready to cook, place rolls on a rack on a large baking pan. Pour in water to a depth just below the rack. Cover the pan and steam for 25 minutes in a 325° F. oven. Serve laulaus with Ginger Sauce.

Ginger Sauce

1 small onion, chopped
1 clove garlic, minced
1 tablespoon curry powder
2 tablespoons butter
2 tablespoons flour

1 teaspoon beef bouillon granules
   (or 1 cube)
1-1/4 cups water
1/4 cup chopped crystallized ginger

Saute onion and garlic in curry powder and butter. Cook until onion is soft. Stir in flour. Mix bouillon with water and add to pan, cooking and stirring until sauce thickens. When clear, take off heat and add ginger. Makes about 1-1/2 cups.

*Cashew Pork Papaya***

Unlike walnuts and almonds, cashews don't take well to long periods of cooking. To keep the curly little devils crisp, be sure they get tossed in at the last minute. That way, the nuts — and you — maintain integrity.

2 beaten eggs	1/2 cup brown sugar
1 cup flour	1/4 cup cornstarch
1 teaspoon salt	1/2 cup pineapple juice
3/4 cup ice water	1 large clove of garlic, minced
1-1/2 pounds pork shoulder, cut	1 large ripe papaya, peeled
in 1-inch cubes	and cubed
Oil	3/4 cup whole cashews
1/2 cup vinegar	Hot cooked white rice

Combine eggs, flour, salt and 1/4-cup water in a large bowl. Blend well. Then toss in the pork cubes, turning to coat well on all sides. Heat 2 inches of oil in heavy skillet. When it starts to smoke, add the pork pieces and cook until lightly browned. Remove meat with a slotted spoon and set aside.

Combine vinegar, sugar, garlic and remaining water. When well mixed, pour into skillet in which pork was cooked, stirring to loosen browned bits. As mixture comes to a boil, stir cornstarch into pineapple juice and add to pan, stirring vigorously. When sauce thickens, add the pork, cashews and papaya. Heat and serve over rice. Serves 4 to 6.

*Smoky Ribs Burgundy***

Smoky spareribs spiked with Burgundy make a tasty treat to pick up and munch out-of-hand.

3 pounds lean pork spareribs,	Pepper
cut in 3-inch pieces	2 to 3 cloves of garlic
Liquid smoke or smoke-flavored	
salt	

Rub ribs with cut cloves of garlic. Then sprinkle with liquid smoke or smoke-flavored salt. Pepper liberally and spread ribs on a rack in a shallow roasting pan. Cook at 450° F. for 20 to 30 minutes. Meantime prepare Burgundy Sauce.

Burgundy Sauce

1/2 cup catsup	1/2 teaspoon each salt and dry
3/4 cup Burgundy wine	mustard
3 tablespoons cider vinegar	1/2 teaspoon chili powder
1/4 cup water	1 clove garlic, minced
1 tablespoon brown sugar	1/2 onion, finely chopped
1 tablespoon Worcestershire	
sauce	

Combine ingredients and pour over ribs after all surplus fat has been drained off. Bake at 350° F. for 45 minutes. Serves 4.

German Pork Chops*

Pork chops, like spareribs, are a natural go-along for sauerkraut. In this case, the kraut takes on a rosy glow from tomato sauce.

4 pork chops, 1/2-inch thick	1 8-ounce can tomato sauce
1/2 cup chopped onion	3 tablespoons brown sugar
1 1-pound can sauerkraut	2 teaspoons caraway seeds (optional)

Brown chops on both sides in a hot skillet. Add the onion and cook until tender, about 8 to 10 minutes. Pour off excess fat.

Drain and rinse sauerkraut in cold water. Add to the pan along with the tomato sauce, brown sugar and caraway seeds. Turn over with a fork so the chops are covered with kraut. Cover and turn the heat low. Simmer 45 minutes. Serves 4.

Veal Piccate**

In this next one, lemon juice gives the veal a pleasant zap. Artichoke hearts and mushrooms make it fancy. Save this one for company — company you want to **impress.**

2 pounds veal scallops	Juice of 2 lemons
Flour seasoned with salt and	1 cup artichoke hearts (not
pepper	marinated), sliced
1/4 cup oil	1 cup sliced mushrooms
1/2 cup white wine	2 tablespoons butter

Pound scallops between sheets of waxed paper or plastic until very thin. Dredge in seasoned flour and then saute in hot oil about 2 minutes on each side, or until lightly browned and tender. Place meat on a heated platter.

Pour excess oil from pan, then add the wine and lemon juice. Bring to a boil, scraping the pan of any browned bits on the bottom. Cook, gently, until the sauce is slightly reduced. Return veal to the pan along with the sliced artichoke hearts and mushrooms. Saute for 3 minutes in 3 tablespoons butter and serve. Serves 6.

Humble Ham Loaf*

Meat loaves, poor things, are widely maligned — mostly because they can be dry as sawdust or so greasy they come out of the oven floating. And that is too bad, for a good meat loaf makes a very respectable family dinner, to say nothing of superb leftovers.

The following meat loaf made with ham is really quite superior the first time around, and for sandwiches later it is unexcelled.

1 pound smoked ham, ground	1 cup cracker crumbs
2 pounds fresh ham, ground	1/2 green pepper, chopped
2 eggs, beaten	2 tablespoons chopped green onion
1/2 teaspoon salt	

Lightly mix meats and combine with remaining ingredients. Form a loaf and place in a greased loaf pan and bake at 325° F. for 2 hours. If meat gets too brown during the last half hour or so, cover with aluminum foil. Serves 8.

Hawaiian Ham Steak*

Ham, bless it, is something the greenest of cooks can't really hurt. A thick ham steak is an excellent choice for a one-star (*) cook's first company dinner. Just one word of caution: sweet glazes tend to burn easily, so keep an eye on the works.

1/4 to 1/2 teaspoon ginger	1 center-cut ham steak, 2 inches
2 tablespoons cornstarch	thick
2 cups pineapple juice	1 small can pineapple chunks
1/2 cup honey	3 tablespoons margarine

Mix ginger with cornstarch. Blend in a little pineapple juice, stirring until smooth. Add the honey and the remaining pineapple juice and cook over a low heat, stirring constantly until the mixture is thickened and clear.

Slash edges of ham to prevent curling. Place over hot coals or 6 inches under the broiler. As it cooks, brush with pineapple glaze. Grill or broil slowly, taking care that the ham doesn't burn. Brush now and then with more of the glaze, and keep turning the ham until thoroughly cooked through, about 30 minutes.

Just before serving, melt butter in a small skillet and add the drained pineapple chunks. Cook, turning until the chunks are lightly browned. Serve the ham topped with pineapple. Serves 6.

Monday Ham Balls**

Have a big baked ham for dinner Sunday and you are apt to end up, on Monday, staring balefully at a large bone with more leftover ham attached than you planned. Do not despair. There are a lot worse things to be saddled with than ham that can be neatly shaped into Monday Ham Balls.

3 cups ground cooked ham	1 tablespoon brown sugar
1/2 cup dry bread crumbs,	2 tablespoons cornstarch
finely crumbled	1/4 cup vinegar
1 egg	2 large green peppers cut in 1/2-
1/4 cup oil	inch wedges
Pinch ginger	1 large onion, cut in 1/2-inch
1 14-ounce can pineapple chunks	squares or wedges
3 tablespoons soy sauce	

Mix ground ham with crumbs and egg. Shape gently into 12 large balls. Heat oil in a heavy skillet. When hot, brown balls, turning to cook evenly. When nicely browned, remove with a slotted spoon and set aside.

Drain syrup from pineapple, reserving juice. To the juice add the soy, ginger, sugar and enough water to make 4 cups of liquid. Stir this into the drippings left from the ham balls. Cook and stir, briefly, then cover skillet and allow to simmer 15 minutes. Mix cornstarch with vinegar. Stir into the simmering liquid and cook, stirring constantly, until clear and thickened. Add ham balls, drained pineapple chunks, peppers and onions. Cook 5 minutes. Serve over rice. Serves 6.

Roast Leg of Lamb*

Roast leg of lamb is one of the best — and easiest to prepare — cuts of meat you can buy. Stud it with garlic and, please, don't overcook it!

3 to 4 pounds of young lamb	**Flour**
3 cloves of garlic	**Salt and pepper**

Heat oven to 325° F. Rinse lamb under cold water and pat dry. Holding the lamb over the sink, dredge with flour, patting it all over. Sprinkle liberally with salt and pepper. Then, with a sharp, pointed knife, make small slits in the meat and insert slivers of fresh garlic. Place lamb in a baking pan and bake it 30 minutes per pound.

Lamb Gravy**

When the lamb is almost done, move it into another baking pan. To the pan with drippings, add 1 tablespoon shortening if the fat from the lamb measures less than 3 tablespoons. Place the baking pan over medium heat and add 2 tablespoons of flour to the hot drippings. Stir well, then gradually add 1 cup water to the pan. Allow gravy to boil and thicken. Add more water, if necessary.

If the gravy is a bit pale (and isn't too salty), add a tablespoon of soy sauce. This will give the gravy a lovely caramel color.

Escalope de Veau Chasseur***

"Veau" means veal in French cookbooks and on fancy French menus. Purchased by the pound, the price would seem prohibitive, but remember: it doesn't take much to fill the bill. Veal is like liver — a little goes a long way.

One of the best sources for prime veal is Kosher meat markets. So take yourself forth (and take money).

12 thin slices of veal scallopine	**1/4 pound mushrooms, sliced**
1-1/4 teaspoons salt	**1/2 cup dry white wine**
1/4 teaspoons ground pepper	**1-1/2 cups canned tomatoes, drained**
1/4 cup flour	**1/2 teaspoon basil**
3 tablespoons olive oil	**3 tablespoons butter**
1 onion, finely chopped	**1 tablespoon minced parsley**

Dip veal slices in flour seasoned with salt and pepper. Refrigerate until ready to cook. Meantime, in a saucepan saute mushrooms and onion in olive oil until limp. Add wine and cook over high heat until liquid is reduced to half. Add the tomatoes and basil. Season to taste with additional salt and pepper. Cover and simmer 30 minutes.

Melt butter in skillet. Saute veal slices 5 minutes on each side, being careful to not overbrown the meat. Arrange on a heated platter and keep warm. Pour mushroom-tomato sauce into the skillet and cook over high heat 1 minute, scraping browned particles from bottom of pan. Add parsley. Serves 6.

What's Ahead in Fish

Fish

. . . Looking the Flounder in the Eye

Cooking fish is easy. A quick dip in and out of the pan and a squeeze of lemon are often all it takes to bring out the best in a fresh fillet.

The same goes for shellfish. They may cost a bundle, but nothing is easier for the novice to tackle. King crab legs, for example, need only a quick run under the broiler and a pot of melted butter to rate raves. And California's Dungeness crab served on cracked ice with fresh mayonnaise is another superb treat.

California cooks are apt to be more familiar with shellfish than fresh water or ocean fish varieties. Supermarkets in these parts tend to carry only a limited variety of fresh fish, and then only when they are in season.

One winter I lived in Maine and experienced what New England housewives take for granted: fish markets everywhere, all of them abundantly supplied with fresh seafood. I still remember lugging home a whole six-pound cod wrapped in newspapers and wondering what to do next.

Those fish were fresh. No doubt about it. **But anytime you aren't sure, you should look the critter straight in the eye, and if the eye that stares back is nice and clear, the fish is nice and fresh.** See?

Of course that isn't much help in supermarkets where fish comes cut up and neatly snugged in plastic wrap. The only thing you can do is sniff. Fresh fish never smells fishy. It should also be firm to the touch and have good color.

If there is a fresh fish market in the area, by all means try it. You may pay a little more, but it can be well worth the extra pennies. Okay, make that a dollar. It's **still** worth it.

Fillets Saute Meuniere*

Pan-fried fish fillets, which comes under this fancy name in French cookbooks, is really nothing more than fish dredged in seasoned flour and pan-sauteed in butter or a combination of butter and oil. (The latter mix doesn't burn as quickly as plain butter and is a better choice if the fish is thick, requiring longer cooking.)

3 pounds fish fillets	Butter, or butter and oil
3/4 cup milk	Lemon juice
Flour, seasoned with	Chopped parsley
salt and pepper	

Dip fish in milk, then dredge in flour seasoned with salt and pepper. Shake off excess flour and lay the fish on waxed paper. Heat 1/2-inch of oil and butter to sizzling in a large skillet. Place fish in the pan, taking care not to crowd the fillets. Cook until brown on the bottom, then turn with a wide spatula and cook on the other side until brown and the fish flakes easily. Remove fillets to a heated serving platter and sprinkle with lemon juice and chopped parsley. Serves 6.

Fillets Saute Veronique*

Slightly fancier, but no more complicated, are Fillets Saute Veronique. Translated that means fried fish with grapes.

Prepare fish as for Fillets Saute Meuniere. After fillets have been sauteed and are resting on their heated platter, quickly saute 1 cup of seedless green grapes in 6 tablespoons melted butter. When the grapes have heated through, arrange around the fillets. A few parsley sprigs are nice, too.

Hurry-Up Fish Fillets**

Here's another way to oven-bake fish fillets and get the whole thing on the table in 20 minutes flat.

1 cup sour cream	1/4 teaspoon dill weed
2 tablespoons packaged dry onion soup mix	1/4 teaspoon each salt and paprika
1 cup fine dry bread crumbs	2 pounds firm white fish fillets (turbot, halibut, etc.)
3 tablespoons Parmesan cheese	1/4 cup oil
2 tablespoons finely minced parsley	

Blend together the sour cream and soup mix. Toss bread crumbs with Parmesan cheese, parsley and paprika. Sprinkle with salt. Place crumb mixture in a container.

Cut fish into 6 pieces and dip each piece into the sour cream mix and then into the bread crumb mix. As fish is coated in cream and crumbs, place in a shallow baking pan that has been well greased. Drizzle with oil. Bake at 475° F. for about 7 minutes, then turn the fish and continue baking for another 5 minutes. Test fish with a fork. When it flakes, it's done. Serves 6.

Lazy Baker Fish*

Baking fish in the oven is the easy way to get out of washing a crusty skillet or a baked-on broiler.

1 pound fish fillets, about 3/4-inch thick	1 cup dry bread crumbs
	1-1/2 tablespoons melted butter
1/2 cup milk	Salt and pepper
2 teaspoons seasoned salt	Dill weed (optional)

Dip fish fillets into milk and salt; drain. Dredge fillets in bread crumbs and place in an oiled baking pan. Sprinkle with melted butter and then with salt, pepper and dill weed. Bake in 500° F. oven for 10 minutes, or until fish flakes when pierced with a fork. Serves 3.

Fillets Amandine*

This version of Fillets Almondine doesn't require any particular kind of fish as long as it's firm (like halibut) and is fresh as a debutant's kiss. Topped with mayonnaise and a sprinkling of almonds, it's ready for a brief bake in the oven and it's ready to go.

1 pound firm white fish fillets	Salt and pepper
2 tablespoons butter	1/2 cup toasted slivered almonds
1/2 cup mayonnaise	Parsley (or minced chives)
Juice of 1/2 lemon	

Butter an ovenproof baking dish. Place fillets in the dish and slather with mayonnaise. Sprinkle with toasted almonds and sprinkle with lemon juice. Bake at 350° F. for 30 minutes, or until fish flakes with a fork. Serve topped with a drift of parsley and/or chives. Serves 2.

NOTE: Almonds may be toasted in a small skillet with a dab of butter or in a pie pan under the broiler. Either way, keep an eye on things — nuts burn fast.

Red Snapper**

Red Snapper gets extra snap when it is prepared with a zesty garlic-tomato sauce.

2 pounds red snapper fillets	1/2 cup dry white wine
Salt and pepper	4 tomatoes, peeled and chopped
3 tablespoons butter	1 teaspoon minced parsley
1 medium onion, chopped	Pinch tarragon, thyme and basil
1 clove garlic, minced	1/4 cup dry bread crumbs
1-1/2 tablespoons flour	2 tablespoons Parmesan cheese

Grease a flat baking dish. Season fillets with salt and pepper and place in dish. Melt butter, adding onion and garlic, and saute slowly for 3 minutes. Stir in flour, make a smooth roux, then add the wine, whisking until smooth and bubbling. Add tomatoes and herbs. Pour sauce over fish, then sprinkle with crumbs and Parmesan. Bake at 350° F. for 25 to 30 minutes.

Saratoga Sole**

Sole stuffed with shrimp is a subtle taste sensation. This version is sauced with cream of mushroom soup spiked with sherry, and is very, very easy.

8 fillets of sole	1-1/2 cans cream of mushroom soup,
1/4 cup butter	undiluted
1/4 teaspoon pepper	3/4 cup dry sherry
1 pound small fresh or frozen	Juice of 1 lemon
shrimp, thawed	1/2 cup grated Parmesan cheese
	Paprika

Place 1 teaspoon butter on each fish fillet, then sprinkle with pepper. Top with shrimp. Roll up fillets and place, seam side down, in a greased baking dish. Heat soup with sherry and lemon juice and spoon hot sauce over the fish. Sprinkle with Parmesan cheese and paprika. Bake at 350° F. for 30 minutes. Serves 8.

Sole Rolls**

Tucked inside these sole rolls is, of all things, dill pickle. It adds a nice little pucker.

6 fillets of sole	2 tablespoons flour
Salt and pepper	1 cup milk
1 large dill pickle	1/2 teaspoon thyme
2 tablespoons butter or	1 cup grated Cheddar cheese
margarine	2 tablespoons minced parsley

Sprinkle fish with salt and pepper. Cut pickle into 6 lengthwise slices and place one slice in the center of each filet. Roll up and place, seam side down, in a shallow baking pan.

Melt butter, blend in flour and slowly stir in milk. When smooth and thickened, add thyme and cheese, stirring over a low flame until cheese is melted. Pour over fish rolls. Bake at 350° F. for 30 minutes.

NOTE: 1/4 cup white wine may be used in the sauce, in which case reduce the milk to 3/4 cup. Serves 6.

Crunchy Seafood Casserole*

Apart from the fact this next casserole can be put together from ingredients you probably keep in your kitchen cupboard, it has the virtue of being so simple you could make it in·two minutes flat.

1 cup cream of chicken soup	1/2 cup evaporated milk
1 6-1/2-ounce can water-packed	1 5-ounce can shrimp
tuna, drained	1 cup salted almonds
1 cup chopped celery	1 4-ounce can chow mein noodles
1/4 cup chopped onion	

Combine all ingredients except chow mein noodles in a bowl. Gently fold together. When mixed, add about three-fourths of the noodles, folding lightly into the mixture. Spoon into a greased 2-quart casserole and top with the remaining noodles. Bake at 350° F. for 25 to 30 minutes. Serves 5 to 6.

Poached Fresh Salmon**

*Next time salmon is in season, enjoy that most marvelous of all seafood delicacies —
poached salmon. It's a gourmet delight, hot or cold.*

Salmon steaks, 1 to 1-1/4 inches thick	Lemon slices
Water	2 bay leaves
Sauterne or dry vermouth	Salt and pepper

Place salmon in a single layer in a flat baking pan. Top with thin slices of lemon.
Pour liquid (half water, half wine) level with the top of the steaks. Add bay leaves,
about 1 teaspoon salt and pepper and bring to a quick boil. Reduce heat to a
simmer and check the fish after 3 or 4 minutes. As soon as the fish flakes, take off
the heat.

Steaks can sit in the hot bath until ready to serve, but don't cook beyond the
"just done" stage. Serve with Hollandaise sauce or a mixture of half mayonnaise,
half sour cream and 1 teaspoon prepared mustard. Or serve, chilled, with
Mousseline Sauce (a mixture of Hollandaise and whipped cream). Garnish with
capers.

Sara's Christmas Scallops**

*Every Christmas six friends who went to college together have a reunion lunch. The
menu never varies. I bring the champagne because I work, and Sara brings the
scallops au gratin because she **doesn't** work. Here's how she does it.*

6 buttered scallop shells	4 green onions, minced
2 pounds fresh scallops (cut in half if they are large)	1 tablespoon minced parsley
1 cup white wine	Pinch marjoram
1 cup Sherry	Salt
4 tablespoons butter	Cracked pepper
1 cup sliced mushrooms	4 slices soft white bread, crusts cut off
2 tablespoons flour	3 tablespoons butter, melted
2 tablespoons cream	

Heat wines together, then add the scallops and simmer until tender — about 10
minutes. Drain, saving the wine.

In a small saucepan, melt the 4 tablespoons butter and saute the mushrooms
until limp. Remove with a slotted spoon and set aside. Add 2 tablespoons flour to
the pan, stirring to make a smooth roux. Slowly add the reserved wine, stirring
until smooth and thickened. Add cream, mushrooms, onions and parsley. Season
with marjoram and salt and pepper, if needed. Cook over low heat for 3 to 4
minutes.

Spoon scallops into buttered shells and top with sauce. Tear bread into soft
crumbs and toss with 3 tablespoons melted butter. Divide crumbs among shells
and bake in 400° F. oven, 10 to 12 minutes.

Scallops in Lime*

This sumptuous summer luncheon entree needs no cooking, which is something to consider when the sidewalks are sizzling. Like the classic ceviche, this delicacy "cooks" in lime juice.

2 pounds scallops	1 cup lime juice
1 large red onion, thinly sliced	2 tablespoons lemon juice
1 tablespoon white vinegar	Dash salt
Pinch cayenne	

Place scallops in a glass bowl and cover with the remaining ingredients. Cover and chill 6 to 8 hours. Drain and serve on lettuce leaves. Quartered tomatoes, hard-cooked eggs and chilled asparagus spears are nice accompaniments. Serves 6 to 8.

Scallops Amandine**

This scallop and almond combination has a delicious nutty crunch.

1 pound scallops	3/4 cup slivered almonds
1/3 cup flour	1/2 cup dry white wine
1/3 cup dry bread crumbs	3 tablespoons fresh lemon juice
1 teaspoon salt	2 tablespoons parsley, chopped
2 tablespoons oil	Lemon wedges
6 tablespoons butter	

Rinse scallops and pat dry. If some are measurably larger than the others, cut in half. Combine flour, crumbs and salt and coat scallops with this mixture. Heat oil and half of the butter in a heavy skillet until butter stops foaming. Saute scallops in hot butter until golden brown, 5 to 10 minutes. Remove to a warm platter. In the same skillet, add the remaining 3 tablespoons of butter and the almonds, taking care that the nuts do not get too brown. Sprinkle almonds over the scallops. Add wine and lemon juice to the pan, stirring to loosen browned bits from the bottom of the pan. Pour over scallops and nuts. Sprinkle with parsley and serve with lemon wedges. Serves 6 to 8.

Canny Shrimp and Crab Casserole**

Here is another excellent seafood casserole that can be put together with items you may already have on hand.

1 green pepper, chopped	1 teaspoon Worcestershire sauce
1 onion, chopped	1 cup mayonnaise
1 cup celery, chopped	1 2-ounce can mushrooms, drained
1 6-1/2-ounce can crab meat, flaked	1 2-ounce can or jar pimientos (optional)
1 6-1/2-ounce can shrimp, drained	1 4-ounce can water chestnuts, drained and sliced
1/2 teaspoon salt	1 cup buttered bread crumbs
Dash pepper	

Combine everything except crumbs. Spoon into a greased 2-quart casserole and sprinkle with buttered crumbs. Bake at 350° F. for 30 minutes. Serves 4.

Stuffed Deviled Crab**

This simple scallop stuffer can be put together in a snap. If you don't have scallop shells, don't fret. Use individual baking dishes or ramekins. Either works just as well.

6 buttered scallop shells	2 tablespoons parsley, finely minced
3 tablespoons butter	1/2 teaspoon salt
4 green onions, minced	1 cup mayonnaise
1/2 green pepper, diced	2 packages (6 ounces) frozen crab,
1 cup poultry stuffing mix,	thawed
crushed	Paprika

Melt butter and saute onion and green pepper until just tender. Add stuffing mix and toss. Stir in parsley, salt and mayonnaise. Add crab that has been thawed and flaked.

Spoon into 6 buttered scallop shells and sprinkle with paprika. Bake on a cookie sheet at 400° F. for 15 minutes. Serve with lemon wedges. Serves 6.

Hot Crab Salad Stuffer**

A friend of mine served this hot avocado dish to her bridge club and the ladies raved. That's the trouble with a really good recipe — now everyone in the bunch keeps trotting it out again, and again and again . . .

2 cups rich white sauce	2 large firm, ripe avocados
1/2 pound fresh crabmeat	4 tablespoons grated Cheddar or
2 tablespoons Sherry	Swiss cheese
Salt and pepper, to taste	

Heat white sauce and crab in top of double boiler. When piping hot, stir in sherry. Season to taste. Peel and halve avocados and fill cavities with the creamed crab. Sprinkle with cheese and set in a preheated 375° F. oven. Bake 15 minutes — no longer (longer cooking makes the avocados bitter). Serve hot.

NOTE: A sprinkling of toasted almonds over each serving is a nice touch. Pass lemon wedges. Serves 4.

San Francisco Crab Topper**

This recipe for crab and cheese has been kicking around San Francisco Fishermen's Wharf for years.

2 strips bacon	2 drops tabasco sauce
1 onion	1/2 to 3/4 teaspoon curry powder
2 stalks celery	1 cup Cheddar cheese, shredded
1 small can tomato sauce	2 cups crab meat
Juice of 1 lemon	4 cups cooked white rice

Fry bacon until crisp, then remove and place on a paper towel. Crumble and set aside. In reserved bacon fat, saute onion and celery until tender-crisp. Then add remaining ingredients (except cheese and crab) and simmer for 15 minutes. Add crab meat and heat through. Finally, add the shredded cheese. As soon as the cheese melts, serve over steamed rice. Serves 4 to 6.

*Jambalaya***

If you have some leftover ham sitting around doing nothing, here's something positively gorgeous to do with it. It needs a fourth pound of shrimp to round things out, but that's a small price to pay for the lovely jambalaya you get for the money.

1 tablespoon oil	2 small cloves garlic, minced
1/4 pound ham, cut in small cubes	1/2 cup water
1 green pepper, chopped	1 teaspoon Worcestershire sauce
1/2 onion, chopped	Sprinkle dried red pepper flakes
1/4 pound shrimp, peeled and deveined (leave the tails on)	1/2 cup long-grain white rice
	Dash salt
3/4 cup canned tomatoes, chopped	Parsley, chopped

Saute ham, green pepper and onion in hot oil until vegetables are soft. Don't get too brown. Add the shrimp, tomatoes, garlic, water, Worcestershire and red pepper flakes and bring to a boil. Stir in the rice and salt. Taste and add a sprinkle of black pepper, if desired. Cover and turn the heat low. Simmer slowly until liquid is absorbed — about 20 minutes. Serve with a sprinkling of chopped parsley. Serves 4 to 6.

*Fillets en Papillote*** *(Fish in Paper)*

Individual portions of fish wrapped in paper packets is a very impressive tack to take when company comes for dinner. It's simple, too. You will find parchment paper in most housewares shops.

1 pound fresh fillets	Salt and pepper
8 slices boiled ham, sliced paper-thin	1 tablespoon finely minced parsley
3 tablespoons butter	Juice of 1/2 lemon

Cut fillets into 4 pieces. Overlap ham slices to make 4 squares. Place one piece of fish on each ham portion, then dot with butter and sprinkle with salt, pepper and parsley. Drizzle a little lemon juice over each portion, then place on a square of parchment paper twice the size of the fish squares. Fold up like packets, crimping the edges to seal in the juices.

Place packets on a baking sheet and brush each one with melted butter. Place in a 400° F. oven and bake for 15 minutes. Serve the fish in the packets so that each guest can open his own (and savor the juices and fragrance) at the table. Serves 4.

Fast Scampi*

Considering how easy it is to prepare an excellent scampi at home, it is amazing how often it is ruined in restaurants. For my money, anytime the sauce gets gussied up, the dish is doomed. Real butter and gobs of garlic are about all it takes.

1 pound raw jumbo shrimp, shelled and cleaned (tails on)	Pinch oregano
	2 cloves garlic, crushed
1/2 cup butter	1/2 lemon, juiced
Salt and pepper	Chopped parsley

Spread cleaned shrimp in an ovenproof platter or pie plate. Dot liberally with butter, then sprinkle with salt, pepper, and oregano. Squeeze garlic over shrimp and sprinkle with lemon juice. Pop under a hot broiler and cook until shrimp are pink and faintly tinged with brown. Serve with a drift of chopped parsley. Serves 4 to 6. And **do** serve chunks of crusty French bread to mop up the juice!

NOTE: As an interesting touch, try sprinkling the shrimp with a few drops of Pernod and use white wine in place of the lemon juice.

Oyster Lovers' Loaves**

Oyster Loaves are the hamburgers of the Gulf States where shellfish abound. These crusty fishwiches are positively scrumptious and aren't at all difficult to whip up at home.

2 medium size crusty French rolls	1 egg, beaten
	Melted butter — about 1/2 cup
1 dozen fresh oysters	Salt and pepper
1 cup cracker crumbs	Tartar sauce

Slice tops off the rolls lengthwise and pull out part of the soft centers. Brush the cavities of the rolls with melted butter and set aside.

Drain oysters thoroughly, then dip first in beaten egg, and then into the cracker crumbs. Chill for 5 minutes to firm up before frying.

Put rolls in a 375° F. oven to heat and crisp up — don't let them brown.

While rolls heat, bring the remaining butter to a sizzle in a small skillet and quickly pan fry the oysters — taking care not to overcook. As they get browned on one side, flip over and brown the other. Then pop 6 oysters into each of the hollowed-out rolls, sprinkle with salt and pepper. Replace the bread lids and serve. Pass the tartar sauce. This serves 2.

What's Ahead in Chicken

Chicken

. . . and other birds of the barnyard

Apart from debating whether the hen or the egg came first, or why a chicken crosses the road, there are two other things to remember about these fine feathered friends: *one, they are inexpensive and, two, there are more ways to prepare them than you will ever have time to try.*

Chicken can also be sneaky. Supremes — which is the fancy name for skinned and boned chicken breasts — have fooled a lot of people a lot of times into thinking they're eating six-dollar-a-pound veal.

Of course chicken isn't the only bird that beats the high cost of living. Turkeys, once considered once-a-year treats, are year-round penny-pinchers. Ducklings that turn into exotic fancies with fruit and liqueur saucery are well within the bride's budget. And Cornish game hens, plumper than the wee bony birds that hit the market a few years ago, cost but pennies per pound.

You will find all these birds, plucked, packed and ready to go in the fresh and frozen sections of your market where they await you — some of the best bargains in town.

Fried Chicken**

*There must be a million ways to cook chicken but, in the long run, none beats plain fried. If you always thought crispy chicken had to be deep-fried, try this low-fat version that's easier on the cook **and** the calories.*

1/4 cup flour	**1/4 cup oil**
1 3-pound fryer, cut up	**Salt and pepper**

Place flour in a brown paper bag. Add chicken pieces, one at a time, and shake until well coated. Set aside to dry for 15 minutes (chilling in the refrigerator helps keep the flour in place).

Heat oil in a heavy 12-inch frying pan. As soon as the oil ripples when the pan is tilted, brown the chicken pieces, turning to cook evenly. Sprinkle with salt and pepper.

Turn heat to medium, cover the pan and cook for 25 minutes. Uncover and cook chicken until crisp — about another 5 minutes.

Remove chicken to a heated platter and prepare gravy. Serves 4.

Chicken Gravy**

Pour off all but about 1/4 cup fat in skillet. Blend in 1/4 cup flour, scraping up browned bits from the bottom of the pan. When flour turns golden, gradually add 2-1/2 cups milk and stir constantly until gravy comes to a boil and is smooth and thickened. Salt and pepper to taste.

Easy Oven Chicken*

Here's how to get crispy chicken on the table without going through the spattery ritual of pan-frying the bird on top of the stove. All you need is real mayonnaise (salad dressing won't do), seasoned bread crumbs and the chicken parts. You can use thighs, breasts, drumsticks or wings — the results are equally smashing.

3 pounds chicken parts   **1 cup seasoned crumbs**
1 cup mayonnaise

Wash and dry chicken. Slather heavily with mayonnaise, then dip in crumbs. (You may need a bit more. Don't scrimp.) Place coated chicken on an ungreased cooky sheet and bake at 350° F. until done. Wings take about 30 minutes, breasts and thighs a bit longer — 40 to 45 minutes. With a sharp knife, test for doneness.

Oven Luau*

This easy sweet-and-sour chicken casserole is ideal for the beginner cook. Just put it together, slip it in the oven and forget the whole thing for an hour.

1 chicken, cut up   **1 teaspoon finely grated fresh**
1/2 cup oil   **ginger**
1 cup pineapple juice   **1 tablespoon cornstarch**
2 tablespoons brown sugar   **1 tablespoon soy sauce**
2 tablespoons catsup   **1 green pepper, cut in dice**
                                    1 onion, chopped

Saute chicken pieces in hot oil, turning to brown evenly on all sides. Add more oil, if necessary. When browned, arrange chicken in a flat baking dish in one layer. Combine remaining ingredients and pour over chicken. Cover tightly with foil and bake at 350° F. for 1 hour. Serves 4.

Chicken Breasts on Beef*

The idea of teaming chicken with chipped beef surfaced a couple of years ago and has been popular ever since. It's a tasty combination and has the added virtue of being extremely simple.

1 jar chipped beef   **1 can cream of mushroom soup**
2 whole chicken breasts (or 4   **1 small carton sour cream**
halves), boned   **Paprika**

Line a greased casserole with chipped beef. Place chicken breasts on top. Mix undiluted soup with sour cream and heat slightly. Pour over chicken and beef, sprinkle with paprika, and bake at 325° F. for 1-1/2 hours. Serves 4.

NOTE: This is another casserole that improves with day-ahead preparation.

Church Social Dinner-in-a-Dish*

This hefty chicken casserole showed up at a church Lenten supper recently and everyone agreed: it's one of the best potluck put-togethers they ever tasted.

3 cooked whole chicken breasts (6 halves), boned and cubed
2-1/2 cups diced celery
6 hard-cooked eggs, chopped
1/2 cup sliced almonds
2 cans undiluted cream of chicken soup

1-1/2 cups mayonnaise
3 tablespoons lemon juice
Salt and pepper, to taste
2 cups potato chips, crumbled (reserve 1/2 cup)
1 cup grated Swiss or American cheese

In a large bowl mix all ingredients except the grated cheese and the 1/2-cup reserved chips. Toss until mixed, then turn into a greased 3-quart casserole. Top with grated cheese and the remaining potato chips. Bake, uncovered, at 375° F. for 40 minutes. Serves 10.

Mustard Chicken*

Like many chicken dishes, Mustard Chicken is just as good cold as hot, which is something to consider if you're not sure just when dinner's going to be served.

1 chicken (3-1/2 to 4 pounds) cut up
1/4 cup Dijon mustard
3 cloves garlic, minced

2 teaspoons rosemary
1/2 teaspoon thyme
Salt and cracked pepper
1/2 cup Parmesan cheese

Arrange chicken in a baking dish, then brush with a mixture of mustard and garlic. Sprinkle with rosemary, thyme, salt and pepper. Top off with a drift of Parmesan. Bake at 350° F. for 55 minutes, turning once during the baking. Serves 3 to 4.

Curried Coconut Wings**

Curry, coconut and crunch give these cocktail wings distinction. Assemble them early in the day, then pop them into the oven after the party gets underway.

2 dozen chicken wings (4 to 5 pounds)
1 cup milk
1 teaspoon coconut extract
2 cups instant mashed potato flakes

3 teaspoons curry powder
1/2 cup flaked coconut
6 tablespoons melted margarine
2 cloves garlic, pressed

Cut wings apart at both joints, discarding the tips. Marinate wings in mixture of milk and coconut extract. Cover and refrigerate 4 hours or overnight.

In a shallow bowl combine potato flakes, curry powder and coconut. Dredge drained wings in potato-coconut mixture, coating thoroughly. Place wings on a greased baking sheet and drizzle with mixture of margarine and garlic. Bake, uncovered, at 375° F. for 45 minutes, or until well browned and crisp. Serves 4 as a main course, 8 people as an appetizer.

Italian Chicken Almond**

Right now pasta is a very trendy item with would-be gourmets. Before the craze dies out, try this pretty party casserole.

3/4 cup mayonnaise
1/3 cup flour
2 cloves garlic, minced
2 tablespoons dehydrated
  minced onions
1 teaspoon salt
2-1/4 cups milk
1 cup shredded Swiss cheese
1/3 cup white wine

7 ounces spaghetti, cooked to *al
  dente* stage, drained
2 cups chopped cooked chicken
1 10-ounce package frozen chopped
  broccoli, thawed
1 4-ounce can sliced mushrooms,
  drained
1-1/4 cups sliced almonds

Combine mayonnaise, flour, garlic, onions and salt in a saucepan and gradually heat, adding the milk as you stir. When sauce has thickened, add the cheese and wine and stir until the cheese melts. In a large bowl, combine the sauce with the cooked spaghetti, chicken, thawed and drained broccoli, drained mushrooms and a handful of almonds. Toss lightly and pour into a greased 7 x 11-inch baking dish. Top with remaining almonds. Bake at 350° F. for 45 minutes. Serves 6 to 8.

Serve sprinkled with freshly grated Parmesan cheese.

Stuffed Chicken Breasts Florentine**

Here is an elegant party entree that won't deep-six your budget. Note that in this version, the stuffing goes under the chicken skin of the chicken breasts, after which you roll each one into a neat little bundle.

1 onion, minced
1 tablespoon butter
1 10-ounce package frozen
  chopped spinach
1 pound ricotta cheese
1 egg, slightly beaten
1/3 cup minced parsley
1 tablespoon Ranch salad
  dressing mix

Salt and pepper
Dash nutmeg
4 whole chicken breasts (8 halves),
  boned but not skinned
1/2 cup chicken broth (or white
  wine)
3 tablespoons butter

Thaw spinach and press out as much liquid as possible. Saute onion in butter until soft. Combine onion and spinach with cheese, egg, parsley and Ranch dressing mix. Season, to taste, with salt and pepper. (Mix should be highly seasoned.)

Loosen skin on breasts and stuff about 1/3 cup of stuffing into each pocket. Fold skin under the breast, pressing into a smooth, round packet. Place, seam side down, in a buttered baking pan. Bake at 350° F. for 1 hour, basting frequently with butter-broth mixture. Cool 10 minutes before serving. Serves 8.

NOTE: For an added touch, spoon a dollop of Hollandaise over the breasts.

Ginger Chicken Wings**

These gingery chicken wings are the easiest cocktail munchies you will ever turn out. They cook, unattended in the oven (no baby-sitting required), and come forth succulent and spicy. Make plenty — they go fast — and provide plenty of napkins.

3 pounds chicken wings, tips
  removed
1 cup brown sugar
1 cup soy sauce
1 cube margarine

3 to 4 tablespoons grated fresh
  ginger
1 rounded teaspoon dry mustard
1/2 cup sherry
Sesame seeds

Cut tips off chicken wings, then separate wings at joint. (Some people use just the larger section, called the drumette, but I use both pieces. Suit yourself.)

Prepare a marinade of the brown sugar, soy sauce and margarine and bring to a boil. Remove from heat and add the grated ginger. Stir dry mustard into the sherry, then add to the sauce. Pour over chicken and let marinate 2 hours, turning occasionally.

Bake at 350° F. for 30 minutes, turning occasionally. Drain off marinade and sprinkle wings with sesame seeds. Return to the oven and continue baking an additional 15 to 20 minutes, turning once as wings glaze.

Wings can be made ahead and served at room temperature or reheated briefly in a micro oven or conventional oven.

Tuckaway Chicken Bundles***

These chicken nuggets are wrapped in dough, then baked to a golden crisp — an artful maneuver that looks a lot more complicated than it is. Just take care to get all of the filling tucked in and pinched shut.

2 whole chicken breasts
1 cup lightly salted water
2 bunches green onions,
  including the green tops
6 ounces cream cheese, softened

1-1/2 packages refrigerated
  crescent rolls (12 rolls)
2 cans of cream of chicken soup,
  undiluted
1/2 cup chicken broth
1/2 cup Sherry

Simmer chicken in salted water until tender. Cool. Bone and skin the meat and cut into small dice. Mince the onions and combine with cream cheese and chicken. With a tablespoon, form mixture into 12 balls a bit smaller than golfballs. Chill.

Unroll crescent rolls, gently stretching each one at the widest edge to make slightly larger. Place a cheese ball in the center. Fold the two wider points up and over, pressing to seal. Bring last corner up over the top and pinch-seal. Make sure cheese is completely enclosed.

Bake on an ungreased cookie sheet at 375° F. for 15 minutes, or until nicely browned. Serve with sauce made from simmering together the soup, broth and sherry. Serves 6.

Chinese Walnut Chicken***

Like most recipes for Chinese cooking, this one isn't difficult provided you have everything at the ready — chopped and lined up within reach. Once you start stir-frying, if you have to stop and hunt for the bamboo shoots, all is lost. Be prepared!

1 cup coarsely broken walnuts	1 teaspoon sugar
1/4 cup salad oil	1/4 cup soy sauce
2 whole chicken breasts, boned	3 tablespoons sherry
and cut in thin strips	Accent
1/2 teaspoon salt	1 5-ounce can bamboo shoots,
1 cup onion slices	drained
1-1/2 cups bias-cut celery slices	1 5-ounce can water chestnuts,
1-1/4 cups chicken broth	drained and sliced
1 tablespoon cornstarch	Hot cooked rice

Toast walnuts in hot oil, stirring constantly. When lightly browned, remove to a paper towel to drain. Place chicken strips in the same hot oil, sprinkle with salt, and saute until tender — 5 to 6 minutes. Remove and set aside. Saute onion, celery and 1/2 cup chicken broth in skillet, cooking for 5 minutes.

Combine cornstarch, sugar, soy sauce, sherry and accent with remaining chicken broth, stirring well. Pour over celery and onions and cook, stirring, until sauce is clear and thickened. Add chicken, bamboo shoots, water chestnuts and walnuts and heat through. Serve over rice.

Chicken Paella***

Olives, almonds and olive oil give this unusual chicken casserole decidedly Spanish accents. While it bears precious little resemblance to the standard paella that features shellfish, it is very, very good. Cheap, too.

3-1/2 pound chicken, cut up	1 cup dry white wine
1/2 cup olive oil	Salt and pepper, to taste
6 small boiling onions, blanched	1/2 cup salted almonds
and skinned	3/4 cup sliced stuffed olives
2-1/2 cups white rice, uncooked	Pinch oregano
2 cloves garlic, minced	1 pound mushrooms, sliced and
3 cups chicken stock	sauteed in butter

Coat chicken pieces in olive oil and place in a flat baking pan. Bake at 325° F. for 30 minutes. Add the small onions and continue baking for an additional 30 minutes. Add the uncooked rice and chopped garlic to the pan and fluff through with a fork. Add 3 cups stock and 1 cup wine and cover the pan. Continue baking for 1 hour. Season, to taste, with salt and pepper.

Uncover pan and sprinkle almonds, olives and oregano over the rice and chicken. Cook, uncovered, 10 minutes. Add more chicken stock if mixture is too dry. Just before serving, sprinkle sauteed mushrooms over the top. Serves 6.

Short-Cut Chicken Divan**

This is one of the easiest (and best) Chicken Divan recipes you will ever encounter.

3 whole chicken breasts (6
  halves), skinned and boned
Water to cover
Chopped onion and celery (plus
  tops)
1 bunch broccoli, skinned and
  cut into long flowerettes

2 cans cream of chicken soup
1 cup mayonnaise
1 teaspoon curry powder
1 tablespoon lemon juice
1 cup Cheddar cheese, grated
Seasoned bread crumbs

Simmer chicken breasts in water in which you have tossed some chopped onion and celery.

While chicken cooks, skin and strip broccoli and blanch for 6 minutes in boiling salted water. Plunge broccoli into cold water to stop the cooking while the stalks are still bright green. Drain.

Place broccoli in a shallow, round baking dish, arranging so the flowers cluster around the edges in an attractive ring. Cut the cooked chicken into strips and place in the center of the dish. Mix soup with mayonnaise, curry powder, lemon juice, and grated cheese; spoon over the chicken. Sprinkle with crumbs and bake at 350° F. for about 1 hour. Serves 4.

Garlic Pasta a la Chicken Livers**

Chicken livers and garlic-sauced linguini can be thrown together in minutes. The big thing is not to overcook the livers or the pasta. The whole thing should not take more than 10 minutes from start to finish.

1 pound chicken livers
1 tablespoon oil
2 tablespoons butter
8 ounces linguini
4 tablespoons butter

4 large cloves garlic, minced
1/2 cup parsley, minced
1/4 cup fresh basil, minced
1/2 teaspoon oregano

Pan-fry livers in 1 tablespoon oil and 2 tablespoons butter until lightly browned. (Do not overcook. Livers should be pink in the center.) Season with salt and pepper.

Meantime cook linguini in about 3 quarts of vigorously boiling, salted water. Cook **al dente** — from 6 to 9 minutes. Drain, rinse and place in a colander over hot water. Melt 4 tablespoons butter in a small pan and add the garlic, parsley, basil, and oregano. Heat through.

On 4 heated dinner plates, mound hot linguini. Drizzle with butter-parsley sauce, then sprinkle with livers. Serves 4.

Chicken Livers*

If you are positively certain that the people you invited over for dinner Saturday night are chicken liver buffs, by all means try this one. Liver lovers like these little devils pristine plain — just like this.

1 pound chicken livers	4 to 5 slices bacon
Seasoned flour	Minced parsley
10 to 12 large fresh	1/2 cup white wine
mushrooms, sliced	

Rinse and dry livers. Dredge in flour seasoned with salt and pepper. Spread out on a plate and chill 1/2 hour in the refrigerator.

Snip bacon in dice (use scissors) and pan-fry until crisp. Remove with a slotted spoon and drain on paper towels.

Heat bacon fat remaining in skillet and pan-fry livers, turning with a spatula as they firm up. Toss in the mushrooms. Cook until the livers are nicely browned but still red-pink in the centers. Add the wine, cover the pan and steam 2 minutes. Uncover and cook another minute or two. Test. Livers should still be pink in the middle. Sprinkle with reserved bacon bits and parsley. Serves 6.

Little Hens l'Orange**

If wrestling with a whole Cornish game hen strikes you as a bit much for one serving, here is how to plump up a half a hen with mushroom-rice stuffing. Have the butcher saw the little darlings in half (you'd never be able to do this at home).

3 Cornish game hens	1/4 cup orange peel, cut in match-
Salt and pepper, to taste	stick slivers
1 6-ounce package long grain	3 tablespoons brown sugar
and wild rice mix	2 tablespoons cornstarch
1 4-ounce can chopped	2/3 cup orange juice
mushrooms, drained	1/2 cup water
1/2 cup chopped green onions	Dash salt
	1 tablespoon brandy

Ask butcher to cut hens in half lengthwise. Rinse and pat dry. Season with salt and pepper.

Prepare rice mix according to package instructions, then combine with mushrooms and chopped onions. Shape mixture into 6 equal portions in a shallow baking pan. Situate a half-hen on each stuffing mound and bake, uncovered, at 375° F. for 1 hour. If hens get too dry, baste with a little orange juice or white wine.

Simmer orange peel in a small amount of water for 15 minutes. Drain and set aside. Combine brown sugar and cornstarch in a small pan. Stir in orange juice, water and a dash of salt. Cook until clear and thickened. Remove from heat and add the orange peel and brandy.

Place hens and stuffing on heated plates. Spoon sauce over each serving. Pass remaining sauce in a gravy boat. Serves 6.

Fruit-Filled Cornish Game Hens**

Game hens stuffed with a delectable mix of rice, apricots and cranberries are a lovely and inexpensive party entree.

6 Cornish game hens
Salt, to taste
1/3 cup chopped onion
1/3 cup chopped celery
1 tablespoon butter
1 package Rice-a-Roni (chicken flavor)
1 16-ounce can whole cranberry sauce

1 8-ounce can crushed pineapple, drained
1 8-ounce can apricots, drained and chopped
1 5-ounce can water chestnuts, drained and chopped
1/2 teaspoon grated ginger
Soy sauce

Sprinkle inside of hens with salt, then set aside. Cook onion and celery in butter until tender-crisp. Prepare rice according to package instructions. Combine vegetables and rice with remaining ingredients (excepting soy sauce), tossing lightly. Spoon lightly into hens. Place extra stuffing in a small casserole and set aside. Tie the hens' legs together and place, breasts up, in a shallow baking pan. Cover lightly with foil and bake at 350° F. for 30 minutes. Uncover and bake 45 minutes more, basting occasionally with a little soy sauce. Put the casserole of extra stuffing in the oven 45 minutes before the baking time is up. Serves 6.

Pineapple Duck**

This delectable sweet and sour duck involves a two-part operation. First the bird is simmered 'til tender, then richly sauteed and sauced with soy, pineapple and peppers. Serve it over a snowy mound of white rice. And, if you're feeling opulent, top the dish off with a sprinkling of toasted slivered almonds.

1 duckling (about 4 pounds)
2 tablespoons oil
1 teaspoon salt
1/2 teaspoon pepper
1 large green pepper, seeded and cut in 1-inch chunks

4 slices canned pineapple slices, cut in chunks
2 cups chicken broth
1 tablespoon soy sauce
1 tablespoon cornstarch
2 tablespoons cold water

Have butcher cut duck in fourths. Cover with hot water and simmer until tender. Drain, saving the broth.

Cook pieces of duck in hot oil, browning evenly on all sides. Sprinkle with salt and pepper, and add the green pepper and pineapple. Add 2 cups of the broth in which the duck was cooked along with the soy sauce. Simmer, covered, for 10 minutes. Stir cornstarch into cold water, making a smooth paste. Add to simmering broth and whisk until smooth and slightly thickened. Serve with steamed rice. Serves 4.

*Gizzards en Brochette***

Gizzards, poor things, are the chicken's toughest parts. But a little patience and leisurely simmering are all it takes to tenderize these sturdy little nuggets that are not only very good but very easy on the budget.

3 pounds chicken gizzards
2 onions, sliced
1 bay leaf
1/2 teaspoon thyme

1/2 teaspoon dehydrated parsley
6 to 8 slices of bacon
Salt and pepper, to taste

Cover gizzards with water to which the onion, bay leaf, thyme and parsley have been added. Season with salt and bring to a boil. Reduce heat, cover and simmer for 1 hour. Drain and set aside to cool.

When cool enough to handle, trim away tough parts and cut gizzards in half. Spear a skewer through one end of a bacon slice and string gizzards on the skewer until nearly full, winding the bacon in and out around the whole thing and fastening it on the tip of the skewer.

Broil or grill over charcoal or under oven broiler until crisp on all sides. Sprinkle with salt and pepper. Serves 6.

*Easy Duck l'Orange***

Here is an Easy Duck l'Orange recipe for you new cooks to cut your teeth on. Just don't overestimate the mileage you can get out of one of these critters. It takes a five-pound duck to feed four people.

1 5-pound duckling
Salt
1 small apple, peeled
   and quartered
1 medium onion, quartered
2 stalks celery, chopped
1 10-1/2 ounce can beef broth

1 cup orange juice
1/2 cup Cointreau
2 tablespoons cornstarch
1 tablespoon honey
1 teaspoon lemon juice
2 tablespoons thin orange rind, cut
   in slivers

Wash and dry duck. Prick skin all over with a fork. Stuff with apple, orange and celery. Place on a rack on a shallow pan and bake at 325° F. for 2 to 2-1/2 hours.

Combine broth, orange juice, Cointreau, honey, cornstarch and lemon juice in a small saucepan. Cook, stirring, over medium heat, until smooth and thickened. Drain fat from pan in which duck cooked. Stir sauce into the drippings left in the pan, scraping up the browned bits with a spatula. Add slivered orange peel and pour sauce over duck. Cut bird in serving pieces, and pass remaining sauce in a gravy boat. Serves 4.

NOTE: Cutting the duck is infinitely easier if you use poultry shears.

Dunkin' Hens*

In this dippy version of Cornish game hens, the little critters are served up at the table with bowls of honey-orange sauce for dunking. A bit "finger-licking" informal, but very festive.

6 Cornish game hens	1 small can frozen orange juice
Salt and pepper, to taste	concentrate, thawed
1 package long grain and wild	1 cup light corn syrup
rice mix	1 small can mandarin oranges,
	drained

Wash hens and pat dry. Sprinkle lightly inside and out with salt and pepper. Prepare rice according to package instructions. Lightly stuff hens with the rice, tying the hens' legs together. Place in a shallow baking pan, lightly cover with foil and bake at 350° F. for 30 minutes. Remove foil and continue baking for 45 minutes, basting hens occasionally with a mixture of undiluted orange juice concentrate and syrup.

Before serving, pour orange-syrup marinade into 6 small bowls. Divide drained mandarin orange sections between the 6 bowls and serve, along with the hens, for dunking. Serves 6.

Georgene's Gorgeous Turkey*

*This recipe for roast turkey is at least 35 years old, according to my friend Georgene, who says her mother first got it from some people who had a big turkey ranch next door to Knott's Berry Farm. Rubbing and basting the bird with this buttery-gingery glaze produces the juiciest, **best** turkey ever. That's a promise!*

1 turkey — 15 to 20 pounds	2 fat cloves garlic, minced
1 stick butter (or margarine)	1 teaspoon salt
1 rounded teaspoon powdered	
ginger	

Bring bird to room temperature. Slather with a spread made of the butter and seasonings. Situate turkey on roasting rack, drape with foil and bake at 350° F. about 15 to 18 minutes per pound. If you want a crispy skin, uncover the bird during the last 45 minutes.

What's Ahead in
Saucery

Saucery

. . . debunking the French chef myth

I read a French cookbook the other day that said it no longer takes 14 days to prepare a good sauce.

Well, I would **hope** not. In that time you ought to be able to make enough Hollandaise to fill a tub and re-wallpaper the dining room, too.

Why it took Escoffier and his crowd so long to develop a good white sauce escapes me. They must turn over in their graves every time somebody cranks open another can of Aunt Penny's.

Good news for you new cooks is that there are all kinds of shortcuts available that, with a bit of doctoring, produce very palatable sauces. Subtleties of seasonings — a soupçon of spice, a dash of wine, a deft drift of herbs — can lift a canned or packaged mix into the realm of real creativity.

After you have the ready-mades down pat, you can tackle made-from-scratch Hollandaise and Bearnaise . . . the classic lily-gilders that really aren't half as intimidating as the fat French cookbooks would lead you to think.

Having developed a fair feel for saucery, the next thing is to learn when something doesn't need any. A lamb chop or char-broiled porterhouse, for instance, is lovely as-is and swagging either one with sauce is going beyond the pale. A really good *saucier* knows when to leave well enough alone.

Packaged Hollandaise and Bearnaise Sauces

No matter how much the epicurean diehards sniff, packaged Hollandaise and Bearnaise sauces really aren't half bad. I especially like Knorrs', although Durkee's Hollandaise is good too.

Either one profits by the addition of a lump of butter and a quick squeeze of fresh lemon juice. This gives a perky, tart sauce that needn't apologize to anything it tops.

Want to really gild the lily? Fold a half cup of stiffly beaten whipped cream and one beaten egg white into Hollandaise and you get the most opulent sauce of all: Mousseline. Mousseline is positively magnificent over poached salmon, but it would never make it through a Weight Watchers' convention.

Canned Gravy Sauces

Canned gravy is something you must never admit to using. In *haute cuisine* circles, this stuff is *kaput*.

Later, as you earn your stars, you can abandon this canned shortcut. But in the beginning, use it and keep your mouth shut. The experienced *saucier* may get a gastronomical charge out of toiling over his saucepans, but at the outset you won't have the time or inclination for such commitment. For now, a can of beef bouillon or gravy can be a perfectly acceptable launch pad for your saucery.

The one-star (*) recipes that follow are tasty examples. Each is super simple provided it isn't rushed. So slow down and stir a lot. And remember: A good sauce — even from a can — can't be made in a minute..

Chateaubriand Sauce*

1 can beef gravy	3 tablespoons lemon juice
1 cup white wine	1 tablespoon minced parsley
1/4 pound butter	Salt and pepper

Cook gravy and wine slowly until reduced by half. Add remaining ingredients, beating until butter melts. Makes about 1 cup.

Wine Merchant's Sauce*

This robust, red-wine sauce is also great on beef, and does positive wonders for sprucing up slices of yesterday's roast.

6 green onions, chopped	1 can beef gravy
4 tablespoons butter	2 teaspoons Worcestershire
3/4 cup dry red wine	(optional)

Saute onions in butter until soft. Add the wine and simmer slowly until liquid is reduced by one-half. Add the gravy and heat. Dribble with Worcestershire, then taste for seasoning. **Good,** huh?

Bordelaise Sauce*

If you feel like steak but are having hamburger, here's what to do: grill the patties medium-rare, then top them off with this wine-based tarragon sauce that will make you forget all about the filet you couldn't afford.

2 tablespoons finely minced green onion	2 tablespoons lemon juice
2 tablespoons butter	1 teaspoon dried tarragon
3/4 cup red wine	2 tablespoons minced parsley
1 can beef gravy	Salt and cayenne (go easy), to taste

Cook onion in butter until soft. Add the wine and simmer until liquid is reduced by one-half. Add remaining ingredients and heat slowly.

White Sauce from Scratch

Sooner or later, you are going to have to learn to make white sauce (aka Bechamel or cream sauce), for it turns up **everywhere** — in casseroles, crepes, soups and souffles. Fortunately, it's as easy as one, two, three.

The three rules to remember are:

1. Make sure the flour is thoroughly mixed with the butter (or fat) before the liquid is added.

2. After adding the liquid (usually milk or cream), the sauce must be very thoroughly cooked. Undercooked white sauce is kissing cousin to wallpaper paste.

3. The proportion of fat to flour is always exactly the same. No exception. It is the amount of liquid you use that determines the thickness of the sauce.

Basic White Sauce* or Bechamel

2 tablespoons butter or margarine

2 tablespoons flour

1 cup milk or half and half

Salt and white pepper, to taste

Melt butter in a small saucepan with a heavy bottom. When butter sizzles, stir in the flour, making a smooth roux. Cook one minute, then remove from heat and stir in the milk. Whisk vigorously until sauce is smooth and lump-free. Return to heat and bring to a boil, stirring constantly. Lower heat and cook 3 to 5 minutes, until sauce is smooth and thickened. Season with salt and pepper. Makes 1 cup.

How To Make Great Gravy

Making gravy for chops or steak that have been pan fried or for an oven roast is really very simple. Once the meat has been removed from the pan, the drippings left behind provide a rich and wonderful basis for the gravy.

If there is excessive fat, pour it off, leaving a half-cup or so in the pan. Then, place the pan over high heat and add a half-cup flour, mixing to a smooth roux.

After the flour has turned a rich brown, add 2 cups of water or stock to the pan and stir vigorously until the gravy is smooth and glossy. Taste for seasoning — adding a sprinkling of granular bouillon, a dash of soy sauce or a pinch of salt if the gravy needs a bit of perking up.

If you want a clear, non-thickened gravy, simply omit the flour and add liquid — stock, water or wine — to the pan drippings. Generally a 1/2-cup of liquid per person is the right amount.

Taste for seasoning and add a drift of salt or bouillon if indicated. A pinch of herbs can add interest, as well.

Home-Made Hollandaise

Don't be put off by all the horror stories you've ever heard about Hollandaise. Actually, it's a snap to prepare if you have a blender or a simple double boiler.

The only caution is to proceed slowly. After the egg yolks are whipped, add the hot butter by dribbles. Don't hurry the operation and you should get a gorgeous, golden sauce every time.

Once it's made, Hollandise is best served right away. But if you must hold it, a good way to keep it warm is in a wide-necked vacuum bottle. Or you might keep it in a bowl set over warm water. Just take care not to get it too hot lest the mix curdles.

(Note: If, for reasons beyond explanation, the sauce does curdle, take if off the heat and gradually beat in 1 tablespoon hot water.)

Blender Hollandaise**

3 egg yolks, room temperature
2 tablespoon lemon juice
Dash salt

2 drops Tabasco sauce
1 stick butter, melted

Place egg yolks, lemon juice, salt and Tabasco in a blender. Turn the motor on and off at medium speed — zap, zap, zap — just until contents are blended.

Heat butter in a small saucepan until bubbling and very hot (but watch it! — don't let it burn). Remove the blender cover, turn the motor on high, and **slowly** drizzle in the hot butter until all is added. Sauce should thicken and be very smooth. Serve warm. Makes about 1 cup.

NOTE: Do not double or triple this recipe. If you need more, make separate batches.

Double Boiler Hollandaise**

If you don't own a blender, here's how to make Hollandaise in a double boiler. It takes a bit more standing around and stirring, but it's well worth the effort.

2 sticks chilled butter
4 egg yolks

3 tablespoons lemon juice
Dash cayenne pepper

Cut chilled butter in 12 pieces and set aside in the refrigerator.

In the top of a double boiler combine egg yolks, lemon juice and 4 pieces of the butter. Place over simmering water (water should not touch the top pan) and start stirring rapidly with a wire whisk until the butter has melted. Now add the remaining butter pieces, one piece at a time, continuing to stir vigorously until each piece melts before adding another.

When thickened and smooth, add a dash of cayenne and serve immediately. If sauce starts to get too thick before serving, add a tablespoon or two of boiling water and stir briefly. This makes 1-1/2 cups.

*Quick Dilled Hollandaise***

Add 1/2 teaspoon dill weed (or 1 tablespoon fresh dill) to the Hollandaise as the last of the butter dribbles in. Excellent for baked or broiled fish.

*Bearnaise Sauce***

Prepare Hollandaise and, during the last minute or two of blending, add 2 teaspoons fresh minced tarragon or 1 teaspoon dried tarragon that has been steeped in tarragon vinegar, then patted dry.

*Garlic-Tarragon Sauce***

This sauce somewhat resembles Bearnaise and goes equally well with beef or fish. The wine and tarragon are simmered down to a richly reduced zest that is then stirred into mayonnaise.

1/2 cup dry white wine	3 cloves garlic
1/2 cup minced parsley	3 teaspoons dried tarragon
1/4 cup white vinegar	1 cup mayonnaise
1 small onion, chopped	Dash black pepper

Blend wine, parsley, vinegar, onion, garlic and tarragon in a blender until emulsified. Pour into a small saucepan and simmer until reduced to about 1/3 cup. Strain into a small bowl, then return to pan. Add mayonnaise, dash of black pepper, and heat, but don't boil. Sprinkle with snipped parsley, if desired. Makes a great sauce for red meat or fish. Makes approximately 1-1/4 cups.

*Remoulade Sauce***

A slightly dressed-up version of good old Tartar Sauce is called Remoulade Sauce. This is excellent with cold boiled shrimp or lobster.

1 cup mayonnaise	1 teaspoon paprika
1 tablespoon chopped onion	1/2 teaspoon salt
1 tablespoon chopped parsley	4 drops Tabasco sauce
2 tablespoons Dijon mustard	1/4 cup salad oil
1 tablespoon prepared	1 tablespoon wine vinegar
horseradish	1 teaspoon Worcestershire sauce

Combine all ingredients until well blended. Refrigerate. Makes 1-1/2 cups.

Green Sauce**

Here's a creamy, pale green sauce that provides a lovely topping for any kind of cold seafood — chilled poached salmon, for instance. Divine!

1 bunch parsley	1/2 cup watercress leaves
12 spinach leaves	1/2 cup mayonnaise
1/4 cup chopped chives	1 tablespoon lemon juice

Wash parsley thoroughly and remove the stems. Wash and pick over the spinach leaves (the little young ones are the best). Place parsley, spinach, chives and watercress in the bowl of a food processor and chop until finely minced. Blend in mayonnaise and lemon juice and continue processing until mixture is pureed. Makes approximately 1 cup of sauce.

NOTE: A sprinkle of dill weed is a nice addition.

Beer Barbecue Sauce**

This barbecue sauce freezes exceptionally well, so make a big batch and stash it. (Or give some to a friend.) It makes a marvelous marinade for all kinds of meats, particularly ribs.

2 15-ounce cans tomato sauce	2 teaspoons dry mustard
1-1/2 cups catsup	1 teaspoon Tabasco sauce
2 cups tomato juice	2 teaspoons garlic salt
1/4 cup brown sugar	1/2 teaspoon black pepper
3 tablespoons Worcestershire sauce	2 12-ounce cans beer

Combine all ingredients, stirring to blend. Bring to a boil in a heavy saucepan, then lower heat and cook, covered, for 1 hour. Ladle into jars or plastic containers with tightly fitting lids and freeze. Makes 9 half-pints.

Simplest Salsa**

In our house, salsa is something that goes with practically everything . . . hamburgers, scrambled eggs, leftovers of all descriptions, hot dogs — you name it.

3 firm ripe tomatoes, peeled and chopped	1 teaspoon salt
	2 tablespoons vinegar
1 white onion, chopped	1-1/2 tablespoons oil
1 green pepper, chopped	2 tablespoons finely minced cilantro
2 4-ounce cans diced green chiles	(optional)

Combine ingredients, place in a covered jar and refrigerate a minimum of 24 hours to allow flavors to ripen. Makes about 1 pint.

Fresh Mint Sauce*

*My mother, who is very English, wouldn't **dream** of putting a leg of lamb on the Sunday table without providing a cruet of fresh mint sauce. It is very easy to make and seems to have more "authority" than plain old mint jelly.*

1/2 cup cut, fresh-from-the- garden mint	1 tablespoon sugar
	1/4 teaspoon salt
1/4 cup boiling water	1/4 cup malt vinegar

Wash the mint and strip off the leaves. Toss out the stems, then chop the leaves finely (Mother always uses scissors). Put the snipped mint in a small bowl and top off with boiling water. Add the sugar and salt and stir. When the sugar has dissolved, add the vinegar, cover and let "steep" until cool. Serve with lamb.

Sauce Grand Marnier*

Proof, again, that some of the best things in life are the simplest. Try this instant-mix Grand Marnier sauce for chilled summer fruits. Magnificent!

1 cup powdered sugar	1/2 teaspoon vanilla
1 8-ounce package cream cheese	1 ounce Grand Marnier liqueur
1 cup sour cream	

Beat together the sugar, cream cheese and sour cream. When thoroughly blended, stir in the vanilla and Grand Marnier. Chill. Makes about 2-1/2 cups.

Amaretto-Apricot Sauce*

This lovely sauce first surfaced in a cooking class where it was ladled over oven-crisped duck. I have found it is equally good over Cornish game hens or chicken.

1/4 cup unsalted butter	1 cup canned apricot halves
1-1/2 tablespoon thinly sliced shallot	1 tablespoon cognac
	Salt and white pepper, to taste
1/3 cup orange juice	1/2 cup Amaretto
2 tablespoons lemon juice	1/4 cup slivered almonds, toasted
1 tablespoon Dijon mustard	

Melt butter in saucepan. Add shallot, orange juice, lemon juice, mustard, salt and pepper. Cook briefly to soften shallot. Add cognac, Amaretto and apricots and simmer 30 minutes, or until sauce coats a spoon. Stir in almonds and serve. serving.

What's Ahead in
Bread for Beginners

Bread for Beginners

. . . exploring the supermarket shortcuts

Thanks to frozen bread dough and Sara Lee, there are more ways than one to bake a bun.

In the freezer section of your market, all kinds of bread and rolls are available which need only a little TLC to arrive at crusty, fresh-from-the-oven goodness.

Try them. And when you bake one of these warm and wonderful loaves, don't be afraid to take credit for the whole thing. Remember, your reputation as a cook hinges on the illusion that everything that lands on the table is something you do all by yourself. Besides, where would those pallid underdone lumps be without you?

You may feel like a Judas denying Pepperidge Farms when your mother-in-law forks into that flaky-layered turnover, but these are the little fibs you will have to live with until you get this part of the learning curve nailed down.

The Half-Baked Approach

The bread section of your market has an assortment of ready-to-go brown-and-serve breads, buns and rolls. It is amazing what ten minutes in a hot oven can do for these anemic-looking gems.

Once baked, slice with serrated knife and a light hand. Under that crispy crust, the bread is tender as a lover's kiss, and the wrong knife won't cut it.

Refrigerated Biscuits

Biscuits that come in pop-out tubes are one of the most versatile convenience foods ever invented. Apart from the fact they make excellent biscuits, the dough is like Silly Putty — ready to be folded, pinched and squiggled into everything from cocktail munchies to sticky buns.

For the brand-new cook who doesn't know a muffin tin from the dog's dish, these fail-safe biscuits are unbeatable for building instant confidence.

Dead-Run Danish*

Dip each biscuit in melted butter and place on a cooky sheet. Make a thumbprint identification in each one and spoon in a dollop of jam or jelly. Bake at 375° F. until puffed and lightly browned, 13 to 15 minutes.

Zap-in-the-Pan Dougnuts*

Open a can of refrigerated biscuits and poke, or cut, a hole in the center of each one. Heat salad oil to 360° F. (oil should be at least two inches deep), and fry doughnuts, one or two at a time, until golden. Drain well. Sprinkle with sugar or frost with chocolate or vanilla icing.

Pasties Pronto*

Press two refrigerated biscuits together, sandwich style. Roll each pair into a 6-inch circle. Place a rounded tablespoon of tuna and mayonnaise, ham salad or finely chopped cooked roast beef, mayonnaise and sweet pickle on each round, then fold over and press edges together to seal. Bake on a greased cooky sheet for 15 minutes at 350° F.

Ready Roquefort Bites*

1 container refrigerator
  biscuits

1/4 cup melted butter
1/3 cup crumbled Roquefort or Bleu
  cheese

Cut each biscuit in fourths and roll each wedge in melted butter, then in the crumbled cheese. Place on a lightly greased cooky sheet and bake at 400° F. for 10 minutes. Serve hot. Makes 40 appetizers.

Instant Monkey Breads

Here are three ways to take tubes of refrigerated biscuits and convert them — quick as a wink — into pull-apart productions called monkey bread or bubble bread.

Bacon Bubble Bread*

1/2 pound lean bacon, chopped
1/2 cup Parmesan cheese
1/4 cup chopped green pepper

1/4 cup chopped onion
1/2 cup melted butter
2 cans refrigerated biscuits

Fry bacon until crisp, then drain and set aside. Combine Parmesan cheese, green pepper and onion with the melted butter. Add the drained bacon bits and place in a large bowl.

Divide biscuits and cut each one into fourths. Drop the biscuit pieces into the bowl, and roll around gently until each piece is coated with the butter-and-bacon mix. Lightly press the biscuit pieces into a greased 9 x 5-inch baking pan. Bake at 400° F. for about 15 minutes, watching to see that it doesn't get too brown. When golden, remove from oven and allow to sit in pan for 5 minutes before turning out.

Parmesan Monkey Bread*

3 tablespoons margarine
1 tablespoon instant minced
  onion flakes
2 teaspoons dill seeds
2 teaspoons poppy seeds

1 10-ounce can flake-style
  refrigerated biscuits
1/2 cup freshly grated Parmesan
  cheese

Melt margarine in a round 8-inch cake pan. Sprinkle onion flakes, dill and poppy seeds evenly into the pan. Separate biscuits and cut each one into 4 sections. Shake biscuit pieces in a paper bag with the Parmesan cheese. Arrange the pieces in the prepared pan. Top with cheese remaining in the bag. Bake at 400° F. for 15 minutes. Invert pan over a serving plate. Serve warm. Serves 10.

Speedy Spicy Breakfast Ring*

1 cup whole walnut halves
1 container refrigerated
  biscuits
1/2 cup melted butter

1/3 cup brown sugar
1 teaspoon cinnamon
1 teaspoon nutmeg
2 tablespoons raisins

Butter a 5-1/2 cup ring mold. Arrange the walnut halves in the bottom of the mold. Open the biscuits and dip each one in the melted butter. Then roll the biscuits in a mixture of brown sugar, cinnamon and nutmeg. Place the biscuits in the mold, overlapping them a little and tucking raisins in between. Bake at 425° F. for 15 to 20 minutes, or until puffed up and golden-brown. Let stand 3 or 4 minutes before turning ring out onto a serving plate.

Barbara's Bundt Pan Coffee Cake*

The lady who gave me the bundt pan coffee cake recipe swears by it — says it's a snap to make for anyone who's all thumbs when it comes to making yeast dough from scratch. She also said the original recipe called for everything to go into one bundt pan, but she thinks it's better to divide the frozen dough balls between two pans.

1 package Bridgeford frozen
Parkerhouse rolls
1 stick melted butter (or
  margarine)
1 cup chopped nuts (walnuts
  or pecans)

3/4 package dry butterscotch
  pudding mix
1/2 cup brown sugar
1 teaspoon cinnamon
1/4 cup raisins

Butter two bundt pans. Dip frozen rolls in melted butter (or margarine) and place in the pans, dividing equally between the two. Combine remaining ingredients and drizzle over the rolls, turning them a bit to distribute the glaze. Cover pans and let stand overnight until dough has puffed up and filled the pans. Bake at 350° F. for 35 to 40 minutes. Turn onto a serving plate and serve warm.

Crusty Herb Sticks*

Herb Sticks make a quick and crunchy accompaniment for a soup lunch. For best results, bake just before serving.

1 can refrigerated biscuits	Caraway seeds
1/2 cup melted butter	Sesame seeds
Celery seeds	

Roll biscuits in long cylinders (roll them between your palms). Dip each roll in melted butter, then in seeds which have been mixed together. Bake according to package instructions. Makes 10 sticks.

Pineapple Hula Buns*

Press refrigerated biscuits into small muffin cups sweetened with a layer of pineapple and you get Hula Buns for breakfast.

3/4 cup crushed pineapple, drained	1 teaspoon cinnamon
1/2 cup soft margarine	1/2 cup chopped nuts
1 cup brown sugar	1 can refrigerated biscuits

Combine drained pineapple with margarine, sugar, cinnamon, and nuts. Spoon the mixture into 10 well-greased muffin cups. Separate biscuits and press one into each of the cups. Bake at 350° F. for 20 minutes. Let stand for 5 minutes on a rack before removing muffins from the cups. Serve warm. Makes 10 muffins.

French Bread Fancies

The things one can do with a crusty loaf of French bread are virtually endless. Look how the standard butter-garlic-and-Parmesan cheese medley can be varied.

Tijuana Toast*

1 loaf French bread	1/4 cup mayonnaise
1 cup Jack cheese, shredded	1/2 can chopped green chiles
1/4 cup margarine	

Cut bread in thick slices and arrange on a baking sheet. Mix grated cheese with margarine and mayonnaise; spread mixture on bread. Top with chopped chiles and bake at 350° F. for 10 to 12 minutes, or until cheese has melted and slices are toasted. Serves 8.

Souffle Slices*

1 long loaf French bread	3/4 cup Parmesan cheese
1 cup mayonnaise	Paprika
2 cloves garlic, minced	

Split loaf lengthwise and spread with mayonnaise that has been mixed with garlic. Sprinkle with Parmesan cheese and paprika and bake at 425° F. for 12 to 15 minutes. The bread should be lightly toasted and bubbly. Serves 6 to 8.

Cheese Bread*

The salad seasoning called for in the next recipe is the kind sold in the spice section of your supermarket. It comes in a bottle, contains a lot of sesame seeds and paprika — hence its deep orange color. You will find it does a snappy job of spicing up this toasty cheese bread.

1 long loaf French bread	**1 tablespoon salad seasoning mix**
1/2 cup margarine	**3/4 cup Cheddar cheese, shredded**
2 cloves garlic, minced	

Cut loaf lengthwise and spread with mixture of margarine, garlic and cheese. Sprinkle with salad seasoning. Bake on a cooky sheet at 425° F. for 12 minutes, or until nicely toasted. Serves 6 to 8.

Marshmallow Puffs**

If you are a marshmallow buff, these sweet puffs have your name on them. Just make sure the marshmallows are snugly sealed in their crescent dough wrappers before baking. If you leave gaps, these little goodies really ooze goo.

1/4 cup sugar	**1/4 cup margarine, melted**
1 teaspoon cinnamon	**1/2 cup powdered sugar**
2 cans refrigerated quick	**2-1/2 teaspoons milk**
crescent rolls	**1/2 teaspoon vanilla**
16 large marshmallows	**1/2 cup chopped nuts**

Combine sugar and cinnamon. Separate rolls into 16 triangles, stretching each slightly to enlarge dough. Dip marshmallows in the melted margarine, then into the sugar-cinnamon mixture.

Place one marshmallow on the short side of each dough triangle. Fold the corners up over the marshmallow and roll to the opposite point, completely covering the marshmallow. Pinch the edges to seal. Dip each bundle in melted margarine and place in muffin cups. Set muffin cups or tins on a larger cooky sheet and bake at 375° F. for 10 to 15 minutes. When golden brown, immediately turn the puffs out of the cups or tins and set onto a rack to cool. While still warm, drizzle with glaze made by combining powdered sugar, vanilla and milk. Finally sprinkle the glazed puffs with finely chopped nuts. Makes 16 puffs.

What's Ahead in
Batter Breads

... quick breads for fast learners

The nice thing about batter breads — the kinds that use baking powder and soda to get their lift — is that they don't have to sit around all day, taking their own sweet time rising. Another plus: they are *easy*.

Batter breads — also called quick breads — include muffins, biscuits, nut and fruit loaves and some coffee cakes.

The only caution with making quick breads is the danger of over-mixing. The batter should never be beaten — just stirred — and only until the ingredients are barely blended.

A good rule of thumb is to sift the dry ingredients together, then dump in the liquid ingredients all at once, stirring very briefly. Use a spoon. Electric mixers over-mix. And don't let a few lumps in the batter throw you. They all straighten out in the baking.

Once you have baked a gorgeous loaf, the temptation to whack into the hot-from-the-oven bread is something only the most resolute can resist. But be forewarned: hot batter breads crumble. If possible, exercise patience and let the loaves set a day before slicing. Then attack with cream cheese and butter and enjoy, enjoy!

Beer Bread*

*Joyce, my society editor friend, cheerfully admits she can't cook a lick. The one thing she **does** do well is Beer Bread. Directions, which are a snap even for my one-star (*) chum, follow.*

3 cups self-rising flour	**1 12-ounce can beer**
2 tablespoons sugar	

Combine all three ingredients, mixing only until the flour is dampened. Pour batter into a well greased loaf tin and let stand for 10 or 15 minutes before baking. Bake for 1 hour at 350° F. Makes one loaf.

NOTE: Joyce says this makes great toast.

Butterscotch Beer Bread**

Butterscotch Beer Bread is a delight thinly sliced and spread with cream cheese and marmalade.

2-1/4 cups flour
1-1/4 teaspoons baking powder
1/2 teaspoon salt
3/4 teaspoon soda
1 cup chopped nuts

1 egg, lightly beaten
1 cup brown sugar
1 tablespoon melted butter
1 cup beer

Sift flour with baking powder, salt and soda. Add nuts. In another bowl, combine the egg, brown sugar, butter and beer. Add this mixture, all at once, to the flour, mixing only until ingredients are moistened. Spoon batter into a greased 9 x 5-inch loaf pan. Bake at 350° F. for 1 hour, or until a toothpick inserted in the center comes out clean. Invert baked loaf on a rack, cool, then wrap in a lightly dampened cloth for 1 hour before serving. (This makes the bread deliciously moist and easy to slice.)

Beer Biscuits**

Bet you thought we were through with the beer bit, didn't you? Well, not quite yet. Here we have beer biscuits. They are very, very tender and light. (The beer does it.)

2 cups buttermilk biscuit mix
1/2 cup shredded Jack cheese
6 green onions (tops, too),
    finely chopped

1/2 cup beer
3 tablespoons melted margarine
Sesame seeds

Combine biscuit mix, cheese and onions in a mixing bowl. Add the beer, mixing with a fork only until the ingredients are moistened. Pat out on a lightly floured board and cut with a biscuit cutter. Dip each biscuit in melted margarine, then in sesame seeds. Place on a greased cooky sheet and bake at 450° F. for 12 to 15 minutes. Makes about a dozen large biscuits.

Fresh Apple Bread**

Chunks of crisp pippin apples go into this quick-mix tea bread. Spread it with cream cheese (or peanut butter) and thin slices of fresh apple for a crunchy tea time treat.

1 cup oil
2 cups sugar
4 eggs
1/4 cup sour cream
4 cups flour
1 teaspoon salt

1/2 teaspoon nutmeg
2 teaspoons baking soda
1 cup chopped pecans
2 cups pippin apples, peeled
    and coarsely chopped
2 teaspoons vanilla

Combine oil and sugar. Beat in eggs one at a time. Blend in sour cream. Sift flour with salt, nutmeg and baking soda. Add to egg mixture along with vanilla, apples and nuts. Place in 2 buttered and floured 9 x 5-inch loaf pans. Bake at 350° F. for 1 hour and 15 minutes.

*Coconut Carrot Bread***

I am hooked on coconut. If this is one of your weaknesses, you, too, will love Coconut Carrot Bread.

2 cups flour
2 teaspoons baking powder
2-1/2 teaspoons cinnamon
1/2 teaspoon salt
1/2 cup nuts, chopped
1 cup oil

1 teaspoon vanilla
1-1/2 cups white sugar
2 cups finely grated carrots
1 cup grated coconut
1 cup raisins
3 eggs, slightly beaten

Sift flour, baking powder, cinnamon, and salt together. Make a well in the middle of the dry ingredients and pour in the remaining ingredients that have been mixed together. With a spoon quickly blend the whole thing together, taking care not to over-mix. Spoon batter into a greased 9 x 5-inch loaf pan and bake at 350° F. for 40 minutes, or until a cake tester comes out clean.

This bread freezes well. Before serving a loaf that has been frozen, place it in a warm oven (200° F.) for an hour.

*Pineapple Nut Bread***

Nuts and raisins stud this moist pineapple tea bread.

1-1/3 cups flour
1/2 teaspoon salt
2 teaspoons baking powder
1/4 teaspoon soda
1/2 cup raisins
3/4 cup sugar
3 tablespoons soft margarine

2 eggs, unbeaten
3/4 cup chopped nuts
1 8-ounce can crushed pineapple, undrained
2 tablespoons sugar
1 teaspoon cinnamon

Sift flour with salt, baking powder and soda. Set aside. Plump raisins in boiling water for 10 minutes, then dry and dust liberally with flour.

Beat sugar into margarine. Beat in eggs, one at a time. Add the nuts and raisins. Sift in half of the flour mixture, but do not beat. Stir only until the mixture is moistened. Add the undrained pineapple, then fold in the rest of the flour. Spoon batter into a greased 9 x 5-inch loaf pan.

Sprinkle with a topping of 2 tablespoons sugar and 1 teaspoon cinnamon. Bake at 350° F. for 60 to 70 minutes, or until a cake tester comes out clean. Cool 5 minutes, then turn out on a rack. Bread cuts best after it has stood overnight.

Date-Apricot-Nut Bread**

Dried apricots give this date bread special zing. Spread with cream cheese and apricot preserves. It makes a nice midday snack with a steaming cup of tea.

1/2 cup dried apricots	3 teaspoons baking powder
1/2 cup dates	1/2 teaspoon cinnamon
3/4 cup chopped walnuts	1 cup brown sugar
3 cups sifted flour	1-1/2 cups milk
1-1/2 teaspoon salt	1 egg
1/4 teaspoon soda	

Let apricots stand in hot water for 20 minutes. Drain well and cut with kitchen scissors into strips. Chop the dates and mix them with the nuts and apricot strips. Sift flour, salt, soda, baking powder and cinnamon into a mixing bowl. Add the fruit and nut mixture, then the brown sugar. Blend milk with the beaten egg and add this all at once to the fruit and nut mixture, stirring only until the ingredients are moistened. Pour batter into a well-greased 9 x 5-inch loaf tin and let rest 15 minutes. Then bake in a 350° F. oven for 1-1/4 hours. Test with a toothpick for doneness. Set loaf on a rack to cool before removing from the pan.

Ripe Olive Bread**

Ripe Olive Bread isn't really a bread, at least not the kind you stand up and slice. This is a flat, patted-out concoction that is a great munchie for a buffet.

1 cup ripe olives	1/4 teaspoon salt
1 egg, lightly beaten	2-1/2 cups grated Cheddar cheese
1/3 cup margarine	3 cups biscuit mix
1 tablespoon instant onion soup mix	1 cup milk (mixed with 1/4 cup water)
1 teaspoon Worcestershire sauce	1 teaspoon sesame or caraway seeds

Cut olives into large pieces, then add egg, margarine, onion soup mix, Worcestershire sauce, salt, and cheese. Set mixture aside while preparing dough.

Combine biscuit mix with milk and water mixture; stir to a soft dough. Spread dough **very** thin in a greased 10 x 15-inch baking pan. Spoon topping over dough and sprinkle lightly with seeds. Bake in a hot 425° F. oven for 15 to 20 minutes, or until well browned. Cut in squares and serve hot. Serves 6 to 8.

Swiss and Olive Snackbread**

This is another flat party bread that makes a neat hors d'oeuvre.

2 tablespoons butter	1-1/2 cups pitted black olives, cut in wedges
1-1/2 cups onions, chopped	
2 cups biscuit mix	1 large tomato, peeled and cut in small pieces
1-1/2 cups shredded Swiss cheese	
	3 tablespoons chopped parsley

Cook onion in butter until transparent but not brown. Prepare biscuit mix according to package directions, kneading the cooked onions into the soft dough. Pat dough into a 9 x 12-inch rectangle on a greased baking sheet.

Bake the dough for 5 minutes at 425° F. Then remove and sprinkle with the grated cheese, chopped olives, tomato and parsley. Return to the oven and bake an additional 12 to 15 minutes, or until the cheese is melted and the bread is golden brown. Cut in squares and serve.

Blueberry Bread**

Try serving this fragrant, berry-filled bread with honey butter. What a divine treat for a mid-afternoon snack!

2 eggs
1 cup sugar
1 cup milk
1/4 cup melted butter (or
     margarine)
3 cups sifted flour

1 teaspoon salt
4 teaspoons baking powder
2 cups fresh or frozen blueberries
     (without syrup)
1 teaspoon finely grated lemon peel

Beat eggs with sugar until thick. Add milk and melted butter. Sift dry ingredients together and add to the egg mixture. Mix lightly — don't worry about a few lumps. Sprinkle flour over the blueberries and toss lightly. Then add the berries to the batter, shaking them as you add to remove excess flour. Add the lemon peel and mix. Spoon batter into 2 small well-greased loaf tins. Bake at 350° F. for 30 to 35 minutes, testing for doneness with a cake tester. Serve with honey butter.

Pineapple-Zucchini Bread**

A sweet departure from the garden variety of zucchini bread is this version that adds pineapple for good measure. This recipe makes two loaves. Freeze the second one or — better yet — treat a friend.

3 eggs
1 cup oil
2 cups sugar
2 teaspoons vanilla
2 cups coarsely shredded
     zucchini
1 8-ounce can crushed
     pineapple, drained

3 cups flour
2 teaspoons soda
1 teaspoon salt
1/2 teaspoon baking powder
2 teaspoons cinnamon
3/4 teaspoon nutmeg
1 cup chopped nuts

Beat eggs. Add oil, sugar and vanilla; beat. Fold in shredded zucchini and pineapple. Combine dry ingredients and nuts, and add to the zucchini-pineapple mixture, stirring only until the dry ingredients are mixed. Don't over-stir. Spoon batter into 2 well-greased 9 x 5-inch loaf pans and bake at 350° F. for 1 hour.

Coffee Cakes

Come we now to the coffee cakes . . . sweet delights that make such special treats for Sunday morning's breakfast or a leisurely midday brunch.

Coconut Coffee Cake*

This easiest-ever coffee cake gets a head start with a package of muffin mix.

1 package muffin mix	1 teaspoon coconut flavoring
1/3 cup brown sugar	2 tablespoons melted butter
1/4 cup chopped nuts	1 tablespoon milk
1/2 cup coconut	

Prepare muffin mix according to package instructions. Pour into a well greased 8-inch round cake pan. Bake at 400° F. for 20 minutes. Meanwhile mix all the remaining ingredients together in a small bowl and spread over the partially baked cake. Place pan back in the oven for an additional 8 to 10 minutes, or until lightly browned.

Chocolate Chip Coffee Cake**

For dedicated chocoholics, chocolate can't show up too early, too late or too often. For them, a coffee cake studded with gooey chocolate chips is a winner for breakfast or brunch.

2 cups flour	1 tablespoon vanilla
1-1/2 cups sugar	2 teaspoons baking powder
2 sticks margarine, melted	1 teaspoon baking soda
1 cup sour cream	1/2 teaspoon salt
2 eggs	1 6-ounce package chocolate chips
2 tablespoons evaporated milk (or light cream)	

Butter a 12-inch tube pan. Combine the flour, sugar, margarine, sour cream, eggs, milk (or cream), vanilla, baking powder, baking soda, and salt in a large mixing bowl. Mix on low speed until batter is smooth and well blended. Fold in chocolate chips. Spoon batter into the greased pan and bake at 350° F. until tester comes out clean (about 45 minutes). Cool in pan 10 minutes before inverting on a rack. When cool, drizzle with powdered sugar icing (optional).

Powdered Sugar Icing*

1 cup powdered sugar	2 tablespoons milk

Mix until smooth.

Heath-nish Coffee Cake**

Crunchy chocolate-covered English toffee-type candy bars go into this one.

1/4 pound butter
2 cups flour
1 cup brown sugar
1/2 cup white sugar
1 cup buttermilk
1 teaspoon soda

1 egg
1 teaspoon vanilla extract
1/2 teaspoon almond extract
4 1-ounce Heath bars
1/2 cup chopped pecans

Cut butter into flour, brown and white sugars. When crumbly, remove 1/2-cup of the mixture and set aside.

To the remaining butter-flour mixture, add the buttermilk, soda, egg, vanilla and almond extracts. Mix well and pour into a greased 10 x 14-inch baking pan.

Crush candy bars and add the nuts and the 1/2-cup reserved crumb mixture. Sprinkle this over the batter and bake at 350° F. for 30 minutes. Cut into squares; serve warm or cold.

Layered Angel Coffee Cake**

This sour cream coffee cake is filled and topped with layers of cinnamon and chocolate chips, then baked in an angle food cake pan — hence its name.

1 stick margarine
1 cup sugar
2 eggs
1 pint sour cream
2 cups cake flour

1 teaspoon soda
1 teaspoon baking powder
Dash salt
1 teaspoon nutmeg
1 teaspoon vanilla

Filling*

1/2 cup sugar
1 teaspoon cinnamon
Dash nutmeg

3/4 cups nuts
3/4 cup chocolate bits

Cream margarine with sugar. Add eggs and sour cream. Sift flour with soda, baking powder, salt and nutmeg and add to the creamed mixture. Add vanilla. Set batter aside.

Mix sugar, cinnamon, nutmeg, nuts, and chocolate chips in a small bowl.

Grease an angel food cake pan and spoon in half the batter. Top with half the nut mixture. Repeat layers, finishing with nuts and chocolate bits. Bake at 350° F. for 40 minutes.

Christmas Kringler***

My friend Paul, who is an accountant, relaxes on weekends baking goodies for his family. This easy kringler is one of his favorites. The topping puffs way up, then sinks down. But it's supposed to, so don't fret.

1 cup flour	2 tablespoons ice water
1/2 cup butter (or margarine)	

With a pastry blender, cut butter into flour. When mixture is crumbly, dribble in the water, a bit at a time, fluffing with a fork until flour is moistened. Divide dough in half, patting into two balls. On an ungreased baking sheet, press each portion into a 12 x 3-inch strip.

Topping

1 cup water	3 eggs
1/2 cup butter	1 teaspoon almond extract
1 cup flour	

In a small saucepan, heat water and butter to boiling. Take off heat and stir in flour, beating with a wooden spoon until soft mass forms. Add eggs, one at a time, beating well after each addition. Stir in almond extract. Spoon batter over the two unbaked crusts, spreading topping to within 3/4 inch of the eges. Bake at 350° F. until puffed and lightly browned. Cool.

Frosting

1 cup powdered sugar	3 tablespoons condensed milk (or
1 tablespoon butter	cream)
1/2 teaspoon almond extract	1/2 cup sliced almonds

When coffee cakes have cooled, spread with an icing made by combining the frosting ingredients. Sprinkle with nuts. Each cake can be cut into 8 to 10 slices.

Cottage Brunch Bread**

Ready to go packaged biscuit mix provides the base for this hearty brunch bread that's topped with a cheese layer of pan-fried onions. Serve with a bowl of soup and you're set!

2 cups packaged biscuit mix	3/4 cup cottage cheese
1 egg, beaten	1/4 cup milk
3/4 cup milk	1/2 teaspoon salt
2 tablespoons poppy seeds	1 egg
2 cups chopped onions	Dash pepper
2 tablespoons butter	1 cup grated Cheddar cheese

Stir egg, milk and poppy seeds into biscuit mix. Turn into a well-greased 9 x 9-inch baking pan.

Saute onions in butter until limp but not brown. Spread over dough.

Beat cottage cheese and milk until smooth. Add egg, salt and pepper and beat well. Spread over onions. Sprinkle with grated cheese, then bake at 375° F. for 25 minutes, or until puffed and crusty. Cool 5 minutes, then cut in squares and serve hot. Serves 4 to 6.

Muffin Maneuvers

Once you have a good basic recipe for plain muffins nailed down, you can toss in all kinds of goodies — from fruit to nuts — to vary the theme.

Basically Beautiful Muffins**

2 cups sifted flour	1 cup milk
1/3 cup sugar	1/3 cup oil
3 teaspoons baking powder	1 egg
1/2 teaspoon salt	

Grease muffin tins (or place paper liners in muffin cups). Sift the flour, sugar, baking powder and salt into a large bowl. In another bowl mix the milk, oil and egg together. When the liquids are well blended, make a well in the center of the dry ingredients and pour in the milk-egg mixture all at once, stirring only until the flour is dampened. Do **not** over-mix (batter will be lumpy).

Spoon batter into prepared cups, filling each one no more than 3/4 full. Bake 25 minutes at 350° F. or until muffins are golden brown and a cake tester inserted in the center comes out clean. This makes approximately twelve 3-inch muffins.

Blueberry Muffins**

Add 1 cup fresh blueberries (or 3/4 cup thawed frozen berries) to the basic muffin mix. Bake as directed.

Apricot-Pineapple Muffins**

Spoon 1 tablespoon basic batter in muffin cups, then add 1 rounded teaspoon apricot-pineapple jam. Top off with remaining batter and bake. This can be varied with strawberry jam and raspberry preserves.

Orange-Nut Muffins**

Add 1/2 cup chopped nuts and 1 tablespoon grated orange rind to basic muffin batter. Bake. While muffins are still warm, drizzle with Orange Glaze (1 cup sugar mixed with 1/2 cup orange juice).

Raisin-Nut Muffins**

To the basic muffin batter add 1/2 cup chopped nuts and 1/2 cup raisins that have been plumped in boiling water, then drained and patted dry with paper towels.

Cheese Muffins**

Add 1/2-cup grated Cheddar cheese to the basic muffin mix, reducing the sugar to 2-1/2 tablespoons and the oil by 1 tablespoon.

Bacon-Cheese Muffins**

Add 1/3-cup crisp bacon bits and 1/3-cup grated Cheddar cheese to the basic muffin mix. Reduce sugar to 1-1/2 tablespoons and the oil by 1 tablespoon.

Apricot Muffins**

Add 1/2 cup finely chopped dried apricots to the basic muffin mix.

Apple Muffins**

Add 1/2 cup finely chopped apples, 1/2 teaspoon cinnamon, and 1/2 teaspoon nutmeg to the basic muffin mix.

Coconut-Nut Muffins**

Add 1/3 cup flaked coconut and 1/3 cup chopped nuts to the basic muffin mix.

Cherry-Nut Muffins**

Add 1/3 cup chopped and drained Maraschino cherries and 1/3 cup chopped nuts to the basic muffin mix.

Cinnamon Muffins**

Combine 2-1/2 teaspoons cinnamon and 1/4 cup sugar. Sprinkle mix on top of muffins before baking for a crunchy top. Or half-fill muffin cups with batter, sprinkle with sugar-cinnamon mixture, top with remaining batter and bake.

Bran Muffins

Being a devotee of bran muffins, it was impossible for me to eliminate any of the following . . . a moist muffin full of shredded carrot, another one sweetened with honey and pineapple, or an easy muffin batter than can be stored in the fridge (and baked into impromptu muffins) up to six weeks.

Any of them can be baked in little pleated paper liners or spooned into muffin cups or tins that have been slathered with glaze. The latter technique produces a super moist and gooey confection . . . just the way a good muffin, in my estimation, should be.

The goop used to glaze your muffin cups can feature honey, molasses or a combination of the two. A good basic mix follows. Try it, then improvise a bit . . . make up the glaze that suits you best.

Muffin Cup Glaze*

1/4 cup margarine, softened	**2 tablespoons molasses**
6 tablespoons brown sugar	**1 tablespoon sugar**
4 tablespoons honey	**1 tablespoon sugar**
	1 tablespoon water

Mix ingredients together and use to coat bottom and sides of 12 muffin cups liberally.

Carrot-Bran Molasses Muffins**

If you are a true bran muffin buff, be sure to try this super-gooey, vitamin-packed version. Real rib-stickers, these!

1-1/2 cups unprocessed bran
1/4 cup wheat germ
1 cup whole wheat flour,
   unsifted
1 teaspoon baking powder
1 teaspoon baking soda
1/2 teaspoon salt
1 cup shredded carrots

1 cup raisins
1/2 cup chopped nuts
1 egg
3/4 cup buttermilk
3/4 cup dark molasses
1/2 cup syrup
3 tablespoons soft margarine

Mix together the bran, wheat germ, flour, baking powder, baking soda and salt. Stir in the shredded carrots, raisins and nuts. Make a well in the center of this mixture and pour into it, all at once, the egg and the remaining ingredients. Stir until blended. The batter will be very stiff.

Prepare glaze (see page 190). Liberally spread glaze over bottom and sides of 12 deep muffin cups. Spoon muffin batter into prepared cups and set on baking sheet. Bake at 400° F., 15 to 18 minutes. When a pick inserted in center comes out clean, the muffins are done. Turn out of cups and let cool. Makes 1 dozen large muffins.

Mrs. Pringle's Good Bran Muffins**

Bran muffins range all the way from dry-as-dust catastrophes to wonderfully chewy confections that are as good as they are good for you. Mrs. Pringle's Bran Muffins fall happily into that latter category — moist, plumped out with nuts and raisins and richly glazed with honey.

1 cup unprocessed bran (sold
   in health food stores)
1 cup flour
1 teaspoon soda
1 teaspoon salt
2/3 cup sugar
2 eggs, slightly beaten

3/4 cup buttermilk
2 tablespoons oil
2 tablespoons molasses
3 tablespoons honey
3/4 cup raisins (dredged in 1
   tablespoon flour)
3/4 cup chopped nuts

Sift dry ingredients together. Beat eggs slightly, then add oil, molasses, honey and buttermilk. Add liquid ingredients to the bran, alternating with flour. Add nuts and raisins. Do not over mix. Spoon batter into 12 muffin cups that have been liberally slathered with muffin glaze. Bake at 400° F. for 15 minutes, or until browned. Makes 1 dozen muffins.

Famous Six-Week Bran Muffins**

You can keep this muffin mixture in the fridge, ready to bake for impromptu breakfast treats. As the name suggests, the batter saves for six weeks.

1 15-ounce package raisin bran cereal	1 teaspoon salt
3 cups sugar	1 cup raisins
4 cups flour	4 eggs, beaten
1 cup unprocessed bran	1 cup oil
5 teaspoons soda	1 quart buttermilk
	1 cup chopped nuts (optional)

Mix the first 7 ingredients together in a bowl. When combined, add the eggs, oil, and buttermilk. Fold in nuts, if desired. Store this batter in a covered container in the refrigerator. Will keep up to 6 weeks. As needed, spoon batter into well-greased muffin cups or papers, filling 2/3 full. Bake 15 minutes at 400° F. Makes 3-1/2 to 4 dozen.

Almost-As-Famous Six-Week Applesauce Muffins**

2 sticks margarine	1 teaspoon ground cloves
2 cups sugar	2 teaspoons soda
1 teaspoon vanilla	1 1-pound can applesauce
4 cups flour	1 cup buttermilk
3 teaspoons cinnamon	1 cup chopped nuts
2 teaspoons allspice	

Cream margarine together with the sugar and vanilla. Sift flour and spices together. Stir soda into the applesauce. Then combine everything in a big bowl and stir in the buttermilk. Fold nuts into the batter and store it in a covered container. Bake, as needed, in well-greased or paper-lined muffin cups, filling each cup about 2/3 full. Bake at 375° F. for about 20 minutes. Like the Six-Week Bran Muffins, this recipe also makes from 3-1/2 to 4 dozen.

Scones*

The highlight of any English tea is scones served with clotted cream and thick strawberry preserves. (For the clotted cream, try a mix of whipped cream and whipped, softened sweet butter.) This is one of life's sweetest indulgences — for breakfast, brunch or lunch.

1-3/4 cups flour	1/4 cup butter
2 teaspoons baking powder	2 eggs, beaten
1 tablespoons sugar	1/3 cup half and half
1/2 teaspoon salt	1 teaspoon sugar

Sift flour, baking powder, sugar and salt into a mixing bowl. Cut in butter until mixture has the consistency of rolled oats. In another bowl, beat eggs, then add cream. Pour into dry ingredients and quickly mix with a fork, taking care not to overmix.

Divide dough into 2 balls. Pat each portion out on a floured board into a circle about 3/4 inch thick. Cut into 6 wedges. Place on a lightly buttered baking sheet and brush lightly with a little milk or beaten egg white. Sprinkle with 1 teaspoon sugar. Bake at 450° F. for 15 minutes. When lightly golden, serve hot. Makes 12.

*Popovers**

Why so much hype surrounds the making of popovers, I cannot imagine. There really is nothing to these little critters save a quick stir and a little restraint (you can't open the oven door midstream). So exercise patience. Let them pop without peeking, okay?

1 cup unsifted flour	**2 eggs, unbeaten**
1/2 teaspoon salt	**1 cup milk**

Liberally grease 6 glass muffin cups and set them on a baking sheet. Preheat the oven to 450° F.

Put all the ingredients into a bowl and give them a quick mix with an egg beater or whisk — 10 to 15 seconds. Fill the cups about half full and slide into the hot oven.

Shut the door and don't peek for 20 minutes. Then lower the temperature to 350° F. and bake 25 minutes more. **Now** you may sneak a peek.

If you want the popovers dry on the inside rather than moist and chewy, prick them on the sides with a fork (to let the steam escape) and give them another 5 minutes in the oven. Makes 6 fat popovers.

NOTE: If you are still a bit antsy about making popovers, try this recipe using Wondra flour. Popovers made with this extraordinary flour are **always** sky-high.

*Hot-Shot Yorkshire Pudding***

Yorkshire pudding is something like a custardy, flattened-out popover you make when you have a roast beef browning in the oven. This English treat is a taste of heaven topped with gravy made from the pan drippings.

2 eggs	**4 tablespoons drippings from roast**
1 cup milk	**beef**
Dash salt	**1 cup flour**

Beat eggs, then add the milk and salt. Blend in 2 tablespoons of the beef drippings and the flour, beating to a thin, smooth batter. Put remaining 2 tablespoons of drippings in a thin cake pan and place in the oven until sizzling hot. Quickly pour the batter into the pan and bake for 10 minutes at 450° F. Then lower oven heat to 350° F. and continue cooking for 15 minutes more. (While the pudding bakes that last 15 minutes, the roast can continue cooking under its own heat on the sink.) Serves 4.

What's Ahead in Yeast Breads

Yeast Breads

... kneading the staff of life

Directions for making yeast breads read something like "Goldilocks and the Three Bears."

First you mix the yeast with water, making sure the water is not too hot and not too cold, but just right.

Then, after the dough has been pummeled and punched, it has to be put in a place that is not too hot and not too cold, but just right.

For a couple of loaves of bread, this might strike you as a bit much — especially if you're a beginner and not on speaking terms with yeast.

Well, let me tell you: bread making is one of the most satisfying tasks you will ever set to in the kitchen, and you could have a lot of fun trying your hand at it. The main ingredients — flour, yeast and water — cost mere pennies, so if you have a few flops along the way, what have you lost?

Admittedly, yeast breads take time, but even this can be weasled around if you play it right. I always make bread on Saturday, so when the dough is rising, I find plenty of time to run to the dry cleaners or check out the neighbor's garage sale. You don't **have** to stand around waiting. Just don't take off for the weekend.

Actually, there is nothing at all complicated about bread making. To see how simple it is, let us go through the six stages of making bread one step at a time.

1. Proofing. This is where you test the yeast to see if it has enough oomph to do the job. To "proof" it you have to have water hot enough to activate the yeast but not so hot it kills it. Stick your finger in the water. If it feels hot — but not too hot — it's probably about right. If you have a thermometer, 110° F. is what you're after.

Another thing: adding 1 teaspoon of flour and 1 teaspoon of sugar to the water helps feed the yeast and get things going.

After about five minutes, the yeast should be bubbling and foamy. If it isn't, it is probably too pooped to do the job. Dump it and start over.

2. Mixing. Here is where you pour the proofed yeast and other liquid ingredients into the flour and start mixing. You need a big bowl and a wooden spoon.

Remember that the amount of flour called for in any bread recipe is only approximate, so just plug along, adding a bit as you go. When the dough gets too stiff to stir, start kneading.

3. Kneading. This is where you get up to your elbows in goo and the phone rings. (It never fails. Sometimes it's the doorbell.)

As you get into the swing of kneading, you will develop a rhythmic push-pull action where you press into the dough with the heels of your hands, flop the mass over, give it a quarter turn or so, and keep going . . . all the while working in just enough flour to make a manageable mass.

When the dough is no longer sticky and has a nice springy feeling (give it a good whack and see if it swells back into shape), the dough is ready for its first rising.

4. Rising. Swirl a tablespoon of oil in the bottom of a large bowl, and turn the dough around in it until the entire surface is oiled. Then cover the bowl with a damp towel and set it in a warm place to rise.

The pilot in an unlit gas oven will provide the right degree of warmth. An electric oven is okay, too, provided the oven light stays on during the rising. (If the light goes out when the door is shut, wedge a pencil in the hinge — just enough to keep the door ajar and the light on.)

Now find something to do for an hour.

When the dough has doubled in size, gently poke two fingers into it. If the impressions remain, it's ready to be shaped into loaves.

5. Loafing. Make a fist and give the dough a swift punch in the middle, and turn the deflated mass out onto a lightly floured board. Divide it into two or three portions (depending on how many loaves you are making), and hand-pat each piece into a flattish rectangle.

Now tightly roll each piece into a snug loaf, tucking the ends under, and fitting each one into a greased loaf pan. The bread is now ready for its second rising which will take less time than the first.

After 30 to 40 minutes, start checking. The loaves should be double in bulk, but no more. Bread that rises too high tends to collapse and get an uneven crown.

6. Baking. If the tops get too brown midway through the baking, cover the loaves loosely with foil. When the baking time is up, test the bread for doneness by rapping the loaves with your knuckles. (They're supposed to sound kind of hollow. If you're not sure what hollow bread sounds like, eye-ball it.) Turn one of the loaves out of the pan and check the bottom. Is it crusty and brown? If the bottom and sides seem nice and firm, chances are, it's done. Turn the loaves out on a rack to cool.

There. That's all there is to it.

Once you get turned onto bread baking, you will never feel the same about storebought loaves. Your breakfast toast will take on a gorgeous new dimension, and friends and family will think you're a genius!

And I'll bet your kitchen never smelled so heavenly!

Flour: What's the Difference?

After using special-for-bread flour for my weekend baking for three years, I made a discovery: that plain unbleached flour works just as well.

Earlier on I had discovered that high gluten flour especially milled for bread making was positively no good at all for any dough to be rolled — for pie crusts, croissants, sweet rolls, etc. But I thought I needed it for my crusty sourdoughs, rye breads and sesame buns. Not so.

Unbleached flour (which is more nutritional and almost as snowy-white as the bleached stuff) is great for bread and good for pie crust, too.

Actually, for any recipe calling for white flour, this is all you need.

Getting Variety in the Mix

Once you have gained confidence making plain white bread, you will be ready to improvise.

Toss in a handful of raisins. Add cracked wheat. Maybe some grated cheese. Or stir in some regular or stone-ground oats. Almost anything can be added to a basic white bread recipe with interesting, and successful, results.

The flours can be varied, too. As you knead along, try adding rye, whole wheat or graham flours to the works. Wheat germ is another ingredient that can be added by itself or in tandem with other flours. All you need to remember is that dark, whole grain flours produce heavier, stickier doughs that take longer to rise, and make denser, heftier loaves. Bread like this makes absolutely heavenly toast.

Once you get into this free-wheeling, personalized bread baking, you may never again follow a recipe. Playing it by ear is fun. And it's **very** creative.

White Bread***

Plain white bread is a good place for the novice baker to make his (or her) kneads known. The dough is soft and pliable, and it rises faster than breads containing rye or whole wheat flours.

2 packages yeast	1/2 cup shortening, melted
1 teaspoon flour	6 to 7 cups unbleached flour
1 teaspoon sugar	1 tablespoon salt
1 cup warm water (110° F.)	2 tablespoons oil
1 cup scalded milk, cooled	
to lukewarm	

Stir yeast into warm water to which 1 teaspoon flour and sugar have been added. Set aside until mixture puffs and bubbles.

Scald milk, add the shortening and cool to lukewarm. Pour into a large bowl. Add the proofed yeast and start adding the flour along with 1 tablespoon salt.

Keep adding flour until too stiff to stir and dough mass can be lifted onto a lightly floured board. Punch and knead until smooth and satiny, adding flour a bit at a time as you go — and only until the dough is no longer sticking to the board. Place dough in a large bowl with 2 tablespoons oil. Turn so the entire surface is oiled; cover and place in warm place to rise until doubled.

Punch down. Shape into two 9 x 5-inch loaves and place them in two greased bread tins. Set in warm place to double in bulk. Bake loaves at 375° F. for 40 to 50 minutes . . . until crusty brown and firm on the bottom.

Honey Wheat Bread***

After you have plain white bread down pat, you will want to progress to a whole wheat loaf. This is a good one to explore — fragrant, lightly sweetened with honey and a gorgeous choice for tomorrow morning's breakfast toast.

2 packages yeast	2-1/2 cups water
1/2 cup warm water (110° F.)	3-1/2 to 4-1/2 cups unbleached flour
1 teaspoon flour	1 tablespoon salt
1 teaspoon sugar	2 cups stone-ground whole
3/4 cup honey	wheat flour
2 tablespoons shortening	

Dissolve yeast in 1/2 cup warm water into which 1 teaspoon flour and 1 teaspoon sugar have been added. Set aside to proof.

Combine shortening and honey. Add proofed yeast and remaining 2-1/2 cups water. Add 2 cups unbleached flour and salt to yeast mixture, stirring well. Add 1 cup whole wheat flour. Beat until thick. Stir in remaining 1 cup whole wheat flour. Gradually add remaining unbleached flour, a bit at a time, until dough gets too thick to stir.

Turn out onto a lightly floured board and start kneading. Knead 5 to 10 minutes, adding only as much flour as is necessary to keep the dough from sticking to the board. Place in a lightly oiled bowl, cover and set in an unlit oven to rise.

When doubled in bulk, punch down and shape dough into two smooth loaves. Place in greased 9 x 5-inch loaf pans and let rise again until doubled in bulk. Bake at 400° F. for 30 to 40 minutes, or until done. Cover with foil if tops get too brown during the baking. Makes 2 loaves.

Ann Larsen's Rye Bread***

This is one of those old family recipes that has been handed down from generation to generation. My friend Ann got it from her Swedish grandmother, and now Ann's son, a young attorney, makes it regularly on weekends.

1 package yeast	1/2 cup brown sugar
1 cup warm water (110° F.)	1/2 cup molasses
1 teaspoon flour	1/2 cup shortening, melted
1 teaspoon sugar	3 cups warm water
3 cups whole wheat flour	1 tablespoon salt
1 cup pure rye flour	Unbleached white flour

Stir yeast into 1 cup warm water to which 1 teaspoon flour and 1 teaspoon sugar have been added. Set aside to proof.

Combine whole wheat and rye flours, sugar, molasses, shortening, warm water and salt in a large mixing bowl and beat well. Add the proofed yeast. Add enough white flour to make a workable dough, then knead 10 minutes. Place in a greased bowl, cover and set aside to double in bulk. Punch down, shape into 2 loaves, place in greased 9 x 5-inch bread pans and let rise again until doubled. Bake 40 to 50 minutes at 375° F. Cover with foil if the loaves get too brown toward the end of the baking. Makes 2 loaves.

Pumpernickel-Raisin Bread***

Years ago I used to stop at a little Jewish bakery and buy plump loaves of glazed Pumpernickel Raisin Bread. On the way home, I would tear off a big chewy hunk and devour it en route. Now I make it at home and the whole family tears in. Warm from the oven, this stuff is better than cake!

1-1/2 cups very warm water (110° F.)	2 cups light rye flour
1/2 cup dark molasses	1 tablespoon cocoa
2 packages yeast	2 cups whole wheat flour
1 tablespoon flour	2 cups unbleached flour
1 tablespoon instant coffee granules	2 tablespoons oil
	1-1/2 cups raisins
1 tablespoon salt	4 tablespoons yellow cornmeal
	1 egg white

Place warm water in a mixing bowl, then stir in molasses, yeast and 1 tablespoon flour. Set aside to proof.

When mixture is bubbling, add coffee granules, rye flour and salt. Stir well, then add cocoa and whole wheat flour. Beat well. Add 1 cup bread flour, mixing to make a sticky dough. Turn out onto a floured board and gradually add the remaining flour, a bit at a time. Knead about 8 to 10 minutes.

Place dough in a greased bowl, cover and set in a warm place to double in bulk.

Spread dough into a large rectangle and sprinkle with raisins. Knead until raisins are evenly distributed. Cover and let rise again until doubled. Turn dough onto a board and cut into 3 even pieces. Shape each piece into a round loaf. Sprinkle a baking sheet with cornmeal and set the loaves on the sheet, leaving space between. Cover and let rise. Brush with beaten egg white and bake at 400° F. for 35 to 40 minutes.

Quick Cloverleaf Rolls**

A cloverleaf roll is a plump little bun with three knobs that break apart easily for buttering. They're easily shaped by rolling the dough into walnut-sized balls and placing three, side by side, in a greased muffin cup. This recipe requires only one rising, so the rolls can be easily whipped out in a couple of hours.

2 tablespoons sugar	1 cup warm milk
1 egg	1 teaspoon salt
Oil	3 to 4 cups unbleached flour
1 package yeast	

Place sugar and egg in a measuring cup and fill to the top with oil. Dissolve yeast in warm milk. Add salt and flour to the milk-yeast mixture, mixing well. Add egg-oil mixture and stir. Turn out on a floured board and knead until smooth and elastic.

Pinch off bits of dough, shaping each piece into a smooth 1-inch ball. Place three balls in each greased muffin cup. Set aside to double in bulk. Bake at 375° F. for 15 to 20 minutes, or until nicely browned. Makes 2 dozen.

Swedish Limpa Bread***

Swedish Limpa Bread is a delectable treat spiced with orange peel and studded with caraway and anise seeds. If you like grainy, fragrant loaves, this one's for you.

1-3/4 cups boiling water	1 teaspoon anise seeds
1/2 cup firmly packed brown sugar	1/4 cup very warm water (110° F.)
1/4 cup quick-cooking oatmeal	1 envelope dry yeast
1/2 stick margarine	3 cups unbleached flour
1/4 cup dark molasses	3 cups rye flour
1 tablespoon salt	1 tablespoon grated orange peel
2 teaspoons caraway seeds	1 egg white
	Caraway seeds

Combine boiling water with sugar, oatmeal, margarine, molasses, salt, caraway and anise seeds in a mixing bowl. Stir and let stand until lukewarm. Proof yeast in 1/4 cup warm water. When bubbling, add to the other ingredients.

Beat in 2-1/2 cups flour, then add rye flour. Add orange peel and additional flour to make a soft dough. Turn out onto a lightly floured board and knead until smooth and satiny. Place in a greased bowl, cover and set in a warm place to rise. When double, punch down and let rise again — about 30 minutes.

Punch down again, and shape dough into 2 loaves. Place in a warm place until doubled in bulk. Brush loaves with beaten egg white and sprinkle with caraway seeds. Bake at 375° F. for 35 to 40 minutes. Makes 2 loaves.

Sweet 'n Swift Crescents***

These flaky crescents are as buttery as the traditional croissant without all the fuss and bother of layering, rolling and re-rolling. Another thing: they can be mixed up, placed in the refrigerator overnight and rolled out in a jiffy the next day.

1/2 pound butter	1 5-ounce can evaporated milk
1 package dry yeast	3-1/2 cups unbleached flour
1/4 cup warm water (110° F.)	8 tablespoons apricot jam
2 tablespoons sugar	3/4 cup chopped pecans
3 egg yolks, slightly beaten	

Melt butter and cool slightly. Dissolve yeast in warm water. When yeast has dissolved, stir in the sugar, egg yolks, milk and cooled butter. Stir this into the flour and mix well. Cover and place in the refrigerator overnight.

Next day, divide dough into thirds. On a well-floured board, roll each portion into a 12-inch circle. Spread with jam and nuts. Cut each circle into 12 pie-shaped triangles and roll up, from the wide end, toward the points. Place, point side down, on a greased cookie sheet and curve each roll into a crescent. Let rise 30 minutes. Bake at 375° F. for about 15 minutes. Makes 3 dozen.

Easiest Bear Claws***

This rich buttery dough makes lovely overnight bear claws. The mix requires no kneading — just a little patience to get the mix thoroughly chilled. The filling is a rich almond confection made from almond paste. The gourmet section of your supermarket should carry it.

1 package dry yeast	3 egg yolks
1/4 cup warm water (110° F.)	1/2 teaspoon salt
1 teaspoon flour	1 5-ounce can evaporated milk
1/4 cup (rounded) sugar	3-1/2 cups unbleached flour
1/2 pound butter or margarine	

Filling

1/4 pound butter or margarine	1 cup almond paste
1-1/2 cups powdered sugar	2 egg whites (reserved from
Pinch salt	dough mixture)
2/3 cup flour	3/4 cup chopped almonds

Dissolve yeast in warm water to which 1 teaspoon of flour and 1 teaspoon of the sugar have been added. Set aside to proof.

Melt butter, then set aside to cool. Stir in 1/4 cup sugar, egg yolks, salt, milk and yeast. Blend, then stir into the flour with a wooden spoon. Mix well. Cover and chill overnight (or up to 3 days).

To shape dough, roll out to a rectangle approximately 13 x 27 inches on a well-floured board. Keep the sides as straight as possible. Cut the dough into 3 long strips, each about 4-1/2 inches wide.

Prepare filling. Divide into 3 parts and form each one into a long rope (about 27 inches long) on a floured surface. Place one strip of filling along the center of each piece of dough. Flatten slightly.

Fold dough over filling, overlapping long edges slightly. Then cut each strip into 6 sections, each about 4-1/2 inches long. Arrange seam side down, on 3 greased baking sheets. With a sharp knife, make 6 cuts halfway across each roll and spread "claws" apart slightly. Curve rolls slightly to make fan shape.

Brush tops of rolls with 1 beaten egg white and sprinkle lightly with sugar. Let rise until doubled, then bake at 375° F. for about 15 minutes. Cool on wire racks. Makes 18 bear claws.

To make filling: Blend butter and powdered sugar until well mixed. Add flour and almond paste. Mixture will be very stiff. Beat in egg whites and chopped nuts. Chill until firm (overnight if possible).

*Basic Sweet Dough****

This simple sweet dough can be rolled, folded and braided into an endless variety of breakfast, brunch and tea time treats.

2 packages yeast	1 cup milk, scalded
1 cup warm water (110° F.)	2 eggs, lightly beaten
1 teaspoon flour	1/2 cup sugar
1 teaspoon sugar	6 to 7 cups unbleached flour
1/2 stick butter (or margarine)	1 tablespoon salt

Proof yeast in warm water into which 1 teaspoon flour and 1 teaspoon sugar have been stirred. Set aside until mixture puffs and bubbles.

Add the butter to milk and cool to lukewarm. Pour into a large mixing bowl. Add the proofed yeast, eggs and sugar and start adding the flour along with the salt.

Add flour until the dough is too stiff to stir, then turn out onto a lightly floured board. Knead, adding a little flour as you go, until dough is smooth and no longer sticks to the board. Place dough in a deep bowl into which you have placed 2 tablespoons of oil. Turn the dough so that the entire surface is well oiled. Cover bowl with plastic wrap, cover with a damp towel and set in a draft-free place to double in bulk.

When dough has doubled, punch down and turn out onto a lightly floured board and shape into crescents, Parker House rolls or roll out for cinnamon rolls.

*Cinnamon Rolls****

Roll Basic Sweet Dough into a flat sheet about 1/2 inch thick. Slather the dough with Cinnamon Filling, then roll up and cut in slices 3/4-inch thick. Place in pie tins that have been well greased and sprinkled with 1/2 cup brown sugar and 1 tablespoon water (the water keeps the rolls from sticking).

Arrange the rolls in the prepared pans (don't crowd), and let rise until doubled. Bake at 375° F. for 15 to 20 minutes, or until rolls are puffed and golden brown.

As soon as the pans are taken from the oven, place a plate over the pans and quickly invert. After the cinnamon rolls have cooled, they can be wrapped in plastic and refrigerated or frozen.

*Cinnamon Filling**

1 package regular pudding mix (vanilla or butterscotch)	1/2 cup soft butter or margarine
1 cup brown sugar	2 teaspoons cinnamon

Mix ingredients to a thick paste. Spread over dough, roll up and cut into slices.

Super Goo*

*For **extra** sticky cinnamon rolls, prepare Super Goo and spread in the pans before the rolls go in. This makes a gloriously goopy topping.*

1-1/2 cups brown sugar
4 tablespoons white corn
   syrup
6 tablespoons water

6 tablespoons butter
1 cup coarsely chopped walnuts
   or pecans

Cook sugar, syrup, water and butter to the soft-ball stage (235° F.) Pour into a 9 x 13-inch pan and sprinkle with nuts. Place rolls in pan and let rise until doubled. Bake at 375° F. for 15 to 20 minutes.

*Pizza Pan Coffee Cake****

A nice change from the standard coil-and-cut cinnamon buns are Pizza Pan Coffee Cakes — fragrant, crispy cartwheels loaded with apple slices.

1/2 recipe Basic Sweet Dough
   (page 202)
3 egg yolks
1/3 cup sugar
1 tablespoon butter
1-1/2 teaspoons grated
   lemon peel
1 teaspoon vanilla
1 8-ounce package cream
   cheese, softened

1/2 teaspoon almond flavoring
1 egg white
1 tablespoon water
1 can (20-ounces) apple pie slices,
   drained
2 tablespoons white sugar
2 tablespoons brown sugar
1-1/2 teaspoons cinnamon
1 teaspoon nutmeg

Grease two 12-inch pizza pans and set aside.

While dough is rising, beat egg yolks with sugar, butter, lemon peel and vanilla. Add the cream cheese and almond flavoring and beat until fluffy. Set aside.

Punch dough down and divide in half. On a lightly floured board, roll half the dough in a 12-inch circle. Pat into one of the pans, pressing to form a slight ridge around the edge. Repeat with the remaining dough.

Whip egg white into the tablespoon of water. With a pastry brush, use this egg wash to "glaze" the two crusts. Let stand 5 minutes, then spread the cheese mixture evenly over the two crusts and top with the apple slices. Sprinkle with white and brown sugars, cinnamon and nutmeg. Cover with waxed paper and let rise in a warm place until doubled — about 1 hour. Bake in a preheated 375° F. oven for about 15 minutes. Serve warm, cut into wedges.

What's Ahead in
Sandwiches

Sandwiches

. . . *trendy tips for tailgates, brownbags, and peanut butter junkies*

If you think about it, the sandwich is more American than apple pie ever thought of being. Every morning a million peanut butter sandwiches get tucked into school kids' lunchpails. Hot dogs dripping mustard are a must at ballgames. Hamburgers sizzle at backyard barbecues, while submarines star at tailgate picnics.

Watercress sandwiches shed their crusts for ladies' teas. In Kosher delis, corned beef and pastrami are piled high on Jewish rye. Or, if you are feeling fancy, you can lunch in a French restaurant where Croque Monsieurs and Monte Cristos go over big with the upper crust.

But plain or fancy, a sandwich is a sandwich is a sandwich. And most of them are a snap to put together.

For informal occasions, breads with spreads are great. And for those times when you'd rather be shot than cook, they're a Godsend.

Basic Cream Cheese Sandwich Spread*

When my good friend Nancy, who has a thriving catering business, makes sandwiches for a party, she mixes up the best basic spread in captivity: cream cheese spiked with plenty of minced green onion. *It's so much better than plain butter or mayonnaise,* there's just no comparison.

After spreading the cream cheese mix thickly on whole wheat bread or dollar-size sesame rolls, she piles on the filling — sliced meats, vegetable combinations, what-have-you. The sandwiches are positively **scrumptious.**

Peanut Butter Club*

Peanut butter — the favorite of every kid on the block — gets a grown-up treatment in this next club that is neatly stacked with Swiss cheese, onions, cucumbers and, would you believe, tomatoes?

8 slices whole grain bread	4 thin red onion slices
1/2 cup chunky peanut butter	1 unpared cucumber, sliced
4 slices Swiss cheese	Salt and pepper
4 large tomato slices	Mayonnaise

Spread peanut butter on 4 slices of bread. Top with slices of cheese, tomato, onion, and cucumbers. Sprinkle with salt and pepper. Spread remaining 4 slices of bread with mayonnaise, top and cut into quarters. (Toothpicks help keep the stacks intact.) Serves 4.

Gunky Peanut Butter Spread*

This is a real rib-sticker. Good for you, too. (Health nuts thrive on stuff like this.)

1 4-ounce package cream cheese, room temperature	1/4 cup finely chopped nuts
	1/4 cup dried apricots, finely snipped
1/2 cup extra chunky peanut butter	1/4 cup flaked coconut
2 tablespoons milk	12 slices whole wheat bread
1 tablespoon honey	

Whip cream cheese and peanut butter together. Add milk and honey. Beat until smooth. Stir in nuts and apricots. Spread on 6 slices of bread. Sprinkle with coconut, and top with remaining 6 slices. Cut in triangles. Makes 1-1/2 cups spread, enough for 6 sandwiches.

Creamy-Crunchy Peanut Butter Sandwiches*

Regular peanut butter sandwiches are even healthier when half the bread is spread with this crunchy cream cheese mix. The filling can be mixed up well ahead of time, refrigerated and ready to go at a moment's notice. Great for a brownbag lunch.

1 8-ounce package cream cheese, room temperature	3 tablespoons toasted sesame seeds
	16 slices wheat bread
2 tablespoons milk	Lettuce
1/2 cup shredded carrot	Crunchy peanut butter
1-1/2 cups finely chopped celery	

Whip cream cheese and milk together until fluffy. Add carrot, celery and sesame seeds. Chill.

Spread cream cheese mixture on 8 slices of bread. Top with lettuce leaf. On the remaining slices of bread, spread peanut butter. Assemble into 8 sandwiches.

Health Nut Sandwich*

You don't have to be a health food buff to go for this next one. Forget how good it is for you . . . just dig in and enjoy.

12 slices whole grain bread	2 cups alfalfa sprouts
2 ripe avocados, mashed	12 thin slices tomato
1 tablespoon lemon juice	1 8-ounce package cream cheese,
1 tablespoon mayonnaise	softened
1/2 teaspoon salt	3 tablespoons walnuts, chopped
1 cucumber, peeled and	
thinly sliced	

Toast bread. Combine avocado with lemon juice, mayonnaise, and salt. Spread over 6 slices of toasted bread, topping each slice with cucumber, sprouts and 2 slices of tomato. Mix cream cheese with nuts and spread on the remaining 6 slices.

Assemble sandwiches, cut diagonally in half, and secure with toothpicks. Makes 6.

Deli Tuna**

These open-face tuna sandwiches bedded with avocado and heaped with sprouts are the kinds of specialties you encounter in whole earth-type restaurants.

1 6-1/2-ounce can water-	1 avocado, mashed
packed white tuna, drained	1 tablespoon lemon juice
1/3 cup sour cream	1 teaspoon hickory (or seasoned)
1/2 cup peeled and diced	salt
cucumber	4 slices rye bread, toasted
2 green onions, minced	Alfalfa sprouts
Salt and pepper	1/4 cup chopped cashews

Mix tuna with sour cream, cucumber and onion. Season with salt and pepper. Mash avocado with lemon juice and hickory salt. Spread on all 4 slices of toast. Top with sprouts, then tuna mixture. Sprinkle with chopped cashews and serve open face. Makes 4.

Dieter's Tuna Sandwich*

Face it, there comes a time in every food-lover's life when calorie cutting is in order. The dreariness of such a prospect can be substantially lightened if you can find a few really good things to eat that don't pack on the pounds. Like this next one. You can brownbag this one to work for a week and feel very virtuous.

1 6-1/2-ounce can white tuna	3 tablespoons minced parsley
in water, drained	1/4 cup mayonnaise
1 cup low-fat cottage cheese	1/2 teaspoon pepper
2 hard-cooked eggs, chopped	2 teaspoons lemon juice
1/4 cup celery	Dash salt
1/4 cup chopped green onions	

Combine ingredients and refrigerate. Makes enough filling for 6 sandwiches.

Bacon-Curry Sandwich*

If you've never heard of bacon-banana sandwiches, now is the time to get acquainted. Spiked with curry, this easy-to-assemble treat has an unexperienced combination of flavors.

4 slices whole wheat bread   2 tablespoons mayonnaise
1 banana, sliced   1/2 teaspoon curry powder
3 slices bacon, fried until crisp
    and crumbled

Place banana slices on two pieces of bread. Sprinkle with crumbled bacon. Mix mayonnaise with curry powder and spread on remaining bread. Cut sandwiches into triangles. Makes two sandwiches.

Day-After-Thanksgiving Dagwood*

What tastes better than Thanksgiving dinner? The next day's leftovers, of course. Here is a neat way to serve them up, in a man-size dagwood that puts everything into the works — even the stuffing.

2 3-ounce packages cream cheese   Cranberry sauce
1/4 cup crumbled bleu cheese   Lettuce
1/4 small onion, finely minced   Salt and pepper
6 slices whole wheat bread   Mayonnaise
6 slices cooked turkey   6 slices white bread
Stuffing

Mix cream cheese, bleu cheese and onion. Spread on whole wheat bread. Cover with turkey slices and as much stuffing as the sandwich will hold. Spread with cranberry sauce, top with lettuce and sprinkle with salt and pepper. Spread white bread with mayonnaise, invert over sandwiches and secure with toothpicks. Cut in half, diagonally. Makes 6 sandwiches.

Bombay Club Chicken Sandwiches**

Cashew-studded chicken sandwiches make a sumptuous luncheon entree. Serve them with Daiquiris the next time you want to make a smashing noontime impression on someone.

3 half chicken breasts   3/4 cup mayonnaise
1 onion, quartered   1 teaspoon curry powder
Salt and pepper   1/2 teaspoon seasoned salt
Water to cover   3/4 cup coarsely chopped cashews

Simmer chicken with onion in water seasoned with salt and pepper. Simmer until tender. Remove meat and cool. Skin, remove bones and cut into dice.

Add mayonnaise, curry powder and salt. Cover and refrigerate overnight. Next day, add the cashews just before serving. Spread generously on whole wheat bread. Makes enough spread for 12 sandwiches.

NOTE: The addition of thin slices of avocado and a sprinkling of alfalfa sprouts produces a mile-high sandwich of the kind that whole earth-type restaurants offer as specialties (for a big price).

Football Sandwiches*

Next fall, when the men in your life are glued to the tube, try prying them loose with Football Sandwiches (so named for the fact that they go so well at half time). Needless to add, they are best washed down with beer. And another thing: the meat needs overnight marinating, so plan ahead.

2 pounds sirloin steak	1 green pepper, cut into strips
1 cup Italian dressing	Salt and pepper
2 tablespoons oil	4 crusty Italian or French rolls
1 thinly sliced red or	
brown onion	

The night before, slice steak into thin strips (this is easier to do if the meat is placed in the freezer long enough to firm up). Cover with dressing and place in refrigerator. Next day, saute the onion and pepper in oil, until tender-crisp. Heat rolls in 250° F. oven.

Drain meat strips and add to the pan with the onion and pepper, cooking over high heat until medium rare. Add salt and pepper, to taste. While meat cooks, cut ends off each roll and scoop out the soft centers. Fill hollowed-out rolls with meat mixture. Serves 4.

Baked Breadloaf**

Here is another version of the stuffed and baked-type sandwich — a mouth-watering meltaway that makes a perfect snack for a late Sunday afternoon when anything more complicated would be too much bother.

1 small unsliced round loaf of	4 tablespoons chile sauce
French bread	1/2 teaspoon chili powder
3/4 pound ground beef	Garlic powder
1/2 onion, chopped	1 teaspoon Italian seasoning
1/2 green pepper, chopped	Salt and pepper
Bread crumbs (crumbled from	Parmesan cheese
the inside of the French loaf)	

Slice a shallow top off the loaf of bread. With a sharp knife or a spoon, carefully scoop out the center of the bread, leaving a crusty shell. Reserve the crumbs.

Brown the ground beef in a skillet, draining off the fat as it accumulates. Add onions and peppers and continue cooking until the onion is limp and tender-crisp. Add the bread crumbs, chile sauce, chili and garlic powders, seasoning, salt and pepper, to taste. Blend well; stuff mixture into the bread shell. Cover with cheese and replace the top slice.

Wrap the whole thing in foil, sealing it tight. Place in a 425° F. oven and bake for 15 to 20 minutes, or until piping hot. Cut into four fat wedges. Serves 4.

Monte Cristo Sandwich***

There is something absolutely decadent about Monte Cristo sandwiches . . .
sinfully delicious and ruinous to one's diet. All the same, everyone owes himself one
of these terribly wonderful treats once in a while.

3 slices white bread	Cristo Batter
1 thin slice ham	Oil
1 slice breast of turkey	Powdered sugar
1 slice Swiss or American	Currant jelly
cheese	

Place sliced ham and turkey on one slice of bread. Top the second slice of bread with cheese. Stack and top with the third piece of bread, making a three-decker sandwich. Cut sandwich on the diagonal and anchor with toothpicks.

Dip each half in Cristo Batter and drain briefly.

In a heavy frying pan, heat 1 inch of oil to 375° F. Fry sandwich halves golden-brown on both sides. Drain on paper towels. Dust with powdered sugar and serve with a small bowl of currant jelly for dipping. Makes 1 sandwich.

NOTE: Tradition dictates that a properly constructed Monte Cristo sandwich be served loosely wrapped in a snowy white linen napkin. If you can't come up with linen, a cotton napkin works okay, too.

Cristo Batter*

1/2 cup sifted flour	1/2 teaspoon vanilla extract
2 eggs	Pinch salt
1/4 cup milk	

Combine ingredients in a small bowl, beating lightly. Chill. Makes enough batter for two sandwiches.

Croque Monsieur**

For all its fancy airs, a Croque Monsieur is really nothing more than a takeoff on
the old grilled ham and cheese sandwich. Typically, it is dipped in an egg batter,
then fried in butter — just like a Monte Cristo minus the turkey. This version offers
a topping cheese sauce that really gilds the lily.

2 cups grated Swiss cheese	2 eggs, beaten
1/4 cup half-and-half (or milk)	2 tablespoons half-and-half
10 slices white bread	1/2 teaspoon nutmeg
5 slices boiled ham	2 tablespoons butter

Mix cheese with half-and-half. Trim crusts from bread and spread 5 slices with the cheese mixture. Top with ham. Assemble sandwiches and cut in half diagonally.

Make a batter of the eggs, half-and-half and nutmeg. Dip the sandwiches in the batter. Melt butter in a heavy skillet. When sizzling, brown the sandwiches on both sides until golden. If desired, top with Cheese Sauce Monsieur.

Cheese Sauce Monsieur*

1 cup medium white sauce	Dash white pepper
3/4 cup grated Swiss cheese	Pinch dry mustard
1/4 teaspoon salt	

Add cheese and seasoning to white sauce. Stir over low heat until smooth and melted. Serve hot over Croque Monsieurs.

Pita Pockets**

Hot pita bread sandwiches are great to munch out-of-hand. Next time you make them, try shredded spinach in place of lettuce. Alfalfa sprouts are good for tucking in, too.

12 eggs	6 pita breads
1/2 cup milk	2 cups shredded lettuce
1 teaspoon salt	1/2 cup chopped ripe olives
1/2 teaspoon pepper	12 slices onion
1/4 cup butter	12 slices tomato

Beat eggs with milk, salt and pepper. Heat butter in a heavy frying pan until sizzling. Pour in eggs, turn heat to low and gently cook eggs until set, drawing a wooden spoon or pancake turner through the mass to make moist, soft curds (do not overcook!). While eggs are still creamy, cut slits in pita rounds and gently tear partway open. Stuff with shredded lettuce, olives, an onion slice and a tomato slice, then spoon eggs into each one. Serve hot. Makes 6.

Oven Burgers*

Having a mob over for an informal party and you don't want to get stuck cooking? Serve these make-ahead, bake-later Oven Burgers and you will be in and out of the kitchen in no time flat.

3 pounds ground beef	2 rounded tablespoons chili
2 large onions, chopped	powder
3 4-ounce cans diced green	2 teaspoons garlic salt
chiles	1 dozen hamburger buns
1 pound sharp cheese, grated	

Saute beef in 1-pound batches, breaking up with a fork as it browns. Remove meat and drain off excess fat. Add onions to the pan, cover and cook until tender-crisp. Remove from heat; stir in meat, chiles, cheese, chili powder and garlic salt. Cool, then pile meat mixture on hamburger buns and wrap individually in foil.

Hamburgers can be made and refrigerated ahead of time. When ready to serve, pop into a 275° F. oven for one hour. Serve hot. Makes 12.

Building the Basic Submarine**

Submarine sandwiches — variously known as grinders, hoagies, etc. — abound in all parts of the country with only minor variations on their ingredients and construction.

Generally speaking, a sub, or grinder, starts with a hard, crusty French or Italian roll, then packs in as much meat and cheese as it will hold.

A good imported salami is a must; use several slices. From there, bologna, thinly sliced ham and various other sandwich meats can go into the works.

Sliced onions are an absolute necessity. Tomatoes are more optional. If you use them (and I always do), gently squeeze out the excess juice, then "sandwich" the tomato slices in between the meat layers so the tomato can't soak into the bread.

Now for the finishing touches.

Get a bottle of pepperoncini, those not-too-hot Italian peppers, and plunk a couple down the middle of the sandwich. Don't leave them whole — slit the peppers open and spread them out flat over the meat and cheese.

Then — and this is the real coup de grace — mix a couple teaspoons of the pepper juice with equal parts olive oil, and use this dressing to sprinkle liberally over the inside of the sandwich just before it's eaten. This eliminates any possibility of the submarine being too dry — a failing of many of these meals-in-buns.

If you are making the sandwiches ahead for a picnic or tailgate party, take the oil-vinegar dressing along in a small bottle or jar. When it's time to eat, pass out the subs and let everyone anoint his own. They'll love it.

Open-Face Hot Olive Slabs*

In a quandary as to what to serve the poker club? Fret no more. This sandwich slab goes together in a flash and needs nothing more than a pitcher of cold beer to keep everyone happy.

1 1-pound loaf French bread	1/2 cup chopped green onions
3 2-ounce cans sliced ripe	1 cup shredded Jack cheese
olives	2 teaspoons mustard
1/2 cup mayonnaise	

Cut loaf in half horizontally and place halves, side by side, on a large baking sheet.

Mix olives, mayonnaise, onions, cheese, and mustard. Spread on bread and bake at 375° F. for 15 minutes, or until bubbling. Cut in wedges. Serves 8.

Roll-'Em-Up Sandwich Loaf***

This novel sandwich loaf made from store-bought frozen bread dough is equally good warm or cold. But if you want it warm and you have a way to go, wrap the hot loaf in foil, then insulate in several layers of newspaper. Then get a move on and it will still be warm when you get to the picnic site.

1 1-pound loaf of frozen bread
  dough
1 pound Italian sausage, hot
  or mild
1 large onion, chopped
1/2 green pepper, finely minced
1 10-ounce package frozen
  chopped spinach, thawed

Salt and pepper
1 teaspoon hot pepper sauce
3/4 cup freshly grated Parmesan
  cheese
1 2-1/4-ounce can sliced ripe
  olives
2 tablespoons melted margarine

While bread dough thaws, crumble sausage into a skillet and cook with onion and green pepper until the meat is browned and the onion is limp. Press moisture out of spinach, then add to the skillet. Season with salt, pepper, and hot sauce.

On a floured board, roll the thawed bread dough into an 11 x 14-inch rectangle. Spread meat mixture to within one inch of the edges; sprinkle with Parmesan cheese and olives. Starting from the long side, make a right roll, pinching the seam and tucking the ends under. Place the roll, seam side down, on a greased baking sheet. Brush with melted margarine. Bake at 350° F. until lightly browned — about 35 minutes. Serve hot, warm, or cold in thick slices. Serves 6.

*Tailgate Stuffer***

This overstuffed king-size sandwich is served cold, making it a good bet for tailgates and park picnics where travel time has to be considered.

1 8-ounce package cream
  cheese
1/3 cup finely chopped walnuts
1/3 cup finely minced green
  onions
Dash garlic salt
1 large loaf unsliced French
  bread

Margarine
3/4 pound sliced boiled ham
1/4 pound fresh spinach, stems
  removed
1/2 pound sliced Swiss or Provolone
  cheese
1/2 cup alfalfa sprouts
1/2 cup sliced ripe olives

Blend cream cheese with walnuts, green onions and garlic salt. Set aside.

With a serrated knife, slice the top off the bread; set top slice aside.

Pull out the soft center of the bread, creating a shell about 1/2-inch thick. Spread the inside of the shell with margarine; then line the cavity with ham slices, allowing the slices to overlap the edge of the crust. Place half of the spinach and the sliced cheese in the cavity and spread with half the cream cheese mixture. Top with alfalfa sprouts and olives.

Layer the remaining cheese and spinach on top. Fold the exposed ham slices over the filling, then replace the top slice of bread. Wrap tightly in a large sheet of foil, crimping to seal. Refrigerate overnight. To serve, cut in thick slices with a serrated knife, and pass Thousand Island dressing to those that want it. Serves 8.

*Crusty Country-Fried Sandwiches***

There's nothing dainty about these he-man sandwiches. Served with a side of French fries and a frosty ale, they are guaranteed to please the men in your life (or in anyone else's life, for that matter).

1-1/2 pounds top round steak, 1/2-inch thick	1 teaspoon Tabasco sauce
2 tablespoons oil	1 egg, beaten
2 tablespoons red wine	2 tablespoons milk
2 teaspoons Worcestershire sauce	1 cup fine cracker crumbs
1/2 teaspoon basil	1 large onion, sliced in rings
2 cloves garlic, crushed	1 large tomato, thinly sliced
	Lettuce leaves
	6 Kaiser rolls, lightly toasted

Cut meat in 6 pieces and pound to 1/4-inch thickness with a meat mallet.

Marinate 1 hour in a mixture of oil, red wine, Worcestershire, basil, garlic and tabasco sauce. Turn meat occasionally (piercing it with a fork will help the marinade penetrate).

Drain meat well. In a shallow bowl, mix egg with milk. Dip pieces of meat in egg mixture, drain briefly, then dip in cracker crumbs. Fry meat, a few pieces at a time, in a large skillet in hot oil 1/8-inch deep. Cook each piece about 2 minutes, or until golden on both sides. Remove and keep warm until all pieces are cooked. Serve on toasted Kaiser rolls with sliced onion, tomato and lettuce. Dress, as desired, with catsup, mustard or steak sauce. Serves 6.

*Broiled Quesadillas***

If fried foods raise the eyebrows of your health food purists, keep them happy by broiling these tortilla treats instead of frying them the traditional way. (Makes less mess, too.) Make sure the tortillas are very fresh and "bendable."

1/4 cup shredded Jack cheese	1 to 2 tablespoons chopped canned green chiles
1/4 cup shredded Cheddar cheese	1 medium-size (about 8 inches) flour tortilla
1 to 2 tablespoons minced onion	3 teaspoons melted margarine

Sprinkle cheeses, onion and chiles over half the tortilla, leaving 1/2 inch border clear. Fold in half; brush top with melted margarine. Invert onto a small baking pan and brush second side with margarine. Broil under high heat for about 2 minutes, or until top is lightly browned. Flip over and broil until second side is golden. Serves 1.

NOTE: Just about anything that strikes your fancy can be tossed into one of these flipped-over concoctions. Meat, sausage, olives, avocados . . . you name it, add it.

Tortilla Burger**

Here is a burger on a corn tortilla, topped with a fried egg and dolloped with shredded cheese and sour cream. A real meal-in-itself with spicy Mexican overtones.

6 fresh corn tortillas	Salt and pepper
1 pound ground beef	1 cup shredded lettuce
1 16-ounce can refried beans	1 8-ounce jar taco sauce
2 tablespoons butter	1/2 cup shredded Jack cheese
6 eggs	1 cup sour cream

Shape ground beef into 6 patties and cook, medium rare, in a heavy skillet, turning once.

While the meat cooks, heat the refried beans in a small saucepan and keep warm. Wrap tortillas in foil and place in a 325° F. oven.

Melt butter in a 10-inch skillet. When sizzling, fry eggs, 3 at a time, until whites are set but yolks are still soft. Sprinkle with salt and pepper.

To serve, place a tortilla on a heated plate, spread with refried beans, top with shredded lettuce, then a beef patty. Pour taco sauce over all, top with a fried egg, and sprinkle with shredded cheese. Spoon a dollop of sour cream on top and serve. Repeat with remaining tortillas. Serves 6.

Sweet 'n Sour Burgers**

For a hearty main-dish sandwich that takes a novel turn, try this Polynesian burger on a big bun.

1 pound ground beef	1/3 cup brown sugar
1 teaspoon garlic salt	1 tablespoons Worcestershire
1/4 teaspoon pepper	sauce
6 slices canned pineapple,	1/3 cup red wine
drained	6 green pepper rings
1 tablespoon soy sauce	6 onion (or Kaiser) rolls

Season beef with garlic salt and pepper, and lightly shape into 6 patties. Quickly brown on both sides in a heavy skillet and pour off excess fat. On each patty place a slice of pineapple and a green pepper ring. Combine soy sauce, sugar, Worcestershire sauce and red wine. Pour over meat and cover skillet.

Simmer slowly for 8 to 10 minutes, testing meat with a fork to check on the degree of doneness you want.

Split heated bun and place a patty in each one. Drizzle with a little additional pan juices. Serves 6.

Mu Shu Burgers**

In Chinese eateries, mu shu pork — a garlicky pork-and-sprout combination (pronounced moo-shee) comes served in delicate tortilla-like wrappers. By substituting fresh flour tortillas for the Chinese wrappers, you can duplicate close to the real thing at home.

1 pound lean ground pork	1/2 teaspoon grated fresh ginger
1 small onion, chopped	3/4 cup hoisin sauce (available in
1/4 cup dry bread crumbs	Oriental markets)
1 egg	1 cup green onions, slit into
1/2 cup finely chopped water	matchstick pieces
chestnuts	1 cup bean sprouts
2 cloves garlic, minced	1/2 cup chopped cilantro
2 tablespoons soy sauce	8 fresh 8-inch flour tortillas

Combine pork, onion, crumbs, egg, water chestnuts, garlic, soy sauce and ginger. Mix well and shape into 8 small cigar-shaped rolls about 3 inches long. Cook in a heavy skillet, turning to brown on all sides until meat is no longer pink in the middle. For ease of assembly, place the hoisin sauce, green onions, sprouts and cilantro in saucers on your work surface.

Lightly moisten both sides of the tortillas, then place on a hot griddle long enough to heat through. (The tortillas must be very soft to roll properly.)

Spread each tortilla with hoisin sauce, place a pork roll near the lower edge and top with onions, sprouts and cilantro. Fold edges of tortilla over filling, then tightly roll to encase the filling. Serve with plum sauce or additional hoisin for dunking. Makes 8.

Chile Burrito**

Burritos — "little burros" — are Mexico's answer to the burger. Served warm and eaten, precariously, out of hand, a burrito is easy to assemble provided the tortillas are soft and fresh enough to roll easily.

2 tomatoes, chopped	Salt and pepper
1 cup finely chopped green	2 cups canned chile con carne
onions	4 large (about 10 inches) flour
2 to 3 canned green chiles,	tortillas
chopped	Shredded Jack cheese
2 tablespoons minced cilantro	Guacamole
(optional)	1/2 cup sour cream

Combine tomatoes, onions, chiles, cilantro (optional), and salt and pepper in a bowl. Cover and set aside until serving time.

Simmer the chile con carne over low heat until most of the liquid has evaporated and mixture thickens.

Heat tortillas on an ungreased griddle until warm and pliable. Over the lower third of each tortilla spread the thickened chile con carne, then top with cheese, guacamole, sour cream and the salsa. Roll up, tucking in the sides as you go. Wrap burritos in waxed paper and serve at once. Serves 4.

Hot Dogs in Beer*

*Next time you have a gang over to watch the World Series, try serving Hot Dogs in Beer. Snugged down in Beer Buns, these plump franks prove you really **can** teach an old dog a new trick!*

Marinate as many frankfurters as you plan to serve in enough beer to cover. Marinate for several hours. At serving time, place the franks — in the beer — over medium heat, adding a chopped onion to the pot. Bring to a boil and quickly remove from heat. Cover the pan and let the franks sit in the hot brew for 5 minutes. Drain and serve on plain buns or, better yet, Beer Buns.

Beer Buns*

1 13-3/4-ounce package hot roll mix	1/4 cup grated Parmesan cheese
1 tablespoon instant onion flakes	3/4 cup beer
1 teaspoon paprika	1 egg

Open the packaged hot roll mix and remove the yeast. To the dry mix add the dried onion flakes, paprika, and Parmesan cheese.

Heat beer in a small saucepan until lukewarm (don't get it too hot), then stir in the yeast. When blended, add the egg. Stir this into the dry ingredients, mixing until a soft dough is formed. Cover bowl and let the mix rise in a warm place until doubled in bulk.

Punch down and knead lightly on a floured board until smooth. Cut dough into 10 pieces. Roll each piece into a smooth oblong, about 7 inches long. Place on a lightly greased cookie sheet and let rise until doubled. Bake in a 375° F. oven for 15 to 20 minutes, or until nicely browned. Makes 10 beer buns.

Texas Chili Dogs**

Can't decide if you want a hog dog or a hamburger? Here is a blockbuster that heaps ground beef over franks, giving you the best of both worlds in a single bun.

1/2 pound ground beef	1 teaspoon salt
2 Bermuda onions, chopped	1/2 teaspoon ground cumin
1 16-ounce can whole tomatoes, undrained	8 frankfurters
1-1/2 tablespoons chili powder	8 crusty French rolls, heated
1 teaspoon brown sugar	1/4 pound grated Cheddar cheese
	1/2 large onion, diced

Combine beef with chopped onion; cook in a heavy skillet over medium heat until onion is transparent. Drain off fat. Add tomatoes, chili powder, brown sugar, salt, and cumin — breaking up tomatoes with a spoon. Bring to a boil, reduce heat and simmer, covered, for 10 minutes.

Steam frankfurters.

Split rolls without cutting all the way through. Press open and tear out part of the soft centers, leaving hollowed-out shells.

Place a frankfurter in each roll and cover with meat-tomato sauce; heap with cheese and onion. Serves 8.

Deli Chopped Liver**

One of the great treats of all time is the chopped liver that Jewish delis serve up in thick mounds on rye bread. This recipe comes from a Kosher family that says, for best results, you need absolutely top-quality beef or calf liver.

1 large onion, sliced	2 teaspoons water
2 cloves garlic, minced	2 tablespoons mayonnaise
1 tablespoon oil	Salt and pepper
1-1/2 pounds beef liver	

Saute onion and garlic in oil until onion is transparent. Add the liver and cook until nicely browned on both sides, but pink in the center. Do not overcook. Cool.

Cut the liver into chunks and put through a meat grinder along with the onions and garlic. (If you use a food processor, do not over-chop.

Mix the liver with water, mayonnaise, salt and pepper. If mix is too dry, add a few drops of oil. Makes enough spread for 8 to 10 sandwiches.

Chicken-Liver Bagels**

Here's another lunchtime treat with Kosher overtones.

1/2 pound (about 1 cup) chicken livers	2 hard-cooked eggs
	2 teaspoons minced parsley
3 tablespoons margarine	Salt and pepper
1 onion, minced	4 bagels

Saute livers in margarine until lightly browned, but still pink in the middle. Add onion and cook another 3 to 5 minutes. Chop livers, onions and hard-cooked eggs by hand, or in a food processor, taking care not to over-process. Add minced parsley and season, to taste, with salt and pepper. Spread thickly on split, warmed bagels.

Paisano Sandwich*

These Italian sausage sandwiches are gorgeously gooey. Serve with big paper napkins and plenty of red wine.

1 pound hot Italian sausage	5 cups spaghetti sauce
3 green peppers, chopped	1/2 teaspoon basil
2 cloves garlic, minced	4 crusty French rolls
2 onions, chopped	1 cup water
3 tablespoons olive oil	1/4 cup olive oil

Simmer sausages in a skillet with 1 cup water for 10 minutes. Pour off water and brown sausages in the same pan, turning as they cook. When browned, remove and set aside. In the same skillet, saute garlic, green pepper and onion in 3 tablespoons olive oil. Cook until tender but not browned. Add spaghetti sauce and basil and bring to a slow simmer. Place sausages in a baking dish and cover with sauce. Bake at 350° F. for 1 hour. Warm rolls and cut in half lengthwise. Fill rolls with sausages and spoon on plenty of sauce. Serves 4.

Reuben Toast-Toppers**

If you like Reuben Sandwiches, you'll love this next one. The combination of sauerkraut and corned beef can be made ahead of time, leaving nothing to do later but heat and heap the mix on rye toast.

1 27-ounce can sauerkraut	1 12-ounce can corned beef,
1 large tomato, chopped	diced
1/4 cup catsup	6 slices Jewish rye bread, lightly
1/2 cup mayonnaise	toasted
1/2 cup finely minced onion	1/2 pound Swiss cheese, shredded
1/2 teaspoon caraway seeds	

Combine everything but the toast and shredded cheese; mix well. Spoon into a greased 9-inch square baking pan and heat at 425° F. for 20 minutes. When mix is hot and bubbling, spread over toast and top with shredded cheese. Pass the horseradish. Serves 6 bountifully.

Econo-Reubens*

This pseudo-Reuben sandwich calls for ground beef which can be easier on the budget than corned beef.

1 pound ground beef	1 8-ounce can sauerkraut, drained
1 rounded tablespoon dry onion	1/2 cup chile sauce (or catsup)
soup mix	4 slices Swiss or Jack cheese
1 tablespoon mustard	8 slices rye bread, toasted
Dash Worcestershire sauce	

Combine beef with onion soup mix, mustard, and Worcestershire. Shape into 4 patties and fry medium-rare in a heavy skillet.

Top each patty with one-fourth of the sauerkraut, drizzle with chili sauce (or catsup), and top with cheese. Cover the pan and cook until the cheese melts. Place on toast, topping with second slice. Cut sandwiches on the diagonal. Serves 4.

Milwaukee Wurst Grills*

Also somewhat reminiscent of the standard Reuben is this grilled sandwich that features knockwurst, onions and melted cheese.

6 knockwurst	12 slices Swiss cheese
12 thick slices sour dough	1 large onion, thinly sliced
bread	Butter
1/2 cup Thousand Island	
Dressing	

Simmer knockwurst in small amount of water for 6 to 8 minutes. Remove and cut sausage lengthwise into 4 slices.

Spread dressing on 12 pieces of bread. On 6 slices layer the knockwurst, 2 slices of cheese and onion. Top with remaining bread. Butter sandwiches on both sides and grill until golden on both sides and cheese is melted. Makes 6.

What's Ahead in
The Watering Hole

The Watering Hole

. . . a basic primer of party potables

What follows here is a modest collection of beverages (including a few non-alcoholic quaffs) that are quick to mix, easy on the pocketbook and unique enough to fall outside the standard bar guide.

Understand that this is by no means a complete reference piece. Rather we will skip lightly over and around the subject of booze and beverage — a small sip here, a wee nip there — just enough to have a good time exploring.

But first a couple of broad generalizations are worth stating.

Booze, like perfume, is a very personal thing. This is especially true of wine.

You will notice that some of the trendiest people in town will loll about, sipping supermarket jug wines, while others —,especially those who have just completed a weekend wine-tasting course — will demand French imports, then spend the evening sniffing and gargling as if they have something caught on their cuspids.

Obviously, with wine, it's everyone for himself. And no matter what the books say, a good one need not be expensive. Unfortunately, the same thing doesn't hold for the hard stuff.

A good Scotch doesn't have to be the costliest brand on the shelf, but it better not be the least expensive, either. The same goes for gins, bourbons and vodka. And a cheap tequila can **kill**.

If you are in a swivet about what constitutes a reliable brand, **ask**. A good bartender is usually a dependable source of information.

Fruit drinks, punches and fizzes are okay for parties and ladies' luncheons. But, beyond that, it seems to me that a good Scotch or bourbon — which is expensive — is best served plain, with water, soda or straight mix.

If, God forbid, you want to make Pink Ladies or some exotic rum drink served with a flower and a teeny paper parasol, get a bar book. And give it a second thought before you cast off and ruin a lot of good booze.

Sweet and Sour Mix*

Many bar drinks, punches and fruit drinks call for sweet and sour mix and simple syrup. Both are easily made at home. Make ahead and keep refrigerated.

2 cups fresh lemon juice   1 cup sugar

Stir together until sugar dissolves, then refrigerate. Makes 2-1/2 cups.

Simple Syrup*

1 cup water   1 cup sugar

Mix until sugar dissolves. Refrigerate. Makes 2 cups.

Kir*

A favorite before-dinner drink with Europeans is a light beverage that combines dry white wine and creme de cassis, a sweet black currant liqueur. The combination is called Kir (pronounced keer) and is rapidly gaining in popularity in these parts with people interested in lighter, less alcoholic aperitifs.

The proportions can vary, but while you are concocting, bear in mind that the more cassis you use, the sweeter the drink. A good mix for most tastes is one tablespoon creme de cassis to four ounces of white wine.

For an ultra-fancy approach, decant the cassis into iced tulip glasses, then fill with chilled champagne.

Bacardi Crush*

Try this one on the ladies. They'll love it!

3 slices canned or fresh   2 jiggers lemon juice
  pineapple   6 jiggers light Bacardi rum
2 cups finely crushed ice   4 maraschino cherries, with stems
1 jigger grenadine

Place pineapple and crushed ice in a blender. Process as you add the grenadine, lemon juice and rum. Serve the slush in sherbet glasses garnished with cherries. Serves 4.

Strawberry Champagne Sipper*

This next one packs a lot of punch if you don't dilute the mix with a little club soda. (Whether or not you do is up to you and the constitution of the people you are serving. Either way, it's a winner.)

1 pound fresh strawberries   1 bottle champagne, chilled
1 cup sugar   3 bottles Rhine wine, chilled
1 cup brandy   Club soda (optional)

Place washed and stemmed strawberries in a large bowl, add sugar and brandy and refrigerate 1 hour. Place berries and brandy in a punch bowl, add the champagne and wine. Dilute, if you wish, with chilled club soda.

Frothy Pina Colada*

The coconut milk called for in tropical libations such as Pina Coladas is available in liquor stores.

1/2 cup coconut milk	4 ice cubes, cracked
1 cup pineapple juice	Pineapple chunks
3/4 cup light rum	Maraschino cherries
1 teaspoon coconut flavoring	

Process coconut milk, juice, rum and coconut flavoring with cracked ice in a blender until smooth and frothy. Pour into stemmed glasses and garnish with pineapple chunks and cherries threaded on wood picks. Makes 4 drinks.

Scrumptious Strawberry Daiquiris*

Love strawberry daiquiris? No need to wait 'til berry season. This version uses frozen berries in tandem with bananas — a year-round treat you can whip up in a wink.

1 cup light rum, well chilled	2 cups frozen strawberries,
3/4 cup lime juice	unthawed
1/4 cup sugar	2 cups chopped bananas

Process rum and lime juice with sugar in a blender. When sugar has dissolved, add the frozen berries and bananas. Blend until smooth. Serve in frosted glasses. Serves 6.

Derby Daiquiris*

The man who gave me this recipe says this makes the best daiquiri in captivity. I've made them, and I am not going to argue that point.

1 ounce orange juice	1-1/2 ounces light rum
1/2 ounce lime juice (preferably	1 ounce simple syrup (Page 222)
Key limes)	1 cup crushed ice

Blend orange juice, lime juice, rum and syrup in a blender. Add crushed ice and process on high speed for 10 seconds. Serves 2.

These outstanding daiquiris shouldn't be doubled up. Mix no more than two drinks per batch.

Make-Ahead Frozen Daiquiris*

Apart from the fact that Daiquiris are about the most refreshing hot-weather drink imaginable, another plus is that this version can be made up in batches and frozen ahead of time. Saves last-minute measuring and messing around.

1 6-ounce can frozen limeade	18 ounces light rum
1 6-ounce can water	1 quart carbonated grapefruit mix

Combine and freeze until slushy. Stir quickly and spoon into short cocktail glasses. Serves 12 to 14.

Peaches Elegant*

Here is the most elegant (and easiest) of all after-dinner drinks — chilled champagne and peaches.

4 firm, ripe peaches   **1 bottle chilled champagne**
1/2 cup brandy

Peel peaches and pierce gently with a fork. Set in a small bowl, drizzle with brandy and let marinate in the refrigerator until well-permeated.

To serve, chill champagne glasses, then place 2 teaspoons of the brandy in each glass. Add a peach, then fill the glasses with chilled champagne. (And **do** provide slender spoons so that guests may eat the peaches!) Serves 4.

Pimm's Cup*

No English pub worth a tuppence would be caught without Pimm's Cup — a light and frisky mix that is a nice change from the standard collins-type drinks. To make Pimm's Cups at home, you need a bottle of Pimm's No. 1 (most liquor stores stock it) and a couple of cucumber sticks to use as swizzles.

16 ounces collins mix   **2 ounces lemon-lime soda**
8 ounces Pimm's No. 1   **2 unpeeled cucumbers, quartered
                                              lengthwise**

Combine first three ingredients in a large pitcher and stir. Pour into collins glasses filled with crushed ice. Garnish each glass with a cucumber swizzle. Serves 8.

Lovely Fizzes . . . Take Your Pick

Everyone in our family loves Ramos Fizzes. Over the years it has become a custom to whip them up for Christmas morning brunch, a light and lovely way to toast the long day ahead. Here, for your pleasure, are three different versions.

New Orleans Ramos Fizz*

1-1/2 ounces gin   **1/2 teaspoon vanilla**
1 teaspoon powdered sugar   **1 egg white**
1/2 teaspoon orange flower   **3 ounces half-and-half**
**   water**   **Soda**

Mix everything but soda in a blender. Add 1/2-cup crushed ice. Blend. Pour into a highball glass and fill with soda. Serves 2.

Roaring 20's Ramos Fizz*

Juice of 1 lemon   **1-1/2 ounces whipping cream**
1-1/2 tablespoons powdered   **1 teaspoon orange flower water**
sugar   **6 ice cubes, cracked**
2 ounces gin   **Iced champagne**
1 egg white

Combine lemon juice and sugar and stir. Add gin, egg white, cream and orange flower water and pour into a blender. Add ice and process briefly until ice is pulverized. Pour into champagne flutes, filling part way. Top off with chilled champagne and serve. Serves 2.

Three Can Fizz*

This easy, fruity fizz is one of our favorites. Make plenty. Everyone always wants two.

1 8-ounce can frozen lemonade	1/3 can orange juice
1 can vodka	1 egg white
1 can light cream (or half-and-half)	1 teaspoon vanilla
	6 ice cubes

Process in a blender until frothy. Serves 4 — amply.

Spoon'en Eggnog**

Connoisseurs of holiday eggnogs contend the mix has to be so stiff you eat it with a spoon. That being the case, this next recipe really fills the bill. Try one and you will be well-filled, too.

12 egg yolks	1 quart whipping cream, whipped stiff
3 cups sugar	6 egg whites, whipped stiff
1 quart straight whiskey	Grated nutmeg, optional

Beat yolks, then add 1-1/2 cups sugar. Mix well; then stir in the whiskey. Add the cream that has been whipped with another 1/2 cup sugar. Finally, fold in egg whites that have been beaten with the remaining 1 cup sugar. Spoon into small cups and serve with a spoon. Sprinkle each serving with a light drift of nutmeg, if desired. Serves 12 to 14.

After Dinner Drinks

The problem of what to serve for dessert can be neatly solved if you skip it entirely and simply serve an opulent after-dinner drink that richly fills the bill. Like Sherried Coffee. Or Coffee Royale. Or Kahlua Chocolate Toddy. These and a couple of other sweet treats follow.

Sherried Coffee*

2 tablespoons sherry	2 cups strong hot coffee
2 tablespoons brandy	Whipped cream
1/2 cup chocolate ice cream	Nutmeg

Heat two cups with boiling water, then empty and dry. In each cup place 1 tablespoon each of sherry and brandy. Then add 1/4 cup rich chocolate ice cream and fill with steaming hot coffee. Top with a dollop of lightly sweetened whipped cream and dust with freshly grated nutmeg. Serves 2.

Coffee Royale*

Fill heated cups half full with strong, hot coffee. Add 2 tablespoons brandy and garnish with a dollop of whipped cream and a sprinkling of finely grated orange peel.

Kahlua Chocolate Toddy*

Skip the cheesecake and apple pie a la mode. Instead, squander the calories on this sumptuous blend of Kahlua, chocolate and cream.

1 ounce semi-sweet chocolate	1 cup half-and-half, heated to a
2 tablespoons sugar	simmer
1 cup boiling water	1 cup fresh hot coffee
1 teaspoon vanilla extract	Whipped cream
2 tablespoons kahlua	Dash nutmeg

Melt chocolate and sugar in boiling water. Add vanilla and kahlua; mix well. Add half-and-half and coffee. Serve in mugs; top off with whipped cream and a drift of nutmeg. Serves 4.

Irish Coffee*

If you didn't know better, you could really be faked out of trying to make Irish Coffee, with all that hoopla about warming the glasses, melting the sugar and like that. Well, you don't have to go to all that bother. Here's the easy way.

Simply combine 1-1/2 teaspoons sugar and a couple tablespoons of hot coffee in an Irish coffee glass or stemmed glass, stirring until the sugar dissolves. Then add 1/4 cup of Irish whiskey and fill the glass to within 1 inch of the top with strong, hot coffee. Float fat globs of sweetened whipped cream on each glass and dust with nutmeg. Makes one serving.

Espresso Inferno*

If you like espresso, don't be conned into thinking you need a machine to crank out these after-dinner treats. Instant espresso coffee powder or crystals are available in the gourmet section of most supermarkets. Unlike run-of-the-mill instant coffee powders, these espressos are really very good.

3 cups strong espresso coffee	1 cup whipping cream
4 tablespoons amaretto	2 tablespoons powdered sugar
4 tablespoons chocolate syrup	

Prepare espresso with instant granules according to package instructions. Rinse four demitasse cups with hot water, then place 1 tablespoon amaretto in each one. Add 1 tablespoon chocolate syrup to each cup and fill with hot espresso. Top with a dollop of whipped cream sweetened with powdered sugar. Serves 4.

Acapulco Coffee Mix*

If you liked that last one, you might consider making up a batch of after-dinner coffee mix that can be stashed on the shelf, ready to use at a moment's notice — no fuss, no bother. You will need another bottle of instant espresso coffee powder and some powdered coffee creamer for this blend.

3/4 cup instant espresso
  coffee powder
1 cup sugar

1/2 cup powdered coffee creamer
1/2 cup unsweetened cocoa

Mix ingredients until blended, then store in a tightly covered container. Makes about 1-1/2 cups mix.

Use 2 tablespoons mix and 1 cup boiling water, and serve with a cinnamon stick swizzle. Makes 1 cup after-dinner drink.

NOTE: A jar of the superb coffee mix would make a lovely hostess gift packaged in a pretty jar or bottle. A neat trick is to tie a half-dozen cinnamon stick "swizzles" onto the jar with a big, fat bow.

Tijuana Punch Bowl*

This punch is not for the tenderhearted. Reserve this one for those friends who can eat chile peppers whole and keep right on smiling. Enough said?

1 quart vodka
2 cups sweet and sour mix
  (page 222)

1 quart club soda
1 12-ounce can beer

Mix ingredients in a small punch bowl. An ice ring studded with sliced limes makes a lovely — and cooling — touch. Serves 20 to 25.

Shandygaff*

When it's 105 degrees in the shade, try a Shandygaff — ginger ale with an unexpected whammy.

Chilled beer

Chilled ginger ale

Fill a frosted pilsner glass half way with cold beer. Top off with ginger ale. Skoal!

Tomato Beer*

A popular hot weather drink at our house has always been Tomato Beer. Just be sure to have the beer and tomato juice icy-cold. You really can't add ice to this one.

Chilled tomato juice
Chilled beer
Worcestershire sauce (to taste)

Tabasco sauce, to taste
Sprinkle of salt (optional)

Fill a tall glass half full of tomato juice, then top off with beer. Add Worcestershire sauce, to taste (1 teaspoon is about right), and enough Tabasco to add zap. Judge for yourself if it needs salt.

Close-to-Julius Orange Drink*

Speculation keeps surfacing regarding the formula for Orange Julius — the creamy orange drink that used to be vended from bright orange stands on every other street corner. So far, no one has been able to ferret out the secret ingredient, although stalwarts keep trying. This version puts vanilla pudding in the mix and claims to come as close as any to the real McCoy.

2 cups crushed ice   1 teaspoon vanilla
1 cup orange juice   3/4 cup simple syrup (page 222)
1 rounded tablespoon vanilla
  pudding (or custard) mix

Place ingredients in a blender and process until blended — but stop while ice crystals still have "crunch." Serves 4.

Orange Juliana Mix*

For another reasonable facsimile of those Julius treats we all loved as kids, make a big batch of this ready-to-go mix and keep it handy for quick pick-ups.

1-3/4 cups dry milk powder   3/4 cup sugar
1 9-ounce jar orange-flavored   2-1/2 teaspoons vanilla
  breakfast drink powder

Mix ingredients and store in a closed container. Makes 4 cups mix.
For one serving, process 1/3 cup mix, 1/2 cup water and 4 ice cubes in a blender. Blend on high speed until smooth.

Boozy Julius*

This version of the Julius puts a little gin in the works, and isn't a bit the worse for it.

1-1/2 ounces gin   Juice of 1/4 lime
1/2 cup orange sherbet   2 teaspoons powdered sugar
2 ounces frozen orange   1 ounce cream
  juice concentrate   2 ice cubes
4 ounces lemon-lime
  carbonated soda

Whip ingredients in a blender until frothy. Serves 2. Or 1, if you are really thirsty.

Dessert-in-a-Goblet*

These next two goodies feature ice cream liberally laced with liqueurs. Serve them in frosted goblets, and please pass spoons.

6 ounces kahlua   1/2 gallon vanilla ice cream
3 ounces brandy   1 cup crushed ice

Process in batches in a blender until mix is thick but pourable. Serve in frosted goblets with a faint dusting of nutmeg. Serves 6 to 8.

Golden Torpedos*

1 ounce Galliano
1/2 ounce Amaretto

2 scoops ice cream

Combine in a blender until smooth. Serves 1.

Margarita Punch*

Next time you plan a big Mexican-themed party, you might simplify the bar and booze problem by simply stirring up a giant batch of margaritas and decanting them from a punch bowl.

3 quarts tequila
1 quart Triple Sec
2 cups lemon juice
2 cups fresh lime juice

2 quarts club soda
Kosher salt
Lemon wedges

Combine tequila, Triple Sec, juices and soda; chill thoroughly. To serve, pour chilled mixture into a punch bowl over a large block of ice. In a small bowl or saucer, pour one inch of coarse Kosher salt. Run lemon wedges around the rim of stemmed glasses and press rims into the salt. Ladle punch into the salt-rimmed glasses and serve. Serves approximately 50.

Sunshine Spritzer*

A marvelous Sunday morning eye-opener and appetite-whetter is this bright and bubbly non-alcoholic spritzer . . . a great way to get things going.

1 6-ounce can frozen orange
   juice
1 6-ounce can frozen
   pineapple juice
12 ounces water

2 small bottles club soda, chilled
Dash Angostura bitters
Maraschino cherries
Orange slices

Blend frozen juices with water, soda and bitters. Fasten cherries to half-slices of oranges with toothpicks, "Old Fashioned" style. Place skewered fruit in champagne or old-fashioned glasses and fill with soda-fruit juice mix. Cheers!

Hangover Shakes*

I don't know if this is pure hearsay or hair of the dog, but someone said that a gentle blend of ice cream and booze can be a real lifesaver the morning after the night before. You might try it some Sunday morning when you're not sure you'll ever live to see Monday.

3 jiggers brandy
1/2 pint vanilla ice cream
1/2 cup whole milk

1/2 teaspoon vanilla
Grated nutmeg

Divide brandy between two tall glasses. Whip ice cream and milk in a blender until frothy. Add vanilla and pour into the glasses. Top with drifts of grated nutmeg. And get well. Saves 2.

Pineapple Cheesecake-in-a-Glass*

If you like pineapple cheesecake, you will flip over this one!

1 15-ounce can pineapple   **1 pint vanilla ice cream**
  chunks, undrained   **1 teaspoon vanilla flavoring**
1 cup buttermilk

Chill pineapple, then pour — with juice — into a blender container. Add the buttermilk and ice cream by spoonfuls. Add vanilla flavoring and process on high speed until smooth. Serves 4.

Cucumber Smoothie*

Suffering from the mid-morning blahs? Perk up! Here is a great pick-up to take to work in a thermos.

1 medium cucumber, peeled   **Dash dillweed**
  and sliced   **1/4 teaspoon salt**
2 cups chilled buttermilk

Cucumber should measure about 1-2/3 cups, thinly peeled. Place cucumber and remaining ingredients in a blender and process until smooth. Chill well before serving or decanting into a thermos. Makes 2 large drinks.

Mocha Coffee*

Instant coffee powder gets a leg up in this distinctive mix that gets a flavor assist from cinnamon and orange peel.

4 ounces instant   **1/2 cup dry nonfat milk powder**
  coffee powder   **1 teaspoon cinnamon**
1/2 cup cocoa   **1-1/2 teaspoons dried orange peel**

Mix all ingredients together and store in a tightly covered container. For 1 serving, blend 3 teaspoons mix into 1 cup boiling water.

Make-Ahead Lemonade Syrup*

No need to squeeze lemons every time a big thirst hits next summer. This syrup made from fresh lemons keeps for weeks in the refrigerator — ready at a moment's notice to make frosty pitchers of lemonade.

6 large lemons   **2 cups sugar**
2 cups water

With a swivel-type peeler, cut the yellow rind off the lemons in thin strips. Bring water and sugar to boil in a heavy saucepan; drop in the rind and simmer, covered, for 5 minutes. Discard the rind and set the syrup aside to cool.

Squeeze juice from the lemons; strain and add to the cooled syrup. Store in a covered bottle in the refrigerator.

To make lemonade, combine 1 cup syrup with 3 cups ice water, stirring well. Add ice and serve.

Instanter Iced Tea*

For ice tea addicts, this wait-and-see recipe is a real treasure. There's no steeping, boiling or messing about required. Just an overnight layover in the fridge is all it takes to turn out a crystal-clear, hassle-free brew.

1 quart cold water	5 heaping teaspoons tea

Stir dry tea into 1 quart of cold water, cover and place in the refrigerator overnight. The next day, it's ready if you are. Just like that!

Mint Tea*

Hot and spicy tea can be brewed in a minute if you keep this minty mix handy in the cupboard.

1/2 pound orange pekoe tea	2 tablespoons whole cloves
2 tablespoons dried mint	1 tablespoon dried lemon peel

Mix all ingredients together and store in a tightly covered container. For 1 serving, steep 1 teaspoon of the mixture in 1 cup boiling water for 6 to 10 minutes.

May Day Punch*

Face it, most champagne punches are only so-so. A notable exception is this one that is very simple and very good — a great choice for a wedding reception or bridal shower.

1 12-ounce can frozen orange juice, thawed	4 tablespoons simple syrup (page 222)
4-1/2 cups water	2 bottles chilled champagne
4 teaspoons rose water	

Combine orange juice concentrate and water in a large punch bowl. Add rose water and simple syrup. Slowly add champagne, pouring down side of bowl. Stir gently. Add ice. Makes 12 servings.

Coco Palms Famous Mai Tais*

One of the most elegant resort hotels in the world is the lush Coco Palms in Kauai. For a taste of the Coco Palms at home, try one of their famous Mai Tais.

1 cup sweet and sour mix (page 222)	1 tablespoon grenadine
	Dark rum
1 cup pineapple juice	Light rum
2 cups orange juice	Pineapple spears

Combine sweet-and-sour mix, juices and grenadine. Store in the refrigerator. For one drink, gently pour 1 jigger of dark rum, then 1 jigger of light rum into a tall glass. Fill to 1 inch of the top with juice mixture, then pack with cracked ice. Garnish with a pineapple spear.

This mixture is enough for about 6 Mai Tais.

Margarita Froth**

*Trying to estimate how many recipes are floating around these parts for the "perfect margarita" would be like guessing how many beans are in a 10-gallon drum. Everyone has his own favorite mix. However, aficionados all agree on one thing: the good margarita **must** be made from scratch — so ditch those bottled and packaged pre-mixes.*

1 lime, cut in quarters	1 cup Triple Sec
Coarse salt	1/4 cup pineapple juice
1/2 cup tequila	1/4 cup fresh lemon juice
1/2 cup sweet and sour mix	3 egg whites
(Page 222)	6 to 8 ice cubes

Run lime around the rim of 3 stemmed glasses. Dip rims in salt.
Measure remaining ingredients in a blender and process until frothy. Serves 3.
NOTE: If you prefer more substance than froth, omit the egg white.

Strawberry Margarita*

Follow directions for Margarita Froth (above), substituting 1/2 cup sliced, fresh strawberries for the pineapple juice.

Caribbean Banana Beer*

This make-ahead frozen fruit slush is great to have on hand for instant thirst-quenchers when the weather gets hot. Kids love it. For the adults, you might try adding a jigger of vodka to each glass.

5 bananas, mashed	5 cups sugar
Juice of 5 oranges	7 cups water
Juice of 5 lemons	Ginger ale

Blend bananas with juices, sugar and water. Spoon into ice cube trays and freeze. To serve, fill glasses 1/3 full with the frozen juice mix, then top with chilled ginger ale. Mix briefly, then serve. Makes enough frozen mix for approximately 30 drinks.

Coffee Liqueur*

A few years ago, a mania for making homemade liqueurs surfaced. These "home brews" make great little gifts around the holidays. Start now to save pretty bottles.

4 cups boiling water	1 quart 80-proof vodka
2 cups instant coffee granules	2 vanilla beans
7 cups sugar	

Pour boiling water over coffee granules and sugar. Stir until dissolved. When cool, add vodka. Decant into a 1/2-gallon bottle. Add vanilla beans. Seal and allow to ripen 3 to 4 weeks. Makes 2-1/2 quarts.

Galliano-Type Liqueur*

You need Strega extract for this next one. Look for it in an Italian import grocery store or deli.

4 cups sugar
2 cups water
16 ounces 100-proof vodka

1/2-ounce bottle Strega extract
Dash yellow food coloring

Bring sugar and water to a boil, lower heat and simmer until syrupy — 10 to 15 minutes. Cool. Add vodka, Strega extract and a few drops of coloring. Mix well, bottle and let stand 30 days before using.

Irish Liqueur*

1 cup Irish whiskey
1 14-ounce can sweetened
   condensed milk
2 tablespoons vanilla extract

2 tablespoons chocolate extract
1 tablespoon coconut extract
1 tablespoon powdered espresso
   instant coffee

Blend together all ingredients until smooth. Decant into bottles and refrigerate. Liqueur is ready to serve in 24 hours. Shake well and serve chilled.

Irish Cream*

2 cups 80-proof Irish whiskey
1 cup light corn syrup

1/4 cup sugar
1 cup heavy cream

Mix whiskey, syrup and sugar, stirring until sugar dissolves. Add cream. Shake well, then cover and refrigerate until well chilled. Shake before serving.

Apricot Liqueur*

This next recipe offers a nice serendipity. After the apricots have done their stint in the mix, they can be fished out and used as a tasty garnish for a meat platter — especially ham — or as a topping for ice cream.

2 6-ounce packages
   dried apricots
3 cups water
1 cup sugar

2 cups 80-proof vodka
1-1/2 cups light corn syrup
1/2 cup brandy

In a glass bowl, mix apricots with water and set aside for 15 minutes. Then cover and gently simmer for 10 minutes. Take off heat and stir in sugar until dissolved. Add vodka, syrup and brandy. Cool to lukewarm, stirring occasionally. Pour into a large glass jar, loosely cover and let stand at room temperature for one week.

Drain off liqueur and set aside. Place apricots in a strainer and gently extract juice without pressing pulp through the strainer. Pour liqueur through 4 thicknesses of dampened cheesecloth placed over a colander. Store in the refrigerator. Refrigerate apricots for later use.

What's Ahead in
Cakes

A Piece of Cake

. . . it is if you do it right

Quick! What comes to mind when someone mentions "cake?" Party, of course.
The time will come when your best friend gets a raise, has a baby or wins a case in small claims court and you will want to make a cake. Happily, the cake mix people have made the whole thing — even the frosting — a cinch.

Chocolate fudge layers, feathery angel foods, sponge cakes and crunchy snack cakes all come neatly boxed and ready for the beginner cook to crank out.

Not that making a cake from the ground up isn't sweet satisfaction for the novice. It **is**! And it needn't be all that difficult either.

Just don't let your mother or Aunt Em con you into thinking that the only good cakes are the ones you sift, stir and sweat out from scratch. T'aint so. Some marvelously toothsome and tender confections come straight out of boxes. And with a little improvisation on your part, they can be just as personalized as Aunt Em's double-dark, extra-special devils food. *And half the bother.*

Italian Torte*

This blissful blend of whipped cream, pistachios and anise seed atop angel food cake is a beautiful way to wind down an Italian dinner. It's an easy treat, and if you buy a ready-made cake, it's a real snap.

1 angel food cake	1 teaspoon anise seed, crushed
1 cup whipping cream	1/2 cup golden raisins
1 teaspoon vanilla	1/2 cup chopped pistachio nuts
Confectioners' sugar	

Split cake into three layers. Whip cream until stiff, add vanilla, then sweeten, to taste, with confectioners' sugar. Divide cream into three small bowls.

Fold anise seeds into one portion and spread over the first layer. Add golden raisins to the second portion of cream, and spread over the next two layers. Top cake with whipped cream remaining in the third bowl and sprinkle with pistachio nuts. Chill until ready to serve.

*Peanut Brittle Angel Cake**

Angel food cake is a snap to make with any of the boxed mixes available in the supermarket. Directions differ with the different brands, but they all turn out beautifully — so well one would wonder why anyone would bother with the old multi-egg method.

An even snappier tactic is to buy a plain angel food cake at the corner bakery and gussy it up from there.

1 angel food cake	3 tablespoons powdered sugar
1/2 cup whipping cream	1/4 pound fresh peanut brittle

Whip cream until stiff peaks form and sweeten to taste with powdered sugar. Crush peanut brittle between sheets of waxed paper, then fold the crumbs into the whipped cream. Serve angel food cake in wedges topped with fat dabs of the peanut brittle cream.

*Peppermint Crunch Angel Cake**

Substitute 1/4 pound butter mints for the peanut brittle in Peanut Brittle Angel Cake. Chocolate shavings make a pretty garnish.

*Pistachio Pudding Cake***

Whoever said a cake mix has to be white, yellow, pink or chocolate? Here's how to whip out a pale green cake subtly touched with almond.

1 2-layer size package white cake mix (without pudding)	1/2 cup water
	1/2 cup Amaretto liqueur
1 3-ounce package instant pistachio pudding mix	3/4 teaspoon almond extract
	1/3 teaspoon green food coloring
4 eggs, slightly beaten	Choco-Almond Icing

Combine cake mix with pudding mix, eggs, water, liqueur, almond extract and food coloring. Mix, then beat thoroughly — 5 to 6 minutes. Pour batter into a well-buttered and floured 12-cup bundt cake pan. Bake at 350° F. for 45 minutes. Cool and frost with Choco-Almond Icing.

*Choco-Almond Icing**

2 1-ounce squares unsweetened chocolate	2 cups powdered sugar
	1 tablespoon milk or cream
1/4 cup margarine	1/3 teaspoon almond extract

Melt chocolate and margarine over simmering water. Cool, then add powdered sugar. Gradually add milk, stirring until smooth. (Add a drop or two more liquid if necessary to make a spreadable frosting.) Add extract, beating well.

Beulah's Scrumptious Coconut Cake**

*This next one is for coconut freaks. You start out with a box cake and go crazy — ending up with a three-layer cake that looks fancy as a bakery confection. Just be sure to get the right kind of cake mix — the kind that doesn't already have pudding in it. (Read the label. You want a **plain** cake mix.)*

1 2-layer-size package yellow cake mix	4 eggs
	1/4 cup oil
1 4-serving-size package vanilla instant pudding mix	2 cups flaked coconut
	1 cup chopped pecans
1-1/2 cups water	Coconut Cream Cheese Frosting

Mix cake mix, pudding mix, water, eggs and oil in a large mixing bowl. Beat at medium speed for 4 minutes. Stir in coconut and nuts. Spoon batter into 3 greased and floured 9-inch cake pans and bake at 350° F. for 35 minutes. Cool in pans for 15 minutes, then turn out onto a rack. When layers are completely cooled, fill and frost with Coconut Cream Cheese Frosting.

Coconut Cream Cheese Frosting**

4 tablespoons butter	2 teaspoons milk
2 cups flaked coconut	3-1/2 cups powdered sugar, sifted
1 8-ounce package cream cheese	1/2 teaspoon vanilla

Melt 2 tablespoons of the butter in a skillet. Add coconut and cook, stirring constantly, over low heat until golden brown. Spread the coconut out on a paper towel to cool. Meantime, cream remaining 2 tablespoons butter with cream cheese, blending well. Add milk and beat in sugar gradually. Blend in vanilla and 1-1/3 cups of the toasted coconut. Spread between layers and on top and sides of Beulah's Scrumptious Coconut Cake. Sprinkle with the remaining coconut.

Double Banana Chocolate Chip Cake**

A good banana cake is great as-is. This one is even better with the addition of chocolate chips. (Some day I am going to put some chopped maraschino cherries in the batter, top the cake with whipped cream and call it a Banana Split Bakeoff!)

1 18-ounce package banana cake mix	Dash cinnamon
	3 ripe bananas, mashed
1/4 cup milk	1/2 cup chopped nuts
3 eggs	1 6-ounce package chocolate chips
1/4 cup margarine, softened	Powdered sugar
1/4 cup brown sugar	

In a large mixing bowl, place everything but the nuts; chocolate chips and powdered sugar. Beat well — at least four minutes. Then fold in the nuts and chocolate chips. Spoon batter into a greased and floured 9 x 13-inch pan and bake at 350° F. for 35 minutes. Cool, then sprinkle with powdered sugar. Serves 14 to 16.

Cassata alla Siciliana**

Here is another treat with a fancy Italian name that is really nothing more than angel food cake liberally dolloped with rum and ricotta cheese. Easy elegance, this, for the one-star (*) cook.

1 angel food cake	1/4 cup chopped candied cherries
6 tablespoons rum	1/2 teaspoon cinnamon
1-1/2 pounds ricotta cheese	3/4 cup chopped toasted almonds
3/4 cup powdered sugar	1 can ready-made white icing
1/4 cup grated semi- sweet chocolate	

Slice cake into 4 horizontal layers, using a serrated knife and a gentle sawing motion. Beat ricotta cheese with rum until fluffy.

Beat in sugar until dissolved. Divide into 3 small bowls. Add grated chocolate to one, cherries and cinnamon to another and almonds to the third.

On first cake layer, spread chocolate-cheese filling. Top with second cake layer and spread with cherry mixture. Add third layer and spread with almond-cheese filling. Top with fourth layer. Frost top and sides of cake with white icing. Refrigerate 6 to 8 hours before serving. Serves 8 to 10.

Yogurt Cake**

You can make this next one-bowl cake with any flavor yogurt that strikes your fancy. The friend who gave me this recipe says she likes raspberry best, but then she loves anything pink.

1 cup margarine	1 teaspoon vanilla
2 cups sugar	2-1/4 cups flour
3 eggs	1/2 teaspoon baking soda
1 8-ounce carton flavored yogurt	1/2 teaspoon salt Glaze

Cream margarine with sugar until fluffy. Add the eggs and the yogurt. Stir in the vanilla. Sift flour, baking soda and salt together, then add all at once to the first mixture. Beat well. Spoon batter into a greased bundt pan and bake at 325° F. for 50 to 60 minutes. Cool slightly, remove from pan and glaze.

Glaze*

1 cup powdered sugar	1 teaspoons cinnamon
2 tablespoons milk	

Combine all ingredients and spread over warm Yogurt Cake.

Hands-Off Cake**

Hands-Off Cake is not something you can whip up for dinner tonight. This one takes a five-day head start, but it's worth it if you can find enough room in the refrigerator to keep it safely stashed.

1 pound shredded coconut	**1 cup sugar**
1 pint sour cream	**1 box plain yellow cake mix**

Five days before you plan to serve the cake, combine the coconut, sour cream and sugar. Cover and refrigerate overnight.

Next day, prepare cake mix according to package instructions, baking in two 9-inch layers. When cool, slice each layer horizontally, making four layers. spread the tops of each layer (not the sides) with the prepared icing. Stack and loosely cover with plastic wrap. Refrigerate four days.

While the cake languishes for four days, warn everyone to keep his hands off. When the time's up, serve with pride to the family that will no doubt ask what all the delay was about. (Tell them the hangup contributed to the cake's consistency which may, or may not be a good enough answer.) ·

Cointreau Cake**

If you can bring yourself to squander a cupful of cointreau in this next recipe, you will have a truly elegant made-from-scratch, one-bowl cake.

2-3/4 cups sifted cake flour	**1 teaspoon vanilla**
3/4 teaspoon baking soda	**5 eggs**
1/2 teaspoon salt	**4 1-ounce squares unsweetened**
1 cup butter (or margarine)	**chocolate, melted**
1-3/4 cups sugar	**1/2 cup buttermilk**
1/2 cup light corn syrup	**1 cup cointreau**

Sift flour, add baking soda and salt; sift again. In another bowl, cream butter and sugar until very fluffy, then add syrup and vanilla. Add eggs, one at a time, mixing well after each addition. Add melted chocolate.

Alternately, add flour mixture and buttermilk, mixed with 1/2 cup of cointreau, to the batter until smooth and well-blended. Pour batter into a greased and floured bundt cake pan and bake at 325° F. for 1 hour and 10 minutes. Remove cake from pan and cool on a rack. While cake is still warm, baste with 1/4 cup cointreau. When completely cool, turn over and baste with remaining 1/4 cup liqueur.

Coke Cake**

This easy-to-make one-bowl cake folds cola beverage into the mix.

1 cup softened margarine	1-1/2 teaspoons vanilla
2 cups sifted all-	2 eggs
purpose flour	1/2 cup buttermilk
1-3/4 cups sugar	1 cup carbonated cola beverage
3 tablespoons cocoa	1-1/2 cups miniature marshmallows
1 teaspoon soda	Coke Frosting

Combine all ingredients except the cola beverage and marshmallows in a large bowl. Blend at low speed until ingredients are well-blended, then turn up speed to medium and continue beating for 1 minute. Add the cola beverage and blend.

By hand, fold in marshmallows, then spoon batter into a greased and floured 9 x 13-inch cake pan. Bake at 350° F. for 40 to 45 minutes, or until a cake tester inserted in the middle comes out clean. Frost with Coke Frosting.

Coke Frosting*

1/2 cup softened margarine	4 cups powdered sugar
3 tablespoons cocoa	1/2 cup chopped pecans
1/3 cup cola beverage	1/2 cup chopped dates

Blend all ingredients in a small bowl. Makes enough frosting for the Coke Cake.

Lemon Butter Angel Fluff**

Considering how easy it is, this has to be one of the most opulent-looking desserts you'll ever whip up. Start with a bakery angel food cake or make one from a boxed mix (they are all very good). From there, you simply slice the cake into three layers — use a long serrated knife and try to come out reasonably even — then layer and frost the whole thing with this fluffy whipped cream filling.

Angel food cake, cut in	Lemon rind
3 layers	1/4 cup butter
3 eggs, beaten	Pinch salt
1 cup sugar	1 cup whipping cream
Juice of 2 lemons	

Place eggs, sugar and lemon juice in top of double boiler. Beat until blended. Add rind. Place over boiling water and cook, stirring occasionally, until thick. Add butter and pinch of salt. Cool, then chill.

Whip cream until stiff peaks form. Gently fold into chilled lemon mixture. Makes enough filling for three layers of cake plus top and sides. If desired, thickly coat top and sides of cake with flaked coconut.

Creme de Menthe Cake*

Creme de menthe goes into this green cake that tastes beautifully minty and would be an excellent choice for next St. Patrick's Day (or any other day if you're keen on green).

1 2-layer size white cake mix	1 pint Cool Whip
1/4 cup green creme de menthe	2 tablespoons creme de menthe
1 can fudge frosting mix	

Prepare cake according to directions on the box, adding 1/4 cup green creme de menthe to the mix. Bake as directed for a 9 x 13-inch cake pan. Cool. Top cooled cake with 1 can fudge frosting mix. Fold 2 tablespoons creme de menthe into the Cool Whip and spread lavishly over the fudge topping.

Creme de Cacao Cake*

Proceed as for Creme de Menthe Cake, substituting a 2-layer chocolate or fudge cake mix for white cake. In place of creme de menthe, use 1/4 cup creme de cacao. Top with a fudge layer, then spread with Cool Whip mixed with 2 tablespoons creme de cacao.

Pina Colada Cake**

The popularity of putting booze in cakes presumably peaked when someone came up with this exotic brainstorm: Pina Colada Cake. It's a rich and rummy confection that is not the least bit difficult to throw together.

1 2-layer-size package plain white cake mix (without pudding)	1/3 cup dark rum
	1/4 cup oil
	1 cup flaked coconut
4 eggs	Pina Colada Frosting
1/4 cup water	
1 4-serving-size package instant coconut cream pudding mix	

Place cake mix in a large bowl. Add the eggs, water, pudding mix, rum and oil; beat on medium speed for 4 minutes. Fold in coconut. Pour batter into two greased and floured 9-inch cake pans. Bake at 350° F. for 25 to 30 minutes. Cool in pans for 15 minutes before turning out on racks to cool. Spread with Pina Colada Frosting.

Pina Colada Frosting*

1 8-ounce can crushed pineapple, undrained	1/3 cup rum
1 4-serving-size package instant coconut creme pudding mix	1 9-ounce container frozen whipped topping, thawed
	Coconut (optional)

Combine pineapple with pudding mix and rum. Fold in thawed topping. Spread between layers and on top of Pina Colada Cake. If desired, sprinkle with additional coconut.

Banana Split Cake**

And here we have a Banana Split Cake that, strictly speaking, isn't really a cake at all. It isn't a bona fide banana split, either. So what is it? A confection that is gloriously gooey and a weight watcher's nightmare, that's what.

1-3/4 cups graham cracker crumbs	1 20-ounce can crushed pineapple, drained
1/2 cup sugar	1 small carton whipping cream, whipped
1/2 cup melted butter	Chopped nuts
2 cups powdered sugar	1/3 cup chocolate syrup
2 sticks butter (or margarine)	8 maraschino cherries, cut in half
2 eggs	
4 to 5 sliced ripe bananas	

Combine crumbs with sugar, then add 1/2 cup melted butter. Mix well and press into a 9 x 13-inch baking pan. Bake at 375° F. for 8 minutes, then set aside to cool.

Combine powdered sugar, butter and eggs and whip with an electric beater for 15 minutes, or until very light and fluffy. Spread this over the cooled crust.

Over the filling layer the following in the order given: Sliced bananas, well-drained pineapple, whipped cream, and chopped nuts. Finally drizzle chocolate syrup over all and sprinkle with cherries. Refrigerate overnight. Serves 14.

Apple Kuchen***

Apple Kuchen is one of those old-world goodies that is well within the reach of the novice cook. Take enough time in the assembly to line up the apple slices in even "apple pie" order. The pieces should have the symmetry of a nice mosaic.

2 cups sifted flour	3 tablespoons water
1/4 teaspoon salt	1 tablespoon melted butter
2-1/4 teaspoons baking powder	4 medium-size apples, cut into 1/2-inch wedges
2/3 cup sugar	1/2 cup raisins
1/2 cup butter (or margarine)	3/4 cup sugar
1 egg, slightly beaten	1 tablespoon grated lemon peel

Sift together flour, salt, baking powder and 2/3 cup sugar. Add 1/4 cup butter and cut into dry ingredients until mixture is crumbly. Stir in egg and water. Work in liquid by hand until dough clings together. Knead three or four times on a lightly floured board, then roll dough out to fit a 10 x 15-inch jellyroll pan. Brush with melted butter.

Peel and slice apples and place in overlapping rows over dough. Sprinkle with raisins. Blend remaining 1/4 cup butter with 3/4 cup sugar and lemon peel and sprinkle over apples. Bake at 375° F. for 40 minutes. Cut into 18 serving-size squares. Serve with rich cream or ice cream, if desired.

Robin's Carrot Cake**

All carrot cakes are good, but the ones — like Robin's — that have pineapple in the mix are even better.

1-1/2 cups oil	1-1/2 teaspoons soda
2 cups sugar	1 8-ounce can crushed pineapple,
4 eggs, slightly beaten	undrained
2 cups flour	4 ounces flaked coconut
2 teaspoons cinnamon	2-1/2 cups grated carrot (about 6,
1-1/2 teaspoons salt	medium-size)
2 teaspoons baking powder	2 cups chopped nuts

In a large bowl, combine the oil, sugar and eggs. Sift together the flour, cinnamon, salt, baking powder and soda. Combine the dry ingredients with the egg-oil mixture. Add undrained pineapple, coconut, carrots and nuts and beat until well-blended. Bake in a well-greased 9 x 12-inch baking pan at 350° F. for 35 minutes. Cool and frost with Cream Cheese Frosting (page 253). If desired, sprinkle with additional chopped nuts.

Mississippi Mud Cake**

Mississippi Mud Cake is dense, dark and achingly rich. Chocolate lovers go cuckoo over it. There is no leavening in the recipe — no baking powder, soda or anything. The batter just sits there, getting gooier by the minute, but the end result is mighty fine, indeed.

2 cups sugar	1 tablespoon vanilla
1 stick margarine	1/2 cup nuts, chopped
2 tablespoons cocoa	1-1/2 cups coconut
4 eggs	1 7-ounce jar marshmallow creme
1-1/2 cups flour	Mississippi Mud Cake Icing

Cream sugar, margarine and cocoa together. Add eggs and beat well. Add flour and vanilla to batter, mixing to blend. Then fold in the nuts and coconut. Pour batter into a greased 9 x 12-inch baking pan and bake at 350° F. for 30 to 40 minutes, or until toothpick inserted in the middle comes out clean. While the cake is still hot, pour over the jar of marshmallow creme — it will ooze in. When the cake is cool, ice with Mississippi Mud Cake Icing.

Mississippi Mud Cake Icing*

Mix 1 stick margarine with 1/3 cup cocoa, 1 tablespoon vanilla and 1 box of powdered sugar. Add just enough cream or condensed milk to make the frosting spreadable. Spread on cooled Mississippi Mud Cake.

*Beer and Kraut Fudge Cake***

Beer and sauerkraut in chocolate cake, you say? Well, don't scoff and don't sniff. Both ingredients add mysterious dimension to a cake that will titillate chocolate lovers and drive them nutty trying to figure out what's in it.

2/3 cup margarine	1 teaspoon soda
1-1/2 cups sugar	1/4 teaspoon salt
3 eggs	1 cup beer
1 teaspoon vanilla	2/3 cup well-drained sauerkraut,
2-1/4 cups sifted flour	finely chopped
1/3 cup cocoa	Cream Cheese Frosting
1 teaspoon baking powder	

Beat margarine and sugar together until fluffy. Beat in eggs and vanilla. Sift flour with cocoa, baking powder, soda and salt; add to the butter-sugar mixture, alternately with beer, ending with dry ingredients. Fold in chopped sauerkraut. Pour batter into two greased 8-inch round pans and bake at 350° F. for 40 minutes. Frost with Cream Cheese Frosting (page 253).*

*Beer Spice Cake***

Here's another moist and spicy cake that gets a leg up from beer. It is surprising what a little brew does for these sweet treats.

1/2 cup shortening	3/4 teaspoon cinnamon
1 cup brown sugar	1/2 teaspoon nutmeg
1 egg	1/4 teaspoon ginger
1-1/2 cups sifted flour	Pinch ground cloves
1 teaspoon baking powder	1 cup beer
1/4 teaspoon soda	1/2 cup chopped nuts
1/2 teaspoon salt	

With an electric mixer, cream shortening and sugar together until fluffy — about 10 minutes. Add the egg and continue beating. Sift flour with rest of the dry ingredients. Add alternately with beer to shortening mixture. Beat well, then add nuts.

Turn batter into a well-greased and floured 8-inch square baking pan and bake at 350° F. for 50 minutes, or until cake springs back when lightly touched. Cool in pan and frost with white icing.

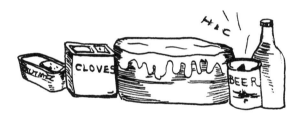

The Cheesecake Controversy

Everyone loves cheesecake, so there's no controversy about that. The big problem is where to look for them in a cookbook — with the pies (if they're made in a pie shell), or in with the cakes (if they stand tall and slice like a cake)?

Well, since they are called cheesecakes, no matter what they look like, this is where they're going. So please don't point out that the kind baked in a pie shell is sometimes called cheese **pie**. That's only confusing the issue.

Beyond that, there are only a couple of things that might leave the new cook in a quandary. The first is how to tell when a cheesecake is done (when the outside edges puff up and the center is barely set, maybe still a bit jiggly, that's it — the middle will continue to firm up as the cake cools).

The other question is how to cut the cheescake — how to do it, that is, without getting the knife all gummed up and mucking up that glorious filling. The answer is easy: use dental floss. Honest.

Just draw a length of waxed or unwaxed floss across and down through the cake and pull it straight out at the bottom — slick as a whistle. No mess, no crumbs, no goo.

If you don't have dental floss (shame on you), use a sharp, thin-bladed knife dipped in hot water.

What follows is a fair sampling of cheesecakes — two that are baked in pie crusts (and are easy to cut), a half-dozen or so that rise to cake-like heights in springform pans plus an unbaked version that combines ice cream with cream cheese.

All are pure and decadent elegance (calories be damned) and, for the most part, they are quite easy to make. The one-star (*) cook can ease into production by starting out with ready-made pie shells, filling them up and advancing from there.

Pineapple Cheesecake*

Here is a good place for the beginner to start. This recipe goes together in minutes and makes enough for two 9-inch pies (make one for yourself, the second for a friend). Use store-bought crumb crusts if you're in a real swivet. No one will know the difference.

2 8-ounce packages cream cheese	1 large can crushed pineapple, drained
3 eggs	2 ready-made graham cracker pie crusts
3/4 cup sugar	1 pint sour cream
2 teaspoons lemon juice	1/2 cup sugar
1 teaspoon vanilla	1 teaspoon vanilla

Place cream cheese, eggs, sugar, lemon juice and vanilla in a blender or beat with a mixer until blended. Stir in drained pineapple. Pour into two graham cracker crusts and bake at 375° F. for 25 minutes. Take from oven and spread with a mixture of sour cream, 1/2 cup sugar and vanilla. Return to the oven and bake an additional 10 minutes. Refrigerate overnight or long enough to chill thoroughly.

Classic Cheesecake Pie**

*This never-fail cheesecake is another good one for the beginner. Note that the crumb crust gets mooshed together and pressed into a pie pan, not a springform pan (making this a cheese **pie**, if you want to get technical). If you plan to use a ready-made crust, skip the first four ingredients and simply whip up the filling.*

1-1/2 cups graham cracker crumbs	2 eggs
1/4 cup sugar	1/2 cup sugar
1/2 teaspoon cinnamon (optional)	Pinch salt
1/3 cup melted butter	1 teaspoon finely grated lemon peel
2 8-ounce packages cream cheese, room temperature	1/2 pint sour cream
	3 tablespoons sugar
	1 teaspoon vanilla

Combine crumbs, cinnamon and sugar. Add melted butter, mix, and pat onto bottom and up sides of a 9-inch pie pan. Bake 8 minutes in a 375° F. oven.

Beat cream cheese with eggs, sugar, salt and rind. Pour into prepared crust. Bake at 350° F. for 35 minutes. Cool 15 minutes. Top with mixture of sour cream, 3 tablespoons sugar and vanilla. Bake at 400° F. for 15 minutes. Cool, then chill before serving.

Opulent Cheesecake**

Sour cream is the traditional topping for this smooth-as-silk springform cheesecake, although the kinds of glazes you can use are almost endless. Browse through the recipes that follow and take your pick.

1-1/2 cups graham cracker crumbs	1/2 teaspoon salt
1/4 cup sugar	2 teaspoons vanilla
1/3 cup melted butter	4 eggs
3 8-ounce packages cream cheese, room temperature	1 cup sugar
	1 pint sour cream
	3 tablespoons sugar

Combine crumbs and sugar. Add melted butter. Mix, then press onto bottom and 2 inches up sides of a springform pan. Bake 8 minutes at 375° F.

Beat cheese, salt and vanilla until fluffy. Add eggs one at a time, beating well after each addition. By tablespoon, add sugar gradually, continuing to beat. Pour into prepared crust.

Bake at 350° F. for 35 minutes. Remove from oven. Let stand 10 minutes.

Blend 2 tablespoons sugar into sour cream. Spread over warm cheesecake and return to 450° F. oven for 6 minutes. Cool completely before refrigerating.

Apricot Amber Cheesecake Glaze*

1 cup dried apricots	1/2 cup light corn syrup
1/2 cup water	1 teaspoon almond flavoring
1/3 cup sugar	

Simmer apricots in water until very soft. Beat until smooth. Add sugar and syrup and cook over low heat until sugar dissolves. Add flavoring. Cool to room temperature, spread over cooled cheesecake and chill.

Cherry Cheesecake Topping*

1 17-ounce jar or can pitted sweet cherries in heavy syrup	Pinch salt
	1/4 cup water
	1 teaspoon almond flavoring
2 tablespoons sugar	1 teaspoon lemon juice
1 tablespoon cornstarch	Red food coloring (optional)

Drain cherries, saving 1/2 cup juice. Combine sugar and cornstarch in a small saucepan. Add reserved cherry juice and lemon juice. Cook over low heat, stirring, until thickened and clear. Take off heat. Add cherries, salt, flavoring and lemon juice. Cool to room temperature and spread over cheesecake. Chill before serving.

Strawberry Cheesecake Glaze*

1 quart fresh strawberries	1/4 cup water
1/2 cup sugar	2 teaspoons butter
2 tablespoons cornstarch	2 teaspoons lemon juice
Pinch salt	

Wash berries, setting aside the prettiest ones for the top of the cake. Cut these in half. (You should have enough to cover the cake.)

Crush enough of the remaining berries to make 1 cup pulp.

Mix cornstarch, salt and sugar in a small saucepan. Add water and crushed berries and stir. Set over medium heat and bring to a boil. Cook 2 minutes, or until thickened and clear. Remove from heat and add lemon juice and butter.

Decorate top of cheesecake with halved berries. When glaze is lukewarm, spoon over strawberries. Chill before serving.

Pineapple Cheesecake Topping*

1/2 cup sugar	1 tablespoon lemon juice
2 tablespoons cornstarch	Pinch salt
1 20-ounce can crushed pineapple	2 teaspoons butter

Drain pineapple, saving juice. Combine sugar and cornstarch in a small saucepan. Add reserved pineapple juice and lemon juice and place over medium heat. Cook, stirring, until mixture comes to a boil. Add salt and stir until mixture is thick and clear.

Take off heat and stir in drained pineapple and butter. Cool to room temperature, then spread over cheesecake. Chill before serving.

Rich Chocolate Cheesecake**

This dark chocolate cheesecake is as rich and dense as fudge. Even chocophiles will be stalled after one slice, so keep the servings thin.

1-1/2 cups vanilla wafer crumbs	3 8-ounce packages cream cheese
1/4 cup sugar	3/4 cup sugar
6 tablespoons softened butter or margarine	3 eggs
5 squares of semi-sweet chocolate	1 teaspoon vanilla
	1 cup sour cream
	1/2 teaspoon salt

Combine cookie crumbs with sugar. Add butter and mix. Press on bottom and 2 inches up sides of a 9-inch springform pan. Bake at 350° F. for 8 minutes.

Melt chocolate over warm water. When melted, set aside to cool.

With an electric mixer, beat cream cheese with sugar, eggs and vanilla until smooth and fluffy. Stir in cooled melted chocolate and sour cream. Add a pinch of salt and beat until throroughly blended. Pour into prepared crust. Bake at 275° F. for 1 hour and 45 minutes. Turn off heat and allow cake to cool in the oven with oven door ajar. When cool enough to handle, place cake on a rack to cool to room temperature. Then refrigerate overnight. Garnish with whipped cream. Serves 16.

Lemon Luscious Cheesecake**

I had a hard time prying this recipe out of the lady who considers it part of her personal fief, but she finally gave up and gave it to me.

Well, I guess you can't blame people for holding onto their private triumphs (but it sure is fun getting them to shake loose!).

1 cup walnuts	4 tablespoons lemon juice
2 8-ounce and 1 3-ounce package cream cheese, room temperature	1 cup sour cream
	2 tablespoons sugar
	2 tablespoons lemon juice
1 cup sugar	2 tablespoons grated lemon peel
4 eggs	

Put walnuts in a blender and process to fine crumbs. Press ground nuts onto the bottom of a 9-inch springform pan. Bake at 350° F. for 8 minutes, watching closely so the nuts don't burn. Cool.

Whip cream cheese until fluffy. Add sugar, beating well. Add eggs, one at a time, beating after each addition. Add 4 tablespoons lemon juice and pour filling into prepared crust. Bake at 350° F. for 1 hour, or until softly set in middle. Remove from oven and cool 30 minutes.

Combine sour cream with 2 tablespoons sugar, 2 tablespoons lemon juice and peel. Spread over cheesecake, then bake at 375° F. for 8 minutes. Cool, then chill. Serves 12.

Beer and Cheddar Cheesecake**

Cheddar cheese and, of all things, beer distinguish this dense cheesecake that is hefty enough to serve 20. (Well, make that 16 if you have a lot of hearty appetites in the crowd and no one's counting calories.)

1 6-ounce box zwieback crackers, crushed	1-1/2 cups finely grated Cheddar cheese
1/4 cup sugar	1-3/4 cups sugar
1/3 cup melted butter	5 eggs
4 8-ounce packages cream cheese, room temperature	1/3 cup beer
	1/4 cup evaporated milk or heavy cream

Combine zwieback crumbs with sugar. Stir in melted margarine. Press onto the bottom and part way up the sides of a buttered 9-inch springform pan. Chill.

Beat cheeses with an electric mixer until blended. Gradually add the sugar, continuing to beat until mixture is light and smooth. Add eggs, one at a time, beating well after each addition. Beat in beer and evaporated milk.

Pour into pan and bake at 300° F. for 2 hours. Turn off heat and leave cake in the oven, with the door ajar, for another 30 minutes. Cool, then refrigerate overnight.

Serve at room temperature. Refrigerate leftovers.

Chocolate Chip Ice Cream Cheesecake**

If you are hankering for cheesecake but your oven's on the bum, here is an unbaked version that has chocolate ice cream in the mix. Make this well ahead and remember to let it soften up a trifle before serving.

1-1/2 cups graham cracker crumbs	1 8-ounce and 1 3-ounce package cream cheese, room temperature
1/2 cup sugar	1 quart rich chocolate ice cream
2 tablespoons unsweetened cocoa	3/4 cup semi-sweet chocolate chips, chopped
1/2 cup melted butter	Whipped cream

Combine crumbs with sugar and cocoa. Add melted butter. Pat onto bottom and 2 inches up sides of a buttered 9-inch springform pan. Chill.

Beat cream cheese until fluffy. In another bowl, stir ice cream until slightly softened. Add ice cream to cream cheese, beating until smooth. Fold in chopped chips. Spoon into chilled crust, cover and freeze overnight.

Before serving, let stand at room temperature about 20 minutes. Garnish with whipped cream. Serves 10. Freeze leftovers if you have any (fat chance!).

*Mini Cherry Cheesecakes***

*These pretty little miniature cheesecakes would be a marvelous treat for Valentine's Day or old George's birthday. There is no crust, as such — just a couple dozen sugar wafers fitted into tiny fluted paper cups. Very dainty (and **very** easy).*

24 small vanilla wafers
2 8-ounce packages cream
  cheese
3/4 cup sugar
2 eggs
1 tablespoon lemon juice

1 teaspoon vanilla extract
Pinch salt
1/2 teaspoon almond extract
1 21-ounce can cherry pie filling
3 drops red food coloring (optional)

Line 24 small muffin tins with petit four-size paper baking cups (available in gourmet kitchen shops). Place a vanilla wafer in each cup.

Beat cream cheese with sugar, eggs, lemon juice and vanilla, whipping until very light and fluffy. Fill the cups 3/4 full with the mixture. Bake at 350° F. for 15 to 20 minutes, or until set.

Stir almond extract into the cherry pie filling and, if desired, add a drop or two of red food coloring. Spoon 1 tablespoon into each cup and chill. Makes 2 dozen.

*Inside Job Cupcakes***

As these chocolate cupcakes bake, a mixture of cream cheese and chocolate chips sinks to the middle of the little cakes, making a surprise center.

1 package two-layer chocolate
  cake mix
1 8-ounce package cream
  cheese
1/2 cup sugar

1 egg, beaten
Dash salt
1 6-ounce package chocolate chips

Prepare cake mix according to package instructions. Fit 30 paper liners in cupcake pans and fill each one 3/4 full with the cake mix. Mix cream cheese with sugar, egg, salt and chocolate chips. Spoon 1 rounded tablespoon of the cheese mixture into the cupcakes. Bake at 350° F. for 20 minutes.

Gorgeous Genoise — What It Is and How to Do It

As you get deeper and deeper into the pure joy of cooking, you will probably be unable to resist the lure of gourmet cookware shops. Once inside, you will be helpless to resist buying some exotic gadget or pan that (you tell yourself) you can't live without.

Well, not only would you be able to live quite well without it, chances are you will wonder what to do with it once you get home.

Take, for example, those pretty, fluted tart pans with the raised centers. They are irresistible. *I know, because I bought one and then wondered what to do next.*

If, perchance, you have one of these cute inside-out pans, here is how to turn out one of those picture-perfect kiwi, strawberry, peach or apricot kind of glazed tarts sold in posh patisseries.

It's a three-part operation that isn't as difficult as it is diddling. First you make a simple sponge cake. This gets filled with a kind of custard called Creme Patissiere. Finally you top off the whole thing with a lovely mosaic of fresh fruit. And it is gorgeous. (It would also cost an arm and a leg at a bakery.)

If your idea of dessert is eating cling peaches out of a can, skip this one — it'd be too much trouble. But if you're eager to develop into a real virtuoso, here's how. With three stars (***) to your credit, you can do it — **I promise.**

Genoise Sponge Cake***

4 eggs	1 cup flour
1/2 cup sugar	1/2 cup butter
1/2 teaspoon vanilla	

Combine eggs and sugar in top of double boiler. Over hot, but not boiling, water, whisk until very thick and light. When mixture is of proper consistency, take off heat and beat with an electric mixture.

Add vanilla and continue beating until very stiff. Sift flour, then fold into the batter with gentle up-and-down motion.

Melt butter, cool to tepid, and add all at once to the batter. Pour into a well-buttered and floured cake tin and bake at 350° F. for 45 minutes. Cool slightly before turning out.

NOTE: To be absolutely authentic about this, you should dribble some liqueur — Grand Marnier, Amaretto or Cointreau — over the cake while it's still warm. Just a sprinkle, mind you — don't soak.

Creme Patissiere***

Creme Patissiere is the creamy filling that goes onto the Genoise.

4 tablespoons sugar	1 cup milk
3 tablespoons flour	1/2 teaspoon vanilla
Pinch salt	1/2 cup whipping cream
1 egg yolk	1 tablespoon sugar

Combine 4 tablespoons sugar, flour, and salt in a small bowl. Add the egg yolk and beat until mixture is thick. Heat milk just to boiling, but don't let it boil. Add slowly to the egg yolk mixture, whipping constantly. Pour into a heavy saucepan and cook, stirring constantly, until mixture is very thick. Take off heat and add vanilla.

Place a piece of waxed paper over the surface of the sauce to keep a skin from forming, and set aside to cool. When cool, refrigerate until well-chilled.

Beat cream with 1 tablespoon sugar. When stiff, stir a small amount of the cream into the chilled custard mixture. When blended, lightly fold in the remaining whipped cream. Makes 2 cups.

Fill depressed center of cake with Creme Patissiere, then arrange circles of fruit in a carefully arranged pattern. Glaze with 1/2 cup pineapple-apricot jam that has been heated until liquid in a small saucepan. Apply glaze with a soft brush, taking care to completely cover fruit.

Frostings

Cake frostings range all the way from simple butter creams (powdered sugar, butter and a dab of milk) to more involved confections that require cooking, stirring and keen temperature control lest they turn to stone before your very eyes. (I have yet to make a Seven Minute Frosting that didn't turn into plaster of Paris the minute it cooled.)

What we have here is a collection of recipes for frostings, or icings that is gorgeously goof-proof.

Witness this first one. It's nothing more, really, than a blend of sour cream and powdered sugar. Very nice atop spice cake.

Sour Cream Frosting*

1 1-pound box powdered sugar	1 teaspoon vanilla
1/2 cup sour cream	1/4 teaspoon salt
	1/2 stick soft margarine

Blend everything together and beat until smooth and creamy. Makes enough to frost the top and sides of a 2-layer cake.

Mock Whipped Cream Frosting**

This is a very handy recipe to have on hand anytime you need a whipped cream-type frosting that's going to have to stand around a bit. My friend Nancy, the caterer, always uses it on her Black Forest Tortes because this stuff, unlike whipped cream, doesn't wilt.

2-1/2 tablespoons flour	3/4 cup powdered sugar
1/2 cup milk	2 teaspoons vanilla
2 tablespoons butter	

Blend flour and milk in a small saucepan. Cook over low heat, stirring constantly, until thickened. Remove from heat and allow to cool. Add butter, mixing well. Beat in powdered sugar until frosting is as fluffy as whipped cream. Add vanilla. Makes enough to liberally frost a loaf cake. Double the recipe for a layer cake.

Chocolate Fudge Icing**

This thick and super-chocolaty icing is spectacular on a white layer cake. And on fudge or devils food, it is positively wicked.

3 ounces unsweetened chocolate	1/2 cup margarine
1 14-ounce can sweetened condensed milk	1 egg yolk, beaten
	2 teaspoons vanilla
	Pinch salt

In a double boiler, melt chocolate. Stir in condensed milk and butter. Beat until smooth. Take off heat. Add egg yolk, continuing to beat. Add vanilla and salt.

Rocky Road Frosting**

Nuts and marshmallows plump out this topping.

2 1-ounce squares unsweetened chocolate	1/4 cup water
2 cups miniature marshmallows	2 cups sifted powdered sugar
1/4 cup margarine	1 teaspoon vanilla
	1/4 cup broken walnuts

Place chocolate, 1 cup marshmallows, margarine and water together in a small saucepan. Heat and stir until well-blended. Cool slightly and add sugar and vanilla, beating until smooth and slightly thickened — about 2 minutes. Stir in reserved marshmallows and walnuts. Enough to frost top of a 9 x 13-inch cake.

Marshmallow Dream Frosting**

If your experience with cooked frostings has been less than a howling success, try this one. The addition of marshmallows keeps the stuff from setting up like cement.

1 cup sugar	Dash salt
1/2 teaspoon cream of tartar	9 marshmallows, cut up
3 tablespoons water	1 teaspoon vanilla
2 egg whites	

Put everything but marshmallows in top of double boiler. Place over boiling water and begin beating with a hand-held electric mixer. As soft peaks form, add marshmallows (snipped into pieces with wet scissors). Continue beating until smooth, marshmallows are melted and frosting is of good spreading consistency. Makes enough for the top and sides of a two-layer cake.

Coconut Walnut Icing**

Lots of coconut and walnuts give this frosting crunch and munch.

1 cup evaporated milk	1 teapoon vanilla
1 cup sugar	1-1/3 cups flaked coconut
3 egg yolks	1 cup chopped walnuts
1/4 pound margarine	

Combine milk, sugar, egg yolks, margarine and vanilla in a saucepan. Cook, stirring constantly, for about 12 minutes, or until mixture thickens. Remove from heat and add coconut and walnuts. Beat until cooled and of spreadable consistency. Makes enough to frost and fill two 8-inch layers.

Cream Cheese Frosting*

2 3-ounce packages of cream cheese, room temperature	2 cups sifted powdered sugar
2 tablespoons cream	1/4 teaspoon salt
	1 teaspoon vanilla (optional)

Beat softened cream cheese with cream. Slowly add powdered sugar, whipping until smooth. Add salt and, if desired, 1 teaspoon vanilla. Vanilla lends a nice flavor, although it tends to darken slightly this otherwise snow-white frosting.

What's Ahead in
Pies

Easy as Pie

. . . look, Ma, I'm rolling my own

The person who first said something was "easy as pie" probably never tried making one. Pies — made from scratch, anyway — are lots of things, but **easy** isn't one of them.

Which isn't to say that proper pie-making can't be learned. It can, and we will. All the same, it should be approached in the same spirit one learns to roller skate: be prepared to take a few flops along the way.

Fortunately, with all the self-helps on the market today — ready-made pie shells and ready-to-roll pastry sticks — the most inexperienced cook can start from ground zero with perfect pies every time.

From there we can advance, hand in hand, to the business of making perfectly wonderful pie crusts like Mama used to make. Or like the one she **wishes** she used to make.

Roll-Your-Own Pie Crust

After you and ready-made pie shells have waltzed around the block a dozen or more times, sooner or later you are going to have to come to grips with the real nitty-gritty: Honest to goodness, old-fashioned pie crust.

Except for a little water, there are only three ingredients to pie dough — flour, salt and shortening. The ingredients are very simple. It's putting them together that causes all the trouble. It isn't complicated so much as it's tricky.

A book can tell you how to do it, but from there you have to run your own experimental station. After a couple of passes, you should be getting the hang of it.

Just remember, if your first attempt fails, don't despair. Your busted crust didn't cost that much, and a tolerable substitute is as close as the corner grocery store.

Perfect Pie Crust***
(Enough for a double-crust pie)

Okay, here it is — a pie crust that's perfect if you do it right. And if you don't . . . oh, well.

Keeping the ingredients icy-cold and handling the dough as little as possible seems to be the trick. A manhandled crust is a tough crust, so this is no place to take out your aggressions.

2-1/2 cups all-purpose flour	**12 tablespoons shortening, chilled**
1 teaspoon salt	**in the freezer**
	3 to 4 tablespoons ice water

Sift flour and salt into a large bowl. Add the well-chilled shortening and cut it into the flour with a pastry cutter. (If you don't have one, use a couple of criss-crossed knives — whick, whick, whick — until the mixture is crumbly, like coarse cornmeal.)

Starting off with two tablespoons, add ice water. With your fingers, lightly mix the water into the flour by swirling the mass in a gentle circular motion. Your touch must be very light — positively **wispy.**

As the mix begins to clump up a bit, add another tablespoon of water, continuing to swish through the mix until it can be pressed gently into a mass.

Mold into 2 smooth balls, wrap in plastic and refrigerate.

Two-Crust Pies

For a double-crust pie, pat the dough into two balls, wrap them in plastic and refrigerate 30 minutes. *Chilling makes the dough easier to roll.*

Another thing that makes it easier to roll is a pastry kit — a heavy canvas cloth and a stockinet kind of slipcover for your rolling pin.

Lightly sprinkle the cloth with flour and start maneuvering the first dough ball into a circle — rolling with a light touch and always in the same direction. Keep turning the pastry cloth, but don't roll back and forth. That puts too much stretch on the dough.

When the dough is 12 inches in diameter (for a 9-inch pie), lift the cloth and flop the dough in half. Pick it up and position it so that the fold lies across the center of the pie pan. Unfold and gently ease the dough into the pan. Press it around the rim and, with a knife or scissors, trim the crust.

Spoon the filling into the bottom crust and roll out the top crust. Once that is accomplished, slightly moisten the rim of the bottom crust before positioning the top crust over the pie.

Seal the top crust to the bottom by pinching the edges together with your fingers — making a sort of scalloped edge — or pressing around the pie rim with the tines of a fork, giving a rick-racky kind of edge.

Cut a few slits in the top crust to prevent your masterpiece from blowing its top, and you are ready to bake your pie.

One-Crust Pies

You make a single-crust pie just like a double-crust pie except that it takes roughly half that amount of dough. You roll it, fold it, and snug it down in the pie pan the very same way.

Bake the pie shell on the center rack of a hot (425° F.) oven for 8 to 12 minutes. But watch it — you don't want an over-browned crust. Another thing: crusts brown faster in glass pie plates than in aluminum pie tins, so be forewarned. After 6 or 7 minutes, start checking.

Unfilled pie shells have an annoying habit of shrinking during the baking. This can be helped by filling the unbaked shell with some dried beans or rice (put a circle of waxed paper in the pie shell first). Three or 4 minutes before the pie shell is ready, remove the paper and the beans and put the crust back in the oven so the bottom can get crisp.

And save the beans. You can use them over and over for this same purpose.

Absolutely No-Fail Pie Crust**
(Enough for Two Double-Crust Pies)

If you have tried and tried to master plain flour-and-shortening pie crust and you're still striking out, do not give up. Help is at hand!

By adding an egg and one tablespoon of vinegar to the mix, magical things happen. The pastry is easy to roll (it doesn't tear, break or dry out), and you should have no problem at all fitting it into a pie tin and even pinching up a nice stand-up rim. This recipe makes enough crust for 2 pies.

4 cups flour	1 tablespoon vinegar
1-3/4 cups shortening	1 egg
1 tablespoon sugar	1/2 cup water
2 teaspoons salt	

Mix together the flour, shortening, sugar and salt. Use a fork or pastry blender. Mix until crumbly.

In a small bowl, beat egg, vinegar and water together with a fork. When blended, dump all at once into flour mixture. Stir with a fork until flour is dampened and you can press the mixture into two balls. Wrap each piece in plastic wrap and refrigerate 15 minutes. (This pie crust handles so well that it isn't even essential to chill it — something to remember if you're in a hurry.)

The dough can be refrigerated up to 3 days or frozen almost indefinitely.

Frozen dough should thaw to room temperature before rolling.

Quick Coconut Cream Pie*

*Here is a dandy place for the brand-new bride or uncertain student to launch into pie baking. Notice I didn't say pie **making**. If you aren't up to rolling your own, buy a ready-to-go pie shell at the supermarket. That way you don't make it, just **bake** it.*

1 baked 9-inch pie shell	1/4 teaspoon almond flavoring
2 envelopes whipped	2 4-ounce packages instant coconut
topping mix	cream pudding mix
2-3/4 cups cold milk	1-1/3 cups flaked coconut
1 teaspoon vanilla	

Whip topping mix, using 1 cup cold milk. Add the vanilla and almond flavoring.

Prepare the pudding mix with the remaining 1-3/4 cups cold milk. Then fold the whipped topping into the pudding, folding gently by hand. Next fold in the coconut. Spoon mixture into the pie shell and refrigerate 4 to 5 hours.

A nice added touch is to serve the pie under a cloud of whipped cream sprinkled with toasted coconut.

Mom's Apple Pie***

Everybody has his own idea of what the perfect apple pie should look and taste like. I suspect the prejudice traces back to the kinds of pies our mothers used to make.

Apple pie at our house was a fragrant cinnamon and lemon-laced wonder, crisp of crust and juicy enough to spill a little when it was cut. My mother served it warm with thin slices of sharp Cheddar. I don't think anyone ever made better pie.

Pastry for a 2-crust pie	Pinch salt
1 cup sugar	2 teaspoons lemon juice
2 tablespoons flour	2 pounds tart green apples (7 to 8)
1/2 teaspoon cinnamon	2 tablespoons butter
1/4 teaspoon nutmeg	

Peel apples and thinly slice. Toss with sugar, flour, spices and salt. Sprinkle with lemon juice, then pile into unbaked pie shell. Dot with butter. Cut vents in top crust and place over bottom crust. Pinch or crimp edges. Sprinkle crust lightly with sugar. Bake at 375° F. for 45 to 50 minutes.

NOTE: For first 25 minutes, place a ring of foil over the pie to keep the edges from getting too brown. Remove foil for the last 20 to 25 minutes.

Cherry Pie***

"Can she bake a cherry pie, Billy Boy?" You bet she can, if she follows this recipe that makes a ruby jewel of a pie.

Pastry for a 2-crust pie	3 or 4 drops red food coloring
2 16-ounce cans water-pack	2 teaspoons lemon juice
red cherries	Pinch salt
1-1/2 cups sugar	3 drops almond extract
1/3 cup cornstarch	

Drain cherries in a sieve, saving 1 cup of the juice.

Mix 1/2 cup of the sugar with cornstarch. Stir in the reserved cherry juice, mixing well. Cook, stirring, until thickened and clear. Take off heat and add cherries, remaining sugar, red food coloring, lemon juice, salt and almond extract. Pour into unbaked pie shell.

Adjust top crust, pinching or crimping the edges. Cut vents in top crust and sprinkle lightly with sugar. Place a ring of foil over the pie to keep the edges from getting too brown. Bake at 375° F. for 25 minutes. Remove foil and bake an additional 20 minutes.

Pineapple Fluff Pie**

This is one of my mother's favorite pies (it sounds weird but it's really wonderful). Besides being feather-light and brightly studded with maraschino cherries, it has another big plus going for it: it is made from pantry items a smart cook always has on hand. No last-minute jogging to the grocery store for this one.

1 10- or 12-inch baked pie shell	1 tablespoon lemon juice
1-1/4 cups crushed canned pineapple, *not* drained	Dash salt
	Grated rind of 1 lemon
3/4 cup sugar	12 maraschino cherries, cut in thin slices
1 3-ounce package lemon gelatin	1/2 cup chopped nuts (optional)
1 cup evaporated milk, chilled in the freezer	

Bring pineapple and sugar to a boil, remove from heat and stir in gelatin. Chill until thickened. Chill evaporated milk in the freezer until ice crystals form.

Whip cold milk until peaks begin to form. Fold in lemon juice, salt and grated lemon rind. Fold in thickened gelatin mixture; add sliced cherries. Pour into pie shell and chill before serving.

NOTE: The addition of chopped nuts is a delicious addition to this filling.

Margarita Pie**

Margarita lovers love this one.

1 baked pie shell	1/2 cup sugar
1 package lemon pie filling (not instant)	1/2 cup tequila
	1/4 cup cointreau
1-1/2 cups water	1 small carton whipping cream
2 eggs, separated	Lemon or lime peel (optional)

Combine lemon pie filling with water, beaten egg yolks and sugar. Cook until thickened. Cool and add tequila and cointreau. Beat egg whites until stiff. Beat cream until stiff peaks form. Fold whites and beaten cream into cooled filling and pile lightly in baked pie shell. Chill. Garnish, if desired, with shreds of lemon or lime peel.

Marvelous Macadamia Pie**

This sumptuous pie was developed in Honolulu in one of the island's plushest hotels.

1 9-inch baked pie shell	1 tablespoon butter
1/2 cup sugar	1-1/2 cups whipping cream
1/4 cup cornstarch	2-1/2 tablespoon kahlua
1/4 teaspoon salt	1 teaspoon vanilla
3 egg yolks	1/2 cup chopped macadamia nuts
2 cups milk	Powdered sugar

Beat sugar, cornstarch, salt and egg yolks together until fluffy. Heat milk just to boiling point without letting it boil. Quickly stir sugar mixture into the hot milk and put the pan back on the stove. Stirring constantly, cook until the mixture thickens — about 3 minutes. Remove from heat, stir in the butter, then place a sheet of plastic over the surface of the pudding to prevent a skin from forming. Refrigerate.

When pudding is thoroughly chilled, beat 1/2 cup cream until stiff. Fold cream gently into chilled pudding along with kahlua and vanilla; add chopped nuts. Spoon into pastry shell and chill. Before serving, whip remaining 1 cup cream until stiff, sweeten to taste with powdered sugar, then spread over pie.

Down-South Pecan Pie**

Pecan pies are extremely easy to make. But before launching forth, you would be well-advised to cut a ring of foil, sized to fit over the rim of the pie crust in case it starts to brown too quickly in the baking. (Don't wait until the pie is in the oven to do this, or the crust could burn while you are hunting for the scissors.)

1 9-inch unbaked pie shell	1 cup white corn syrup
1/4 cup butter	1 tablespoon lemon juice
1/2 cup sugar	1 teaspoon vanilla
3 eggs, beaten	2 cups pecans

Brush pie shell with a teaspoon of the beaten eggs and set aside. Cream butter and sugar until fluffy. Add beaten eggs, syrup, lemon juice and vanilla. Mix only until blended. Fold in nuts and turn mixture into crust. Bake at 450° F. for 10 minutes, then reduce heat to 350° F. Continue baking for 45 to 50 minutes, or until set. This is great served with vanilla ice cream.

Coconut-Walnut Pie*

Coconut-Walnut Pie closely resembles pecan pie and, regrettably, is just as ruinous to one's diet. But worth it. This one also tends to get pretty brown in the crust during the baking, so better follow the instructions for Down-South Pecan Pie and prepare an aluminum foil ring — just in case.

1 unbaked 9-inch pie shell	1 teaspoon vanilla
3 eggs	1 cup coconut
1-1/2 cups sugar	1 cup walnuts, diced
1 stick butter, melted	

Bake pie shell for 2 minutes at 400° F., then set aside.

Beat eggs with sugar until light. Add butter and vanilla to egg mixture, blending thoroughly. Fold in coconut and walnuts. Spoon into pie shell and bake at 400° F. for 10 minutes, then lower heat to 350° F. and cook approximately 35 minutes (or until filling is set). Serve warm with whipped cream or vanilla ice cream.

Mincemeat Cheese Pie**

If you are thinking of this pie for Thanksgiving dinner, be forewarned: it is very, very rich. It might be better to bring it forth after a more modest spread.

1 9-inch unbaked pie shell	1 tablespoon lemon juice
4 3-ounce packages	2 cups prepared mincemeat
cream cheese	1 cup sour cream
2 eggs	2 tablespoons sugar
1/2 cup sugar	1/2 teaspoon vanilla
Grated rind of 1 lemon	

Whip cream cheese, eggs, sugar, lemon rind and juice together until very fluffy. Spoon mincemeat into prepared pie shell and spread cream cheese mixture over the top. Bake at 375° F. for 30 minutes.

Meanwhile, blend 2 tablespoons sugar and vanilla into sour cream. Remove pie from oven and top with sour cream mixture. Return to oven and continue baking for an additional 10 minutes. Chill pie before serving.

Gommie's Mile-High Fresh Strawberry Pie***

*You will see many recipes for fresh strawberry pie. What you will **not** see is one as good as the one Grandma has been making every spring for years.*

1 baked 9-inch pie shell	1 cup sugar
2-1/2 boxes perfect	Pinch salt
strawberries	1-1/2 tablespoons lemon juice
1/2 cup water	1 tablespoon butter
3 tablespoons cornstarch	Red food coloring

Clean and hull berries just before making pie. Set aside enough soft berries to make 1/2 cup of pulp. Set the rest of the perfect berries on a paper towel to dry.

Add 1/2 cup water to the 1/2 cup mashed berries. Set aside.

Blend cornstarch and sugar. Add salt, lemon juice and butter. Add the mashed berries, mix and cook over a low fire until thick and clear. Add enough red coloring to make a brilliant crimson. Cool to lukewarm.

Carefully dip the whole perfect berries into the red glaze, then place the berries in a perfect "mosaic" pattern in the pie shell. Keep adding the berries that have been dipped in the glaze, piling the berries higher as you work toward the center. Spoon the remaining glaze over the berries, filling in the chinks. (If glaze is too thick, gently warm before glazing the pie.) Refrigerate until serving time, then top with whipped cream.

Banana Cream Pie**

The custard filling in this Banana Cream pie is smooth as velvet. Just don't lose any time spooning it over the banana slices before they discolor. (Ordinarily you can prevent bananas from turning dark by dousing them with lemon juice, but in the case of cream pies, I don't care for that added tart.)

1 9- or 10-inch baked	3 egg yolks, beaten
pie shell	slightly
2/3 cup sugar	2 tablespoons butter
1/3 cup flour	1/2 teaspoon vanilla
1/4 teaspoon salt	3 bananas, sliced
2 cups scalded milk	3 egg whites

Mix sugar, flour and salt in the top of a double boiler. Gradually add scalded milk, stirring constantly over simmering water, until thick and smooth. Beat 3 tablespoons of the hot custard into the beaten egg yolks, then rapidly stir the yolks back into the custard. Cook, stirring, for 5 minutes, then set off to cool. When lukewarm, add the butter and vanilla.

Place sliced bananas in the baked pie shell and cover with custard. Top with meringue made with 3 egg whites (page 263). Bake as directed.

Sour Cream Raisin Pie**

Raisin Pie is one of those down-home treats that never sounds as good as it really is. And that's too bad because a good raisin pie is easily one of the best pies in captivity. This tried-and-true recipe has been in our family for generations.

1 9-inch baked pie shell	1 cup sour cream
1 cup raisins	1 teaspoon vinegar
2 teaspoons flour, rounded	2 egg yolks, beaten
2 teaspoons cornstarch	1/2 cup chopped nuts
1 cup sugar	Meringue

Plump raisins in boiling water for 10 to 15 minutes. Then drain well and toss with a mixture of flour, cornstarch and sugar. Blend sour cream with vinegar and beaten egg yolks and add to raisin mixture. Cook in a double boiler, stirring constantly, until filling thickens and is smooth. Add the chopped nuts and set aside to cool.

Turn cooled filling into a baked pie shell and top with a meringue made with 3 egg whites (page 263). Bake as directed.

Grandma's Pink Rhubarb Meringue Pie**

My mother's rhubarb pie is a maverick, topped with a cloud of meringue instead of a top crust. This is an elegant, pale pink pie that never fails to dazzle company. Just be sure to buy bright red rhubarb. That anemic-looking kind just won't cut it.

1 9-inch baked pie shell	1 cup sugar
2-1/2 cups strawberry rhubarb	3 eggs, separated
1-1/2 tablespoons flour	Lemon rind
1/4 teaspoon salt	2 tablespoons butter

Cut rhubarb into 1-inch lengths and cover with boiling water. Let stand for 5 minutes. Drain. Place in top of double boiler and add flour, salt and sugar. Cook and stir until mixture gets soft and slightly thickened. Add a little of the hot rhubarb to the beaten yolks, then blend yolks back into the same double boiler, stirring to keep mixture smooth. Add rind. Cool slightly and add butter.

Pour into pie shell and top with meringue made with the 3 egg whites (this page, below).

NOTE: If your rhubarb is a bit on the pale side, add a few drops of red coloring along with the lemon rind.

Ethel's Fresh Peach Pie**

Fresh peach pie is like those divine sky-high fresh strawberry pies . . . with heaps of fresh fruit topped off with a clear, sweetened glaze. Served with a drift of whipped cream or a scoop of vanilla ice cream, this has to be one of the nicest things that ever happened to a summer.

1 9-inch baked pie shell	**2 tablespoons lemon juice**
8 to 10 plump ripe peaches	**1 teaspoon almond extract**
3/4 cup sugar (plus 2 table-	**Pinch salt**
spoons if fruit is tart)	**1 tablespoon butter, rounded**
2-1/2 tablespoons cornstarch	

Peel peaches. Mash the pulp of 2 peaches, adding enough water to the pulp to make 1 cup. Add sugar, cornstarch, lemon juice, extract, and salt to the pulp and cook, stirring constantly, until thickened and clear. Remove from heat and add butter. Cut remaining peaches in 1/2-inch slices and place in a pinwheel pattern in baked pie shell. Spoon cooked glaze over the peaches, spreading to completely cover the fruit. Refrigerate until cold. Serve with whipped cream or ice cream.

Marvelous Meringue**

3 egg whites, room	**3 teaspoons ice water**
temperature	**4 tablespoons sugar**
1/2 teaspoon cream of tartar	

Sprinkle cream of tartar over egg whites and add the ice water. Beat whites until soft peaks begin to form. Gradually add the sugar, a teaspoon at a time, until all the sugar is incorporated and the whites are very stiff.

Spread over pie filling with a light, swirling touch. Make sure that meringue is sealed all around the edges. Bake at 350° F. for 10 to 15 minutes, watching closely so that the meringue doesn't over-brown.

Spiffy-Stiff Meringue**

This version differs from the traditional beat-to-peaks meringue recipe by tossing a little cornstarch in the with the egg whites. This produces a topping that is a bit more droop-proof if the pie has any standing around to do.

3 tablespoons sugar	3 egg whites, room
1 tablespoon cornstarch	temperature
1/2 cup water	6 tablespoons sugar
Dash salt	1/2 teaspoon vanilla

Mix sugar and cornstarch with water and salt in a small saucepan and cook until thick. Cool.

Beat room-temperature egg whites until soft peaks form. Gradually add 6 tablespoons sugar, beating thoroughly after each addition. Add vanilla. Add cooled cornstarch mixture and continue beating until mixture is very stiff. Pile on pie and bake at 350° F. for 10 to 15 minutes.

Crumb Crusts

Unlike flaky pastry shells, a crumb crust is something the greenest cook can put together with confidence.

It takes only a flick of the wrist to reduce cookies or crackers to crumbs in a blender or, lacking that, mere minutes to bash them into crumbs in a plastic bag with a rolling pin. But if even that is too much bother, a store-bought crust will work very nicely. Just fetch and fill.

Crumb crusts can be briefly baked before filling or simply chilled. A crust that is baked for 8 to 10 minutes at 350° F. tends to be a bit crisper and better able to hold its edge. But unless a recipe specifically calls for the crust to be baked, simply slip into the refrigerator to firm up and let it go at that.

The only note of caution I would give you is to avoid making these crusts too thick, especially at the edges where the bottom meets the outer rim of the pan. You won't have a clumsy crust if you keep patting and pressing until the crumbs are only cardboard thick.

Graham Cracker Pie Crust*

Enough for a 9-inch pie shell.

1-1/2 cups graham	1/2 cup sugar
cracker crumbs	1/2 cup melted butter
	(or margarine)

Use prepared graham cracker crumbs (or make your own by rolling crackers between sheets of waxed paper). Combine crumbs with sugar, then add the melted butter. Pat into a greased 9-inch pie plate. Chill until firm (or bake at 350° F. for 5 to 8 minutes, then chill).

Pecan Crunch Crust*

Add 1/2 cup finely chopped pecans to recipe for Graham Cracker Crust and increase melted butter to 3/4 cup.

Rice Crispies Crust*

Prepare as for Graham Cracker Crust, using 2 cups Rice Crispies (crushed), 1/4 cup sugar and 1/3 cup melted butter.

Zwieback Crumb Crust*

This crust is frequently called for in cheesecake recipes. Combine crumbs from 2 6-ounce packages of zwieback with 1/2 cup sugar and 1/2 cup melted butter.

Pretzel Crumb Crust*

Sooner or later you may come across a recipe calling for a pretzel crumb crust. And you may like it, although it's a bit salty for my taste. But if sodium isn't on your hit list, by all means proceed — just use pretzel crumbs in place of graham cracker crumbs in that first recipe.

Coconut Pie Crust*

1-1/2 cups Angel Flake coconut

4 tablespoons melted butter (or margarine)

Mix coconut with butter and press into a 9-inch pie plate. Bake 8 minutes at 350° F. Watch very carefully to prevent over-browning.

Nuts and Coconut Pie Crust*

Prepare as for Coconut Pie Crust, reducing coconut to 1 cup and adding 1/2 cup chopped nuts.

Coconut Crumb Crust*

1-1/2 cups shredded coconut
1/4 cup melted butter (or margarine)

1/4 cup graham cracker crumbs
1/2 cup finely chopped pecans

Combine ingredients and press into a buttered 10-inch pie plate. Bake at 350° F. for 8 to 9 minutes. Take care that it doesn't get too brown.

Chocolate Cookie Crust I*

20 Hydrox creme-filled chocolate cookies, crushed

3 tablespoons melted butter (or margarine)

Mix crumbs with butter (or margarine) and press into buttered 9- or 10-inch pie plate. Chill. This makes a very rich, black crust.

Chocolate Cookie Crust II*

1-1/2 cups chocolate cookie wafers, crushed

1/4 cup melted butter (or margarine)
2 tablespoons sugar

Prepare as for Chocolate Cookie Crust I. This crust is a bit crisper, less dense.

Chocolate Crunch Crust*

2 6-ounce packages
  chocolate chips
2 tablespoons butter
  (or margarine)

2 cups puffed rice cereal
1/2 cup chopped nuts

Melt chocolate chips with butter (or margarine) in a double boiler over hot water. When melted, remove from heat and stir in cereal and nuts. Spread over bottom and sides of a buttered pie pan. Chill. This makes a thick, crunchy crust.

Date Coconut Pie Crust*

I recently discovered this unusual pie shell when it was served at a very tony dinner party. (The filling was a feathery combination of pistachio pudding and whipped cream, but any light, unbaked filling would be good.) When I finally pried the recipe out of the host, I was amazed how simple the whole thing is. Just keep the servings small. This one is **rich.**

2 cups dates, snipped into
  fine dice (use wet scissors)

2 cups Angel Flake coconut
1 cup finely diced walnuts

Mix ingredients well. With damp hands press mixture into a ball. Then pat into a buttered 9- or 10-inch pie pan and chill thoroughly.

Crumb Crust Pies

On the assumption that you are now well-versed in the vagaries of crumb crusts, here is how you can turn any one of them into a quick-as-a-wink pie.

Ruby Red Cherry Cheese Pie*

This recipe has been floating around forever, but it never ceases to make a dazzling entrance. I got the recipe years ago from a lady whose culinary accomplishments began and ended with this quick-fix pie. That ought to tell you how easy it is.

1 9-inch graham cracker
  pie crust
2 8-ounce packages cream
  cheese, softened
1 cup whipping cream
3 tablespoons powdered sugar

1 teaspoon vanilla extract
1 16-ounce can cherry pie filling,
  chilled
1 teaspoon almond extract
3 drops red food coloring

Beat cheese until fluffy. Whip cream with powdered sugar until stiff. Add vanilla. With rubber spatula, gently fold whipped cream into cheese. Spoon into pie crust. Refrigerate.

Stir almond flavoring and red coloring into cherry pie filling. Spoon topping over cream layer and refrigerate until firm — about 3 hours.

NOTE: This pie also works very nicely with a pre-baked conventional pie shell. So if you are up to *here* with crumb crusts, you might consider this second option.

Chocolate Mousse Pie**

*This scandalous mousse-in-a-crust is so rich it'll make the staunchest chocoholic blanch. But if you are looking for a knock'em dead dessert, this is it. Just keep the slices thin. Too much is really **too** much.*

1 chocolate crumb crust	2 cups whipping cream
1 pound semi-sweet chocolate	6 tablespoons powdered sugar
2 eggs	4 egg whites, room temperature
4 egg yolks	

Soften chocolate in top of double boiler. Cool to lukewarm. Add whole eggs and mix well. Add yolks and mix thoroughly.

Whip cream with powdered sugar, beating to soft peaks. Beat egg whites until stiff peaks form (but not dry). Stir a little of the whipped cream and the egg whites into the chocolate mixture. Then gently fold in the remaining cream and whites. Spoon into prepared chocolate crumb crust and chill until set.

Grasshopper Pie*

Grasshopper Pie has been around the party circuit long enough for the novelty to wear off, but it still makes a lovely way to wind down dinner on a light note. Again, crumb your own crust or buy a ready-made at the store.

1 chocolate cookie crust (page 265)	1-1/2 ounces green creme de menthe
1 cup milk	1 cup whipping cream
10 large marshmallows	1 teaspoon vanilla
1-1/2 ounces white creme de cacao	Aerosol can whipped cream Bittersweet chocolate

Heat milk gradually in a heavy saucepan. Add marshmallows that have been snipped in small pieces (use wet scissors). Stir until marshmallows have melted and sauce is smooth. Remove from heat and add liqueurs. Cool.

Whip cream until it holds stiff peaks, then add vanilla.

Fold whipped cream into marshmallow mixture and spoon into crust. Chill until firm. Garnish pie with swirls of whipped cream piped out of an aersol can. Sprinkle with bittersweet chocolate shavings.

Velvet Hammer Pie**

You can whip up this light-as-a-cloud party pie by following the recipe for Grasshopper Pie, substituting Cointreau for the green creme de menthe.

*Sparkle Plenty Party Pie***

An interesting mix of colors and textures shows up in this recipe that my friend, Tak, always volunteers for potlucks. It is very easy to make, requiring only a little patience so that one layer can firm up before adding another. NOTE: This "pie" is baked in a 9 x 13-inch pan — big enough for 10 to 12 servings.

Crust

1-1/2 cubes margarine	1-1/2 cups flour
1/2 cup brown sugar	1-1/2 cups chopped nuts

Mix margarine with sugar, flour and nuts. Press into a well-buttered 9 x 13-inch pan. Bake at 375° F. for about 10 minutes, or until lightly browned.

Cheese Layer

1 3-ounce package lemon gelatin	1 envelope whipped topping mix (or 8-ounce carton prepared topping)
1 cup boiling water	
3/4 cup sugar	
1 8-ounce package cream cheese, room temperature	

Dissolve gelatin in 1 cup boiling water and set aside to cool. Beat cream cheese, add sugar and beat again; add to whipped topping prepared from an envelope of mix (or use 8-ounce carton of whipped topping). Blend in the cooled gelatin, mix well and spread over the cooled crust. Be sure to cover the crust completely so the gelatin topping won't seep through. Refrigerate until firm, about 45 minutes.

Top Layer

1 6-ounce package cherry gelatin	3 cups boiling water

Meantime, prepare the 6-ounce package of cherry-flavored gelatin by dissolving in boiling water. Set aside until cool. When gelatin has cooled and the pie filling has firmed up in the refrigerator, carefully spoon the gelatin over the creamed cheese filling, being very, very careful not to poke a hole in the cheese layer. Chill until firm. Serves 10 to 12.

*Chocolate Pudding Layer Pie***

Similar to Sparkle Plenty Pie is this next king-size pie that is just as sensational — maybe more so if chocolate is your downfall.

1 stick margarine, softened	1 cup flour
1/2 cup brown sugar	1 cup chopped nuts

Mix margarine with sugar, flour, and nuts. Press into a 9 x 13-inch baking pan. Bake at 375° F. for 10 minutes, or until lightly browned. Cool.

Cheese Layer

1 8-ounce package cream cheese, softened	1 cup prepared whipped topping 1/2 cup powdered sugar

Whip cream cheese, then fold in 1 cup whipped topping. Mix in powdered sugar and blend well. Spread over cooled crust.

Top Layer

1 6-ounce package instant chocolate pudding mix 2-1/2 cups milk	Whipped topping (remaining from Cream Cheese Layer) 1/2 cup chopped nuts

Prepare instant pudding, using 2-1/2 cups milk. Spread over cream cheese layer. Top with remaining whipped topping and sprinkle with chopped nuts. Refrigerate 3 hours before serving. Serves 10 to 12.

Peanut Butter Chiffon Pie**

Rich and wickedly loaded with calories, Peanut Butter Chiffon Pie has to be one of the most decadent downfalls a dieter will ever encounter.

1 graham cracker crust (page 264) 1 envelope unflavored gelatin 1/4 cup sugar 1/4 teaspoon salt 1 cup milk 2 egg yolks, slightly beaten	1/4 cup creamy peanut butter 2 egg whites 1/4 cup sugar 2 cups frozen whipped topping, thawed Grated chocolate

Mix gelatin, 1/4 cup sugar, and salt in saucepan; add milk and yolks. Cook and stir over medium heat until mixture comes to a boil. Add peanut butter and stir until blended. Refrigerate until thoroughly chilled.

Beat chilled peanut butter mixture and set aside.

Whip egg whites until foamy, and gradually add 1/4 cup sugar. Continue beating until stiff peaks form. Fold into peanut butter mixture. Then fold in whipped topping. Spoon into crust and chill until firm. Garnish with grated chocolate.

Mud Pie*

Calories be damned! Here comes Mud Pie, one of the gooeyest, wickedly rich desserts ever invented.

1 9-inch chocolate crumb crust (page 265) 1 quart coffee ice cream	2 ounces kahlua Mud-Fudge Topping (page 270) Whipped cream

Into slightly softened ice cream, stir the kahlua. Pat into crumb crust and freeze until solid. Top with Mud-Fudge Topping and re-freeze. Serve in wedges (make them **skinny** wedges) topped with whipped cream.

Mud-Fudge Topping*

1 cup thick hot fudge topping   1-1/2 ounces orange-flavored
                                      liqueur (or Grand Marnier)

Get the thickest canned or bottled hot fudge topping available. Open the container and set it in a small pan of hot water. Heat gently until topping is soft enough to spread. Add liqueur, mix well, and spoon over the frozen ice cream pie. Smooth with a wet knife and place in the freezer.

Peppermint Ice Cream Sundae Pie*

Super-easy Peppermint Ice Cream Sundae Pie features that lovely marriage of flavors, chocolate and peppermint.

1 chocolate crumb crust   3/4 cup prepared fudge topping*
  (page 265)   Whipped cream
1 quart peppermint stick   1/2 cup chopped nuts
  ice cream

Fill crumb crust with scoops of ice cream, mounting high in the center. Pour fudge topping over the ice cream, then place in the freezer. Just before serving, top with dollops of whipped cream and sprinkle with chopped nuts.

*Prepared fudge toppings are sold in jars and in cans. If the fudge is too thick to pour, open the container, set it in a pan of hot water and place over low heat — just long enough to soften slightly.

Fudge Sundae Pie**

1 graham cracker pie crust   1 cup miniature marshmallows
  (page 265)   1/4 teaspoon salt
1 cup evaporated milk   1 quart butter pecan (or vanilla)
1 6-ounce package semi-   ice cream
  sweet chocolate bits   Pecan halves

In a heavy saucepan place evaporated milk, chocolate bits, marshmallows and salt. Stir over low heat until marshmallows have melted and mixture thickens. Cool to room temperature. Let ice cream soften slightly.

Spoon half the ice cream into the prepared shell. Smooth, and top with half of the chocolate mixture. Then spoon in the remaining ice cream. Top with remaining chocolate mixture and sprinkle with pecan halves. Freeze until firm — 3 to 5 hours.

Meringue Shells

While they will never take the place of good old apple pie, meringue pies — with their puffy shells and airy fillings — can be a pretty spectacular achievement for the new cook. They can, however, be subject to fits of temperament.

The main pitfall is temperature: keep it low and let the pie shell sit in the unlit oven until they both cool off. That helps insure a nice, crispy, dry meringue.

Another thing: never try to make a meringue shell on a damp or rainy day. If it's humid, don't hazard it. Meringue absorbs dampness like a sponge, and a pie like a sponge is **not** what you're after.

*Meringue Pie Shell**

4 egg whites, room   1/4 teaspoon cream of tartar
  temperature   1 cup sugar

Grease and flour a 9-inch pie plate. Beat egg whites until frothy, then add the cream of tartar, beating constantly. As soft peaks start to form, very gradually start adding the sugar — a tablespoon at a time — until it's all absorbed. (Rub a little meringue between your fingers. If it feels gritty, keep beating — the sugar should be dissolved.)

Spread meringue in the pie plate, building up the sides. Bake in a pre-heated 275° F. oven for 1 hour. Turn off the heat, open the oven door and allow the pie shell to cool in the oven for 1 hour. Cool, remove gently from pie plate and chill before filling.

*Chocolate Bar Angel Pie***

I once knew a young man whose favorite dessert was a fluffy chocolate pie in a meringue shell. Every birthday and anniversary, his bride would make him one. And, just as predictably, he would barge into the office the next day raving about those light-as-puff pies.

This is the candy bar confection he was so mad about.

1 meringue pie shell   3 tablespoons water
3 milk chocolate candy bars   1 teaspoon vanilla
  (1-1/2 ounces each)   1 cup whipping cream
  without almonds   Chocolate curls or shaved chocolate

Melt candy bars with water in top of a double boiler over simmering water. Stir in vanilla, then let cool. Fold in cream that has been stiffly beaten and spoon into meringue shell. Chill a minimum of 24 hours before serving. Decorate with chocolate curls, if desired. (Whipped cream wouldn't hurt, either.)

*Angel Lemon Cream Filling***

Here's a novel twist — a lemon meringue pie with the meringue on the bottom.

1 meringue pie shell   1/3 cup lemon juice
4 egg yolks   Dash salt
2/3 cup sugar   1 cup whipping cream
Grated rind of 2 lemons

Beat egg yolks with sugar in top of double boiler. When mixture is light and fluffy, add the lemon rind, juice and salt. Cook over simmering water until thickened, stirring constantly. Set off to cool.

Whip cream until stiff. Spread half the cream in the meringue shell. Top with cooled lemon mixture. Cover with remaining cream. Refrigerate 2 hours before serving.

What's Ahead in Splendid Endings

. . . *the rest of the sweet temptations*

Having cut through the pies and cakes, we come now to the miscellaneous mousses and meringues, puddings and parfaits that can wind down dinner on a sweet and even keel.

Actually a dessert doesn't have to be sweet. Nuts and cheese, for example, are a classy exception. They're easy, too. And for the beginning cook, that is one thing dessert should always be: **easy.**

Next to simplicity, the next thing you need is something that can be prepared well ahead of time. In the hands of an inexperienced cook, a last-minute dazzler can turn into a split-second disaster, so why chance it?

Ideally, before dinner begins, dessert should be cooling its heels in the fridge or behaving itself on the sideboard.

If there's one thing you don't need it is to be hung up in the kitchen wrestling with a stuck bombe or a half-baked Alaska while everyone is ho-humming in the dining room and wondering what happened to the cook.

Parfait a la Nutz*

Naked and unadorned, vanilla pudding is pretty dull stuff. But you'd be surprised how easily you can zap it into something special with a few minor embellishments. In this case, peanut brittle and kahlua do the noble deed.

1 3-1/2-ounce package
   vanilla pudding
   (not instant)
1 cup crushed peanut brittle
	1 tablespoon kahlua (or creme
	   de cacao)
	Whipped cream
	Chopped almonds (or pecans)

Prepare pudding according to package instructions. Cool slightly, then fold in the crushed peanut brittle and the kahlua. Place a piece of waxed paper over the surface of the pudding as it cools, then refrigerate.

When thoroughly chilled, spoon into tall (and preferably frosted) parfait glasses, alternating with dollops of sweetened whipped cream. Top off with chopped nuts. Makes enough for 4 parfait-glass servings.

Rocky Road Pudding*

Here's how to give chocolate pudding mix a leg up.

1 3-1/4-ounce package chocolate pudding mix (not instant)	1/4 cup brandy
	1 cup miniature marshmallows
	1/2 cup chopped walnuts
1-1/2 cups milk	1/2 cup whipping cream, whipped

Combine pudding mix and milk in a small, heavy saucepan. Stir over low heat until thick and smooth. Remove from heat and stir in brandy. Place a piece of waxed paper over pudding surface to prevent skin from forming.

When cooled to room temperature, fold in marshmallows and nuts. Cover and chill. Before serving, spoon pudding into parfait or sherbet glasses alternately with sweetened whipped cream. Serves 6.

Speedy Spumoni*

*The next time you have friends over for one of your world-famous spaghetti dinners, try winding things down with this make-ahead Italian ice cream. It's very authentic and **very** easy.*

1 quart vanilla ice cream	1/3 cup drained and chopped maraschino cherries
1/2 cup toasted slivered almonds	
	1/2 teaspoon shredded orange peel
1 3/4-ounce chocolate candy bar, chopped	1/4 teaspoon shredded lemon peel

Soften ice cream slightly, then stir in remaining ingredients. Place fluted paper cups in muffin tins and spoon ice cream into the cups. Cover and freeze until firm. Makes 10 servings.

Bread Pudding with Rum Sauce**

This recipe for bread pudding comes from one of the finest plantation restaurants in Mississippi. The pudding, by itself, is divine. And the rum sauce that tops it is pure elixir. (If you have any sauce left over, try it on vanilla ice cream.)

6 slices day-old bread	4 eggs
1 teaspoon cinnamon	1/2 cup, rounded, sugar
1/2 cup seedless raisins	2 cups milk
2 tablespoons melted margarine	1 teaspoon vanilla
	Rum sauce

Butter a 1-1/2 quart baking dish. Break bread in small cubes, sprinkle with cinnamon and toss with raisins and melted margarine. Spread on a baking sheet and toast in a 350° F. oven until bread is a pale, golden brown. Spoon into baking dish. Beat eggs with sugar, milk, and vanilla; pour over bread.

Set baking dish in a larger pan and add hot water to a depth of 2 inches. Bake at 350° F. for 30 minutes. Serve warm with Rum Sauce.

Rum Sauce**

2 cups milk	2 teaspoons nutmeg
1/2 cup butter	1 tablespoon vanilla
1/2 cup sugar	Pinch salt
1 tablespoon butter	3 tablespoons rum
2 tablespoons flour	

Combine milk, butter and sugar in small pan. Bring to a boil, then set aside. In another small pan, heat butter. Mix in flour, stirring to make a smooth paste. Add some of the hot milk mixture, blending well. Then return this mixture to the remaining hot milk and cook until the sauce is smooth and thickened. Remove from heat and stir in nutmeg, vanilla, salt and rum. Serve warm over pudding. Makes about 2 cups.

Steamed Persimmon Christmas Pudding**

Christmas at our house could never get off the ground without Steamed Persimmon Pudding with Brandy Sauce. When my college roommate landed a job as food page editor on a major San Francisco newspaper, she ran the recipe one Christmas. Every year after that the paper was flooded with repeat requests for the same recipe.

1 cup flour	1/2 cup milk
1 cup sugar	1 cup persimmon pulp
1 teaspoon salt	1 teaspoon vanilla
1/4 teaspoon cinnamon	1 cup chopped nuts
2 teaspoons soda	1 cup chopped raisins

Sift flour with sugar, salt, cinnamon, and soda. Add milk, persimmon pulp, vanilla, nuts, and raisins. Stir until well-blended, then spoon into two well-greased ovenproof bowls. Cover with a double layer of waxed paper and secure tops with rubber bands.

Place bowls on a rack (metal jar rings can substitute for racks) in a large kettle so that bowls don't rest on the bottom of the pot. Fill half way with water, cover and steam puddings for 1-1/2 hours. Cool, cover tightly and store in the refrigerator. Puddings can be kept for weeks in the refrigerator. Before serving, steam over hot water until piping hot. Serve warm with Brandy Sauce.

Brandy Sauce*

1/2 cup brown sugar	4 tablespoons butter
1/2 cup white sugar	2 teaspoons vanilla
2 tablespoons cornstarch	Dash salt
1 cup boiling water	1/4 cup brandy

Combine sugars, cornstarch, and boiling water in a small saucepan. Cook, stirring, until thickened. Remove from heat and add butter, vanilla, salt, and brandy. Store in the refrigerator, but heat gently before serving. Serve over Steamed Persimmon Christmas Pudding.

Harvey Wallbanger Souffles**

These sky-high souffles don't require any baking nor do they fall down if somebody slams the door. They do, however, take a bit of doing which isn't hard if you stay calm and take your time.

One more thing: these souffles have to be refrigerated in individual stemmed wine glasses, so make sure there's plenty of room in the refrigerator before you embark. (Fridge space is always a big problem at our house.)

1/4 cup sugar	2 cups frozen whipped topping,
1 envelope unflavored gelatin	thawed
1-1/4 cups orange juice	3 egg whites
3 egg yolks	1/4 cup sugar
2 tablespoons orange liqueur	Fresh orange slices
2 tablespoons vodka	Soft butter

Lightly butter the insides of 6 8-ounce wine glasses. Sprinkle with a little sugar. Then place foil collars around each glass, extending above the rims about 1 inch. Secure foil with tape.

Mix 1/4 cup sugar and gelatin in a small saucepan. Add orange juice. Stir over medium heat until sugar dissolves and mixture boils. Take off heat.

Beat egg yolks for 5 minutes with an electric beater. Stir 1/2 cup of the hot gelatin mixture into the yolks. Then add the yolk mixture to the remaining gelatin in the pan, stirring over medium heat until mixture thickens. Take off heat and add orange liqueur and vodka. Refrigerate until partially set. Then fold in whipped topping. In a small bowl, beat egg whites until soft peaks form. Slowly add 1/4 cup sugar, beating into stiff peaks. Fold gelatin mixture into the egg whites, taking care not to deflate the mass.

Spoon mixture into prepared glasses, lightly cover with plastic and refrigerate until firm. Just before serving, remove collars. Garnish with blobs of whipped cream and a twisted orange slice. Serves 6.

Quick Cookie Crumble Ice Cream**

Bet you thought you needed an ice cream freezer to make homemade ice cream, didn't you? Well, you don't. This quick-fix recipe proves the point, very sweetly.

3 egg yolks	3 teaspoons vanilla
1 14-ounce can sweetened	1 cup coarsely crushed Oreo
condensed milk	sandwich cookies
2 tablespoons Amaretto liqueur	1 pint whipping cream, whipped

Beat yolks. Stir in sweetened condensed milk, liqueur and vanilla. Fold in crushed cookies and whipped cream.

Line a 2-quart container with foil (a loaf pan works well) and spoon in mixture. Cover tightly and freeze until firm — about 6 hours. Makes about 1-1/2 quarts.

Fresh Strawberry Trifle**

*At first glance, trifle looks pretty complicated and gooey. But that's only half right. It's gooey, all right, but it really isn't difficult to do. Just take it a step at a time and hang in there. This gives you a chance to get in and really **build** something.*

1 3-1/4-ounce package vanilla pudding mix (not instant)	2 tablespoons red raspberry preserves
2 cups light cream (or half-and-half)	1 round sponge cake (about 2 inches thick)
2 tablespoons rum	1/4 cup brandy
2-1/4 cups whipping cream	1/4 cup sherry
3 tablespoons sugar	3 dozen plump, whole strawberries

Combine pudding mix and cream in a heavy saucepan and cook over low heat until mixture comes to a boil. Stir in rum, then take from the heat and cover pudding with a circle of waxed paper and refrigerate until well-chilled.

Take 1-1/4 cups of the whipping cream and beat, with 1 tablespoon of sugar, until the cream is stiff. Fold this into the chilled pudding.

Chill a 10-inch glass bowl. When cold, paint the inside of the bowl with the raspberry preserves (use a pastry brush). With a serrated knife, cut the sponge cake into 4 thin layers. Put the top slice in the bowl first, crust side up. Cut the other three layers into bars about 2 inches wide and stand up along the inside of the bowl, pressing so the bars of cake adhere to the preserves.

Combine brandy and sherry and sprinkle over the bottom crust in the bowl. Sprinkle in the whipped-cream custard mix.

Beat remaining 1 cup whipping cream with 2 tablespoons sugar, whipping until stiff. Pipe whipped cream around the rim of the bowl and in fat puffs in the center. Decorate with whole, chilled berries. Refrigerate 2 hours before serving. Serves 8.

Almond Trifle*

Lest you be boggled by that last one, here is a simple trifle that goes together in minutes— definitely a good bet for the one-star (*) novice.

2 sponge cake layers	1/2 cup sherry
6 big macaroons, crumbled slightly (stale, if possible)	1/2 pint whipping cream, whipped
1 cup toasted slivered almonds	3 tablespoons powdered sugar

With a serrated knife, cut the sponge cake layers in half horizontally, making four layers in all. Crumble macaroons.

In your prettiest clear glass bowl, place a cake layer, sprinkle with part of the macaroon crumbs and nuts. Repeat layers — using all cake, crumbs, and nuts. Drizzle with sherry. (You might need a drop or two more, but bear in mind that what you're after is dampness, not sog. So go easy.) Cover with plastic and refrigerate several hours. Before serving, pile the bowl with whipped cream, sweetened with powdered sugar, and a sprinkling of almonds. Serves 6.

Cherries Jubilee***

Cherries Jubilee, one of the most spectacular desserts of all, can be easily engineered provided you pay attention to the temperature of the liquor to be ignited and the sauce over which it is to be poured. Both should be warm enough to easily flame.

In this recipe, the cherry sauce can be prepared well ahead, leaving nothing to do at the last minute but to warm up and light up. (With a little luck you will be able to pull this all off without catching the curtains on fire.)

2 16-ounce cans pitted dark sweet cherries	1/4 cup sugar
	1/4 cup currant jelly
1 cup brandy	1 quart vanilla ice cream

Drain cherries into a bowl, reserving 1/2 cup syrup.

Place 1/2 cup cherry syrup, 1/2 cup brandy, and 1/4 cup sugar in a small saucepan. Bring to boil, reduce heat and cook until sauce is reduced to 1/2 cup. Pour over cherries and set aside. Let stand several hours before serving.

Just before serving, heat cherries with currant jelly. Stir in 6 tablespoons brandy. Over low heat, warm the remaining 2 tablespoons of brandy in a large ladle. Ignite and spoon over the warm cherries. As the flames fade, spoon sauce over individual servings of ice cream. Serves 8.

Chocolate Orange Mousse**

A really good mousse is smooth as satin, dense and achingly rich — like this one that puts a trace of orange in with the chocolate. The Grand Marnier is an optional, but smashing, coup de grace.

If you have an elegant cut glass bowl, by all means prepare — and serve — the mousse in it. ***Very*** *showy at the table.*

2 eggs	1 cup whipping cream, whipped
3 egg yolks	6 ounces semi-sweet chocolate
1/2 cup sugar	2 ounces cold water
Rind and juice of 1 orange	1-1/2 tablespoons Grand Marnier
1 package unflavored gelatin	(optional)
	Sweetened whipped cream

Beat eggs, egg yolks and sugar with an electric beater until mixture is very thick (as much as 5 minutes). Add Grand Marnier.

Melt chocolate in 2 ounces water. Grate orange rind and add to the melted chocolate. Squeeze orange juice into a small saucepan. Sprinkle geltain over surface of the juice and let stand until softened, 2 to 3 minutes.

Heat juice and gelatin over low heat, not allowing it to boil. When gelatin is melted, stir into egg mixture. Next, fold melted chocolate into eggs. Finally fold in the lightly whipped cream. Turn into a 1-1/2 quart glass serving bowl and chill a minimum of 4 hours. At serving time garnish with puffs of whipped cream. Serves 6.

Banana Won Tons**

Some menus present a real problem when it comes to dessert. Anything Oriental, for instance. Well, if nothing else seems a fitting ending for your stir-fry or Szechwan specialty, try these sweet and crispy won tons.

1 package won ton skins	1/2 teaspoon cinnamon
2 mashed bananas	1/4 cup raisins
1/3 cup coconut	Oil

Heat oil to 350° F. in an electric skillet. In a bowl, combine bananas, coconut, cinnamon and raisins.

Moisten edges of won ton skins with water. Place 1 teaspoon filling on the center of each piece, then fold into a triangle. (Or, as you get more adept, try folding the edges in, then rolling and sealing the won tons into miniature rolls.) Fry, turning, until golden. Drain on paper towels and dust with powdered sugar. Serve warm.

NOTE: You will have a lot more skins than you will filling. Tightly wrap unused won ton skins in foil or plastic and freeze. Or double the recipe and freeze the filled won tons that can be thawed and fried later.

Baked Alaska Jet Set***

Here it is, the classic of all time — Baked Alaska — that freezer-to-oven grandstander that never fails to flabbergast the uninitiated.

A quick way to knock one out is to buy a ready-made ice cream roll, slather it with meringue and move fast. (And eat it all. Leftovers don't work with this one.)

3 egg whites, beaten stiff	1 frozen ice cream roll, chocolate
2-1/2 tablespoons sugar	(or white)
1/4 teaspoon cream of tartar	1 to 2 tablespoons brandy

Beat egg whites until glossy, then add cream of tartar. Add sugar, a teaspoonful at a time, continuing to beat until stiff peaks form.

Just before serving, slide the firmly frozen cake roll onto a small oven-proof serving platter and brush the cake with brandy. Then, working quickly, "frost" the cake with the meringue and pop into the oven which has been preheated to 450° F. Give it three minutes to turn a toasty brown. Then serve — **pronto.** Serves 8. NOTE: Leftovers are a disaster, so eat heartily.

Peche Melba*

One of the classic desserts of all time, Peche (pronounced p-esh) Melba is nothing more than a happy marriage of peaches and red raspberry sauce. It doesn't always have ice cream but, in my opinion, that just makes a good thing even better.

Place one canned and drained peach half in an individual serving dish, top with a scoop of rich vanilla ice cream and drizzle raspberry sauce over the whole thing. It doesn't need whipped cream, but it's a lovely touch, all the same.

Raspberry sauce: Blend 1 package thawed red raspberries with 2 tablespoons warmed currant jelly. Stir to blend.

Strawberries Romanoff*

Strawberries Romanoff is another tony dessert that is very easy to put together. Light and refreshing, it provides a perfect ending for a company dinner on a springtime evening.

3 baskets of fresh ripe strawberries	1 pint French vanilla ice cream
3 tablespoons sugar	1 cup whipping cream, whipped stiff
1/2 cup cointreau	Juice of 1 lemon

Slice berries, sprinkle with sugar and about 2 tablespoons of cointreau. Chill.

Just before serving, allow ice cream to soften slightly (this can be done by putting the ice cream in the refrigerator section instead of the freezer for about a half hour). Fold whipped cream into the slightly softened ice cream. Fold in the remaining cointreau and the lemon juice. Place berries in a glass serving bowl and pour over the whipped ice cream. Serves 4.

Peaches 'n Cream*

This rummy dessert borrows from Strawberries Romanoff the same topping — vanilla ice cream and whipped cream.

Slice fresh peaches into a pretty bowl, bring it to the table and, before your guests, douse with fruit with rum (3 or 4 healthy swigs). Toss lightly, then spoon into serving dishes. Top with a fluffy combination of whipped cream and ice cream served from a second bowl.

Poires Helene*

Drain canned pears thoroughly, then place the halves, cut side up, on chilled serving plates. Place scoops of vanilla ice cream on each pear half, pipe whipped cream in opulent dollops around the edge, then drizzle with warm chocolate sauce.

Bananas Foster***

This flaming dessert originated in New Orleans where it has been a staple in plush restaurants for two generations.

1/4 cup butter	Dash cinnamon
1/2 cup light brown sugar	1/2 cup white rum
4 ripe bananas, peeled and split lengthwise	1/2 cup banana liqueur (creme de banana)

Melt butter and brown sugar in a chafing dish or a flat skillet. Add the bananas and saute gently until tender, turning once — about 5 minutes, total. Sprinkle with cinnamon.

Meanwhile, gently heat rum and liqueur in a small pan until warm, then ignite with a match. As liquid flames, pour over the bananas. Swirl the skillet until the flames go out. Serve at once over vanilla ice cream. Serves 4.

Rhubarb Cloud**

One of the surest signs of Spring is the emergence of rhubarb. As soon as those pale pink-to-ruby stalks hit the produce stands, my friend Lennie whips out her stemmed wine glasses and spoons up this gorgeous pale-pink dessert.

4 cups strawberry rhubarb
(or any of the pink or red
varieties) cut in 1-inch
pieces
1/2 cup sugar
1/4 cup cranberry juice

1 3-ounce package raspberry
gelatin
1/2 cup cold cranberry juice
1 cup heavy cream, whipped
Fresh strawberries or raspberries
Mint sprigs

Combine rhubarb pieces with sugar and 1/4 cup cranberry juice in a heavy saucepan. Bring to a boil, cover pan and simmer, stirring occasionally, for 8 to 10 minutes. Take off heat and add gelatin. Stir, then put back over medium heat and stir until gelatin is completely dissolved. Stir in 1/2 cup cold cranberry juice. Chill until partially set.

Whip with electric beater until fluffy — beating at least 10 minutes. Fold in whipped cream. Spoon into stemmed wine glasses and chill. Serve garnished with a few fresh berries and mint. Serves 6.

Corn Flake Ice Cream Baskets***

Making ice cream baskets is like weaving a May basket (or a May pole) — it takes time. But it really isn't difficult, and it certainly provides a novel way to serve up ice cream. Kids, especially, love them.

1-1/2 cups corn flakes
1/2 cup chocolate chips
1 tablespoon butter

1 tablespoons light corn syrup
4 large marshmallows, cut in pieces
1/3 cup flaked coconut

Crunch corn flakes into crumbs. You should have about 3/4 cup crumbs. Set aside.

Melt chocolate chips with butter and corn syrup in a double boiler over hot, not boiling, water. Stir constantly while chocolate melts. Add marshmallows, continuing to stir until marshmallows are almost melted. Take from heat and fold in corn flake crumbs and coconut.

Butter 6 muffin cups (about 2-1/2 inches in diameter) and press corn flake mixture onto the bottoms and up the sides of the cups, using the back of a spoon. Refrigerate 1 hour or until cups harden. Just before serving, loosen with a sharp knife. Should any of the baskets stick, wrap a warm, damp towel around the outside of the muffin cups just long enough to free the baskets.

NOTE: Baskets should be filled with ice cream.

A Host of Sundaes

When all else fails (the cake fell, the pie burned or the cookies crumbled), there's always good old ice cream for dessert. Thank goodness, help is as close as the corner drug store. More than once a half gallon of French vanilla has galloped to my personal rescue.

The trick, when you're caught, is to proceed as if ice cream was what you had in mind all the time. From there, you simply have to doctor it up a bit. You know, make it look like **more**.

The solution is swift and simple: Make sundaes.

A tailor-made topping is all you need to make these sweet treats yours, all yours.

Chocolate Sundae Sauce Deluxe**

Here's a rich chocolate sauce you should make up ahead and have on hand in the fridge — not only for company but those times in the middle of the night when you could kill for a chocolate sundae.

1 6-ounce package semi- sweet chocolate bits	1/2 cup light corn syrup
1/2 stick margarine	1/4 cup boiling water
1 cup sifted powdered sugar	1/4 cup creme de cacao
Pinch salt	1 teaspoon vanilla extract

Melt chocolate in top of double boiler. Remove from heat and add remaining ingredients. Stir until smooth and well blended. Store in the refrigerator. Makes about 2 cups topping for ice cream.

Sunday Sundae Sauce*

Here is a rich and unusual topping that combines dates, figs and walnuts.

1 cup finely chopped dates	1/2 cup corn syrup
1 cup water	3/4 cup coarsely chopped walnuts
1/2 cup finely chopped figs	

Combine all ingredients but the walnuts in a small saucepan and cook over low heat until sauce is well blended and thickened. Remove from heat, stir in nuts. Serve warm over ice cream. Makes about 1-1/2 cups sauce.

Apple Pie Sundaes*

If you adore apple pie with ice cream but have no time to make it, here's a ready option: warm apple pie topping spooned over ice cream.

1 21-ounce can apple pie filling	1/2 teaspoon finely grated lemon peel (optional)
1-1/2 teaspoons cinnamon	Vanilla ice cream

Place pie filling, cinnamon and grated peel in a small saucepan and slowly warm. Spoon over ice cream. Serves 6 to 8.

Brandy Fudge Sauce**

This brandy-laced fudge topping can be gently warmed before serving. And, if you want to zap it a bit more, increase the brandy. (Better give the kids Popsicles when you serve this stuff.)

2 2-ounce squares bitter chocolate	1 tablespoon cornstarch
1/2 cup corn syrup	Dash salt
1/2 cup sugar	3 tablespoons butter
1/2 cup half-and-half	1 teaspoon vanilla extract
	2 tablespoons brandy

In top of double boiler, over hot water, melt the chocolate with corn syrup. Stir sugar into the half-and-half; stir until dissolved. Stir cornstarch and salt into half-and-half mixture. Add to the melted chocolate and cook over simmering water for 10 minutes. Add the butter, vanilla extract, and brandy; mix well. Store tightly covered in the refrigerator.

Brandy Alexander Ice Cream Topping**

Once, when I was quite young (but old enough to know better), I put away three Brandy Alexanders as if they were milk shakes and ended up very sorry, indeed. Brandy Alexander Ice Cream Topping is just as delicious and lots safer.

2 squares bitter chocolate	1 teaspoon vanilla
2 tablespoons butter	Pinch salt
2/3 cup sugar	1/3 cup brandy
1/2 cup evaporated milk	

Melt chocolate with butter over low heat. When melted, add sugar and evaporated milk. Cook over very low heat until the sugar is dissolved and the sauce has thickened. Remove from the heat and add vanilla, a speck of salt, and the brandy. This will keep well in the refrigerator in a tightly covered container. Serve cold or warm over French vanilla ice cream.

Sangria Sundae Topping**

Sangria — that red wine-based fruit cooler that made such a big splash a few summers ago — resurfaces here in an ice cream topping that will score big points for novelty, if nothing else.

1 8-1/4-ounce can pineapple chunks	2 tablespoons frozen lemon concentrate
1 tablespoon cornstarch	2 large navel oranges, peeled and sectioned
1/2 cup red wine	6 maraschino cherries, sliced

Drain pineapple, reserving syrup. Stir cornstarch into the syrup and stir until smooth. Add wine and lemonade concentrate and cook, over a low heat, until smooth and thickened. When sauce is bubbling, add the pineapple chunks, the orange segments and the cherries. This is good served warm or cold over vanilla ice cream. Makes about 1-3/4 cups.

Grasshopper Sundae*

First we had Grasshopper Cocktails, then pies, and now this — Grasshopper Sundaes! Will these boozy wonders never end?

2 scoops French vanilla
  ice cream
1/4 cup coffee cream
1 jigger white creme de cacao

1 jigger green creme de menthe
Toasted almonds, chopped
Maraschino cherries

Spoon scoops of ice cream into two champagne glasses. Combine cream with liqueurs and blend well. Pour over ice cream and top each serving with a liberal sprinkling of chopped almonds and a maraschino cherry.

Apricot Supreme Sundae Sauce*

How often does anyone get treated to a golden apricot sundae? Once you've tried this one, you will have to agree: it isn't nearly often enough.

1 8-ounce package dried
  apricots
1 cup water
1 cup sugar

1 teaspoon lemon juice
1/4 teaspoon almond extract
Few grains salt

Cook apricots in water until tender, about 10 minutes. Add sugar and cook an additional 15 minutes. Add lemon juice, almond extract, and a sprinkle of salt. Process in a blender until smooth. Serve chilled over vanilla ice cream. Makes about 2-1/2 cups.

Honey of a Sundae*

Another quickie topping for ice cream can be engineered by putting 1/2 cup slivered almonds in a pie pan and toasting the nuts under the broiler until lightly browned. Watch closely so they don't burn.

Melt 2 tablespoons butter in a small skillet. Into the bubbling butter, stir 1/2 cup honey. When these have blended together, spoon over vanilla ice cream and sprinkle with toasted almonds. Superb!

Mint Patty Sundae Sauce*

Peppermint buffs love this one. Chocoholics won't turn it down, either.

12 chocolate-covered
  peppermint patties

3 tablespoons cream (or evaporated
  milk)

Put the peppermint patties and cream (or evaporated milk) in the top of a double boiler and melt over simmering water, stirring to blend. Spoon warm over ice cream. Remaining topping may be re-warmed for later use.

Quick Kahlua Fudge Sauce**

Got a fondue pot standing around doing nothing? Use it for this quick-mix sauce that makes marvelous dunking for squares of angel food cake, slices of oranges, pineapple and fresh apple wedges. After you have fondued to your heart's content, save what's left of the sauce for topping ice cream.

6 ounces unsweetened chocolate	1-1/2 cups sugar
1 cup half and half	1/2 cup butter
	3 tablespoons Kahlua

Slowly melt chocolate in half and half. Take off heat and stir in sugar and butter. Stir until sugar is completely melted and sauce is smooth. Add Kahlua. Sauce should be refrigerated until ready to use.

Peanut Butter Sauce for Ice Cream*

Another rich and creamy topping for ice cream employs that old standby, peanut butter.

1 cup sugar	1/2 teaspoon salt
3/4 cup water	1/2 cup peanut butter
2/3 cup light corn syrup	

Combine sugar, water, corn syrup, and salt in a small saucepan and bring to a boil. Reduce heat and cook over low heat for 5 minutes. Remove from heat and stir in peanut butter. Stir until well blended. If necessary, thin with 1 tablespoon water. Serve over vanilla ice cream. Makes 2 cups.

Praline Topping**

3 tablespoons butter	4 tablespoons light corn syrup
2 tablespoon slivered almonds	1/4 teaspoon salt
1 cup light brown sugar	1/2 cup evaporated milk

Melt 1 tablespoon butter in a small heavy skillet and add the nuts. Saute until almonds are golden brown. Add remaining 2 tablespoons butter, brown sugar, syrup and salt. Cook over low heat until sugar dissolves. Remove from heat and stir in the evaporated milk. Serve warm or cool over rum or vanilla ice cream.

Other Ice Cream Quickies

Short of building sundaes for the folks, there are other sleight-of-hand glamourizers to smarten up drugstore ice cream.

When time has run out and your back's to the wall, just remember: something as simple as a splash of liqueur drizzled over, or a handful of nuts or fruit stirred into, store-bought ice cream diminishes its cash-and-carry qualities.

Brandy Creme*

Stir 4 or 5 tablespoons of brandy into one quart of slightly softened vanilla ice cream. Serve in brandy snifters.

Choco-Menthe Parfait*

2 ounces creme de
  menthe (green)
1 pint chocolate chip (or
  chocolate almond) ice cream

2 ounces creme de cacao
Whipped cream
Chopped almonds

Spoon a little creme de menthe in the bottoms of four parfait glasses. Top with small scoops of ice cream, then drizzle with creme de cacao. Top off with whipped cream and chopped almonds. Serves 2.

Coffee Snow*

1/3 cup fresh roasted
  coffee beans
1 quart French vanilla
  ice cream

Whipped cream
Freshly grated nutmeg

Minutes before serving, grind coffee beans as finely as possible in a coffee grinder or blender. Scoop ice cream into 4 well-chilled parfait glasses, sprinkling fine drifts of ground coffee over the ice cream as the glasses fill. Top with whipped cream and a sprinkling of ground nutmeg.

Fresh Fruit Fasties

Some of the loveliest — and lightest — desserts are nothing more than fresh fruits sprinkled with, or steeped in, compatible liqueurs. They come forth looking very fancy, and even someone who has never seen the inside of a kitchen can put one together in jig time.

Consider, for instance, this next one:

Pineapple Kirsch*

1 fresh pineapple, cut
  lengthwise in quarters
4 tablespoons kirsch

Maraschino cherries
Mint sprigs

Cut ripe pineapple in half, then cut each half into two lengthwise sections, taking care to leave some of the green leafy frond on each piece.

With a sharp knife, cut the wedge of pineapple from the outside bark. Trim the woody inner core away from each section. Now cut the pineapple into bite-sized chunks, carefully fitting the wedges back into their shells.

Drizzle each section with kirsch and wrap in plastic. Chill. Serve garnished with maraschino cherries on picks and fresh mint sprigs dipped in sugar.

Bing Cherry Kirsch*

Now that you've sprung for a bottle of kirsch, there's no point letting it stand around tapping its little foot in the cupboard while you ponder what to do next. What you do next follows.

Steep two cups of pitted fresh black bing cherries in kirsch for about an hour in the refrigerator. Just before serving, spoon into pretty glass serving dishes and top with whipped cream. Or you can use the cherries as a topping for vanilla ice cream. Either way, a topping drift of freshly grated nutmeg makes a nice fillip.

Melon Kirsch*

And this is what you do with what's left of the kirsch.

Combine melon balls, pineapple chunks, seedless grapes and strawberries in a bowl. Drizzle with enough kirsch to lace the fruit, then refrigerate — covered — until the fruit is well chilled. Serve in hollowed-out cantaloupe halves or pineapple shells and garnish with mint sprigs.

Gin 'n Fruit*

On the off chance you have a couple of leftover martinis languishing in the fridge, you can always dribble them over fruit and call it dessert. Otherwise start from scratch with plain gin — straight.

1 cup pineapple chunks, with juice	Juice of 1/2 lemon
1 cup fresh grapefruit segments	Pinch salt
Fresh mint sprigs	Sugar, to taste
	Gin

Combine equal amounts of pineapple chunks (plus juice) and grapefruit segments in a bowl. Chop several sprigs of fresh mint and add. Sprinkle with lemon juice, add a pinch of salt and enough sugar to liberally sweeten the mix. Refrigerate overnight. Before serving, pile drained fruit in compotes, add a jigger of gin to each.

If you have some hanging around, you might top each compote with a maraschino cherry.

Brandy Berries*

If you can find some really beautiful plump strawberries that are still wearing their bright green caps and stems, you will have the makings of the quickest dessert in the world.

Serve whole berries — stems attached — alongside two bowls, one filled with brandy, the other heaped with a snowy drift of powdered sugar. The trick is to dip the berries first in the booze, then in the sugar. Ah! Instant ambrosia!

Berries Creme de la Creme*

Another marvelous dip for fresh strawberries is a simple but elegant blend of sour cream and brown sugar. Stir 1/2 cup sugar into 1 cup sour cream and let them "marry" until the sugar dissolves. Chill the cream, then serve in a pretty bowl alongside the berries.

Rasberry Sherbet Royale*

1 package frozen raspberries   1 quart raspberry sherbet
Juice of 1/2 lemon   1 tablespoon white wine

Blend frozen berries with lemon juice and wine in a blender. Spoon over scoops of sherbet in stemmed balloon wine glasses. Serves 8.

Strawberries Grand Marnier*

Strawberries Grand Marnier are just that — grand. Use a blender to whip the mix to a frosty froth.

2 baskets of strawberries   1 cup lemon sherbet
1/2 cup sugar   1/3 cup Grand Marnier

Wash and hull berries and let dry on paper towels. Place berries with sugar in blender and process until liquid. Freeze in ice cube trays. Just before serving, put the frozen berry slush back in the blender and add the sherbet and Grand Marnier. This will probably take two batches. Serve in tall wine glasses with spoons. Serves 6 to 8.

Bomb Shell*

Next summer when you are asked to provide a goody for the class picnic, remember this one. People will say they have never tasted such a fun watermelon.

1 watermelon, well chilled   Cointreau or Triple Sec liqueur
Vodka

With a sharp knife, cut a triangular plug in the melon (cut a hefty wedge — at least 2 inches per side). Save the plug.

Mix approximately 3/4 cup vodka with 1/4 cup Cointreau. Gradually pour this into the hole in the melon. (You may have to spread the 'pour and seep' operation over a 15 to 20 minute period. It takes time for the melon to absorb the booze.)

Replace the plug and chill the melon overnight.

Chocolate Pots de Creme**

One Christmas, after getting six adorable little Haviland pots de creme — those cunning china cups with the lids — I was stuck for a good recipe for the rich mousse-like filling one typically serves in these mini-pots. The following recipe is one of the best I've found — very dark and rich.

2 eggs   2 6-ounce packages semi-sweet
1/4 teaspoon salt   chocolate bits
1/4 cup sugar   2 teaspoons vanilla
1-1/2 cups milk   Whipped cream
                                      Chocolate curls

Combine eggs, salt, and sugar in the top of a double boiler. Over simmering water, beat the mixture until thick. When thickened, add the milk and continue stirring for another 5 minutes. Remove the top of the double boiler and add the chocolate bits and vanilla, stirring until smooth. When the chocolate has melted, pour into 6 to 8 pots de creme or demitasse cups. Chill thoroughly and serve with dollops of whipped cream and chocolate curls. Serves 6 to 8.

White Chocolate Mousse**

One usually expects to find something chocolate under the lid of those dainty little pots de creme. Well, here's a variation on that theme — a blond mousse of white chocolate. Surprise!

6 ounces white chocolate	2 egg whites, room temperature
1/4 cup light cream	1 cup whipping cream, whipped
2 tablespoons butter	1 teaspoon vanilla

In top of double boiler, over simmering water, melt chocolate with cream. Stir until smooth. Take off heat and stir in butter. Cool slightly. Beat egg whites until stiff. Carefully fold chocolate mixture into whites, taking care not to deflate the mass. Season whipped cream with vanilla and fold into the mousse. Spoon into pots de creme or small serving dishes and chill thoroughly before serving. Serves 4 to 6.

Camembert with Wine and Almonds*

When it shows up at dessert, Camembert cheese is usually served as-is — in small wedges along with fruit and maybe a few nuts. This next version provides an exotic option: the Camembert is marinated overnight in white wine, then mixed to a creamy blend with butter and cognac. Superb!

1 small cake of Camembert cheese	1/4 cup soft butter
White wine	2 teaspoons cognac
	Finely chopped toasted almonds

Cover cheese with wine — about 1/4 cup — and let stand overnight. Next day, drain and cut away darkest portion of the crust, taking care not to cut too deeply into the cheese. Blend the cheese with the butter and cognac. Chill thoroughly and then shape into a block. Cover with toasted chopped almonds. Serve with wheat crackers and apple or pear wedges.

Hot Brie with Walnuts*

*Brie cheese gently warmed and sprinkled with walnuts is **heavenly**. Just be careful and don't get the cheese too warm. Brie has a very low melting point.*

1 package Brie cheese	Chopped walnuts (or almonds)

Sprinkle nuts evenly over cheese and place on an ovenproof serving dish. Heat briefly in a 350° F. oven, just until cheese starts to puff. Remove immediately. Serve with crisp crackers, pears and apple wedges.

What's Ahead in Cookies

Cookies

. . . bake a batch and beat the blahs

I read someplace that baking cookies is like basket weaving — great therapy for depression. Well, that's **one** way to rationalize the soaring cost of chocolate chips: they're still cheaper than tranquilizers.

Eating cookies can be comforting, too. The soothing effect of a plump molasses cookie, warm from the oven, can do wonderful things for man and boy alike.

When our last offspring, the cookie maker, went off to college, the production of brownies and oatmeal clumps came to a screeching halt. And for weeks after, my spouse would prowl through the kitchen at bedtime — a glass of milk in one hand and the other one stuck in an empty cookie jar — with this forlorn look on his face. Deprived cookie eaters can get pretty depressed, too.

Fortunately, cookies are easy sweets to make. What follows is a fair sampling of how the various kinds crumble . . . from sugar cookies like Mama used to make to such exotica as Kahlua Brownies. Take your pick. And enjoy.

No-Bake Snow Balls*

As cooks go, my cousin Blanche is given to somewhat complex combinations. Imagine my surprise when I sampled her party Snow Balls and found out the little critters aren't even cooked!

1 cup peanut butter	1 teaspoon vanilla
1/2 cup chopped nuts	1 cup powdered sugar
1 cup powdered sugar	1/4 cup milk
1 cup puffed rice cereal	Angel Flake coconut
1 tablespoon margarine	

Mix peanut butter with nuts, 1 cup powdered sugar, rice cereal, margarine and vanilla. Roll into small balls.

Mix 1 cup powdered sugar with milk, blending until smooth. Roll balls in the icing, then coat with coconut. Refrigerate until serving.

Coconut Fingers*

Need a sweet treat in a hurry? Here's how to convert simple slices of store-bought white bread into sleight-of-hand Coconut Fingers.

8 slices soft white bread   **3 cups flaked coconut**
1 can sweetened condensed
  milk

Cut crusts from bread, then cut slices into 4 strips, or "fingers". Roll each piece in the sweetened condensed milk, then dredge in coconut. Bake on a well-greased cookie sheet at 375° F. for 8 to 10 minutes, or until toasty. Makes 24.

Coconut Rum Balls*

If somebody volunteered you to take cookies to the office Christmas party, and you are too hassled to even turn on the oven, try these. They are rich and rummy and come out looking like they took a lot more effort than they did.

1 12-ounce box of vanilla   **1 3-1/2-ounce can flaked coconut**
  wafers, crushed   **1 can sweetened condensed milk**
1 cup chopped walnuts   **1/2 cup rum**

Mix all ingredients until thoroughly blended, then chill overnight.
Dip hands in powdered sugar and shape into 1-inch balls. Roll in coconut. Cover and store in refrigerator.

Skillet Cookies*

You won't have to turn the oven on for this one, either. These chewy top-of-the-stove goodies are great for the beginner cook and fun for kids to make, too.

1 stick margarine (or butter)   **1 cup walnuts, chopped**
3/4 cup sugar   **2 cups Rice Krispies**
1 egg, beaten   **1 teaspoon vanilla**
1/2 pound dates, chopped   **1 cup coconut**

Combine margarine (or butter), sugar, egg, and dates in a skillet. Cook over low heat for about 10 minutes, stirring occasionally to keep the mixture from sticking. Remove skillet from heat and stir in the walnuts, Rice Krispies, and vanilla. When mixture is cool enough to handle, form into small balls and roll in the coconut. Makes about 4 dozen.

Mint Snowballs**

If you don't mind a little stuffing and shaping, you will love these unusual Christmas cookies that look like mini snowballs with cherries tucked inside.

1 cup butter	2 cups sifted flour
1/2 cup sifted confectioners	1 cup rolled oats
sugar	54 red or green candied cherries
1/2 teaspoon salt	Mint Frosting
1 teaspoon vanilla	2 cups flaked coconut
1 tablespoon water	

Combine butter, sugar, salt, vanilla and water; cream well. Add the flour and blend. Stir in the oats. Shape small bits of dough around the cherries, making balls about 1 inch in diameter. Place on ungreased cookie sheets and bake at 325° F. for 18 to 20 minutes. Cool cookies, then dip in frosting and roll in coconut.

Mint Frosting*

2 cups confectioners sugar	Few drops mint extract
1/4 cup milk	

Combine and beat until smooth.

Cream Cheese 'n Prune Brownies*

Once you one-star (*) cooks have gotten well-acquainted with packaged brownie mixes, you can go a step further — adding a bit of this and that to the basic dough. In this case, cream cheese and chopped prunes go into the works before being baked up like cupcakes in paper-lined muffin cups.

2 3-ounce packages	1 cup chopped prunes
cream cheese	1/2 cup chopped nuts
1 egg	1 15-ounce package brownie mix
2 teaspoons grated orange	1 tablespoon orange-flavored
peel	liqueur

Beat cream cheese, egg and orange peel until smooth and thoroughly blended. Fold in prunes and nuts.

Prepare brownie mix according to package instructions, adding orange-flavored liqueur to the blend. Spoon 1 rounded tablespoon of the brownie mix into 12 paper-lined muffin cups. Top each with 2 tablespoons of the cheese-prune mixture. Then top off with the remaining brownie mix. Bake at 350° F. for 30 minutes or until brownies spring back when pressed. Cool in cups before removing. Makes a dozen cupcake brownies.

*Super Scrumptious Brownies***

These brownies are loaded with chocolate and filled with nuts . . . perfect for people who like them rich and chewy.

1/2 pound margarine	Pinch salt
4 squares bitter chocolate	1 teaspoon vanilla
2-1/3 cups granulated sugar	1/4 teaspoon almond flavoring
4 large eggs	1-1/2 cups chopped nuts
1-1/2 cups flour	

Melt margarine and chocolate in the top of a double boiler. When melted, add the sugar, stirring constantly for 5 minutes. Remove from heat and add the eggs, one at a time, stirring well. Add the sifted flour and salt, beating with a spoon. (Do not use a mixer.) Add the flavorings and 1 cup nuts.

Pour into a greased 9 x 13-inch pan. Sprinkle with remaining nuts that have been finely chopped. Bake at 375° F. for 10 minutes. Lower heat to 350° F. and continue baking for another 20 minutes. Score into squares while warm. Remove cookies from pan when cool.

*Boozy Brownies***

You will love Boozy Brownies. Just don't put them in the kids' lunchpails.

3/4 cups sifted flour	1 6-ounce package chocolate bits
1/4 teaspoon soda	1 teaspoon vanilla
1/4 teaspoon salt	2 eggs
1/3 cup shortening	1-1/2 cups walnuts
1/2 cup sugar	1/3 cup bourbon (or rum)
2 tablespoons water	Bourbon Frosting

Sift flour with soda and salt, and set aside. Melt shortening and add sugar and water. Stir until dissolved, then add the chocolate bits and vanilla. Cook slowly until smooth. Cool.

Beat eggs, then beat in the chocolate mixture. Add the flour mixture and the nuts. Mix well, then spoon batter into a greased 9-inch square pan. Bake at 325° F. for 30 minutes. Sprinkle hot brownies with bourbon or rum. When cool, spread with Bourbon Frosting.

*Bourbon Frosting**

1/2 cup butter (or margarine)	2 teaspoons bourbon (or rum)
2-1/2 cups powdered sugar	

Cream everything together and beat until smooth.

Harry's Humorers**

My good friend Joyce is happily married to a man named Harry whom she variously refers to as Harry the Helpful, Harry the Hangdog or Harry the Hopeful — depending on what mood she (or he) is in. This is his favorite cookie recipe. Joyce calls them Harry's Humorers.

1 cup margarine	2 teaspoons cinnamon
2 cups sugar	1-1/2 teaspoons baking soda
2 eggs	2 cups quick-cooking oats
1 tablespoon molasses	2/3 cup raisins
2 teaspoons vanilla	1 cup chopped nuts
2 cups flour	3/4 cup chocolate chips

Cream margarine with sugar. Add eggs, molasses and vanilla. Combine flour, cinnamon and soda and add gradually to the creamed mixture. Stir in oats, raisins, nuts and chocolate chips. Drop by teaspoonfuls on a greased cookie sheet. Bake at 350° F. for 12 minutes or until lightly browned. Makes 6 dozen.

Carrot-Oatmeal Cookies**

Carrots and peanut butter go into these chewy, nutritious cookies that are great for the kids' lunch pails.

1/3 cup margarine	1 teaspoon vanilla
1/3 cup chunky peanut butter	1-1/2 cups oatmeal
	1 cup flour
1/2 cup brown sugar	3/4 teaspoon baking soda
6 tablespoons granulated sugar	1 teaspoon salt
	1 cup chopped nuts
2 eggs	1 cup shredded carrots

Combine margarine, peanut butter, brown sugar, granulated sugar, eggs and vanilla in a large bowl and beat until fluffy.

Combine oatmeal, flour, baking soda and salt. Add to the peanut butter mixture and mix thoroughly. Stir in nuts and carrots and blend well. Drop by rounded teaspoons onto a greased cookie sheet, placing cookies about 2 inches apart. Bake at 350° F. for 12 minutes, or until lightly browned. Makes 3 dozen.

Myrt's Oatmeal Clumpies**

Years ago a lady named Myrt used to bring homemade oatmeal cookies to the office once or twice a month. The fact was, we all loved Myrt for her clumpies. We'd wait around like ghouls for coffee break, then dig in and plow through six dozen in two minutes flat.

3 cups flour	1-1/2 cups walnuts, chopped
1-1/2 teaspoons baking soda	3 teaspoons vanilla
1 cup shortening	1 teaspoon salt
3/4 cup brown sugar	1-1/2 cups white sugar
2 6-ounce packages chocolate	3 eggs, beaten slightly
chips	1 cup quick-cooking oatmeal

Mix everything but the oatmeal into a stiff mass, then add the oats. (The dough will be stiff.) Drop by rounded tablespoons onto a greased cookie sheet and bake at 325° F. for 10 to 12 minutes. The cookies should be light brown and hefty in size. Makes about 8 dozen cookies.

Randy's Sunflower Seed Cookies**

Randy, our in-house cookie maker, thinks this is one of the best cookie recipes in town. The sunflower seeds, she says, make them good for you. (Go ahead, have another.)

1 cup sugar	1-1/2 teaspoons baking powder
1 cup brown sugar	1 teaspoon soda
1 cup margarine	1 cup coconut
2 eggs	1 cup sunflower seeds
1 teaspoon vanilla	2 cups old-fashioned oats
2 cups flour	

Beat sugar, brown sugar, margarine, eggs and vanilla together until fluffy. Sift flour with baking powder and soda. Add this, with sunflower seeds, oats and coconut to sugar-egg mixture. Mix well.

Drop by rounded teaspoonfuls onto lightly greased cookie sheets. Bake at 350° F. for 12 to 15 minutes. Makes 4 dozen.

Poppy Seed Cookies**

If you're into seedy cookies, here's another one you should try. This is a refrigerated dough that bakes into crisp, dainty little tidbits.

1 cup soft margarine	1 cup poppy seeds
1 cup sugar	2-1/4 cups flour
1 egg yolk, well beaten	1/2 teaspoon cinnamon
2 teaspoons vanilla	1/4 teaspoon salt
1 cup chopped walnuts	Pinch ground ginger

Cream margarine and sugar together. Beat in egg yolk, nuts and poppy seeds.

Sift flour with cinnamon, salt and ginger and add gradually to creamed ingredients.

Shape mixture by hand into 2 long rolls about 2 inches thick. Wrap in plastic or waxed paper and refrigerate overnight or until very firm.

With a sharp knife, cut rolls into slices 1/4 inch thick and place on ungreased cookie sheets. Bake at 325° F. for 10 to 15 minutes or until pale gold. Makes about 4 dozen.

Aggression Cookies*

Feeling frustrated, ready to climb the curtains? One way to work off your hostility is to beat out a batch of Aggression Cookies. The dough loves being punched out, so go to it. The more you whack, mash and knead, the better it gets.

*If you are really frustrated, make the whole recipe (it makes 15 dozen great cookies). If you aren't **that** mad, cut the recipe in half.*

3 cups brown sugar	1 teaspoon salt
3 cups margarine	1 tablespoon baking soda
6 cups oatmeal	3 cups flour

Mash, pound, pummel ingredients into a well-mixed mass (use a big bowl). Roll into walnut-sized balls and distribute over ungreased cookies sheets.

Smear margarine over the bottom of a small glass, dip in sugar, then press onto cookies, mashing them fairly flat. (Keep re-sugaring the glass as you press. You'll only need to re-butter once or twice.)

Bake cookies at 350° F. for 10 to 12 minutes.

NOTE: Nothing says you can't add some finely chopped nuts to the dough if you feel like it, but remember: this stuff is supposed to be therapeutic, not fancy.

Sweet and Salty Nut Bars**

These scrumptious nut-encrusted cookies look more like candy bars than cookies. You need whole mixed nuts for the topping, preferably a blend that doesn't include peanuts. (I know, it's expensive, but please don't chisel.)

3 cups flour	1/2 cup corn syrup
1-1/2 cups brown sugar	2-1/2 tablespoons margarine
1 teaspoon salt	1 tablespoon water
1/2 teaspoon cinnamon	1 6-ounce package peanut butter
1 cup soft margarine	chips
2 cups mixed salted nuts	

Combine flour with brown sugar, salt, cinnamon and 1 cup margarine; mix well. Press into an ungreased 10 x 15-inch jelly roll pan and bake at 350° F. for 10 to 12 minutes. Distribute nuts evenly over the baked crust and set aside.

In a small, heavy saucepan bring to a boil the corn syrup, 2-1/2 tablespoons margarine, water and peanut butter chips; boil 2 minutes, stirring constantly. Pour hot syrup over the nuts, spread evenly and bake an additional 10 to 12 minutes. Cool completely before cutting into squares or bars.

NOTE: Do not chop the nuts. Whole nutmeats, in this case, make a more attractive presentation.

Master Icebox Cookie Dough**

This basic icebox cookie recipe can be varied at will — depending on what's on hand and what you feel like adding. (Suggestions for how the basic dough can be modifed follow.)

Please note: this recipe makes an awful lot of cookies — about 20 dozen — but don't let that throw you. Just keep the dough stashed in the freezer and take out as much as you want when you want it.

6 cups flour	2 cups white sugar
1 teaspoon soda	1 cup brown sugar
1 teaspoon cinnamon	3 eggs, lightly beaten
1/2 teaspoon nutmeg	2 teaspoons vanilla
1/4 teaspoon salt	1 cup nuts, finely chopped
1 pound margarine	

Sift flour, soda, cinnamon, nutmeg and salt together. Set aside. In a large mixing bowl, beat the margarine and sugars together until fluffy. Beat in eggs and vanilla, mixing well. Add nuts.

Divide dough into 6 equal parts. (Here is where you can add various other ingredients to vary the cookies.) Shape each segment into smooth rolls, about 1-1/2 inches in diameter. Wrap snugly in plastic, then in foil and freeze.

When ready to bake, slice the solidly frozen rolls into thin 1/4-inch slices (use a sharp, wet knife). Arrange on an ungreased cookie sheet and bake at 375° F. for 10 minutes, or until lightly browned. Each roll makes about 3-1/2 dozen cookies.

Master Icebox Cookie Variations

Coconut — add 3/4 cup flaked coconut and 1/2 teaspoon coconut flavoring to one-sixth basic dough mix.

Pecan — add 1/2 cup finely chopped pecans and 1/2 teaspoon maple flavoring to one-sixth basic dough mix.

Orange-Date — Add 1/2 cup finely chopped dates and 1 tablespoon finely grated orange peel to one-sixth basic dough mix.

Spice — add 1/2 teaspoon cinnamon, 1/2 teaspoon nutmeg and 1/4 teaspoon cloves to one-sixth basic dough mix.

Chocolate — add 1 envelope pre-melted baking chocolate to one-sixth basic dough mix.

Black Walnut — add 1/2 cup finely chopped black walnuts and 1/2 teaspoon black walnut flavoring to one-sixth basic dough mix.

Susan's Toffee Cookie Mix**

Here is a mix you can keep in the fridge almost indefinitely and dig out any time the mood to make fresh cookies moves you. The Toffee Bars made from the mix are superb . . . vaguely resembling English toffee candy.

4 cups sifted flour	2 cups sugar
2 teaspoons soda	2 cups soft shortening
2 teaspoons salt	4 cups oatmeal

Sift the flour, soda, and salt. Add sugar, and cut in shortening until mixture resembles fine crumbs. Blend in oats. Store in a covered container in the refrigerator. Makes about 14 cups of dough.

Susan's Super Toffee Bars**

2 cups Susan's Toffee Cookie Mix	1 teaspoon vanilla
1/3 cup corn syrup	1/2 cup melted chocolate bits
	1/2 cup chopped nuts

Into the cookie mix, blend syrup and vanilla. Pat into a well-greased 8-inch square pan. Bake at 450° F. for 8 to 10 minutes, watching to see the mix doesn't get over-brown. Take out of the oven and flatten the edges. Cool, then cover and chill several hours.

When cold, spread with the melted chocolate chips and sprinkle with chopped nuts. Chill. Cut into squares. Keep refrigerated.

Espresso Cookies***

*Espresso Nut Cookies are not for the kiddies' lunch pails. Bring these out with ice cream, an ice or sorbet when you have guests over for dinner. **Very** trendy.*

1 stick butter, room temperature	2 cups all-purpose flour
1 cup sugar	1 teaspoon baking powder
1 tablespoon instant espresso powder	Dash salt
1 tablespoon hot water	1/2 teaspoon vanilla extract
1 egg	1/2 cup finely chopped pecans (or walnuts)

Cream butter, then gradually add the sugar, beating until fluffy. Dissolve espresso powder in hot water; set aside.

Add the egg and cooled espresso to the creamed mixture, stirring to blend. Sift flour, baking powder and salt into the bowl and beat to combine dry and creamed ingredients. Stir in the vanilla and nuts. Divide dough into two portions and make into rolls about 2 inches in diameter. Wrap in plastic wrap and refrigerate (or freeze).

When ready to bake, slice rolls into 1/4-inch slices and bake on ungreased cookie sheets at 275° F. for about 8 minutes. Store in an airtight container.

Anise Cookies**

Anise-flavored sugar tops these crisp cookies.

3/4 cup sugar	3 cups all-purpose flour
2 teaspoons anise seeds	1 teaspoon baking powder
1/2 pound margarine	1/2 teaspoon salt
1 egg	1/2 teaspoon cinnamon
2 tablespoons brandy	

Combine sugar and anise seeds. Cover tightly and let stand at least 24 hours. Combine 1/2 cup of the anise-sugar with the margarine. Beat until light and fluffy. Beat in egg and brandy. Combine flour, baking powder, salt and cinnamon. Gradually add the dry ingredients to the creamed mixture, mixing well. Shape into a ball, wrap with plastic and refrigerate until dough is firm.

Roll out on lightly floured board to 1/8-inch thickness. Cut with a 2-inch round cookie cutter. Arrange 1 inch apart on a lightly greased cookie sheet. Sift remaining anise seed-sugar mix over the cookies, placing about 1/4 teaspoon on each round. Bake at 350° F. for about 12 minutes or until golden brown. Makes about 6 dozen.

Night-Before Macaroons*

As the name suggests, Night-Before Macaroons need a 12-hour headstart to arrive at the proper "ripeness" for baking. If you mix up a batch tonight, all you need to do tomorrow is stir, season and bake.

4 cups quick cooking oats	1 teaspoon salt
2 cups brown sugar	1 teaspoon cinnamon
1 cup oil	1 teaspoon almond extract
2 eggs, beaten	

The night before, mix the oats, brown sugar and oil in a bowl and set aside. The next day, add the beaten eggs, salt and seasonings. Stir well, then drop by teaspoon onto a greased cookie sheet. Bake at 325° F. for 15 minutes.

Chocolate Macaroon Chews*

It's quick! It's chewy! And it's very, very easy . . . a treat the one-star (*) cook can knock out with ease.

1 14-ounce package flaked coconut	2 teaspoons vanilla
	Pinch salt
1 14-ounce can sweetened condensed milk	4 squares unsweetened chocolate, melted

Combine everything in a bowl, then drop by teaspoon onto a well-greased cookie sheet, placing cookies about 1 inch apart. Bake at 350° F. for 10 to 12 minutes. Makes 8 dozen.

Coconut Macaroons*

It doesn't take any particular talent to turn out these gorgeous coconut macaroons — just patience. If you don't mind standing by the stove stirring the mix for 10 minutes, it's an easy enough task to tackle. No fair dropping everything to chat on the phone or talk to the mailman. Keep stirring!

3 egg whites, stiffly beaten	1/4 teaspoon salt
1 cup sugar	2 cups packaged flaked coconut
1 tablespoon cornstarch	1/2 teaspoon almond extract

Preheat oven to 300° F. Lightly grease 2 cookie sheets.

In top of double boiler combine the stiffly beaten egg whites, sugar and cornstarch. Cook over gently boiling water, stirring constantly, for 10 minutes.

Remove from heat and add salt, coconut and almond extract. Stir until well combined. Drop by teaspoonfuls, 1/2 inch apart, onto cookies sheets. Bake at 300° F. for 20 to 25 minutes, or until pale golden brown. Remove to wire rack. Makes 2 dozen.

Coconut Crunchies**

Nuts, oatmeal and coconut give these drop cookies nutritious heft.

1 cup sifted flour	1/2 cup brown sugar
1/4 teaspoon soda	1 egg, unbeaten
1/2 teaspoon baking powder	1/2 teaspoon vanilla
Dash salt	1 cup oatmeal
1/2 cup soft margarine	1 cup nuts
1/2 cup sugar	1 cup flaked coconut

Sift together flour, soda, baking powder and salt. Combine margarine, sugars, egg and vanilla. Add the flour mixture to the margarine-egg mixture and beat. Blend in the oatmeal, nuts and coconut. Drop by teaspoon on a greased cookie sheet. Bake at 325° F. for 15 minutes. Makes about 4 dozen cookies.

Corn Flake Macaroons**

There's no flour in these crispy macaroons, just cornflake crumbs. And that is enough to give them a light-as-air quality you will love.

3 egg whites	2/3 cup nonfat dry milk powder
1/2 teaspoon cream of tartar	3 cups corn flakes
1/2 teaspoon salt	1 cup walnuts
1 cup sugar	1-1/2 cups coconut
1 teaspoon vanilla	

Beat egg whites with cream of tartar and salt until soft peaks form. Add sugar gradually, beating until very stiff. Add vanilla and gradually beat in the milk powder. Fold in cornflakes, nuts and coconut. Drop by teaspoonfuls onto a greased cookie sheet. Bake at 300° F. for 20 to 25 minutes.

Amaretti Cookies**

*Almond-flavored Amaretti Cookies are as tender as a teenager's first kiss. Wouldn't you just **know** these romantic little confections would be Italian? For perfectly formed cookies, you will need a pastry bag fitted with a plain round tip.*

1 8-ounce can of almond paste	1-1/4 teaspoons vanilla
2 egg whites	1 cup sifted powdered sugar
Pinch salt	1 tablespoon granulated sugar

Grease two cookie sheets. Dust with flour and tap off the excess. Set aside.

Break up almond paste with a fork in a small bowl. Add unbeaten egg whites, salt and vanilla and beat with an electric mixer until smooth. Add the powdered sugar a teaspoon at a time, continuously beating. Spoon soft dough into a pastry bag fitted with a small round tip. Pipe dough out in small rounds onto the cookie sheets. With wet fingers, gently pat tops of cookies and sprinkle lightly with granulated sugar. Bake at 325° F. for 45 minutes or until cookies are pale golden brown. Store in an airtight tin. Makes about 3 dozen.

Coconut-Date Macaroons*

Interested in a moist, chewy cookie you can whip out in 15 minutes flat? Here it is. (That's five minutes to shape, and 10 minutes to bake.)

1 cup flaked coconut	2/3 cup sweetened condensed milk
1 cup chopped pecans	1-1/2 teaspoon vanilla extract
1 cup chopped dates	

Mix ingredients and shape into balls the size of walnuts. Place 1 inch apart on a greased cookie sheet. Bake at 350° F. for 10 to 12 minutes. Makes 2 dozen.

Haystacks**

If the very sight of these fat, cupcake-size coconut macaroons in the bakery case makes you weak in the knees, you'll be happy to know you can make the very same thing at home. Easy, too.

3 cups shredded coconut	8 candied cherries, diced
2/3 cup sugar	(optional)
3 egg whites	1/2 cup pecans, finely diced
6 tablespoons cake flour	(optional)
1/2 teaspoon baking powder	4 whole candied cherries, cut in
1 teaspoon salt	half
1/2 teaspoon almond extract	

Combine coconut, 1/3 cup sugar, and 1 egg white in the top of a double boiler. Cook over simmering water until the mixture is hot. Stir occasionally. Take off heat and add flour, baking powder and salt. Blend well. Add the almond extract and fold in diced cherries and pecans, if desired.

Beat the remaining 2 egg whites stiff, adding the remaining 1/3 cup sugar as you whip. Fold beaten whites into the coconut mixture and spoon into 8 paper-lined muffin cups. Top each haystack with a half cherry. Bake at 325° F. for 25 minutes. Makes 8 big haystacks.

Mounds Bars Cookies**

I absolutely **adore** *Mounds Bars, which explains why I'm so goofy over Mounds Bar Cookies. If you, too, are a coconut freak, try them. It's the next best thing to a candy bar from the corner store.*

2 cups graham cracker crumbs	1 can flaked coconut
1/4 cup sugar	1/2 bar German sweet chocolate
1/2 cup melted butter	1 6-ounce package chocolate chips
1 can sweetened condensed milk	1/2 cup cream (or half-and-half)

Mix cracker crumbs with sugar and butter. Press mixture into the bottom of an 8 x 13-inch baking pan. Bake at 350° F. for 10 minutes.

Meanwhile, mix condensed milk with coconut. Spread this over the crumb crust and bake an additional 20 minutes. While this layer is baking, melt the bar chocolate and the chocolate bits over boiling water. Add the cream and blend. Take cookies from the oven and, while warm, spread with the chocolate layer. Cut in squares while room temperature, then chill.

Lemon Chilly Bars**

These buttery, sweet-sour cookies bars are one of our family's all-time favorites. If you are having a party, you can double the recipe and bake the whole batch in 9 x 13-inch pan.

1 cup sifted flour	3 tablespoons lemon juice
1/4 cup powdered sugar	1 teaspoon grated lemon rind
1/2 cup butter, chilled	2 tablespoons flour
2 eggs	1/2 teaspoon baking powder
1 cup granulated sugar	Powdered sugar or Lemon Ice Icing

Sift together 1 cup flour with 1/4 cup powdered sugar. Cut in butter until mixture resemble coarse meal. Pat into an ungreased 8-inch square baking pan. Bake at 350° F. for 20 minutes.

Meanwhile, beat eggs and slowly add the granulated sugar. Blend in 1 lemon juice and rind, and beat thoroughly.

Sift 2 tablespoons flour with baking powder, then stir into the egg mixture. Pour over the slightly cooled crust and bake at 350° F. for 25 minutes. Sift powdered sugar over the top and cool.

You can stop here, or go one step farther — spread the cookies with Lemon Ice Icing. Either way, you get about 20 bars.

Lemon Ice Icing*

2 tablespoons soft butter	1 tablespoon lemon juice
1 cup powdered sugar	

Blend together until smooth. Measurement of sugar is approximate — you may need more to make a spreadable icing. And vary the amount of lemon juice according to the tartness desired.

Apricot Chews**

These moist apricot squares would make a lovely gift for anyone who doesn't do much baking. They travel well, too, which is a bonus if they have far to go.

3/4 cup butter	3/4 pound dried apricots
1 cup brown sugar	1 cup water
1-1/2 cups flour	3/4 cup sugar
1-1/2 cups oatmeal	1 tablespoon apricot liqueur
1 teaspoon soda	1/4 cup grated coconut

Melt butter and add brown sugar, flour, oatmeal and soda. Mix until well blended and pat half the mixture into a greased 9-inch baking pan.

Simmer apricots in water and sugar for 30 minutes. Add the liqueur after the apricots have cooked 20 minutes. Spoon the apricots over the crumb layer, then top with coconut. Pat remaining crumb mixture over all and bake at 350° F. for 25 to 30 minutes or until golden. While still warm, cut into squares. Turn out from pan when cookies are completely cooled.

All-Seasons Fruit Bars**

Lennie, my old college roommate, serves these cream cheese-frosted cookies at holiday parties, coffees, meetings, brunches and luncheons. That has to tell you two things — how good they are and how busy she is.

1-1/2 cups flour	2 eggs
1 teaspoon salt	1 teaspoon vanilla
3/4 teaspoon baking soda	1 8-ounce can crushed pineapple,
1/2 teaspoon nutmeg	drained
1/2 teaspoon cinnamon	1 cup finely chopped unpeeled
1/2 teaspoon allspice	apples
1/4 cup margarine	1/2 cup golden raisins
3/4 cup sugar	

Stir together the flour, salt, baking soda, nutmeg, cinnamon and allspice. In another bowl, cream the margarine with sugar. Add the eggs and vanilla and beat. Stir in pineapple, apple and raisins. Add flour mixture and mix thoroughly. Spray a 10 x 15-inch jellyroll pan and spread batter evenly in pan. Bake 20 minutes at 350° F., or until toothpick tests clean. Remove from oven and cool slightly. While still warm, spread with Lemon Cream Cheese Icing.

Lemon Cream Cheese Icing*

1 3-ounce package cream	1 teaspoon grated lemon rind
cheese, room temperature	1 teaspoon milk
2 tablespoons margarine	2 cups powdered sugar
1 teaspoon lemon juice	

Blend cream cheese with margarine until smooth. Add juice, peel and milk. Add powdered sugar, stirring until mixture is smooth and spreadable. This may require an additional drop or two of lemon juice. Spread over cooled cookie sheet. Cut into bars. Makes approximately 64 pieces.

*Pepper Cookies***

These crisp peppery cookies are not for the faint of heart. Better start off with 1 teaspoon of pepper for openers. Then, if you're game, you can up the ante with the next batch.

1 cup butter	1 tablespoon ginger
2 teaspoons pepper (or	1-1/2 cups sugar
1 teaspoon if you aren't sure)	1 egg
1/2 teaspoon cloves	3 cups sifted flour
2 teaspoons cinnamon	2 teaspoons baking powder
1 teaspoon nutmeg	1/2 teaspoon salt

Beat butter with the spices until fluffy. Gradually add sugar, beating continuously. Add egg and beat. Sift flour, with baking powder and salt, into the egg mixture. Beat well. Chill dough until firm.

Roll dough out into a thin sheet and cut out with cookie cutters. Place cookies on a baking sheet lined with brown paper. Bake at 375° F. for 8 to 10 minutes.

*Frizbee Cookies***

These giant, platter-size cookies make a big hit with people who like their cookies big and hefty. This recipe makes more than 4 dozen king-sized munchies.

1/2 cup margarine	1 18-ounce box rolled oats
1-1/2 cups brown sugar	1 6-ounce package chocolate chips
4 eggs	1 cup chopped nuts
1 teaspoon vanilla	2-1/2 teaspoons soda
1 18-ounce jar chunky peanut butter	

In a large bowl, beat together butter and sugars until fluffy. Beat in eggs, soda and vanilla. Mix in peanut butter. Stir in oats, nuts and chocolate bits. Spoon batter in 1/4-cup measure and space about 4 inches apart on ungreased cookie sheets. Flatten dough with a fork to about 2-1/2 inches in diameter. Bake at 350° F. for 10 to 12 minutes. Cool 1 minute on the sheets, then remove to wire racks to cool. Makes about 4-1/2 dozen. Store in a tightly covered container.

What's Ahead in
Giveaways

The Great Giveaway Program

. . . let 'em eat cake. Or bourbon balls. Or a nice jar of pickles, maybe?

There is something very touching about gifts you make with your own little hands, especially if you barely know your way around the kitchen.

You would be surprised what a crockful of brandied cheese or fudge can do for your image as a talented and thoughty person.

People love to get these highly personal presents, although some handmades admittedly go over better than others. *Come Christmas, you are more apt to make points with a cannister of caramel corn than, say, a painfully homemade tie or crocheted coat hanger.*

Another thing: those craft class projects usually take a lot longer to make than something swift and nifty from your kitchen.

What follows are recipes that range all the way from spiced nuts to marmalade like Mama made — every one of them geared to make your gourmet friends sit up and beg for more.

Just remember, no matter what month it is, there are only so many days left 'til Christmas, and you can't start too early to make your presents known later.

Cocktail Pecans*

These seasoned pecans make a great hostess gift and a marvelous munchie to have on hand at home. So make a double batch — save half, share the rest.

1/3 cup butter	**1 teaspoon seasoned salt**
1 pound (about 4 cups) whole pecan halves	

Toast nuts and butter in a roasting pan in a 325° F. for about 15 minutes. Give the nuts a couple of stirs as they toast. Sprinkle with seasoned salt and continue baking for another 10 to 15 minutes. Cool, then pack in airtight containers. Keep refrigerated. Makes about 4 cups.

NOTE: Use prepared seasoned salt or just sprinkle on a blend of salt, pepper and garlic powder.

Potted Caraway Cheese*

Here's another spread that improves with standing.

1 pound Cheddar cheese,
　grated
1 small package cream cheese
1/4 cup salad oil
1 teaspoon dry mustard

1 teaspoon caraway seed
1/4 teaspoon garlic salt
2 tablespoons brandy
2 tablespoons kirsch

Combine all the ingredients and blend well. Pack into a crock and store in the refrigerator to ripen several days. Let come to room temperature before serving.

The Bottomless Crock*

While you are whipping up a crock of Potted Caraway Cheese for giving away, why not make a second batch for yourself? There never was a handier snack to whip forth with crackers, and you can keep the crock going by periodically adding the bits and pieces of miscellaneous cheeses you have on hand.

As the tag-ends of Cheddar, Swiss or what have you accrue, simply grate up and add to the crock along with a dash or two of brandy, wine or kirsch. Stir to blend and keep refrigerated.

Play it right, and your cheese crock will know no end.

Garlic Olives*

These pungent olives make a tasty addition to any antipasto tray. The lady who gave me the recipe says they're great in martinis, too, although I'm not sure I'd go that far.

Drain a large can of jumbo-size black olives and plunk them in a jar along with 3 or 4 peeled whole cloves of garlic. Cover with olive oil and let ripen a week before giving away. The olives are best served at room temperature. (Refrigeration tends to cloud olive oil.)

Green Apple Chutney**

For the curry lovers on your list, here is an excellent and inexpensive chutney made from green apples and pears.

1 cup prunes
2 cups seedless raisins
2 cups peeled and chopped
　green apples
1 cup pared, slightly green
　pears, chopped firm
6 tomatoes, peeled and cut
　into quarters

2-1/2 cups vinegar
3 cups firmly packed brown sugar
1-1/2 teaspoons salt
1/2 cup preserved ginger, chopped
1 cup minced onion
2 small cloves garlic, sliced paper-
　thin
Dash cayenne

Cover prunes with water and cook 10 minutes, then drain and set aside to cool. Pit and chop prunes and combine with remaining ingredients. Place in a heavy saucepan and bring to a boil. Reduce heat and cook very slowly for about 3 hours, stirring occasionally to prevent sticking. Pour chutney into sterilized jars and seal. Makes about 4 pints.

Red-Hot Dynamite Pepper Jelly**

This is that jet-hot jelly that turns up at cocktail parties — usually slathered over cream cheese. Some versions of jalapeno jelly are green. This one is bright red. If you get it confused with currant jelly you are in for a big surprise.

1 cup fresh jalapeno chiles, chopped	7 cups sugar
	1-1/4 cups vinegar
1 quart cranberry juice cocktail	5 ounces liquid fruit pectin
	Red food coloring (optional)

Process chiles with cranberry juice in a blender until fine. Pour through a strainer, discarding pulp. Add sugar, vinegar, pectin and coloring, to taste, and bring to a boil. Boil 5 minutes, then pour into sterilized jars and seal with paraffin. Makes about 8 half-pints.

Hot and Sweet Mustard**

Mustard lovers will welcome a sweet and spicy mix that is sweetened with honey and "hotted up" with red pepper seasoning.

1/2 cup finely chopped onion	1 tablespoon honey
2 cloves garlic, minced	1 teaspoon salt
1 cup dry white wine	Sprinkle MSG
2/3 cup dry mustard	3 to 4 drops liquid red pepper seasoning
1-1/2 teaspoons salad oil	

Simmer onion and garlic in wine over low heat for 5 to 6 minutes. Set mixture aside to cool. When cool, strain into a small saucepan and beat in the dry mustard. When smooth, add the oil, honey, salt, MSG, and pepper sauce. Cook over low heat until the mixture thickens. Set aside to cool. Pour into small jars. Will keep in the refrigerator up to 1 month.

Brandy Apples**

Tell your recipients that Brandy Apples are great over vanilla ice cream and good on pancakes, too. Also tell them to keep it refrigerated.

6 Golden Delicious apples	Pinch salt
1 cup orange juice	3/4 cup sugar
2 cinnamon sticks	1/2 cup brandy

Peel and core apples, then cut in half. Cut each half into four slices. Place in a saucepan and add orange juice and cinnamon sticks. Simmer, covered, for about 10 minutes, or until apples are tender. Add a pinch of salt. Then remove from heat and stir in sugar and brandy. Cool and place in fancy gift containers. Makes about 5 cups.

Gussied Grapefruit Peel**

Candied grapefruit strips make a lovely go-along with after dinner demitasse. For a truly elegant hostess gift, present a jar of espresso coffee along with a pretty container of the candied peel.

6 grapefruit with thick skins	1/2 cup orange liqueur
	Rock sugar (plain will do)
3 cups sugar	1/2 cup melted chocolate chips

Peel grapefruit and cut into 1/4-inch strips. Place in a deep saucepan and cover with water, then add an extra 2 inches. Boil over medium heat for 5 minutes, then drain. Repeat the boil-and-drain process 3 more times.

Drain well and place peel in a large heavy skillet with the sugar. Cook over low heat, stirring occasionally, for 1 hour. At this point, the peel should be coated with a heavy syrup.

Stir in the orange liqueur and cook another 30 minutes. Spread peel on a rack to dry. Roll strips in sugar, then dip one end in melted chocolate. Refrigerate until firm on sheets of waxed paper.

Crackerjack**

What kid — even the grownup kind — doesn't love Crackerjack? You will want to make lots of it, so start now lining up some nice tins or plastic tubs with snap-on lids. And if you really want to emulate the original Crackerjack, tuck a couple of little prizes in each one.

3 sticks margarine	1 teaspoon salt
2 cups light brown sugar	Pinch cream of tartar
1/2 cup light corn syrup	6 quarts popped corn
1/2 teaspoon soda	2 cups peanuts

Bring margarine, sugar and corn syrup to a boil in a heavy saucepan. Boil 5 minutes. Remove from heat and stir in soda, salt, and cream of tartar.

Place popped corn and nuts in a large baking pan, pour over the hot syrup and toss until well coated. Spread on cookie sheets and bake in a slow, 225° F. oven for 1 hour, stirring every 15 minutes. Cool and store in tight containers.

Chocolate Peanut Brittle**

For someone who loves peanut brittle, here is a very extra-special gift idea: Chocolate covered peanut brittle. (Naturally, if your purist prefers his brittle naked, by all means leave the chocolate topping off.)

1-1/2 cups sugar	1 teaspoon soda
2/3 cup water	1 tablespoon cold water
1/2 cup light corn syrup	1 teaspoon vanilla
2 tablespoons butter	1 8-ounce package semi-sweet
1/2 pound peanuts	chocolate chips

Mix sugar, water, and syrup in a heavy saucepan. Over low heat, stir mixture until sugar is dissolved. Then cook, without stirring, until a small amount of the syrup becomes brittle when dropped in cold water (275° F. on a candy thermometer.) Add butter and peanuts and stir until peanuts are lightly browned (296° F.). Dissolve soda in cold water, add vanilla and slowly stir into candy. Pour out on a warm buttered 10 x 15-inch pan, spreading into a smooth, flat sheet. Cool. Melt chocolate and spread over brittle. Cool until firm. Then break into pieces. Makes about 1-3/4 pounds.

Almond Crackle**

Anyone who's nutty about peanut brittle is sure to flip over this brittle studded with almonds.

Follow the recipe for peanut brittle, substituting unblanched whole almonds for the peanuts. Macadamia nuts also make divine brittle.

Chocolate Pretzels*

An easy way to weasel out of all the cookie and candy making that goes on during the holidays is to simply buy a big bag of pretzels, dip them in chocolate and let everyone think you've accomplished something special.

1 6-ounce package chocolate chips	2 tablespoons margarine
2 tablespoons corn syrup	1-1/2 teaspoons water
	25 to 30 pretzels

Place chocolate chips, syrup, margarine, and water in top of double boiler and place over hot, not boiling, water. Stir until smooth. Take off heat but keep warm over hot water. Dip pretzels in mix, and set on wire racks over waxed paper. Chill 10 minutes in the refrigerator, then set out to dry at room temperature.

Fool's Fudge**

Candy isn't one of the easiest things in the world for the beginner cook to tackle. An exception is Fool's Fudge. As long as you keep it firmed up in the fridge, you really can't fail.

3 6-ounce packages semi-sweet chocolate bits	Dash salt
1 8-ounce can sweetened condensed milk	1-1/2 teaspoons vanilla
	3/4 cup chopped nuts

Place chocolate bits in the top of a double boiler over gently simmering water, and melt, stirring occasionally. When chocolate has melted, remove the pan from the heat and stir in the sweetened condensed milk. Sprinkle in the salt and the vanilla and stir until blended. Add nuts. Spread mixture in an 8 x 8-inch pan lined with waxed paper. Chill the fudge for 4 to 5 hours. When firm, cut into squares. Keep candy refrigerated. Makes 1-3/4 pounds.

Caramel Nut Clumps*

'Twas the night before Christmas and you still haven't made any candy. Not to worry. Here's a last-minute quickie to fill the bill.

48 vanilla caramels	**2 cups unsalted peanuts**
Dash of salt	**1 cup semi-sweet chocolate chips**

Melt caramels in the top of a double boiler over simmering water. When melted, stir in salt and peanuts and drop by rounded teaspoons onto a greased cookie sheet. (A wet spoon makes this easier.) Melt chocolate chips over simmering water, then spoon over the caramels. Refrigerate until well chilled. Makes about 4 dozen.

Springerle***

Springerle cookies are once-a-year treats that show up only at Christmas. You need a springerle rolling pin to make the little tile-like cookies, but the pins — carved in old world designs — aren't very expensive. You will find them in most good kitchenware shops.

2 eggs	**2-1/4 cups flour**
1 cup sugar	**Anise seeds**

Beat eggs and sugar together until thick and fluffy. Then stir in flour and mix until well blended. This makes a very stiff dough. Chill the dough 3 hours before rolling.

Lightly flour bread board before rolling dough out about 1/4 inch thick. Then press well-floured springerle rolling pin over the dough, making well-impressed designs on the dough. (Keep the rolling pin lightly dusted with flour to keep from sticking.)

Cut apart designs and place on another board that has been liberally sprinkled with anise seeds. Let the cookies dry overnight. Then transfer to baking sheets that have been lightly greased. Bake at 325° F. about 15 minutes. Don't expect Springerle cookies to brown, because they don't. Store in a covered container until Christmas. (The longer they're stored, the harder they get.)

NOTE: If your family is really big on licorice, you can add a couple of drops of anise flavored extract to the cookie dough. I always do.

Christmas Toffee***

Every Christmas my friend Martha and I make this superb English toffee that is every bit as good as the candy sold in expensive candy stores. For the absolutely best results, you must use butter. Margarine just won't do.

1 cup butter	**1-1/2 cups chopped nuts**
1 cup sugar	**1 6-ounce package semi-sweet**
1 tablespoon white corn syrup	**chocolate bits**
3 tablespoons water	

In a 2-quart saucepan, melt butter. Stir in sugar gradually. Add the syrup and water. Cover and cook over moderate heat, stirring occasionally, to 290° F. on a candy thermometer. Add 1 cup nuts and cook for 3 minutes more, stirring constantly. Pour into a 9-inch buttered pan. Cool.

When cold, remove candy from the pan and place it on a sheet of waxed paper. Melt chocolate over hot, not boiling, water. Coat one side of the toffee with the melted chocolate and sprinkle with finely chopped nuts. Flip over and coat the other side with chocolate and nuts. When the chocolate has set up, break the toffee into pieces. Makes about 1-3/4 pound of candy — the kind that costs $8 per pound in good candy stores.

Susan's Mounds Logs***

Oh, what heavenly candy this is! My young friend Susan cranks these treats out every year at Christmas time . . . complaining that they're a bit of a bother but well worth the effort.

3/4 cup cold mashed potatoes	1 12-ounce package chocolate chips
1 pound flaked coconut	2/3 cup melted paraffin
1 pound powdered sugar	8 squares unsweetened chocolate
3/4 teaspoon almond extract	

Thoroughly mix potatoes with coconut, sugar and almond extract. Refrigerate several hours, or until firm. (In a hurry? Tuck in the freezer for 30 to 40 minutes.) Let mix stand at room temperature until just workable, then roll into small logs the size of Mounds Bars.

For coating, melt chocolate chips, paraffin and unsweetened chocolate in the top of a double boiler. Keep warm over simmering water as you dip the logs.

Let dipped candy cool on waxed paper until coating firms up.

NOTE: If coconut mix gets too soft during the dipping, put back in the refrigerator or freezer for a few minutes.

Peanut Butter Crunch Balls**

These meltaway peanut butter balls taste just like those peanut butter cups that kids — and grownups — are so nutty about. This recipe makes a big batch, which is good. They disappear like snow on a hot sidewalk.

3 sticks margarine	2 8-ounce chocolate bars
24 ounces peanut butter	1 12-ounce package chocolate chips
2 pounds powdered sugar	1/2 bar paraffin
7 cups puffed rice cereal	

Melt margarine and blend into peanut butter. Add powdered sugar and rice cereal, and work until well blended. Mixture will be very stiff, and will take a bit of muscle getting it pressed into small balls the size of walnuts. Arrange the balls on a cookie sheet and chill 3 hours before dipping.

In double boiler melt chocolate bars and chocolate chips. In another small pan, melt paraffin. Add to melted chocolate and stir. Keep mixture over simmering water while dipping the peanut butter balls. Use a teaspoon to dip the balls in the chocolate mixture. Let excess chocolate drip off, then place balls on a sheet of waxed paper to harden. Makes 200 or more balls.

Stuffed Dates*

If you aren't up to the rigors of candy making, you can always stuff a few dates. Just be sure to get the pre-pitted kind. Digging pits out of dates is a sticky job you really don't need.

1 cup walnuts, chopped
1/4 cup brown sugar
2 tablespoons finely minced
candied orange peel

1 tablespoon frozen orange juice
concentrate
1 10-ounce container pitted dates,
split lengthwise
1/4 cup granulated sugar

Mix walnuts, sugar, orange peel, and orange juice concentrate until well blended. Stuff rounded 1/2 teaspoonfuls of the mixture into the dates. Roll in sugar and pack in airtight container. Makes about 32 date confections.

Apple Walnut Candy**

These apple gelatin squares closely resemble that famous apple candy made up in the state of Washington. You will need orange flower water for the proper flavor. You can find it in any liquor store.

1-1/2 pounds apples
(preferably Golden
Delicious)
2 tablespoons water
2 cups sugar
2 envelopes unflavored gelatin

2 teaspoons orange flower water
1 teaspoon lemon peel, grated
1 teaspoon lemon juice
1/2 teaspoon almond extract
2 cups nuts
1/2 cup powdered sugar

Peel and cube apples (makes about 6 cups). Combine apples and water in heavy saucepan and simmer over low heat until apples are tender. Uncover and cook until most of liquid has evaporated. Place apples in a blender and process until smooth, then return to pan and add sugar mixed with the gelatin. Boil gently in the pan, uncovered, stirring constantly for 15 minutes. Mixture should be quite thick.

Remove from heat and add orange flower water, lemon peel, juice, almond extract, and nuts. Pour into a buttered 8-inch pan, cover and refrigerate overnight.

The next day cut candy into 1-inch squares and place on racks to dry for 8 hours, or overnight. Dust with powdered sugar and store in a covered container at room temperature. Makes 64 pieces.

Apricot Gels**

Kissin' cousins to those apple candy squares are Apricot Gels.

2 envelopes unflavored
gelatin
1-1/2 cups sugar
Dash salt
2-1/4 cups (8 ounces) dried
apricots

1/2 cup water
1/2 teaspoon vanilla
1/2 teaspoon almond extract
1/2 cup chopped walnuts
Powdered sugar

Combine gelatin, sugar, and salt in the top of a double boiler. Puree apricots with water in a blender and add puree to the gelatin and sugar mixture. Cook over simmering water for 30 minutes, stirring frequently. Remove from heat and stir in vanilla, almond extract, and nuts.

Pour into a loaf pan that has been rinsed with cold wàter; let stand in the refrigerator overnight. Next day, loosen candy around edges with a sharp knife and turn out onto a board that has been dusted with powdered sugar. Cut into cubes and roll in powdered sugar. Makes about 40 cubes. Store in a cool, dry place.

Peanut Butter and Apricot Granola**

This special granola blend makes a welcome gift for the jogger, health nut or anyone else interested in high-energy pickups. Bag it in plastic and tie it with a big, fat bow.

1 cup raisins	1 teaspoon vanilla
2/3 cup creamy peanut butter	4 cups old-fashioned rolled oats
2/3 cup honey	1/2 cup dried apricots, snipped fine
1/2 teaspoon ground cinnamon	1 cup shelled peanuts

Soak raisins in boiling water until plump — about 10 minutes. Drain and set aside.

Combine peanut butter, honey, and cinnamon in a small saucepan and slowly heat until blended and simmering. Remove from heat and stir in vanilla.

Spread oats in a large, flat baking pan and pour over warm peanut butter-honey mixture, stirring until well coated. Bake at 300° F. for 35 minutes, stirring occasionally. Turn oven off and add the apricots, raisins and peanuts. Let granola dry in the unlit oven for 1-1/2 hours. Fluff with a fork occasionally. Store in tightly covered containers. Makes about 8 cups.

Jingle Balls*

These nutritious fruit balls make a neat energy re-charger and a great gift for anyone who is into health food.

1/2 cup pitted dates	3/4 teaspoon grated orange peel
1/2 cup dried apricots	3 tablespoons frozen orange juice
1/2 cup tiny marshmallows	concentrate
1 cup chopped nuts	1/4 cup dry milk
1/2 cup shredded coconut	1/2 cup finely chopped nuts

With a knife or in a food processor, finely chop the dates, apricots, marshmallows, nuts, and coconut. Blend the grated orange peel, orange juice concentrate, and dry milk and mix into the fruit-nut mixture. Blend until everything is well combined and very lightly moistened.

Sprinkle the chopped nuts on a sheet of waxed paper. With a tablespoon dipped in hot water, shape the fruit-nut mixture into round balls, and roll each one in the chopped nuts. Cover with waxed paper and place in the refrigerator until firm. Store in gift containers in the refrigerator. These treats will keep up to 2 months. Makes about 3 dozen.

Nuts to You*

This is a last-minute gift idea for someone who has everything (except, possibly, enough nuts for indulgent nibbling).

1-1/2 pounds shelled walnuts	1/4 pound shelled sunflower seeds
1/2 pound shelled almonds	1/2 pound shelled raw cashews
1/2 pound shelled pecans	1/2 pound raisins

Combine everything but the raisins and spread on a cookie sheet or in a large roasting pan. Bake at 350° F. about 35 minutes, or until nuts are toasty. Cool, then add the raisins. Store in airtight containers.

Turtles*

Store-bought turtles cost a king's ransom, and look how easy they are to make at home!

For each candy, arrange four whole pecan halves in groups on a greased cookie sheet. Make sure that points of nuts meet in the center, forming an X. Top each cluster with a vanilla caramel square. Place cookie sheet in a 325° F. oven until the caramels soften and begin to spread. This will take about 8 minutes, but maintain a close watch so they don't over-melt.

Remove from oven and top each cluster with 3 semi-sweet chocolate chips. As chips melt, swirl with a knife to spread. Remove turtles to a buttered sheet of waxed paper and allow to cool completely. Store in an airtight container.

Spicy Orange Slices**

Spicy Orange Slices will be appreciated by anyone who likes to cook. Tie a pretty bow around the jar and tell her (or him) that these goodies go particularly well with baked ham or poultry.

10 medium sized thin-	1-1/4 cups white vinegar
skinned oranges	12 whole cloves
5 cups sugar	2 sticks cinnamon
1/2 cup water	

Do not peel oranges. Slice thin — about 1/4 inch. Discard seeds, then place slices in a 6-quart kettle and cover with just enough water to top the oranges. Bring to a boil, then reduce heat and simmer, uncovered, for about 1 hour. Drain.

Add the sugar, 1/2 cup water, vinegar, cloves and cinnamon. Stir over low heat until sugar dissolves. Then simmer gently for about 1-1/2 hours, or until liquid is reduced and slightly thickened. Cool and spoon into glass jars. Oranges will keep in the refrigerator up to 1 month. Makes about 4 pints.

The Size of It

... how to tell when a pinch is plenty

To the truly creative cook — one who presses on by the seat of his or her pants — any kind of precise measuring can be a big bore. On the other hand, sometimes it is necessary to know how much of **this** it takes to make how much of **that** — lest you end up with a kitchen filled with overruns.

The following list is strictly cursory. In fact, it is the skinniest minimum you will need to get by. But at least it will deter you from cooking a pailful of spaghetti when there only two of you for dinner.

1 cube of butter or margarine = 1/2 cup.

1 cup uncooked white rice = 4 to 5 cups cooked (use a big pot). Serves 4.

1 cup quick (pre-cooked) rice = 2 cups cooked. Serves 2.

1 cup uncooked brown rice = 4 cups cooked. Serves 4.

1 cup dried beans = about 2-1/2 cups cooked. Serves 4.

1 8-ounce package spaghetti or macaroni serves 4 to 6.

3 cups dry noodles serves 4.

1/2 pound onions = 2 to 2-1/2 cups sliced.

1/2 pound mushrooms = 1 to 1-1/2 cups sliced

1 pound unshelled walnuts = 1/2 pound nutmeats. *Every holiday I drive myself nutty trying to figure how much I can save by buying nuts in the shell (which never includes labor, of course).*

1 pound unshelled peanuts = 2/3 pound shelled nuts.

1 package frozen vegetables serves 4. *A frozen food knife is handy for halving the package for two.*

1 egg, in a pinch, will serve 1 if it's fried or soft-boiled. *For scrambled, you'll need 2 eggs. One egg, scrambled, looks awfully stingy.*

3 eggs, in an omelet, serves 1 bountifully.

1/4 pound hard cheese (Parmesan, Romano) = 5-1/2 cups grated.

1/4 pound firm cheese (Cheddar, Longhorn) = 1 cup shredded. *And remember, cheese is easier to grate if it's chilled first.*

1/4 to 1/2 chicken serves 1. *This is pretty flexible, depending on how much the bird weighs. A skinny chicken won't go as far as a fat hen.*

A 3-pound whole chicken will serve 3. A 4-pound chicken serves 4, and so on.

One pound per person is the rule of thumb here.

A 3-1/2-pound chicken = 2 cups of diced, cooked meat. *Figure on getting more white meat than dark.*

1/3 to 1/2 pound of rib roast serves 1.

1/4 to 1/3 pound of boneless roast or ground beef serves 1.

1/2 pound of meat with heavy bone serves 1. *As you can see, some low-cost cuts with a lot of bone aren't such great buys, after all.*

1/3 pound fish fillets serves 1. *That's why fish is such a good buy; a little goes a long way.*

1/2 pound beef liver serves 4. *A package of liver can really fool you. You won't believe what $1.50 will buy until you get home and start unfolding it!*

1 ounce solid chocolate = 1/3 cup grated.

1 ounce solid chocolate = 2 tablespoons melted

Beyond those easy equations, there isn't a whole lot you need to know in the measurement department. As you learn your way around the kitchen, you will develop a feel for how much it takes to get the job done. Meanwhile, a little common sense helps.

When a recipe calls for a pinch of something — a pinch being the amount of anything you can squeeze between your thumb and forefinger — you are dealing with a very catch-as-catch-can measurement. If you have a small thumb and you adore pepper, by all means go back for more.

Now, while we are on the subject of size, let us briefly consider the size of cans.

If a recipe calls for a 15-ounce can of tomato sauce or a 6-ounce can of mushrooms, don't tear your hair if the cans in your cupboard happen to contain 15-1/2 ounces of sauce and 5-1/2 ounces of mushrooms. Such measurements are approximate and the outcome of your spaghetti sauce or stew won't be affected one bit by a few extra ounces in, or out of, the pot.

You will also find that ingredients such as chopped nuts, parsley, capers and garlic can be weasled around at will. You can add more, or less, or leave them out entirely without affecting the recipe's chemical balance. So suit yourself. I know a lady who wouldn't put pimiento in anything if you put a gun to her head. You may feel the same way about anchovies. No problem. Leave them out.

The only place you should hold to exact measurement — or sizes — is where an ingredient has physical impact on the outcome of the dish. Baking powder, baking soda and yeast make things rise. Eggs, flour, cornstarch and arrowroot help things thicken.. So it's best if you don't deviate from the prescribed recipe where these things are concerned.

Otherwise, relax. A pinch is a pinch is a pinch, and straying an ounce or two off the track shouldn't derail your efforts one whit.

Nifty Tricks

. . . how to de-lump the gravy when your mother-in-law isn't looking

Along with articles on how to lose weight and save your marriage, ladies' magazines are very big on ways to do things better and quicker around the kitchen. And some of their ideas are quite sound if you discount the crazies. I mean, who in his right mind is going to spread grape jelly on leftover mashed potatoes to "spruce them up"?

What we have here is a collection of quick tricks that is good reading for anyone planning to spend much time in the kitchen. They all work, and some work very well indeed.

GRAVY

Lumpy gravy hint: Strain through a fine sieve, then put the gravy back on the heat and continue cooking. Because you have tossed out part of the flour with the lumps, the mix might be a mite thin. If so, thicken it by mixing a spoonful or two of flour into enough cold water or stock to make a thin roux, then stir this into the bubbling gravy. Cook, stirring constantly, until thickened and glossy.

Another lumpy gravy hint: If the lumps aren't too bad, you may be able to smooth things out by processing the gravy in a blender. If that works, put it back on the stove and cook, stirring, until the gravy is smooth and glossy. Do not undercook. Sauces and gravies containing flour can take up to 10 minutes to get thoroughly cooked.

Make-ahead white sauce hint: To save last-minute dithers, make a batch of white sauce ahead for use later. Just rub a chunk of butter over the surface of the hot sauce before it cools. That makes a seal that prevents a skin from forming. When the sauce is re-heated, the butter melts in and disappears.

MEAT

Juicy hamburger hint: A tablespoon of ice water mixed lightly in with the ground beef makes hamburger patties extra juicy and moist.

Hamburgers-in-a-hurry hint: If you're in a rush for the burgers, poke a hole in the middle of each patty before putting them on the grill. This helps the centers cook faster. And don't worry about the holes. They fill in as the meat cooks.

Pot roast and stew hint: Next time you set a stew on to simmer, use beer in place of water. Beer tenderizes and adds great flavor.

Tough meat marinade hint: Got a tough piece of meat? Add some strong tea to the marinade. Tannin in tea is a great natural tenderizer, and it won't hurt the flavor, either.

Meat carving hint: Always let an oven roast cool its heels on the counter for 15 minutes before carving. This lets the meat settle down a bit, making the carving lots easier. And remember, it will continue to cook in its own heat after it is taken from the oven. Keep a close eye on the thermometer, and take the meat out a degree or two slight of the temperature you want.

Beef browning hint: When pan-frying a large quantity of ground beef or stew meat, do not add the meat all at once to the skillet. This can cause the temperature to drop and the meat to turn watery and grey instead of browning. Brown the meat in small batches, remove and cook the next batch, and so on until it's all browned.

CHICKEN

Chicken cut-up hint: A whole chicken is much easier to cut up if it is put in the freezer long enough to firm up. And do use a razor-sharp knife. A sharp knife is much less apt to slip and cut a finger than a dull one.

Fried chicken hint: After shaking pieces in seasoned flour, set aside to chill for 20 minutes before frying. This applies to all kinds of floured and breaded foods. Chilling helps firm up the coating and makes it less apt to fall off during the frying.

Another fried chicken hint: When frying chicken parts, place the dark pieces (legs and thighs) in the pan first. After a few minutes, add the white pieces. The dark meat takes a bit longer to cook. This way, the whole thing comes out even.

Chicken complexion hint: If your baked chickens look a little anemic, give them a ruddy glow by basting with butter mixed with a tablespoon of soy sauce. Pop back into the oven for a couple of minutes.

Another chicken skin hint: Another way to get a gorgeous skin is to rub the chicken with mayonnaise before it is baked.

SEASONING

Stew seasoning hint: Empty a couple of packets of dried onion soup mix into a glass container and keep it handy with your spices. A spoonful or two of the mix makes a marvelous instant pickup for stews, gravies and soups.

Seasoned flour hint: You probably use seasoned flour (flour mixed with salt and pepper) frequently enough to keep some handy in an over-size sugar shaker. That way, you just shake once instead of three times. One cup of flour, 1/2 teaspoon salt and 1/4 teaspoon pepper is a good mix.

Spice storage hint: Light and heat are ruinous to spices, so don't get conned into buying one of those hanging spice racks with all the cute little glass bottles. If you leave your spices hanging out on the wall long enough you won't be able to tell the saffron and sage from the savory. They'll all taste like old grass cuttings.

Spice (and herb) purchase hint: Resist the urge to buy spices and herbs in wholesale quantities no matter how irresistible the price. These have to be fresh, and the tag end of a bulk quantity of anything is bound to be past the pale.

SALT SENSE

Bean seasoning hint: Do not salt the water in which you cook dried beans. This toughens them, and they won't cook as fast, either.

Corn-on-the-cob hint: Another place not to add salt is to the water for cooking corn on the cob. Salt makes the corn tough. But do add a spoonful of sugar.

Egg seasoning hint: Don't sprinkle salt on eggs as they sizzle in the pan. In fact, never add salt to **any** egg dish during the cooking. This is another place where salt toughens.

Meat seasoning hint: Never season raw beef with salt before cooking. Salt draws out the juices, leaving the meat dry and stringy. Season with herbs and spices, but leave the salt off until the meat is well seared.

Gravy seasoning hint: Instead of salt, try a dash of soy sauce. A teaspoon or two will really enhance the flavor and impart a deep, rich color.

SOUP

Soup stock hint: For a richer, browner soup stock, roast soup bones in a 350° F. oven on an ungreased cookie sheet for 1 hour. Put the browned bones in a soup pot and proceed.

Clear soup stock hint: You can clear up cloudy soup stock by beating one egg white with a couple teaspoons of cold water. Crush the egg shell and add it to the egg white, then pour the whole thing into the soup. Boil the stock for a couple of minutes, then strain through a layer of cheesecloth placed over a strainer.

Soup kettle fat hint: You can easily remove the fat from soup or stew by floating a few lettuce leaves or ice cubes over the surface. The fat will solidify and cling to the leaves (or cubes), making it easy to remove.

TEMPERATURE

Egg temperature hint: Eggs should always be room temperature before using, although eggs right out of the refrigerator separate easier. After separating, set the yolks and whites out to reach room temperature. Warmed egg whites whip to a much greater volume than cold ones.

Eggs in hot mix hint: When a recipe calls for eggs to be added to a hot mixture, never add the eggs directly into the hot ingredients or the eggs will scramble. Instead, stir a little of the hot mixture into the beaten eggs. Then, when thoroughly mixed, slowly add the eggs to the hot mixture.

Pan-frying hint: Always heat the skillet **before** adding butter or oil. Then even eggs won't stick.

Flaming food hint: Liquor that has a high alcoholic content — such as brandy or rum — flames better than liqueurs. If you want to flame something like Grand Marnier or Cointreau, mix with a little straight brandy for better flammability.

Another flaming food hint: When you plan to flambe a dish, be sure that the food, itself, is hot. The flames will last lots longer if poured onto piping hot food.

Heat turnoff hint: Foods cook just as fast in gently boiling water as they do in water heated to a galloping boil. Turn the heat down and conserve a little.

Oven heating hint: It isn't necessary to pre-heat ovens anymore — especially for breads, meats and casseroles. Exceptions are heat-finicky things like meringues and popovers. For everything else, start cold and save energy.

Pasta boilover hint: Adding a lump of butter or fat to the water in which you cook noodles or spaghetti will keep the pot from boiling over. It also helps keep the pasta from sticking together.

Crepe batter hint: Crepes are much better if the batter is chilled a couple of hours before cooking.

Grated cheese hint: Soft cheeses, like Jack, grate much easier if they are put in the freezer long enough to firm up.

VEGETABLES

Artichoke hint: Before cooking artichokes, cover with cold water and add one tablespoon vinegar. Let stand, then cook in the same water. This keeps the artichokes green and tenderizes the flesh, too.

Excess avocado hint: Buried under an avalanche of avocados getting ripe at the same time? Don't despair. Mash and season liberally with lemon juice. Spoon into small plastic containers and freeze. Makes great later-day guacamole. (Unfortunately, plain avocado — without lime or lemon juice — won't keep.)

Asparagus cooking hint: Peel fresh stalks of asparagus with a swivel-handled vegetable peeler. Then gently bend each stalk until it snaps. Asparagus will break at the place it ceases being tender.

Baked potato hint: Ideally, a potato should never be wrapped in foil before baking. This steams the spud and prevents the skins from getting nice and crusty. Just rub a little butter on the skin and let it go at that.

Baked potatoes-in-a-hurry hint: Cut down on the baking time by boiling the potatoes for 10 minutes and then inserting an aluminum nail in each one before finishing up in the oven.

Fresh parsley hint: Wash a bouquet of fresh parsley and push the whole bunch, stems down, into a mason jar. Add enough cold water to cover the stems; cap and refrigerate. As you need fresh parsley, pull it up, snip off what you need and store what's left. This way, parsley will stay fresh and perky for a week or better.

Onion quick-peel hint: Make short work of peeling onions by dunking them in boiling water for 10 to 15 seconds. The skins will slip off without trouble **or** tears.

Weepless onion hint: If you store onions in the fridge, you won't cry when you peel and chop them. Otherwise, give your onions a quick chill in the freezer before chopping.

Mushroom storage hint: Storing mushrooms in plastic bags encourages rot. Keep them stashed in the same cardboard box or paper bag they came in and cover with a slightly damp cloth. And if the mushrooms turn dark, don't toss them. They will still taste good, and can be perked up with a dash of lemon juice.

Crunchy coleslaw hint: Slaw is crispier if the cabbage is chilled in slightly salted ice water before slicing. This makes it easier to shred, as well.

Red cabbage hint: A fourth cup of red wine vinegar added to the cooking water helps set the color. It keeps the cabbage firm and zips up the flavor, as well.

Tomato peeling hint: A tomato plunged in boiling water for 10 to 15 seconds will slip its skin the minute it is held under cold water. The same goes for peaches. Just make sure they aren't left too long in the hot water bath or they'll cook.

Bell pepper hint: Got an especially good buy on peppers? Buy plenty, then either chop in a food processor or cut in squares and freeze in individual plastic sandwich bags. Frozen peppers are just as good as fresh ones in any cooked dish.

Sauerkraut hint: Draining sauerkraut and steeping it in white wine will give it an exceptionally mellow flavor.

Cooked rice hint: Cooked rice can be refrigerated up to four days if stored in a tightly covered container. To reheat, add two tablespoons milk or water and heat over low heat for four to five minutes. Or spoon into a casserole with a tight fitting lid and heat in a 450° F. oven for 5 minutes. Lower the heat and continue heating at 350° F. for 15 to 20 minutes.

FRUIT

Banana saver hint: Bananas getting ripe before you can use them? Peel and wrap them snugly in plastic, then in foil, and pop into the freezer. Frozen bananas, drizzled with chocolate, are a neat treat for the kids.

Fresh strawberries hint: Always wash whole berries before removing the stems. If you take the stems off first, this permits water to soak in and make the berries soggy.

Juicy lemon hint: A lemon plunged into hot water for 10 minutes before being squeezed will yield almost twice as much juice.

Orange section hint: To section oranges for salads and desserts, drop the whole orange in boiling water first, and let it stand for 5 minutes. The white membrane will come off much easier.

COOKIES

Cookie dough hint: After adding flour, stir cookie dough as little as possible. Over-mixing makes cookies tough, as does adding too much flour.

Cookie rolling hint: To prevent putting too much flour in the dough, roll dough between sheets of waxed paper instead of on a floured board. Dough that has been chilled rolls easier, so refrigerate two to three hours before rolling and baking.

Cookie sheet hint: Cookie sheets should be at least two inches smaller on all sides than the oven's dimensions. This allows for a free circulation of heat. As you bake, try to have enough baking sheets available so you aren't forced to use hot-out-of-the-oven pans that make the dough spread out excessively.

Another cookie sheet hint: Next time you make chocolate chip cookies, lightly flour the baking sheet after greasing. This helps keep the chips from sticking and burning when they come in direct contact with the metal. This is especially helpful when the batter is thin.

Frozen cookie dough hint: Save your 6-ounce orange juice cans for freezing cookie dough. Pack dough into cans, wrap tightly and freeze. Later, thaw 15 minutes, then open the bottom of the can and push the dough out. Slice thin and bake.

Cookie storage hint: Crisp cookies should be stored in containers with loose-fitting lids. Soft cookies need tight-fitting lids. And you can't successfully store soft cookies with crisp ones; so do not mix.

BAKING

Muffin and waffle batter hint: Do not over-mix. Stir only until flour is dampened. Lumpy batters make tender waffles and muffins.

Glass baking pan hint: Glass pans brown faster than metal ones, so baking times can be shortened slightly. You might also turn down the heat a bit — say 10 to 15 degrees.

Cake flour from plain flour: Plain flour can be converted into cake flour very easily. For every cup of all-purpose flour, simply remove 1 tablespoon and replace it with 1 tablespoon cornstarch, and sift.

Cake pan liner hint: Save those brown paper bags from the market and use them to line cake pans. Cut paper to fit, slip into pans and simply spoon in the cake batter. There's no need to grease the pans or the liners. When the cake has been baked, simply turn out and peel off the paper — zap! This works like magic.

Cupcake paper hints: You won't have a hard time peeling fluted papers off cupcakes if you take the papers off the cakes while they're still warm.

Anti-sog piecrust hint: Before filling an unbaked pie shell with a custard, pumpkin or quiche filling, brush the crust with a little beaten egg white. This helps keep the filling from soaking into the crust. Another trick is to bake the empty pie shell in a hot oven for five or six minutes — just long enough to firm up before filling.

Non-stick piecrust hint: Lightly spray the pie pan or dish with an aerosol non-stick spray before fitting in the pie dough. The baked pie will slip out of the pan, slick as a wink.

Substitute buttermilk hint: When a recipe calls for buttermilk or sour milk, you can stir up a workable substitute by stirring a tablespoon of vinegar or lemon juice into one cup of sweet milk. Set it aside five minutes to thicken.

Baking powder test: If your baking powder has been languishing on the shelf for longer than you can remember, test its effectiveness by putting a teaspoonful in a half-cup of boiling water. If this doesn't bubble, your baking powder has lost its zap.

Biscuit rolling hint: Roll the dough thin, then fold over once before cutting into biscuits. They will split open easier for buttering after baking.

Waffle iron hint: When you are finished baking waffles, slip a piece of waxed paper in between the hot grids before storing. This helps keep the next batch of waffles from sticking.

CHOCOLATE

Chocolate dipping hint: When dipping strawberries, other fruits or anything containing moisture into melted chocolate, be sure that the fruit (or whatever) is completely dry. Moisture of any kind in the melted chocolate will cause it to harden and become unworkable.

Another chocolate dipping hint: Be sure that the water in the bottom of the double boiler is simmering, not boiling. If the water gets too hot, the chocolate will turn dull and gray and yukky-looking after it hardens.

Chocolate chip hint: Out of chocolate chips? Cut up three or four squares of semi-sweet chocolate into bits and you are ready to make cookies or whatever.

OTHER SLICK TRICKS

Almond blanching hint: Briefly cover with boiling water. The skins will slip right off.

Filbert blanching hint: Filberts — also called hazelnuts — can be easily skinned by placing on a cookie sheet in a 350° F. oven. After 15 minutes the skins will flake right off. Rubbing briskly between rough towels will hurry the process.

Dried fruits and nuts hint: When adding nuts and fruits to baked goods, dredge them first in flour before adding to the batters. This keeps the nuts and fruits from sinking to the bottom of the pans.

Chopped dates and figs hint: You can ease this sticky chore by putting the dates and figs in the freezer for an hour or so before chopping. Also keep dipping your scissors in hot water as you snip.

Leftover champagne hint: Is there a half-bottle of bubbly languishing in the fridge? Do not toss it. Use it to gently poach a couple of chicken breasts or fish fillets in the wine seasoned with salt, pepper and a pinch or two of tarragon or thyme. This makes a divine sauce — with or without bubbles.

Coconut cracking hint: With an ice pick, poke out the holes in the end of the coconut and drain off the juice. Bake the coconut in a 350° F. oven for 30 minutes. Take the hot coconut out on the sidewalk and give it a hard whack with a hammer. Once it is broken open, the meat can be easily pried out with a blunt knife. Use a vegetable peeler to pare off the brown inner husk. From there, grating the coconut is a breeze. Just drop it, in 1/2-inch chunks, in a food processor and grate. The yield: 3 to 4 cups.

Garlic-at-the-ready hint: Shuck skins off a whole head of garlic, peel the buds and stash in a small jar filled with salad oil. When you need a pod or two, just fish it out.

Garlic puree hint: Peel a whole head or two of garlic, put the pods through a garlic press and mix the pulp with a spoonful of olive oil. Store the puree in a covered jar in the refrigerator.

Garlic surplus hint: Freeze it. Frozen garlic is easy to peel and chop.

Quick-gel hint: Gelatin salads and desserts can be hurried by pouring the liquid into a shallow pan and placing it in the freezer for 10 to 15 minutes. Another quickie: in place of cold water, use one cup of crushed ice when preparing the gelatin.

Gelatin unmolding hint: Coat the mold with an aerosol non-stick spray or grease very lightly before filling.

Recycled fat hint: To clarify fat, just drop a few slices of raw potato into the fat and bring it to a quick boil. Then strain through a sieve.

The Joy of Solo Dining

. . . how to eat (alone) in your underwear and love it

Play it right, and eating alone can be one of life's loveliest luxuries.

It can also be a bummer. It all depends on how often you do it (no one wants to eat alone **all** the time), how frazzled you are from cooking for everybody else, plus what kind of goodies you can lay your hands on for dinner.

Now don't start mewling that you don't like to cook for yourself. Do it right, and there's practically no cooking involved.

The prospect of an evening alone can be a very restorative experience if you have been shoveling out meals for friends and family for weeks on end. Everyone, even Julia, needs a night off once in awhile.

When the time comes, treat yourself to whatever personal whimsies pleasure you the most . . . like soaking in a hot tub 'til your fingers crinkle, or watching Merv Griffin in your undies or shuffling off to bed at 7:30 with James Bond and a clutch of jelly beans in your pajama pocket.

If you adore caviar, that is what you should have. Don't whine that it's too expensive. **Nonsense.** You certainly can afford a smidge. You are only feeding one, you know. Indulge yourself!

The success of solo dining is strictly a matter of style so don't scrimp.

Eating leftovers with a bent fork is no way to feed your ego. On the other hand, it's impossible to feel neglected while you're cutting into a wedge of imported Brie with a silver butter knife.

The other big thing is to keep preparation to a nub.

There should be no work associated with dining alone. You are treating yourself, remember?

A typical scenario might go something like this: Arrive home. Talk to the cat. Take off your shoes. Go to the kitchen. Open a can (maybe two). Look in fridge.

Slide something in the oven (if applicable). Take ice out of freezer. Pour favorite libation. Take leave of the kitchen.

KEEP IT SIMPLE

Time it. Five to seven minutes total toil should be max. Not bad for the cook's night off, huh?

From here, you can go soak in the bathtub or catch the 6 o'clock news or sit on the back step and watch the sun set. Pretend you're on the French Riviera. (That probably won't work, but it's a lovely thought.) The idea is to **relax**. Flatten out like an oil slick.

By the time you have poured a second of whatever you started out with, the timer will buzz, signaling it's time to put your steaming dinner on a tray. Or to pan-fry that fillet. Or maybe, if you've worked it right, you needn't cook at all.

So what's for dinner?

How about something murderous — like a big wedge of Camembert cheese and a couple of croissants from the corner patisserie? A half-dozen slices of paper-thin Prosciutto ham wouldn't hurt, either.

Imported pate makes another luxurious mini-meal served with a stack of melba toast. Or try this: Have the butcher grind up a gorgeous little filet and treat yourself to a private portion of steak tartare. All it needs is salt, pepper, some minced onion and a couple of capers to turn into a top-drawer treat.

Now for heartier fare, you might consider the following:

FAST FISH

Don't overlook oysters. Tiny, sweet eastern oysters are one of the sea's most memorable treats (if you like oysters, that is). A half-pint makes a memorable feast. A glass of chilled white wine, a crusty baguette from the neighborhood boulangerie and a pat of butter are all you need to fill this bill.

A tin of salmon is another good bet. Keep a small can ready in the fridge. This goes great with a squirt of lemon, some cracked pepper and a couple slices of rye bread. Sardines work well, too. On the side you need some tender green onions and some salt in which to dunk them. And eat all the onions you want. Who's to notice?

Giant prawns are out of sight. Just the same, you can probably come up with the price of four or five of these succulent beauties. Get the biggest, freshest ones you can find, then handle with care. Very little cooking is required. Either drop them for one minute in vigorously boiling water (add a tad of salt and vinegar) or shell them and broil them under high heat slathered with garlic and **real** butter. This is neither the time nor the place to count calories. Enjoy, enjoy!

Consider investing in one lobster tail. (Don't look at the price per pound. Just close your eyes and buy it.) With kitchen shears, slit it down the middle, dot with butter and slide under a hot broiler. When it's charred around the edges, it's done. Serve with melted butter and a fat slice of French bread for mopping up the juices. An Olympian feast, this, in 5 to 7 minutes flat.

MINUTE MEATS

A kidney veal chop. These chops that have a delicious morsel of kidney attached need little in the way of preparation. Pan-fry on both sides, season with salt and pepper, and top with a glob of sour cream or undiluted mushroom soup. Then cover, turn the heat low, and cook for 15 minutes. NOTE: If you can't get a kidney veal chop, the same process works well with a plain veal chop.

A plump pat of freshly-ground country sausage. Pan-fry briefly on both sides, then cover and steam-fry until cooked through. Served with applesauce and a can of tiny peas, this makes another good meal-in-minutes.

Or how about a one-serving slice of hickory-smoked ham? Plop it in a baking pan, top with any kind of fruit you have hanging around — a sliced apple, banana, a leftover canned peach — dot with butter and brown sugar and slide into a hot oven. Within minutes you have a brown and bubbling ham-and-fruit medley.

Then you have the egg-on-muffin bit. Plunk a poached egg on a toasted English muffin that has been topped with a slice of ham. A couple tablespoons of sour cream or canned Hollandaise on top and a quick run under the broiler turn the whole thing beautifully bubbly.

You can sear a steak in minutes. Forget the barbecue or broiler bit. Just get a small black iron pan smoking, then sear your steak on both sides. The best bet here is a small, perfect filet. If you have a good butcher, you will cut it with a fork. Have a glass of husky red wine. And count your blessings.

Liver is lovely. A slice of baby beef or calves' liver pan-fries in a flash. Chicken livers are another simple-to-prepare gourmet treat that need only a quick pan and a little sherry to arrive at remarkable goodness. One-quarter pound is plenty. Add some canned or fresh mushrooms if they're handy.

LOVELY INDULGENCES

And then you have mushrooms, period. One of the easiest treats of all is to quickly saute a whole basketful of tender white mushrooms in butter. Use **plenty** of butter, sprinkle with salt and pepper and pile on toast. Superb!

Anything out of season is a special treat. Like Spring's first asparagus. It will cost an arm and a leg, but at least it's light — 10 or 12 stalks weigh only ounces. So splurge. Break off the tough bottoms, steam the beauties in a bit of water, then slather with Hollandaise. (Canned or packaged is okay.)

The same thing goes for the season's first corn on the cob. Go ahead. Eat four ears and let the butter dribble off your chin. Isn't scarfing solo wonderful?

CAN DO'S

Canned corned beef hash isn't glamorous, but it's a great quick filler. Press half a can into a small greased ramekin, make a dent in the center, brush with butter and carefully break an egg into the depression. Bake at 350° F. until the egg white has set but the yolk is still soft. Crank black pepper over all and serve with toast.

There's always canned stew. The best brands aren't bad as-is, although a splash of burgundy makes a good thing better. If you have a handful of mushrooms hanging around, toss them in. You need red wine to wash it down. (NOTE: when you stock your pantry with stew for these solo flights, always buy the smallest cans. This stuff goes a long way, and if you crank open a big can, your leftovers will have leftovers.)

WHEN IN DOUBT, SEND OUT

When you're pooped, a home delivery can be the next best thing to room service. Order a pizza and, if you crave anchovies, get extras. There's no one around to yell at you, as they usually do, for such fishy indulgence. Red wine or beer is obligatory for washing down.

If you call out for Chinese, live it up — get a king-size serving of Cashew Chicken or Almond Duck. Forget the bean sprouts and rice.

A deli barbecued chicken makes a neat take-out treat. Buy a half chicken or cut a whole one in half at home with your poultry shears. Place, breast side up, on a baking dish and coat with a mixture of apricot jam and brandy. Heat in the oven until glazed.

WASHING IT DOWN

What you drink with dinner is very important. It should be special. I know a lady accountant who keeps two splits of champagne in the fridge at all times — to be uncorked on those occasions when she's frazzled, fit to be tied and greatly in need of some first-class self-indulgence. A 20-year-old Scotch, iced Perrier or buttermilk may do the same for you.

... AND WINDING IT DOWN

What's for dessert? That's easy. Just stop on the way home at a bakery or French patisserie and buy one — maybe two — of the gooiest pastries in the case. Or indulge in a couple of imported chocolates that sell for $9 a pound. You are only buying two bon bons, so for heaven's sake **splurge**.

How sweet it is if you will only do it right.

The Kitchen Sink, Everything But

. . . things that didn't fit in anyplace else

What we have here is a random clutch of recipes that kept falling through the cracks as the rest of the book came together. And some of them, believe it or not, are real gems.

Of course, you may decide that enough is enough — that you really don't want to make sugar daisies. Or peanut butter pizza. Or anything else that isn't capable of keeping body and soul together on a day-to-day basis.

Fair enough. But do, at least, give this odd-lot collection a fleeting look. Even if your career as a cook never hinges on your ability to turn a camellia leaf into a chocolate dainty, it's nice to know that directions are at hand in case the mood ever moves you.

Please Don't Eat the Sugar Daisies*

*Perky garden-fresh daisies come to the tea table frosted with sugar and looking delicate as a fairy's wing. Their use? Not to **eat**, certainly, but to decorate a cake plate or a tray of mini-sandwiches for a ladies' tea. If you are fresh out of daisies, this lily-gilding technique works with almost any kind of small, fresh flower, although the sturdier varieties work best.*

Small fresh flowers   3 tablespoons sugar
1 egg white, beaten

Dip clean dry flowers in beaten egg white, then into sugar. Shake off excess and let the blossoms dry 10 minutes. Dip again in sugar, then keep in the refrigerator until party-time. These sugar flowers look lovely with fresh ferns.

Chocolate Leaves*

When you are casting about wondering how to gussy up some fancy dessert, you might consider molding a few chocolate leaves. These are very chic and easy to make providing you peel carefully and exercise a little patience.

24 camellia leaves (rose   4 ounces semi-sweet chocolate
   leaves will work in a pinch)

Wash and dry leaves, then place on a baking sheet covered with waxed paper. Melt chocolate in top of a double boiler. With a small flat knife or spatula, spread a little melted chocolate over the underside of each leaf. Place them, coated side up, on the baking sheet. Chill until firm.

Gently separate the chocolate from the leaves by pulling the leaf stems. Out of 24, you should end up with a dozen or so perfectly shaped and molded leaves for garnishing.

Frosted Grapes*

The next time you set about garnishing a meat tray or a salad platter for a party, try this one. Frosted Grapes are positively **opulent** *looking.*

1 pound firm and fresh seed-   1/2 cup granulated sugar
   less green grapes   1/2 teaspoon ground cardamom
1 egg white, slightly beaten   (optional)

Break grapes into small clusters and dip briefly in the egg white, letting the excess drip off. Sprinkle lightly with a mixture of sugar and cardamom and set aside to dry in a cool place.

Chocolate-Dipped Strawberries**

One of summer's loveliest luxuries is plump garden-fresh strawberries. Dipping them in chocolate doesn't necessarily make them better, just fancier. Try to get berries with bright green caps and stems still attached.

1 12-ounce package semi-   Pinch salt
   sweet chocolate pieces   1 teaspoon vanilla
6 tablespoons butter   1 basket plump berries with stems

Melt chocolate in top of double boiler, then add butter, salt and vanilla. Swirl berries in warm chocolate, leaving a small top section of the berries uncovered. Set on waxed paper in a cool place to dry, then chill. These berries are best eaten shortly after they are dipped.

NOTE: When dipping strawberries — or anything — in melted chocolate, be very careful not to get any moisture (water or whatever) in the dip. One drop, and the chocolate won't harden properly.

Frozen Bananas**

Next summer when the kids drive you daffy pleading for popsicles and ice cream cones, try placating them with Frozen Bananas. The ruse should work — for awhile, anyhow.

3 firm, ripe bananas	1 teaspoon butter
3 3-ounce squares semi-sweet chocolate	1/2 cup finely chopped peanuts (optional)

Peel and cut bananas in half crosswise. Push a popsicle stick or wood skewer into the cut ends of the bananas. Wrap each piece snugly in foil or plastic wrap. Freeze a minimum of 1 hour.

Meantime, melt chocolate and butter over low heat. When smooth, roll frozen bananas in chocolate, then the nuts, to cover. Place bananas on a pie tin covered with foil and return to the freezer until chocolate sets up. Makes 6 treats.

Mock Pineapple**

*Collectors of goofy recipes should love this one. And, trust me, you will be **amazed** at the results. Trying to tell the difference between real crushed pineapple and this ersatz version could stump an expert. Try spooning it over vanilla ice cream and run your own taste test.*

1 gallon zucchini, chopped	4 teaspoons pineapple extract
3 cups sugar	4 to 6 drops yellow food coloring
Pinch salt	1 large can pineapple juice

Peel, then grate or chop zucchini. (If you use a food processor, take care not to chop too fine.) In a heavy kettle combine all the ingredients and bring to a boil. When the mixture reaches boiling, time for 20 minutes. Pour into sterilized jars. This will keep in the refrigerator almost indefinitely.

Zucchini Applesauce*

Here is another way to use up the garden's excess zucchini — in applesauce. No one would ever guess it was made with anything but plain apples. It's amazing the masquerades this vegetable can pull off and get away with it.

2 zucchini, peeled and diced	Dash cloves
2 apples, peeled and diced	1/2 teaspoon salt
1/2 cup water	1 tablespoon lemon juice
1/2 cup sugar	1/2 teaspoon cinnamon

Gently bring zucchini, apples, water and sugar to a boil. Add cloves and salt, cover and simmer 20 minutes, stirring occasionally. Stir in lemon juice and cinnamon. Refrigerate. Makes 2 cups.

Kumquat Preserves*

We have a miniature kumquat tree in a pot in the backyard. Every year it comes forth with this phenomenal crop of fruit. Here is one thing we do with the surplus. These preserved beauties, by the way, make an elegant garnish for a holiday meat tray.

2 cups kumquats
1-1/2 cups water
2 cups sugar

3 3-inch sticks bark cinnamon
1 lemon, thinly sliced

Push a large darning needle or an ice pick through each kumquat lengthwise. Cover with water, bring to a boil and drain.

Combine 1-1/2 cups water with sugar and bring to a boil. Add the scalded kumquats, lemon slices, and bark cinnamon. Bring back to boiling, then take off the stove and set aside overnight.

Next day boil again in the same water, then cool to room temperature. Bring back to a boil and pour into hot, sterilized jars. Make sure each jar of fruit is completely covered with syrup. Seal with paraffin.

Personalized Sausage*

There's a lot of hype associated with making your own sausage, but it really isn't one bit difficult provided you make it in patties and don't get conned into trying to stuff it into casings (real hog or otherwise). Once you get into the swing of sausage, you can experiment with various kinds of seasonings. The following is a good basic mix to start with.

1 pound lean ground pork
3/4 teaspoon salt
1 teaspoon dried sage

2 dashes cayenne pepper
1/4 teaspoon thyme
1/2 teaspoon freshly cracked
  black pepper

Have the butcher coarse-grind the pork; or, if you have a food processor, you can chop your own.

With hands or a fork, lightly blend seasonings into the meat. Form into 6 fat patties. Fry gently until golden brown on both sides. Serves 6.

Salami Chubs

Making salami at home is as easy as rolling off a log. And nice little logs, called chubs, are what you get when you make it.

Before you start, locate some curing salt. It is available in places that specialize in commercial butcher supplies. You will also need about a yard of nylon net. You can find that in any yardage store.

4 pounds ground beef
  (no more than 25% fat)
1/4 cup curing salt
2 tablespoons liquid smoke

3 to 4 large cloves garlic, minced
  or crushed
1 teaspoon black pepper
Cracked pepper

Mix first five ingredients. Cover tightly and refrigerate overnight. Next day, shape meat into compact rolls — about 1-1/2 inches in diameter and 4 inches long. Roll chubs in coarsely cracked pepper, coating fairly thickly. Then roll up tightly in 8 x 10-inch squares of net, securing the ends with wire twists or string. Place rolls on a broiler pan or on racks over cookie sheets. Bake for 4 hours at 225° F. Pat with paper towels to remove excess fat, then remove net. Wrap in plastic or foil and freeze or refrigerate.

Mock Capers

Capers are those little pale green pods that turn up on pates and sprinkled over salads in chi-chi restaurants. Real capers are something else, but if you're in a mood to innovate, you can make a dandy substitute from that nasturtium plant going to seed in the backyard. This recipe makes enough to share with friends. (When it comes to capers, a little goes a long way.)

1 quart nasturtium seeds	2 cups wine vinegar
1 tablespoon salt	1 or 2 cloves garlic (optional)
8 peppercorns	

Start picking the naturtium seeds, washing them and placing them in a clean quart jar. Combine the remaining ingredients and pour the brine over the seeds. If you don't have enough pods to fill the jar, cover them and simply add more seeds as they're harvested. When the container is full, cover it tightly and let the contents pickle for 4 weeks. If desired, 1 or 2 cloves of garlic can be added to the mix.

Jack O'Lantern Seeds*

Face it, you really can't celebrate Halloween without carving out a pumpkin. Here is what you can do with the seeds after the candle has gone out and the kids have gone home.

2 cups cleaned pumpkin seeds	1/4 cup melted butter
4 cups water	1 teaspoon seasoned salt
1/2 cup salt	1/2 teaspoon chili powder

Soak cleaned seeds in water with salt. Let stand at room temperature overnight. Drain seeds and spread on a slightly greased cookie sheet. Bake at 200° F. for 1 hour, then turn off oven and let seeds stand in the oven overnight. Next day, melt butter and drizzle over seeds, tossing to coat. Sprinkle with seasoned salt and chili powder. Cool and store in a tightly covered container.

Goober Pizza***

Riddle: what do you get when you cross peanut butter and pizza? Goober Pizza, of course. This big, fat, flat buttery treat will have all the peanut butter buffs grabbing for seconds.

1 envelope yeast	1/4 cup raisins
1 cup very warm water	1/4 cup sunflower seeds
2 teaspoons honey	1/2 cup chopped nuts
1 tablespoon salad oil	1/3 cup shredded coconut
1 teaspoon salt	1 tablespoon finely grated orange
1 cup white flour	peel
1 cup whole wheat flour	3/4 cup shredded Mozzarella and
1 cup crunchy peanut butter	Jack Cheese
1/4 cup honey	

Sprinkle yeast over very warm water. Stir, then add the 2 teaspoons honey, oil and salt. Set aside to proof. When yeast mix is foamy, turn into a large bowl with the flours. Beat until smooth, then turn out onto a lightly floured board and knead about 10 minutes, or until dough is smooth and satiny. Roll out into a 15-inch circle.

Grease a 15-inch pizza pan and fit dough into it, pressing with fingers to flatten. Bake at 450° F. for 15 minutes. Remove pizza shell and lower oven heat to 350° F. Combine peanut butter and 1/4 cup honey. Spread over warm pizza. Sprinkle with raisins, seeds, nuts, coconut, and grated peel. Top with grated cheeses. Return to 350° F. oven for 10 minutes. Serves 6 to 8.

Garlic Puree*

On the off chance you find yourself saddled with a passel of garlic — it happened to me once when I got carried away and planted a whole bagful of garlic bulbs in the backyard — here's what to do with the surplus.

20 whole heads of	1 teaspoon salt
firm garlic	1/4 cup oil

Place whole garlic heads on a large sheet of foil, then wrap snugly. Bake in a hot 425° F. oven for 1 hour. Undo foil and cool garlic.

Gently separate cloves, removing the outer parchment covering without removing skins from the individual sections.

One at a time, press each clove into a fine sieve, forcing the soft puree into a bowl. When all the puree has been collected in the bowl, add salt and oil. Store tightly covered in the refrigerator.

Pseudo Creme Fraiche*

This rich, thick and mildly flavored cream so widely used in French cuisine cannot really be duplicated here, although a reasonable facsimile is at hand for anyone willing to give it a go and anyone with 12 hours to spend on the process.

Basically, the ersatz creme is made by stirring one teaspoonful of commercial buttermilk into 1 cup of heavy cream and allowing the mix to stand at room temperature for 10 to 12 hours. After that, it must be refrigerated, and it will keep a week.

This is as close as we are going to get to the thick, nutty-flavored creme fraiche Frenchmen slather over their fresh fruits. As one cookbook author wistfully observed, the imitation mix wouldn't fool any Frenchman, but for the rest of us, it is a reasonable enough substitute.

Seasoned Crumbs*

You can beat the high cost of seasoned bread crumbs by making your own. If you don't have enough stale white bread to make a batch, just buy an inexpensive loaf of sandwich bread and go from there. The crumbs can be stored almost indefinitely in a covered container in the refrigerator.

1 1-pound loaf white sandwich bread	2 teaspoons basil
1 cup Parmesan or Romano cheese	2 teaspoons rosemary
	2 teaspoons oregano
1/4 cup onion flakes	1/2 cup dried parsley
	1 teaspoon seasoned salt

Put bread slices on a cookie sheet and bake in a slow 200° F. oven for 2 hours or until very hard and dry (not browned). Break dried bread into chunks. Process, by batches, in a food processor or a blender into fine crumbs. Mix with remaining ingredients.

Stabilized Whipped Cream*

*Whipped cream has a tendency to droop without some internal "propping". In this recipe, unflavored gelatin added to the cream helps hold up the works. The secret is in the chilling. Add the gelatin and chill the cream **before** it is whipped.*

1 envelope unflavored gelatin	2 cups heavy cream
2 tablespoons kirsch, rum or water	1/4 cup sugar

Dissolve gelatin in kirsch, rum or water. Stir into cream and add the sugar. Chill a minimum of 20 minutes (more is better) before whipping. Once whipped, gelatin will keep the cream "puffy" for hours.

Whipped Evaporated Milk*

If you are ever in a bind for whipping cream and there isn't any for miles (and you don't feel like going out into the blizzard or whatever), you can make out just fine provided there is a can of evaporated milk stashed in the cupboard. Here's what you do:

Place evaporated milk in a bowl along with the beaters to be used, and put the whole thing in the freezer. Leave it until ice crystals form around the edge of the bowl. Remove and immediately whip until stiff peaks form. Add a dash of lemon juice (to add volume) and sweeten to taste with powdered sugar.

Substitute Sweetened Condensed Milk*

If something calls for sweetened condensed milk and you don't have any, here is an easy substitute. (Another plus: it costs lots less than the store-bought product costs.)

1 cup instant powdered milk	2/3 cup sugar
1/3 cup boiling water	1/2 teaspoon vanilla
3 tablespoons melted butter	Dash salt

Process ingredients in a blender until smooth — 3 to 4 minutes. This is equivalent to a 14-ounce can of regular sweetened condensed milk.

Pomanders*

Strictly speaking, Pomanders fall outside the food category. All the same, they make delightful gifts for people who enjoy heavenly scents for their closets. Just remember, pomanders take six weeks to ripen, so if you are planning to make some of these critters for Christmas, you'd better get cracking.

1 or 2 boxes whole cloves	Ground cinnamon
3 or 4 thin-skinned, firm	Orrisroot (available in pharmacies)
oranges	

While you chat with a friend or watch TV, because this takes time, poke holes in the oranges with an ice pick or a thick darning needle. Insert whole cloves into the holes, tightly studding the oranges with cloves. Roll on equal parts of cinnamon and orrisroot. Pat the powder onto the oranges until liberally coated, then wrap in tissue paper and set aside to ripen for 6 weeks.

Remove the paper, shake off excess cinnamon coating and, with a corsage pin, fasten a bow with long streamers to the top of each pomander.

Present them with pride. The recipients will find that their fragrance will permeate everything — deliciously.

Christmas In-Scents*

There's a special smell about Christmas — of evergreens, cookies baking and spices — that really sets visions of sugarplums dancing in one's head.

You can fill your house with the spicy smell of Christmas by keeping a small pot of cinnamon and cloves simmering slowly on the back burner. As the pan gets dry, add more liquid. And from time to time toss in a few more spices. One batch is good for 3 or 4 days. After that, toss and start over.

1 orange, quartered	1/2 box whole cloves
1 lemon, quartered	2 cups water
4 cinnamon sticks, broken	

Combine everything in a small, heavy pan and set over low heat. (If necessary, use an asbestos pad or a trivet to keep pan from getting too hot.)

As water level evaporates, add a bit more. Next day, sprinkle in a few more pieces of cinnamon and a handful of fresh cloves. After the fourth day, start over.

INDEX

Continued

Continued

Continued

Continued

Continued

S

Continued

BIRD IN HAND
PUBLISHING
P.O. Box 7772
Long Beach, CA 90807

Please send me _____ copies of **OUT OF THE NEST, INTO THE FRYING PAN** at $10.00 plus $1.50 postage and handling per copy.

Enclosed is my check for $ _____ , payable to Bird in Hand Publishing.

Name _____

Street _____

City _____ State _____ Zip _____

....

BIRD IN HAND
PUBLISHING
P.O. Box 7772
Long Beach, CA 90807

Please send me _____ copies of **OUT OF THE NEST, INTO THE FRYING PAN** at $10.00 plus $1.50 postage and handling per copy.

Enclosed is my check for $ _____ , payable to Bird in Hand Publishing.

Name _____

Street _____

City _____ State _____ Zip _____

....

BIRD IN HAND
PUBLISHING
P.O. Box 7772
Long Beach, CA 90807

Please send me _____ copies of **OUT OF THE NEST, INTO THE FRYING PAN** at $10.00 plus $1.50 postage and handling per copy.

Enclosed is my check for $ _____ , payable to Bird in Hand Publishing.

Name _____

Street _____

City _____ State _____ Zip _____